Mastering Embedded Linux Programming

Second Edition

Unleash the full potential of Embedded Linux with Linux 4.9 and Yocto Project 2.2 (Morty) Updates

Chris Simmonds

BIRMINGHAM - MUMBAI

Mastering Embedded Linux Programming

Second Edition

First published: December 2015

Second edition: June 2017

Production reference: 1280617

Published by Packt Publishing Ltd.
Livery Place
35 Livery Street
Birmingham
B3 2PB, UK.
ISBN 978-1-78728-328-2

www.packtpub.com

Credits

Author
Chris Simmonds

Reviewers
Daiane Angolini
Otavio Salvador
Alex Tereschenko

Commissioning Editor
Kartikey Pandey

Acquisition Editor
Prateek Bharadwaj

Content Development Editor
Sharon Raj

Technical Editor
Vishal Kamal Mewada

Copy Editors
Madhusudan Uchil
Stuti Shrivastava

Project Coordinator
Virginia Dias

Proofreader
Safis Editing

Indexer
Rekha Nair

Graphics
Kirk D'Penha

Production Coordinator
Melwyn Dsa

About the Author

Chris Simmonds is a software consultant and trainer living in southern England. He has almost two decades of experience in designing and building open-source embedded systems. He is the founder and chief consultant at 2net Ltd, which provides professional training and mentoring services in embedded Linux, Linux device drivers, and Android platform development. He has trained engineers at many of the biggest companies in the embedded world, including ARM, Qualcomm, Intel, Ericsson, and General Dynamics. He is a frequent presenter at open source and embedded conferences, including the Embedded Linux Conference and Embedded World. You can see some of his work on the Inner Penguin blog at www.2net.co.uk.

I would like to thank Shirley Simmonds for being so supportive during the long hours that I was shut in my home office researching and writing this book. I would also like to thank all the people who have helped me with the research of the technical aspects of this book, whether they realized that is what they were doing or not. In particular, I would like to mention Klaas van Gend, Thomas Petazzoni, and Ralph Nguyen for their help and advice. Lastly, I would like to thank Sharon Raj, Vishal Mewada, and the team at Packt Publishing for keeping me on track and bringing the book to fruition.

About the Reviewers

Daiane Angolini has been working with embedded Linux since 2008. She has been working as an application engineer at NXP, acting on internal development, porting custom applications from Android, and on-customer support for i.MX architectures in areas such as Linux kernel, u-boot, Android, Yocto Project, and user-space applications. However, it was on the Yocto Project that she found her place. She has coauthored the books *Embedded Linux Development with Yocto Project* and *Heading for the Yocto Project*, and learned a lot in the process.

Otavio Salvador loves technology and started his free software activities in 1999. In 2002, he founded O.S. Systems, a company focused on embedded system development services and consultancy worldwide, creating and maintaining customized BSPs, and helping companies with their product's development challenges. This resulted in him joining the OpenEmbedded community in 2008, when he became an active contributor to the OpenEmbedded project. He has coauthored the books *Embedded Linux Development with Yocto Project* and *Heading for the Yocto Project*.

Alex Tereschenko is an embedded systems engineer by day, and an avid maker by night, who is convinced that computers can do a lot of good for people when they are interfaced with real-world objects, as opposed to just crunching data in a dusty corner. That's what's driving him in his projects, and this is why embedded systems and the Internet of Things are the topics he enjoys the most.

www.PacktPub.com

For support files and downloads related to your book, please visit www.PacktPub.com. Did you know that Packt offers eBook versions of every book published, with PDF and ePub files available? You can upgrade to the eBook version at www.PacktPub.comand as a print book customer, you are entitled to a discount on the eBook copy. Get in touch with us at service@packtpub.com for more details. At www.PacktPub.com, you can also read a collection of free technical articles, sign up for a range of free newsletters and receive exclusive discounts and offers on Packt books and eBooks.

https://www.packtpub.com/mapt

Get the most in-demand software skills with Mapt. Mapt gives you full access to all Packt books and video courses, as well as industry-leading tools to help you plan your personal development and advance your career.

Why subscribe?

- Fully searchable across every book published by Packt
- Copy and paste, print, and bookmark content
- On demand and accessible via a web browser

Customer Feedback

Table of Contents

Preface

Linux has been the mainstay of embedded computing for many years. And yet, there are remarkably few books that cover the topic as a whole: this book is intended to fill that gap. The term embedded Linux is not well-defined, and can be applied to the operating system inside a wide range of devices ranging from thermostats to Wi-Fi routers to industrial control units. However, they are all built on the same basic open source software. Those are the technologies that I describe in this book, based on my experience as an engineer and the materials I have developed for my training courses.

Technology does not stand still. The industry based around embedded computing is just as susceptible to Moore's law as mainstream computing. The exponential growth that this implies has meant that a surprisingly large number of things have changed since the first edition of this book was published. This second edition is fully revised to use the latest versions of the major open source components, which include Linux 4.9, Yocto Project 2.2 Morty, and Buildroot 2017.02. Since it is clear that embedded Linux will play an important part in the *Internet of Things*, there is a new chapter on the updating of devices in the field, including Over the Air updates. Another trend is the quest to reduce power consumption, both to extend the battery life of mobile devices and to reduce energy costs. The chapter on power management shows how this is done.

Mastering Embedded Linux Programming covers the topics in roughly the order that you will encounter them in a real-life project. The first 6 chapters are concerned with the early stages of the project, covering basics such as selecting the toolchain, the bootloader, and the kernel. At the conclusion of this this section, I introduce the idea of using an embedded build tool, using Buildroot and the Yocto Project as examples.

The middle part of the book, chapters 7 through to 13, will help you in the implementation phase of the project. It covers the topics of filesystems, the init program, multithreaded programming, software update, and power management. The third section, chapters 14 and 15, show you how to make effective use of the many debug and profiling tools that Linux has to offer in order to detect problems and identify bottlenecks. The final chapter brings together several threads to explain how Linux can be used in real-time applications.

Each chapter introduces a major area of embedded Linux. It describes the background so that you can learn the general principles, but it also includes detailed worked examples that illustrate each of these areas. You can treat this as a book of theory, or a book of examples. It works best if you do both: understand the theory and try it out in real life.

What this book covers

Chapter 1, *Starting Out*, sets the scene by describing the embedded Linux ecosystem and the choices available to you as you start your project.

Chapter 2, *Learning About Toolchains*, describes the components of a toolchain and shows you how to create a toolchain for cross-compiling code for the target board. It describes where to get a toolchain and provides details on how to build one from the source code.

Chapter 3, *All About Bootloaders*, explains the role of the bootloader in loading the Linux kernel into memory, and uses U-Boot and Bareboot as examples. It also introduces device trees as the mechanism used to encode the details of hardware in almost all embedded Linux systems.

Chapter 4, *Configuring and Building the Kernel*, provides information on how to select a Linux kernel for an embedded system and configure it for the hardware within the device. It also covers how to port Linux to the new hardware.

Chapter 5, *Building a Root Filesystem*, introduces the ideas behind the user space part of an embedded Linux implementation by means of a step-by-step guide on how to configure a root filesystem.

Chapter 6, *Selecting a Build System*, covers two commonly used embedded Linux build systems, Buildroot and Yocto Project, which automate the steps described in the previous four chapters.

Chapter 7, *Creating a Storage Strategy*, discusses the challenges created by managing flash memory, including raw flash chips and embedded MMC (eMMC) packages. It describes the filesystems that are applicable to each type of technology.

Chapter 8, *Updating Software in the Field*, examines various ways of updating the software after the device has been deployed, and includes fully managed Over the Air (OTA) updates. The key topics under discussion are reliability and security.

Chapter 9, *Interfacing with Device Drivers*, describes how kernel device drivers interact with the hardware with worked examples of a simple driver. It also describes the various ways of calling device drivers from the user space.

Chapter 10, *Starting Up – The Init Program*, shows how the first user space program--init-- starts the rest of the system. It describes the three versions of the init program, each suitable for a different group of embedded systems, ranging from the simplicity of the BusyBox init, through System V init, to the current state-of-the-art, systemd.

Chapter 11, *Managing Power*, considers the various ways that Linux can be tuned to reduce power consumption, including Dynamic Frequency and Voltage scaling, selecting deeper idle states, and system suspend. The aim is to make devices that run for longer on a battery charge and also run cooler.

Chapter 12, *Learning About Processes and Threads*, describes embedded systems from the point of view of the application programmer. This chapter looks at processes and threads, inter-process communications, and scheduling policies

Chapter 13, *Managing Memory*, introduces the ideas behind virtual memory and how the address space is divided into memory mappings. It also describes how to measure memory usage accurately and how to detect memory leaks.

Chapter 14, *Debugging with GDB*, shows you how to use the GNU debugger, GDB, together with the debug agent, gdbserver, to debug applications running remotely on the target device. It goes on to show how you can extend this model to debug kernel code, making use of the kernel debug stubs, KGDB.

Chapter 15, *Profiling and Tracing*, covers the techniques available to measure the system performance, starting from whole system profiles and then zeroing in on particular areas where bottlenecks are causing poor performance. It also describes how to use Valgrind to check the correctness of an application's use of thread synchronization and memory allocation.

Chapter 16, *Real-Time Programming*, provides a detailed guide to real-time programming on Linux, including the configuration of the kernel and the PREEMPT_RT real-time kernel patch. The kernel trace tool, Ftrace, is used to measure kernel latencies and show the effect of the various kernel configurations.

What you need for this book

The software used in this book is entirely open source. In almost all cases, I have used the latest stable versions available at the time of writing. While I have tried to describe the main features in a manner that is not version-specific, it is inevitable that some of the examples will need adaptation to work with later software.

Embedded development involves two systems: the host, which is used for developing the programs, and the target, which runs them. For the host system, I have used Ubuntu 16.04, but most Linux distributions will work with just a little modification. You may decide to run Linux as a guest in a virtual machine, but you should be aware that some tasks, such as building a distribution using the Yocto Project, are quite demanding and are better run on a native installation of Linux.

I chose two exemplar targets: the QEMU emulator and the BeagleBone Black. Using QEMU means that you can try out most of the examples without having to invest in any additional hardware. On the other hand, some things work better if you do have real hardware, for which, I have chosen the BeagleBone Black because it is not expensive, it is widely available, and it has very good community support. Of course, you are not limited to just these two targets. The idea behind the book is to provide you with general solutions to problems so that you can apply them to a wide range of target boards.

Who this book is for

This book is written for developers who have an interest in embedded computing and Linux, and want to extend their knowledge into the various branches of the subject. In writing the book, I assume a basic understanding of the Linux command line, and in the programming examples, a working knowledge of the C language. Several chapters focus on the hardware that goes into an embedded target board, and, so, a familiarity with hardware and hardware interfaces will be a definite advantage in these cases.

Conventions

In this book, you will find a number of text styles that distinguish between different kinds of information. Here are some examples of these styles and an explanation of their meaning. Code words in text, database table names, folder names, filenames, file extensions, pathnames, dummy URLs, user input, and Twitter handles are shown as follows: "You configure tap0 in exactly the same way as any other interface."

A block of code is set as follows:

```
/ {
  #address-cells = <2>;
  #size-cells = <2>;
  memory@80000000 {
  device_type = "memory";
  reg = <0x00000000 0x80000000 0 0x80000000>;
  };
};
```

Any command-line input or output is written as follows:

```
$ mipsel-unkown-linux-gnu-gcc -dumpmachine
milsel-unknown-linux-gnu
```

New terms and **important words** are shown in bold.

 Warnings or important notes appear in a box like this.

 Tips and tricks appear like this.

Reader feedback

Feedback from our readers is always welcome. Let us know what you think about this book-what you liked or disliked. Reader feedback is important for us as it helps us develop titles that you will really get the most out of. To send us general feedback, simply e-mail feedback@packtpub.com, and mention the book's title in the subject of your message. If there is a topic that you have expertise in and you are interested in either writing or contributing to a book, see our author guide at www.packtpub.com/authors.

Customer support

Now that you are the proud owner of a Packt book, we have a number of things to help you to get the most from your purchase.

Downloading the example code

You can download the example code files for this book from your account at http://www.packtpub.com. If you purchased this book elsewhere, you can visit http://www.packtpub.com/support and register to have the files e-mailed directly to you. You can download the code files by following these steps:

1. Log in or register to our website using your e-mail address and password.
2. Hover the mouse pointer on the **SUPPORT** tab at the top.
3. Click on **Code Downloads & Errata**.
4. Enter the name of the book in the **Search** box.
5. Select the book for which you're looking to download the code files.

6. Choose from the drop-down menu where you purchased this book from.
7. Click on **Code Download**.

Once the file is downloaded, please make sure that you unzip or extract the folder using the latest version of:

- WinRAR / 7-Zip for Windows
- Zipeg / iZip / UnRarX for Mac
- TAR for Linux

The code bundle for the book is also hosted on GitHub at `https://github.com/PacktPubl ishing/Mastering-Embedded-Linux-Programming-Second-Edition`. We also have other code bundles from our rich catalog of books and videos available at `https://github.com/P acktPublishing/`. Check them out!

Downloading the color images of this book

We also provide you with a PDF file that has color images of the screenshots/diagrams used in this book. The color images will help you better understand the changes in the output. You can download this file from `https://www.packtpub.com/sites/default/files/down loads/MasteringEmbeddedLinuxProgrammingSecondEdition_ColorImages.pdf`.

Errata

Although we have taken every care to ensure the accuracy of our content, mistakes do happen. If you find a mistake in one of our books-maybe a mistake in the text or the code-we would be grateful if you could report this to us. By doing so, you can save other readers from frustration and help us improve subsequent versions of this book. If you find any errata, please report them by visiting `http://www.packtpub.com/submit-errata`, selecting your book, clicking on the **Errata Submission Form** link, and entering the details of your errata. Once your errata are verified, your submission will be accepted and the errata will be uploaded to our website or added to any list of existing errata under the Errata section of that title. To view the previously submitted errata, go to `https://www.packtpub.com/book s/content/support` and enter the name of the book in the search field. The required information will appear under the **Errata** section.

Piracy

Piracy of copyrighted material on the Internet is an ongoing problem across all media. At Packt, we take the protection of our copyright and licenses very seriously. If you come across any illegal copies of our works in any form on the Internet, please provide us with the location address or website name immediately so that we can pursue a remedy. Please contact us at copyright@packtpub.com with a link to the suspected pirated material. We appreciate your help in protecting our authors and our ability to bring you valuable content.

Questions

If you have a problem with any aspect of this book, you can contact us at questions@packtpub.com, and we will do our best to address the problem.

1
Starting Out

You are about to begin working on your next project, and this time it is going to be running Linux. What should you think about before you put finger to keyboard? Let's begin with a high-level look at embedded Linux and see why it is popular, what are the implications of open source licenses, and what kind of hardware you will need to run Linux.

Linux first became a viable choice for embedded devices around 1999. That was when Axis (https://www.axis.com), released their first Linux-powered network camera and TiVo (https://business.tivo.com/) their first **Digital Video Recorder** (**DVR**). Since 1999, Linux has become ever more popular, to the point that today it is the operating system of choice for many classes of product. At the time of writing, in 2017, there are about two billion devices running Linux. That includes a large number of smartphones running Android, which uses a Linux kernel, and hundreds of millions of set-top-boxes, smart TVs, and Wi-Fi routers, not to mention a very diverse range of devices such as vehicle diagnostics, weighing scales, industrial devices, and medical monitoring units that ship in smaller volumes.

So, why does your TV run Linux? At first glance, the function of a TV is simple: it has to display a stream of video on a screen. Why is a complex Unix-like operating system like Linux necessary?

The simple answer is Moore's Law: Gordon Moore, co-founder of Intel, observed in 1965 that the density of components on a chip will double approximately every two years. That applies to the devices that we design and use in our everyday lives just as much as it does to desktops, laptops, and servers. At the heart of most embedded devices is a highly integrated chip that contains one or more processor cores and interfaces with main memory, mass storage, and peripherals of many types. This is referred to as a **System on Chip**, or **SoC**, and SoCs are increasing in complexity in accordance with Moore's Law. A typical SoC has a technical reference manual that stretches to thousands of pages. Your TV is not simply displaying a video stream as the old analog sets used to do.

The stream is digital, possibly encrypted, and it needs processing to create an image. Your TV is (or soon will be) connected to the Internet. It can receive content from smartphones, tablets, and home media servers. It can be (or soon will be) used to play games. And so on and so on. You need a full operating system to manage this degree of complexity.

Here are some points that drive the adoption of Linux:

- Linux has the necessary functionality. It has a good scheduler, a good network stack, support for USB, Wi-Fi, Bluetooth, many kinds of storage media, good support for multimedia devices, and so on. It ticks all the boxes.
- Linux has been ported to a wide range of processor architectures, including some that are very commonly found in SoC designs—ARM, MIPS, x86, and PowerPC.
- Linux is open source, so you have the freedom to get the source code and modify it to meet your needs. You, or someone working on your behalf, can create a board support package for your particular SoC board or device. You can add protocols, features, and technologies that may be missing from the mainline source code. You can remove features that you don't need to reduce memory and storage requirements. Linux is flexible.
- Linux has an active community; in the case of the Linux kernel, very active. There is a new release of the kernel every 8 to 10 weeks, and each release contains code from more than 1,000 developers. An active community means that Linux is up to date and supports current hardware, protocols, and standards.
- Open source licenses guarantee that you have access to the source code. There is no vendor tie-in.

For these reasons, Linux is an ideal choice for complex devices. But there are a few caveats I should mention here. Complexity makes it harder to understand. Coupled with the fast moving development process and the decentralized structures of open source, you have to put some effort into learning how to use it and to keep on re-learning as it changes. I hope that this book will help in the process.

Selecting the right operating system

Is Linux suitable for your project? Linux works well where the problem being solved justifies the complexity. It is especially good where connectivity, robustness, and complex user interfaces are required. However, it cannot solve every problem, so here are some things to consider before you jump in:

- Is your hardware up to the job? Compared to a traditional **real-time operating system (RTOS)** such as VxWorks, Linux requires a lot more resources. It needs at least a 32-bit processor and lots more memory. I will go into more detail in the section on typical hardware requirements.

- Do you have the right skill set? The early parts of a project, board bring-up, require detailed knowledge of Linux and how it relates to your hardware. Likewise, when debugging and tuning your application, you will need to be able to interpret the results. If you don't have the skills in-house, you may want to outsource some of the work. Of course, reading this book helps!

- Is your system real-time? Linux can handle many real-time activities so long as you pay attention to certain details, which I will cover in detail in Chapter 16, *Real-Time Programming*.

Consider these points carefully. Probably the best indicator of success is to look around for similar products that run Linux and see how they have done it; follow best practice.

The players

Where does open source software come from? Who writes it? In particular, how does this relate to the key components of embedded development—the toolchain, bootloader, kernel, and basic utilities found in the root filesystem?

The main players are:

- **The open source community**: This, after all, is the engine that generates the software you are going to be using. The community is a loose alliance of developers, many of whom are funded in some way, perhaps by a not-for-profit organization, an academic institution, or a commercial company. They work together to further the aims of the various projects. There are many of them—some small, some large. Some that we will be making use of in the remainder of this book are Linux itself, U-Boot, BusyBox, Buildroot, the Yocto Project, and the many projects under the GNU umbrella.

- **CPU architects**: These are the organizations that design the CPUs we use. The important ones here are ARM/Linaro (ARM-based SoCs), Intel (x86 and x86_64), Imagination Technologies (MIPS), and IBM (PowerPC). They implement or, at the very least, influence support for the basic CPU architecture.

- **SoC vendors** (Atmel, Broadcom, Intel, Qualcomm, TI, and many others). They take the kernel and toolchain from the CPU architects and modify them to support their chips. They also create reference boards: designs that are used by the next level down to create development boards and working products.
- **Board vendors and OEMs**: These people take the reference designs from SoC vendors and build them in to specific products, for instance, set-top-boxes or cameras, or create more general purpose development boards, such as those from Avantech and Kontron. An important category are the cheap development boards such as BeagleBoard/BeagleBone and Raspberry Pi that have created their own ecosystems of software and hardware add-ons.

These form a chain, with your project usually at the end, which means that you do not have a free choice of components. You cannot simply take the latest kernel from https://www.kernel.org/, except in a few rare cases, because it does not have support for the chip or board that you are using.

This is an ongoing problem with embedded development. Ideally, the developers at each link in the chain would push their changes upstream, but they don't. It is not uncommon to find a kernel which has many thousands of patches that are not merged. In addition, SoC vendors tend to actively develop open source components only for their latest chips, meaning that support for any chip more than a couple of years old will be frozen and not receive any updates.

The consequence is that most embedded designs are based on old versions of software. They do not receive security fixes, performance enhancements, or features that are in newer versions. Problems such as Heartbleed (a bug in the OpenSSL libraries) and ShellShock (a bug in the bash shell) go unfixed. I will talk more about this later in this chapter under the topic of security.

What can you do about it? First, ask questions of your vendors: what is their update policy, how often do they revise kernel versions, what is the current kernel version, what was the one before that, and what is their policy for merging changes up-stream? Some vendors are making great strides in this way. You should prefer their chips.

Secondly, you can take steps to make yourself more self-sufficient. The chapters in section 1 explain the dependencies in more detail and show you where you can help yourself. Don't just take the package offered to you by the SoC or board vendor and use it blindly without considering the alternatives.

Project life cycle

This book is divided into four sections that reflect the phases of a project. The phases are not necessarily sequential. Usually they overlap and you will need to jump back to revisit things that were done previously. However, they are representative of a developer's preoccupations as the project progresses:

- Elements of embedded Linux (Chapters 1 to 6) will help you set up the development environment and create a working platform for the later phases. It is often referred to as the **board bring-up** phase.
- System architecture and design choices (Chapters 7 to 11) will help you to look at some of the design decisions you will have to make concerning the storage of programs and data, how to divide work between kernel device drivers and applications, and how to initialize the system.
- Writing embedded applications (Chapters 12 and 13) shows how to make effective use of the Linux process and threads model, and how to manage memory in a resource-constrained device.
- Debugging and optimizing performance (Chapters 14 and 15) describes how to trace, profile, and debug your code in both the applications and the kernel.

The fifth section on real-time (Chapter 16, *Real-Time Programming*) stands somewhat alone because it is a small, but important, category of embedded systems. Designing for real-time behavior has an impact on each of the four main phases.

The four elements of embedded Linux

Every project begins by obtaining, customizing, and deploying these four elements: the toolchain, the bootloader, the kernel, and the root filesystem. This is the topic of the first section of this book.

- **Toolchain**: The compiler and other tools needed to create code for your target device. Everything else depends on the toolchain.
- **Bootloader**: The program that initializes the board and loads the Linux kernel.
- **Kernel**: This is the heart of the system, managing system resources and interfacing with hardware.
- **Root filesystem**: Contains the libraries and programs that are run once the kernel has completed its initialization.

Of course, there is also a fifth element, not mentioned here. That is the collection of programs specific to your embedded application which make the device do whatever it is supposed to do, be it weigh groceries, display movies, control a robot, or fly a drone.

Typically, you will be offered some or all of these elements as a package when you buy your SoC or board. But, for the reasons mentioned in the preceding paragraph, they may not be the best choices for you. I will give you the background to make the right selections in the first six chapters and I will introduce you to two tools that automate the whole process for you: Buildroot and the Yocto Project.

Open source

The components of embedded Linux are open source, so now is a good time to consider what that means, why open sources work the way they do, and how this affects the often proprietary embedded device you will be creating from it.

Licenses

When talking about open source, the word *free* is often used. People new to the subject often take it to mean nothing to pay, and open source software licenses do indeed guarantee that you can use the software to develop and deploy systems for no charge. However, the more important meaning here is freedom, since you are free to obtain the source code, modify it in any way you see fit, and redeploy it in other systems. These licenses give you this right. Compare that with shareware licenses which allow you to copy the binaries for no cost but do not give you the source code, or other licenses that allow you to use the software for free under certain circumstances, for example, for personal use but not commercial. These are not open source.

I will provide the following comments in the interest of helping you understand the implications of working with open source licenses, but I would like to point out that I am an engineer and not a lawyer. What follows is my understanding of the licenses and the way they are interpreted.

Open source licenses fall broadly into two categories: the copyleft licenses such as the **General Public License (GPL)** and the permissive licenses such as those from the **Berkeley Software Distribution (BSD)**, the Apache Foundation, and others.

The permissive licenses say, in essence, that you may modify the source code and use it in systems of your own choosing so long as you do not modify the terms of the license in any way. In other words, with that one restriction, you can do with it what you want, including building it into possibly proprietary systems.

The GPL licenses are similar, but have clauses which compel you to pass the rights to obtain and modify the software on to your end users. In other words, you share your source code. One option is to make it completely public by putting it onto a public server. Another is to offer it only to your end users by means of a written offer to provide the code when requested. The GPL goes further to say that you cannot incorporate GPL code into proprietary programs. Any attempt to do so would make the GPL apply to the whole. In other words, you cannot combine a GPL and proprietary code in one program.

So, what about libraries? If they are licensed with the GPL, any program linked with them becomes GPL also. However, most libraries are licensed under the **Lesser General Public License (LGPL)**. If this is the case, you are allowed to link with them from a proprietary program.

All the preceding description relates specifically to GLP v2 and LGPL v2.1. I should mention the latest versions of GLP v3 and LGPL v3. These are controversial, and I will admit that I don't fully understand the implications. However, the intention is to ensure that the GPLv3 and LGPL v3 components in any system can be replaced by the end user, which is in the spirit of open source software for everyone. It does pose some problems though. Some Linux devices are used to gain access to information according to a subscription level or another restriction, and replacing critical parts of the software may compromise that. Set-top-boxes fit into this category. There are also issues with security. If the owner of a device has access to the system code, then so might an unwelcome intruder. Often the defense is to have kernel images that are signed by an authority, the vendor, so that unauthorized updates are not possible. Is that an infringement of my right to modify my device? Opinions differ.

The TiVo set-top-box is an important part of this debate. It uses a Linux kernel, which is licensed under GPL v2. TiVo have released the source code of their version of the kernel and so comply with the license. TiVo also has a bootloader that will only load a kernel binary that is signed by them. Consequently, you can build a modified kernel for a TiVo box but you cannot load it on the hardware. The **Free Software Foundation (FSF)** takes the position that this is not in the spirit of open source software and refers to this procedure as **Tivoization**. The GPL v3 and LGPL v3 were written to explicitly prevent this happening. Some projects, the Linux kernel in particular, have been reluctant to adopt the version three licenses because of the restrictions it would place on device manufacturers.

Hardware for embedded Linux

If you are designing or selecting hardware for an embedded Linux project, what do you look out for?

Firstly, a CPU architecture that is supported by the kernel—unless you plan to add a new architecture yourself, of course! Looking at the source code for Linux 4.9, there are 31 architectures, each represented by a sub-directory in the arch/ directory. They are all 32- or 64-bit architectures, most with a **memory management unit (MMU)**, but some without. The ones most often found in embedded devices are ARM, MIPS PowerPC, and X86, each in 32- and 64-bit variants, and all of which have memory management units.

Most of this book is written with this class of processor in mind. There is another group that doesn't have an MMU that runs a subset of Linux known as **microcontroller Linux** or **uClinux**. These processor architectures include ARC, Blackfin, MicroBlaze, and Nios. I will mention uClinux from time to time but I will not go into detail because it is a rather specialized topic.

Secondly, you will need a reasonable amount of RAM. 16 MiB is a good minimum, although it is quite possible to run Linux using half that. It is even possible to run Linux with 4 MiB if you are prepared to go to the trouble of optimizing every part of the system. It may even be possible to get lower, but there comes a point at which it is no longer Linux.

Thirdly, there is non-volatile storage, usually flash memory. 8 MiB is enough for a simple device such as a webcam or a simple router. As with RAM, you can create a workable Linux system with less storage if you really want to, but the lower you go, the harder it becomes. Linux has extensive support for flash storage devices, including raw NOR and NAND flash chips, and managed flash in the form of SD cards, eMMC chips, USB flash memory, and so on.

Fourthly, a debug port is very useful, most commonly an RS-232 serial port. It does not have to be fitted on production boards, but makes board bring-up, debugging, and development much easier.

Fifthly, you need some means of loading software when starting from scratch. A few years ago, boards would have been fitted with a **Joint Test Action Group (JTAG)** interface for this purpose, but modern SoCs have the ability to load boot code directly from removable media, especially SD and micro SD cards, or serial interfaces such as RS-232 or USB.

In addition to these basics, there are interfaces to the specific bits of hardware your device needs to get its job done. Mainline Linux comes with open source drivers for many thousands of different devices, and there are drivers (of variable quality) from the SoC manufacturer and from the OEMs of third-party chips that may be included in the design, but remember my comments on the commitment and ability of some manufacturers. As a developer of embedded devices, you will find that you spend quite a lot of time evaluating and adapting third-party code, if you have it, or liaising with the manufacturer if you don't. Finally, you will have to write the device support for interfaces that are unique to the device, or find someone to do it for you.

Hardware used in this book

The worked examples in this book are intended to be generic, but to make them relevant and easy to follow, I have had to choose specific hardware. I have chosen two exemplar devices: the BeagleBone Black and QEMU. The first is a widely-available and cheap development board which can be used in serious embedded hardware. The second is a machine emulator that can be used to create a range of systems that are typical of embedded hardware. It was tempting to use QEMU exclusively, but, like all emulations, it is not quite the same as the real thing. Using a BeagleBone Black, you have the satisfaction of interacting with real hardware and seeing real LEDs flash. I could have selected a board that is more up-to-date than the BeagleBone Black, which is several years old now, but I believe that its popularity gives it a degree of longevity and it means that it will continue to be available for some years yet.

In any case, I encourage you to try out as many of the examples as you can, using either of these two platforms, or indeed any embedded hardware you may have to hand.

The BeagleBone Black

The BeagleBone and the later BeagleBone Black are open hardware designs for a small, credit card sized development board produced by CircuitCo LLC. The main repository of information is at `https://beagleboard.org/`. The main points of the specifications are:

- TI AM335x 1 GHz ARM® Cortex-A8 Sitara SoC
- 512 MiB DDR3 RAM
- 2 or 4 GiB 8-bit eMMC on-board flash storage
- Serial port for debug and development
- MicroSD connector, which can be used as the boot device
- Mini USB OTG client/host port that can also be used to power the board

- Full size USB 2.0 host port
- 10/100 Ethernet port
- HDMI for video and audio output

In addition, there are two 46-pin expansion headers for which there are a great variety of daughter boards, known as **capes**, which allow you to adapt the board to do many different things. However, you do not need to fit any capes in the examples in this book.

In addition to the board itself, you will need:

- A mini USB to full-size USB cable (supplied with the board) to provide power, unless you have the last item on this list.
- An RS-232 cable that can interface with the 6-pin 3.3V TTL level signals provided by the board. The Beagleboard website has links to compatible cables.
- A microSD card and a means of writing to it from your development PC or laptop, which will be needed to load software onto the board.
- An Ethernet cable, as some of the examples require network connectivity.
- Optional, but recommended, a 5V power supply capable of delivering 1 A or more.

QEMU

QEMU is a machine emulator. It comes in a number of different flavors, each of which can emulate a processor architecture and a number of boards built using that architecture. For example, we have the following:

- `qemu-system-arm`: ARM
- `qemu-system-mips`: MIPS
- `qemu-system-ppc`: PowerPC
- `qemu-system-x86`: x86 and x86_64

For each architecture, QEMU emulates a range of hardware, which you can see by using the option—machine help. Each machine emulates most of the hardware that would normally be found on that board. There are options to link hardware to local resources, such as using a local file for the emulated disk drive. Here is a concrete example:

```
$ qemu-system-arm -machine vexpress-a9 -m 256M -drive
  file=rootfs.ext4,sd -net nic -net use -kernel zImage -dtb vexpress-
  v2p-ca9.dtb -append "console=ttyAMA0,115200 root=/dev/mmcblk0" -
  serial stdio -net nic,model=lan9118 -net tap,ifname=tap0
```

The options used in the preceding command line are:

- `-machine vexpress-a9`: Creates an emulation of an ARM Versatile Express development board with a Cortex A-9 processor
- `-m 256M`: Populates it with 256 MiB of RAM
- `-drive file=rootfs.ext4,sd`: Connects the SD interface to the local file `rootfs.ext4` (which contains a filesystem image)
- `-kernel zImage`: Loads the Linux kernel from the local file named `zImage`
- `-dtb vexpress-v2p-ca9.dtb`: Loads the device tree from the local file `vexpress-v2p-ca9.dtb`
- `-append "..."`: Supplies this string as the kernel command-line
- `-serial stdio`: Connects the serial port to the terminal that launched QEMU, usually so that you can log on to the emulated machine via the serial console
- `-net nic,model=lan9118`: Creates a network interface
- `-net tap,ifname=tap0`: Connects the network interface to the virtual network interface `tap0`

To configure the host side of the network, you need the `tunctl` command from the **User Mode Linux (UML)** project; on Debian and Ubuntu, the package is named `uml-utilites`:

```
$ sudo tunctl -u $(whoami) -t tap0
```

This creates a network interface named `tap0` which is connected to the network controller in the emulated QEMU machine. You configure `tap0` in exactly the same way as any other interface.

All of these options are described in detail in the following chapters. I will be using Versatile Express for most of my examples, but it should be easy to use a different machine or architecture.

Software used in this book

I have used only open source software, both for the development tools and the target operating system and applications. I assume that you will be using Linux on your development system. I tested all the host commands using Ubuntu 14.04 and so there is a slight bias towards that particular version, but any modern Linux distribution is likely to work just fine.

Summary

Embedded hardware will continue to get more complex, following the trajectory set by Moore's Law. Linux has the power and the flexibility to make use of hardware in an efficient way.

Linux is just one component of open source software out of the many that you need to create a working product. The fact that the code is freely available means that people and organizations at many different levels can contribute. However, the sheer variety of embedded platforms and the fast pace of development lead to isolated pools of software which are not shared as efficiently as they should be. In many cases, you will become dependent on this software, especially the Linux kernel that is provided by your SoC or Board vendor, and to a lesser extent, the toolchain. Some SoC manufacturers are getting better at pushing their changes upstream and the maintenance of these changes is getting easier.

Fortunately, there are some powerful tools that can help you create and maintain the software for your device. For example, Buildroot is ideal for small systems and the Yocto Project for larger ones. Before I describe these build tools, I will describe the four elements of embedded Linux, which you can apply to all embedded Linux projects, however they are created.

The next chapter is all about the first of these, the toolchain, which you need to compile code for your target platform.

2
Learning About Toolchains

The toolchain is the first element of embedded Linux and the starting point of your project. You will use it to compile all the code that will run on your device. The choices you make at this early stage will have a profound impact on the final outcome. Your toolchain should be capable of making effective use of your hardware by using the optimum instruction set for your processor. It should support the languages that you require, and have a solid implementation of the **Portable Operating System Interface (POSIX)** and other system interfaces. Not only that, but it should be updated when security flaws are discovered or bugs are found. Finally, it should be constant throughout the project. In other words, once you have chosen your toolchain, it is important to stick with it. Changing compilers and development libraries in an inconsistent way during a project will lead to subtle bugs.

Obtaining a toolchain can be as simple as downloading and installing a TAR file, or it can be as complex as building the whole thing from source code. In this chapter, I take the latter approach, with the help of a tool called **crosstool-NG**, so that I can show you the details of creating a toolchain. Later on in Chapter 6, *Selecting a Build System*, I will switch to using the toolchain generated by the build system, which is the more usual means of obtaining a toolchain.

In this chapter, we will cover the following topics:

- Introducing toolchains
- Finding a toolchain
- Building a toolchain using the crosstool-NG tool
- Anatomy of a toolchain
- Linking with libraries—static and dynamic linking
- The art of cross compiling

Introducing toolchains

A toolchain is the set of tools that compiles source code into executables that can run on your target device, and includes a compiler, a linker, and run-time libraries. Initially you need one to build the other three elements of an embedded Linux system: the bootloader, the kernel, and the root filesystem. It has to be able to compile code written in assembly, C, and C++ since these are the languages used in the base open source packages.

Usually, toolchains for Linux are based on components from the GNU project (http://www.gnu.org), and that is still true in the majority of cases at the time of writing. However, over the past few years, the **Clang** compiler and the associated **Low Level Virtual Machine (LLVM)** project (http://llvm.org) have progressed to the point that it is now a viable alternative to a GNU toolchain. One major distinction between LLVM and GNU-based toolchains is the licensing; LLVM has a BSD license while GNU has the GPL. There are some technical advantages to Clang as well, such as faster compilation and better diagnostics, but GNU GCC has the advantage of compatibility with the existing code base and support for a wide range of architectures and operating systems. Indeed, there are still some areas where Clang cannot replace the GNU C compiler, especially when it comes to compiling a mainline Linux kernel. It is probable that, in the next year or so, Clang will be able to compile all the components needed for embedded Linux and so will become an alternative to GNU. There is a good description of how to use Clang for cross compilation at http://clang.llvm.org/docs/CrossCompilation.html. If you would like to use it as part of an embedded Linux build system, the EmbToolkit (https://www.embtoolkit.org) fully supports both GNU and LLVM/Clang toolchains, and various people are working on using Clang with Buildroot and the Yocto Project. I will cover embedded build systems in Chapter 6, *Selecting a Build System*. Meanwhile, this chapter focuses on the GNU toolchain as it is the only complete option at this time.

A standard GNU toolchain consists of three main components:

- **Binutils**: A set of binary utilities including the assembler and the linker. It is available at http://www.gnu.org/software/binutils.
- **GNU Compiler Collection (GCC)**: These are the compilers for C and other languages which, depending on the version of GCC, include C++, Objective-C, Objective-C++, Java, Fortran, Ada, and Go. They all use a common backend which produces assembler code, which is fed to the GNU assembler. It is available at http://gcc.gnu.org/.
- **C library**: A standardized **application program interface (API)** based on the POSIX specification, which is the main interface to the operating system kernel for applications. There are several C libraries to consider, as we shall see later on in this chapter.

As well as these, you will need a copy of the Linux kernel headers, which contain definitions and constants that are needed when accessing the kernel directly. Right now, you need them to be able to compile the C library, but you will also need them later when writing programs or compiling libraries that interact with particular Linux devices, for example, to display graphics via the Linux frame buffer driver. This is not simply a question of making a copy of the header files in the include directory of your kernel source code. Those headers are intended for use in the kernel only and contain definitions that will cause conflicts if used in their raw state to compile regular Linux applications.

Instead, you will need to generate a set of sanitized kernel headers, which I have illustrated in Chapter 5, *Building a Root Filesystem*.

It is not usually crucial whether the kernel headers are generated from the exact version of Linux you are going to be using or not. Since the kernel interfaces are always backwards-compatible, it is only necessary that the headers are from a kernel that is the same as, or older than, the one you are using on the target.

Most people would consider the **GNU Debugger (GDB)** to be part of the toolchain as well, and it is usual that it is built at this point. I will talk about GDB in Chapter 14, *Debugging with GDB*.

Types of toolchains

For our purposes, there are two types of toolchain:

- **Native**: This toolchain runs on the same type of system (sometimes the same actual system) as the programs it generates. This is the usual case for desktops and servers, and it is becoming popular on certain classes of embedded devices. The Raspberry Pi running Debian for ARM, for example, has self-hosted native compilers.
- **Cross**: This toolchain runs on a different type of system than the target, allowing the development to be done on a fast desktop PC and then loaded onto the embedded target for testing.

Almost all embedded Linux development is done using a cross development toolchain, partly because most embedded devices are not well suited to program development since they lack computing power, memory, and storage, but also because it keeps the host and target environments separate. The latter point is especially important when the host and the target are using the same architecture, x86_64, for example. In this case, it is tempting to compile natively on the host and simply copy the binaries to the target.

This works up to a point, but it is likely that the host distribution will receive updates more often than the target, or that different engineers building code for the target will have slightly different versions of the host development libraries. Over time, the development and target systems will diverge and you will violate the principle that the toolchain should remain constant throughout the life of the project. You can make this approach work if you ensure that the host and the target build environments are in lockstep with each other. However, a much better approach is to keep the host and the target separate, and a cross toolchain is the way to do that.

However, there is a counter argument in favor of native development. Cross development creates the burden of cross-compiling all the libraries and tools that you need for your target. We will see later in this chapter that cross-compiling is not always simple because many open source packages are not designed to be built in this way. Integrated build tools, including Buildroot and the Yocto Project, help by encapsulating the rules to cross compile a range of packages that you need in typical embedded systems, but if you want to compile a large number of additional packages, then it is better to natively compile them. For example, building a Debian distribution for the Raspberry Pi or BeagleBone using a cross compiler would be very hard. Instead, they are natively compiled. Creating a native build environment from scratch is not easy. You would still need a cross compiler at first to create the native build environment on the target, which you then use to build the packages. Then, in order to perform the native build in a reasonable amount of time, you would need a build farm of well-provisioned target boards, or you may be able to use QEMU to emulate the target.

Meanwhile, in this chapter, I will focus on the more mainstream cross compiler environment, which is relatively easy to set up and administer.

CPU architectures

The toolchain has to be built according to the capabilities of the target CPU, which includes:

- **CPU architecture**: ARM, MIPS, x86_64, and so on
- **Big- or little-endian operation**: Some CPUs can operate in both modes, but the machine code is different for each
- **Floating point support**: Not all versions of embedded processors implement a hardware floating point unit, in which case the toolchain has to be configured to call a software floating point library instead
- **Application Binary Interface** (**ABI**): The calling convention used for passing parameters between function calls

With many architectures, the ABI is constant across the family of processors. One notable exception is ARM. The ARM architecture transitioned to the **Extended Application Binary Interface (EABI)** in the late 2000s, resulting in the previous ABI being named the **Old Application Binary Interface (OABI)**. While the OABI is now obsolete, you continue to see references to EABI. Since then, the EABI has split into two, based on the way the floating point parameters are passed. The original EABI uses general purpose (integer) registers, while the newer **Extended Application Binary Interface Hard-Float (EABIHF)** uses floating point registers. The EABIHF is significantly faster at floating point operations, since it removes the need for copying between integer and floating point registers, but it is not compatible with CPUs that do not have a floating point unit. The choice, then, is between two incompatible ABIs; you cannot mix and match the two, and so you have to decide at this stage.

GNU uses a prefix to the name of each tool in the toolchain, which identifies the various combinations that can be generated. It consists of a tuple of three or four components separated by dashes, as described here:

- **CPU**: This is the CPU architecture, such as ARM, MIPS, or x86_64. If the CPU has both endian modes, they may be differentiated by adding `el` for little-endian or `eb` for big-endian. Good examples are little-endian MIPS, `mipsel` and big-endian ARM, `armeb`.
- **Vendor**: This identifies the provider of the toolchain. Examples include `buildroot`, `poky`, or just `unknown`. Sometimes it is left out altogether.
- **Kernel**: For our purposes, it is always `linux`.
- **Operating system**: A name for the user space component, which might be `gnu` or `musl`. The ABI may be appended here as well, so for ARM toolchains, you may see `gnueabi`, `gnueabihf`, `musleabi`, or `musleabihf`.

You can find the tuple used when building the toolchain by using the `-dumpmachine` option of `gcc`. For example, you may see the following on the host computer:

```
$ gcc -dumpmachine
x86_64-linux-gnu
```

When a native compiler is installed on a machine, it is normal to create links to each of the tools in the toolchain with no prefixes, so that you can call the C compiler with the `gcc` command.

Here is an example using a cross compiler:

```
$ mipsel-unknown-linux-gnu-gcc -dumpmachine
mipsel-unknown-linux-gnu
```

Choosing the C library

The programming interface to the Unix operating system is defined in the C language, which is now defined by the POSIX standards. The C library is the implementation of that interface; it is the gateway to the kernel for Linux programs, as shown in the following diagram. Even if you are writing programs in another language, maybe Java or Python, the respective run-time support libraries will have to call the **C library** eventually, as shown here:

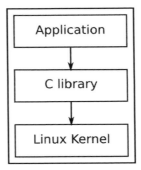

Whenever the C library needs the services of the kernel, it will use the kernel system call interface to transition between user space and kernel space. It is possible to bypass the C library by making the kernel system calls directly, but that is a lot of trouble and almost never necessary.

There are several C libraries to choose from. The main options are as follows:

- **glibc**: This is the standard GNU C library, available at `http://www.gnu.org/software/libc`. It is big and, until recently, not very configurable, but it is the most complete implementation of the POSIX API. The license is LGPL 2.1.
- **musl libc**: This is available at `https://www.musl-libc.org`. The `musl libc` library is comparatively new, but has been gaining a lot of attention as a small and standards-compliant alternative to GNU `libc`. It is a good choice for systems with a limited amount of RAM and storage. It has an MIT license.

- **uClibc-ng**: This is available at `https://uclibc-ng.org/`. u is really a Greek mu character, indicating that this is the micro controller C library. It was first developed to work with uClinux (Linux for CPUs without memory management units), but has since been adapted to be used with full Linux. The `uClibc-ng` library is a fork of the original `uClibc` project (`https://uclibc.org/`), which has unfortunately fallen into disrepair. Both are licensed with LGPL 2.1.
- **eglibc**: This is available at `http://www.eglibc.org/home`. Now obsolete, `eglibc` was a fork of `glibc` with changes to make it more suitable for embedded usage. Among other things, `eglibc` added configuration options and support for architectures not covered by `glibc`, in particular the PowerPC e500 CPU core. The code base from `eglibc` was merged back into `glibc` in version 2.20. The `eglibc` library is no longer maintained.

So, which to choose? My advice is to use `uClibc-ng` only if you are using `uClinux`. If you have very limited amount of storage or RAM, then `musl libc` is a good choice, otherwise, use `glibc`, as shown in this flow chart:

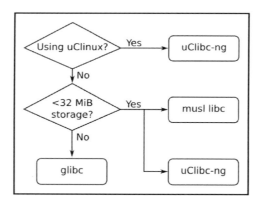

Finding a toolchain

You have three choices for your cross development toolchain: you may find a ready built toolchain that matches your needs, you can use the one generated by an embedded build tool which is covered in `Chapter 6`, *Selecting a Build System*, or you can create one yourself as described later in this chapter.

A pre-built cross toolchain is an attractive option in that you only have to download and install it, but you are limited to the configuration of that particular toolchain and you are dependent on the person or organization you got it from. Most likely, it will be one of these:

- An SoC or board vendor. Most vendors offer a Linux toolchain.
- A consortium dedicated to providing system-level support for a given architecture. For example, Linaro, (https://www.linaro.org/) have pre-built toolchains for the ARM architecture.
- A third-party Linux tool vendor, such as Mentor Graphics, TimeSys, or MontaVista.
- The cross tool packages for your desktop Linux distribution. For example, Debian-based distributions have packages for cross compiling for ARM, MIPS, and PowerPC targets.
- A binary SDK produced by one of the integrated embedded build tools. The Yocto Project has some examples at http://downloads.yoctoproject.org/releases/yocto/yocto-[version]/toolchain.
- A link from a forum that you can't find any more.

In all of these cases, you have to decide whether the pre-built toolchain on offer meets your requirements. Does it use the C library you prefer? Will the provider give you updates for security fixes and bugs, bearing in mind my comments on support and updates from Chapter 1, *Starting Out*. If your answer is no to any of these, then you should consider creating your own.

Unfortunately, building a toolchain is no easy task. If you truly want to do the whole thing yourself, take a look at **Cross Linux From Scratch** (http://trac.clfs.org). There you will find step-by-step instructions on how to create each component.

A simpler alternative is to use crosstool-NG, which encapsulates the process into a set of scripts and has a menu-driven frontend. You still need a fair degree of knowledge, though, just to make the right choices.

It is simpler still to use a build system such as Buildroot or the Yocto Project, since they generate a toolchain as part of the build process. This is my preferred solution, as I have shown in Chapter 6, *Selecting a Build System*.

Building a toolchain using crosstool-NG

Some years ago, Dan Kegel wrote a set of scripts and `makefiles` for generating cross development toolchains and called it crosstool (`http://kegel.com/crosstool/`). In 2007, Yann E. Morin used that base to create the next generation of crosstool, crosstool-NG (`http://crosstool-ng.github.io/`). Today it is by far the most convenient way to create a stand-alone cross toolchain from source.

Installing crosstool-NG

Before you begin, you will need a working native toolchain and build tools on your host PC. To work with crosstool-NG on an Ubuntu host, you will need to install the packages using the following command:

```
$ sudo apt-get install automake bison chrpath flex g++ git gperf \
gawk libexpat1-dev libncurses5-dev libsdl1.2-dev libtool \
python2.7-dev texinfo
```

Next, get the current release from the crosstool-NG Git repository. In my examples, I have used version 1.22.0. Extract it and create the frontend menu system, `ct-ng`, as shown in the following commands:

```
$ git clone https://github.com/crosstool-ng/crosstool-ng.git
$ cd crosstool-ng
$ git checkout crosstool-ng-1.22.0
$ ./bootstrap
$ ./configure --enable-local
$ make
$ make install
```

The `--enable-local` option means that the program will be installed into the current directory, which avoids the need for root permissions, as would be required if you were to install it in the default location `/usr/local/bin`. Type `./ct-ng` from the current directory to launch the crosstool menu.

Building a toolchain for BeagleBone Black

Crosstool-NG can build many different combinations of toolchains. To make the initial configuration easier, it comes with a set of samples that cover many of the common use-cases. Use `./ct-ng list-samples` to generate the list.

The BeagleBone Black has a TI AM335x SoC, which contains an ARM Cortex A8 core and a VFPv3 floating point unit. Since the BeagleBone Black has plenty of RAM and storage, we can use `glibc` as the C library. The closest sample is `arm-cortex_a8-linux-gnueabi`. You can see the default configuration by prefixing the name with `show-`, as demonstrated here:

```
$ ./ct-ng show-arm-cortex_a8-linux-gnueabi
[L..] arm-cortex_a8-linux-gnueabi
 OS : linux-4.3
 Companion libs : gmp-6.0.0a mpfr-3.1.3 mpc-1.0.3 libelf-0.8.13 expat-2.1.0
                  ncurses-6.0
 binutils : binutils-2.25.1
 C compilers : gcc | 5.2.0
 Languages : C,C++
 C library : glibc-2.22 (threads: nptl)
 Tools : dmalloc-5.5.2 duma-2_5_15 gdb-7.10 ltrace-0.7.3 strace-4.10
```

This is a close match with our requirements, except that it using the `eabi` binary interface, which passes floating point arguments in integer registers. We would prefer to use hardware floating point registers for that purpose because it would speed up function calls that have float and double parameter types. You can change the configuration later on, so for now you should select this target configuration:

```
$ ./ct-ng arm-cortex_a8-linux-gnueabi
```

At this point, you can review the configuration and make changes using the configuration menu command `menuconfig`:

```
$ ./ct-ng menuconfig
```

The menu system is based on the Linux kernel `menuconfig`, and so navigation of the user interface will be familiar to anyone who has configured a kernel. If not, refer to Chapter 4, *Configuring and Building the Kernel* for a description of `menuconfig`.

There are two configuration changes that I would recommend you make at this point:

- In **Paths and misc options**, disable **Render the toolchain read-only** (CT_INSTALL_DIR_RO)
- In **Target options** | **Floating point**, select **hardware (FPU)** (CT_ARCH_FLOAT_HW)

The first is necessary if you want to add libraries to the toolchain after it has been installed, which I describe later in this chapter. The second selects the `eabihf` binary interface for the reasons discussed earlier. The names in parentheses are the configuration labels stored in the configuration file. When you have made the changes, exit the `menuconfig` menu and save the configuration as you do so.

Now you can use crosstool-NG to get, configure, and build the components according to your specification, by typing the following command:

```
$ ./ct-ng build
```

The build will take about half an hour, after which you will find your toolchain is present in `~/x-tools/arm-cortex_a8-linux-gnueabihf`.

Building a toolchain for QEMU

On the QEMU target, you will be emulating an ARM-versatile PB evaluation board that has an ARM926EJ-S processor core, which implements the ARMv5TE instruction set. You need to generate a crosstool-NG toolchain that matches with the specification. The procedure is very similar to the one for the BeagleBone Black.

You begin by running `./ct-ng list-samples` to find a good base configuration to work from. There isn't an exact fit, so use a generic target, `arm-unknown-linux-gnueabi`. You select it as shown, running `distclean` first to make sure that there are no artifacts left over from a previous build:

```
$ ./ct-ng distclean
$ ./ct-ng arm-unknown-linux-gnueabi
```

As with the BeagleBone Black, you can review the configuration and make changes using the configuration menu command `./ct-ng menuconfig`. There is only one change necessary:

- In **Paths and misc options**, disable **Render the toolchain read-only** (CT_INSTALL_DIR_RO)

Now, build the toolchain with the command as shown here:

```
$ ./ct-ng build
```

As before, the build will take about half an hour. The toolchain will be installed in `~/x-tools/arm-unknown-linux-gnueabi`.

Anatomy of a toolchain

To get an idea of what is in a typical toolchain, I want to examine the crosstool-NG toolchain you have just created. The examples use the ARM Cortex A8 toolchain created for the BeagleBone Black, which has the prefix `arm-cortex_a8-linux-gnueabihf-`. If you built the ARM926EJ-S toolchain for the QEMU target, then the prefix will be `arm-unknown-linux-gnueabi` instead.

The ARM Cortex A8 toolchain is in the directory `~/x-tools/arm-cortex_a8-linux-gnueabihf/bin`. In there you will find the cross compiler, `arm-cortex_a8-linux-gnueabihf-gcc`. To make use of it, you need to add the directory to your path using the following command:

```
$ PATH=~/x-tools/arm-cortex_a8-linux-gnueabihf/bin:$PATH
```

Now you can take a simple helloworld program, which in the C language looks like this:

```
#include <stdio.h>
#include <stdlib.h>

int main (int argc, char *argv[])
{
    printf ("Hello, world!\n");
    return 0;
}
```

You compile it like this:

```
$ arm-cortex_a8-linux-gnueabihf-gcc helloworld.c -o helloworld
```

You can confirm that it has been cross compiled by using the `file` command to print the type of the file:

```
$ file helloworld
helloworld: ELF 32-bit LSB executable, ARM, EABI5 version 1 (SYSV),
dynamically linked (uses shared libs), for GNU/Linux 4.3.0, not stripped
```

Finding out about your cross compiler

Imagine that you have just received a toolchain and that you would like to know more about how it was configured. You can find out a lot by querying `gcc`. For example, to find the version, you use `--version`:

```
$ arm-cortex_a8-linux-gnueabihf-gcc --version
arm-cortex_a8-linux-gnueabihf-gcc (crosstool-NG crosstool-ng-1.22.0) 5.2.0
Copyright (C) 2015 Free Software Foundation, Inc.
This is free software; see the source for copying conditions. There is NO
warranty; not even for MERCHANTABILITY or FITNESS FOR A PARTICULAR PURPOSE.
```

To find how it was configured, use -v:

```
$ arm-cortex_a8-linux-gnueabihf-gcc -v
Using built-in specs.
COLLECT_GCC=arm-cortex_a8-linux-gnueabihf-gcc
COLLECT_LTO_WRAPPER=/home/chris/x-tools/arm-cortex_a8-linux-
gnueabihf/libexec/gcc/arm-cortex_a8-linux-gnueabihf/5.2.0/lto-wrapper
Target: arm-cortex_a8-linux-gnueabihf
Configured with: /home/chris/crosstool-ng/.build/src/gcc-5.2.0/configure --
build=x86_64-build_pc-linux-gnu --host=x86_64-build_pc-linux-gnu --
target=arm-cortex_a8-linux-gnueabihf --prefix=/home/chris/x-tools/arm-
cortex_a8-linux-gnueabihf --with-sysroot=/home/chris/x-tools/arm-cortex_a8-
linux-gnueabihf/arm-cortex_a8-linux-gnueabihf/sysroot --enable-
languages=c,c++ --with-cpu=cortex-a8 --with-float=hard --with-
pkgversion='crosstool-NG crosstool-ng-1.22.0' --enable-__cxa_atexit --
disable-libmudflap --disable-libgomp --disable-libssp --disable-libquadmath
--disable-libquadmath-support --disable-libsanitizer --with-
gmp=/media/chris/android/home/training/MELP/ch02/crosstool-ng/.build/arm-
cortex_a8-linux-gnueabihf/buildtools --with-
mpfr=/media/chris/android/home/training/MELP/ch02/crosstool-ng/.build/arm-
cortex_a8-linux-gnueabihf/buildtools --with-
mpc=/media/chris/android/home/training/MELP/ch02/crosstool-ng/.build/arm-
cortex_a8-linux-gnueabihf/buildtools --with-
isl=/media/chris/android/home/training/MELP/ch02/crosstool-ng/.build/arm-
cortex_a8-linux-gnueabihf/buildtools --with-
cloog=/media/chris/android/home/training/MELP/ch02/crosstool-ng/.build/arm-
cortex_a8-linux-gnueabihf/buildtools --with-
libelf=/media/chris/android/home/training/MELP/ch02/crosstool-
ng/.build/arm-cortex_a8-linux-gnueabihf/buildtools --enable-lto --with-
host-libstdcxx='-static-libgcc -Wl,-Bstatic,-lstdc++,-Bdynamic -lm' --
enable-threads=posix --enable-target-optspace --enable-plugin --enable-gold
--disable-nls --disable-multilib --with-local-prefix=/home/chris/x-
tools/arm-cortex_a8-linux-gnueabihf/arm-cortex_a8-linux-gnueabihf/sysroot -
-enable-long-long
Thread model: posix
gcc version 5.2.0 (crosstool-NG crosstool-ng-1.22.0)
```

There is a lot of output there, but the interesting things to note are:

- `--with-sysroot=/home/chris/x-tools/arm-cortex_a8-linux-gnueabihf/arm-cortex_a8-linux-gnueabihf/sysroot`: This is the default `sysroot` directory; see the following section for an explanation
- `--enable-languages=c,c++`: Using this, we have both C and C++ languages enabled
- `--with-cpu=cortex-a8`: The code is generated for an ARM Cortex A8 core
- `--with-float=hard`: Generates opcodes for the floating point unit and uses the VFP registers for parameters
- `--enable-threads=posix`: This enables the POSIX threads

These are the default settings for the compiler. You can override most of them on the `gcc` command line. For example, if you want to compile for a different CPU, you can override the configured setting, `--with-cpu`, by adding `-mcpu` to the command line, as follows:

```
$ arm-cortex_a8-linux-gnueabihf-gcc -mcpu=cortex-a5 helloworld.c \
  -o helloworld
```

You can print out the range of architecture-specific options available using `--target-help`, as follows:

```
$ arm-cortex_a8-linux-gnueabihf-gcc --target-help
```

You may be wondering if it matters that you get the configuration exactly right at this point, since you can always change it as shown here. The answer depends on the way you anticipate using it. If you plan to create a new toolchain for each target, then it makes sense to set everything up at the beginning, because it will reduce the risks of getting it wrong later on. Jumping ahead a little to Chapter 6, *Selecting a Build System*, I call this the Buildroot philosophy. If, on the other hand, you want to build a toolchain that is generic and you are prepared to provide the correct settings when you build for a particular target, then you should make the base toolchain generic, which is the way the Yocto Project handles things. The preceding examples follow the Buildroot philosophy.

The sysroot, library, and header files

The toolchain `sysroot` is a directory which contains subdirectories for libraries, header files, and other configuration files. It can be set when the toolchain is configured through `--with-sysroot=`, or it can be set on the command line using `--sysroot=`. You can see the location of the default sysroot by using `-print-sysroot`:

```
$ arm-cortex_a8-linux-gnueabihf-gcc -print-sysroot
/home/chris/x-tools/arm-cortex_a8-linux-gnueabihf/arm-cortex_a8-linux-
gnueabihf/sysroot
```

You will find the following subdirectories in `sysroot`:

- `lib`: Contains the shared objects for the C library and the dynamic linker/loader, `ld-linux`
- `usr/lib`, the static library archive files for the C library, and any other libraries that may be installed subsequently
- `usr/include`: Contains the headers for all the libraries
- `usr/bin`: Contains the utility programs that run on the target, such as the `ldd` command
- `use/share`: Used for localization and internationalization
- `sbin`: Provides the `ldconfig` utility, used to optimize library loading paths

Plainly, some of these are needed on the development host to compile programs, and others - for example, the shared libraries and `ld-linux` - are needed on the target at runtime.

Other tools in the toolchain

The following table shows various other components of a GNU toolchain, together with a brief description:

Command	Description
addr2line	Converts program addresses into filenames and numbers by reading the debug symbol tables in an executable file. It is very useful when decoding addresses printed out in a system crash report.
ar	The archive utility is used to create static libraries.
as	This is the GNU assembler.
c++filt	This is used to demangle C++ and Java symbols.

Command	Description
cpp	This is the C preprocessor and is used to expand `#define`, `#include`, and other similar directives. You seldom need to use this by itself.
elfedit	This is used to update the ELF header of the ELF files.
g++	This is the GNU C++ frontend, which assumes that source files contain C++ code.
gcc	This is the GNU C frontend, which assumes that source files contain C code.
gcov	This is a code coverage tool.
gdb	This is the GNU debugger.
gprof	This is a program profiling tool.
ld	This is the GNU linker.
nm	This lists symbols from object files.
objcopy	This is used to copy and translate object files.
objdump	This is used to display information from object files.
ranlib	This creates or modifies an index in a static library, making the linking stage faster.
readelf	This displays information about files in ELF object format.
size	This lists section sizes and the total size.
strings	This displays strings of printable characters in files.
strip	This is used to strip an object file of debug symbol tables, thus making it smaller. Typically, you would strip all the executable code that is put onto the target.

Looking at the components of the C library

The C library is not a single library file. It is composed of four main parts that together implement the POSIX API:

- `libc`: The main C library that contains the well-known POSIX functions such as `printf`, `open`, `close`, `read`, `write`, and so on
- `libm`: Contains maths functions such as `cos`, `exp`, and `log`

- libpthread: Contains all the POSIX thread functions with names beginning with pthread_
- librt: Has the real-time extensions to POSIX, including shared memory and asynchronous I/O

The first one, libc, is always linked in but the others have to be explicitly linked with the -l option. The parameter to -l is the library name with lib stripped off. For example, a program that calculates a sine function by calling sin() would be linked with libm using -lm:

```
$ arm-cortex_a8-linux-gnueabihf-gcc myprog.c -o myprog -lm
```

You can verify which libraries have been linked in this or any other program by using the readelf command:

```
$ arm-cortex_a8-linux-gnueabihf-readelf -a myprog | grep "Shared library"
0x00000001 (NEEDED) Shared library: [libm.so.6]
0x00000001 (NEEDED) Shared library: [libc.so.6]
```

Shared libraries need a runtime linker, which you can expose using:

```
$ arm-cortex_a8-linux-gnueabihf-readelf -a myprog | grep "program interpreter"
[Requesting program interpreter: /lib/ld-linux-armhf.so.3]
```

This is so useful that I have a script file named list-libs, which you will find in the book code archive in MELP/list-libs. It contains the following commands:

```
#!/bin/sh
${CROSS_COMPILE}readelf -a $1 | grep "program interpreter"
${CROSS_COMPILE}readelf -a $1 | grep "Shared library"
```

Linking with libraries – static and dynamic linking

Any application you write for Linux, whether it be in C or C++, will be linked with the C library libc. This is so fundamental that you don't even have to tell gcc or g++ to do it because it always links libc. Other libraries that you may want to link with have to be explicitly named through the -l option.

The library code can be linked in two different ways: statically, meaning that all the library functions your application calls and their dependencies are pulled from the library archive and bound into your executable; and dynamically, meaning that references to the library files and functions in those files are generated in the code but the actual linking is done dynamically at runtime. You will find the code for the examples that follow in the book code archive in MELP/chapter_02/library.

Static libraries

Static linking is useful in a few circumstances. For example, if you are building a small system which consists of only BusyBox and some script files, it is simpler to link BusyBox statically and avoid having to copy the runtime library files and linker. It will also be smaller because you only link in the code that your application uses rather than supplying the entire C library. Static linking is also useful if you need to run a program before the filesystem that holds the runtime libraries is available.

You tell to link all the libraries statically by adding -static to the command line:

```
$ arm-cortex_a8-linux-gnueabihf-gcc –static helloworld.c –o helloworld-
static
```

You will note that the size of the binary increases dramatically:

```
$ ls –l
-rwxrwxr-x 1 chris chris 5884 Mar 5 09:56 helloworld
-rwxrwxr-x 1 chris chris 614692 Mar 5 10:27 helloworld-static
```

Static linking pulls code from a library archive, usually named lib[name].a. In the preceding case, it is libc.a, which is in [sysroot]/usr/lib:

```
$ export SYSROOT=$(arm-cortex_a8-linux-gnueabihf-gcc –print-sysroot)
$ cd $SYSROOT
$ ls –l usr/lib/libc.a
-rw-r--r-- 1 chris chris 3457004 Mar 3 15:21 usr/lib/libc.a
```

Note that the syntax export SYSROOT=$(arm-cortex_a8-linux-gnueabihf-gcc –print-sysroot) places the path to the sysroot in the shell variable, SYSROOT, which makes the example a little clearer.

Creating a static library is as simple as creating an archive of object files using the ar command. If I have two source files named test1.c and test2.c, and I want to create a static library named libtest.a, then I would do the following:

```
$ arm-cortex_a8-linux-gnueabihf-gcc -c test1.c
$ arm-cortex_a8-linux-gnueabihf-gcc -c test2.c
$ arm-cortex_a8-linux-gnueabihf-ar rc libtest.a test1.o test2.o
$ ls -l
total 24
-rw-rw-r-- 1 chris chris 2392 Oct 9 09:28 libtest.a
-rw-rw-r-- 1 chris chris 116 Oct 9 09:26 test1.c
-rw-rw-r-- 1 chris chris 1080 Oct 9 09:27 test1.o
-rw-rw-r-- 1 chris chris 121 Oct 9 09:26 test2.c
-rw-rw-r-- 1 chris chris 1088 Oct 9 09:27 test2.o
```

Then I could link libtest into my helloworld program, using:

```
$ arm-cortex_a8-linux-gnueabihf-gcc helloworld.c -ltest \
-L../libs -I../libs -o helloworld
```

Shared libraries

A more common way to deploy libraries is as shared objects that are linked at runtime, which makes more efficient use of storage and system memory, since only one copy of the code needs to be loaded. It also makes it easy to update the library files without having to re-link all the programs that use them.

The object code for a shared library must be position-independent, so that the runtime linker is free to locate it in memory at the next free address. To do this, add the -fPIC parameter to gcc, and then link it using the -shared option:

```
$ arm-cortex_a8-linux-gnueabihf-gcc -fPIC -c test1.c
$ arm-cortex_a8-linux-gnueabihf-gcc -fPIC -c test2.c
$ arm-cortex_a8-linux-gnueabihf-gcc -shared -o libtest.so test1.o test2.o
```

This creates the shared library, libtest.so. To link an application with this library, you add -ltest, exactly as in the static case mentioned in the preceding section, but this time the code is not included in the executable. Instead, there is a reference to the library that the runtime linker will have to resolve:

```
$ arm-cortex_a8-linux-gnueabihf-gcc helloworld.c -ltest \
-L../libs -I../libs -o helloworld
$ MELP/list-libs helloworld
[Requesting program interpreter: /lib/ld-linux-armhf.so.3]
0x00000001 (NEEDED) Shared library: [libtest.so]
0x00000001 (NEEDED) Shared library: [libc.so.6]
```

The runtime linker for this program is /lib/ld-linux-armhf.so.3, which must be present in the target's filesystem. The linker will look for libtest.so in the default search path: /lib and /usr/lib. If you want it to look for libraries in other directories as well, you can place a colon-separated list of paths in the shell variable LD_LIBRARY_PATH:

```
# export LD_LIBRARY_PATH=/opt/lib:/opt/usr/lib
```

Understanding shared library version numbers

One of the benefits of shared libraries is that they can be updated independently of the programs that use them. Library updates are of two types: those that fix bugs or add new functions in a backwards-compatible way, and those that break compatibility with existing applications. GNU/Linux has a versioning scheme to handle both these cases.

Each library has a release version and an interface number. The release version is simply a string that is appended to the library name; for example, the JPEG image library libjpeg is currently at release 8.0.2 and so the library is named libjpeg.so.8.0.2. There is a symbolic link named libjpeg.so to libjpeg.so.8.0.2, so that when you compile a program with -ljpeg, you link with the current version. If you install version 8.0.3, the link is updated and you will link with that one instead.

Now suppose that version 9.0.0. comes along and that breaks the backwards compatibility. The link from libjpeg.so now points to libjpeg.so.9.0.0, so that any new programs are linked with the new version, possibly throwing compile errors when the interface to libjpeg changes, which the developer can fix. Any programs on the target that are not recompiled are going to fail in some way, because they are still using the old interface. This is where an object known as the **soname** helps. The soname encodes the interface number when the library was built and is used by the runtime linker when it loads the library. It is formatted as <library name>.so.<interface number>. For libjpeg.so.8.0.2, the soname is libjpeg.so.8:

```
$ readelf -a /usr/lib/libjpeg.so.8.0.2 | grep SONAME
0x000000000000000e (SONAME) Library soname:
  [libjpeg.so.8]
```

Any program compiled with it will request libjpeg.so.8 at runtime, which will be a symbolic link on the target to libjpeg.so.8.0.2. When version 9.0.0 of libjpeg is installed, it will have a soname of libjpeg.so.9, and so it is possible to have two incompatible versions of the same library installed on the same system. Programs that were linked with libjpeg.so.8.*.* will load libjpeg.so.8, and those linked with libjpeg.so.9.*.* will load libjpeg.so.9.

This is why, when you look at the directory listing of `<sysroot>/usr/lib/libjpeg*`, you find these four files:

- `libjpeg.a`: This is the library archive used for static linking
- `libjpeg.so -> libjpeg.so.8.0.2`: This is a symbolic link, used for dynamic linking
- `libjpeg.so.8 -> libjpeg.so.8.0.2`: This is a symbolic link, used when loading the library at runtime
- `libjpeg.so.8.0.2`: This is the actual shared library, used at both compile time and runtime

The first two are only needed on the host computer for building and the last two are needed on the target at runtime.

The art of cross compiling

Having a working cross toolchain is the starting point of a journey, not the end of it. At some point, you will want to begin cross compiling the various tools, applications, and libraries that you need on your target. Many of them will be open source packages—each of which has its own method of compiling and its own peculiarities. There are some common build systems, including:

- Pure `makefiles`, where the toolchain is usually controlled by the make variable `CROSS_COMPILE`
- The GNU build system known as **Autotools**
- CMake (`https://cmake.org/`)

I will cover only the first two here since these are the ones needed for even a basic embedded Linux system. For CMake, there are some excellent resources on the CMake website referenced in the preceding point.

Simple makefiles

Some important packages are very simple to cross compile, including the Linux kernel, the U-Boot bootloader, and BusyBox. For each of these, you only need to put the toolchain prefix in the make variable `CROSS_COMPILE`, for example `arm-cortex_a8-linux-gnueabi-`. Note the trailing dash `-`.

So, to compile BusyBox, you would type:

```
$ make CROSS_COMPILE=arm-cortex_a8-linux-gnueabihf-
```

Or, you can set it as a shell variable:

```
$ export CROSS_COMPILE=arm-cortex_a8-linux-gnueabihf-
$ make
```

In the case of U-Boot and Linux, you also have to set the `make` variable ARCH to one of the machine architectures they support, which I will cover in `Chapter 3`, *All About Bootloaders*, and `Chapter 4`, *Configuring and Building the Kernel*.

Autotools

The name Autotools refers to a group of tools that are used as the build system in many open source projects. The components, together with the appropriate project pages, are:

- GNU Autoconf (`https://www.gnu.org/software/autoconf/autoconf.html`)
- GNU Automake (`https://www.gnu.org/savannah-checkouts/gnu/automake/`)
- GNU Libtool (`https://www.gnu.org/software/libtool/libtool.html`)
- Gnulib (`https://www.gnu.org/software/gnulib/`)

The role of Autotools is to smooth over the differences between the many different types of systems that the package may be compiled for, accounting for different versions of compilers, different versions of libraries, different locations of header files, and dependencies with other packages. Packages that use Autotools come with a script named `configure` that checks dependencies and generates makefiles according to what it finds. The `configure` script may also give you the opportunity to enable or disable certain features. You can find the options on offer by running `./configure --help`.

To configure, build, and install a package for the native operating system, you would typically run the following three commands:

```
$ ./configure
$ make
$ sudo make install
```

Autotools is able to handle cross development as well. You can influence the behavior of the configure script by setting these shell variables:

- CC: The C compiler command
- CFLAGS: Additional C compiler flags

- LDFLAGS: Additional linker flags; for example, if you have libraries in a non-standard directory `<lib dir>`, you would add it to the library search path by adding `-L<lib dir>`
- LIBS: Contains a list of additional libraries to pass to the linker; for instance, `-lm` for the math library
- CPPFLAGS: Contains C/C++ preprocessor flags; for example, you would add `-I<include dir>` to search for headers in a non-standard directory `<include dir>`
- CPP: The C preprocessor to use

Sometimes it is sufficient to set only the CC variable, as follows:

```
$ CC=arm-cortex_a8-linux-gnueabihf-gcc ./configure
```

At other times, that will result in an error like this:

```
[...]
checking whether we are cross compiling... configure: error: in
'/home/chris/MELP/build/sqlite-autoconf-3081101':
configure: error: cannot run C compiled programs.
If you meant to cross compile, use '--host'.
See 'config.log' for more details
```

The reason for the failure is that configure often tries to discover the capabilities of the toolchain by compiling snippets of code and running them to see what happens, which cannot work if the program has been cross compiled. Nevertheless, there is a hint in the error message on how to solve the problem. Autotools understands three different types of machines that may be involved when compiling a package:

- **Build** is the computer that builds the package, which defaults to the current machine.
- **Host** is the computer the program will run on; for a native compile, this is left blank and it defaults to be the same computer as build. When you are cross compiling, set it to be the tuple of your toolchain.
- **Target** is the computer the program will generate code for; you would set this when building a cross compiler, for example.

So, to cross compile, you just need to override the host, as follows:

```
$ CC=arm-cortex_a8-linux-gnueabihf-gcc \
./configure --host=arm-cortex_a8-linux-gnueabihf
```

One final thing to note is that the default install directory is `<sysroot>/usr/local/*`. You would usually install it in `<sysroot>/usr/*`, so that the header files and libraries would be picked up from their default locations. The complete command to configure a typical Autotools package is as follows:

```
$ CC=arm-cortex_a8-linux-gnueabihf-gcc \
./configure --host=arm-cortex_a8-linux-gnueabihf --prefix=/usr
```

An example: SQLite

The SQLite library implements a simple relational database and is quite popular on embedded devices. You begin by getting a copy of SQLite:

```
$ wget http://www.sqlite.org/2015/sqlite-autoconf-3081101.tar.gz
$ tar xf sqlite-autoconf-3081101.tar.gz
$ cd sqlite-autoconf-3081101
```

Next, run the `configure` script:

```
$ CC=arm-cortex_a8-linux-gnueabihf-gcc \
./configure --host=arm-cortex_a8-linux-gnueabihf --prefix=/usr
```

That seems to work! If it had failed, there would be error messages printed to the Terminal and recorded in `config.log`. Note that several makefiles have been created, so now you can build it:

```
$ make
```

Finally, you install it into the toolchain directory by setting the `make` variable `DESTDIR`. If you don't, it will try to install it into the host computer's `/usr` directory, which is not what you want:

```
$ make DESTDIR=$(arm-cortex_a8-linux-gnueabihf-gcc -print-sysroot) install
```

You may find that the final command fails with a file permissions error. A crosstool-NG toolchain is read-only by default, which is why it is useful to set `CT_INSTALL_DIR_RO` to `y` when building it. Another common problem is that the toolchain is installed in a system directory, such as `/opt` or `/usr/local`, in which case you will need `root` permissions when running the install.

After installing, you should find that various files have been added to your toolchain:

- `<sysroot>/usr/bin`: `sqlite3`: This is a command-line interface for SQLite that you can install and run on the target

- `<sysroot>/usr/lib`: `libsqlite3.so.0.8.6`, `libsqlite3.so.0`, `libsqlite3.so`, `libsqlite3.la`, `libsqlite3.a`: These are the shared and static libraries
- `<sysroot>/usr/lib/pkgconfig`: `sqlite3.pc`: This is the package configuration file, as described in the following section
- `<sysroot>/usr/lib/include`: `sqlite3.h`, `sqlite3ext.h`: These are the header files
- `<sysroot>/usr/share/man/man1`: `sqlite3.1`: This is the manual page

Now you can compile programs that use `sqlite3` by adding `-lsqlite3` at the link stage:

```
$ arm-cortex_a8-linux-gnueabihf-gcc -lsqlite3 sqlite-test.c -o sqlite-test
```

Here, `sqlite-test.c` is a hypothetical program that calls SQLite functions. Since `sqlite3` has been installed into the `sysroot`, the compiler will find the header and library files without any problem. If they had been installed elsewhere, you would have had to add `-L<lib dir>` and `-I<include dir>`.

Naturally, there will be runtime dependencies as well, and you will have to install the appropriate files into the target directory as described in Chapter 5, *Building a Root Filesystem*.

Package configuration

Tracking package dependencies is quite complex. The package configuration utility `pkg-config` (https://www.freedesktop.org/wiki/Software/pkg-config/) helps track which packages are installed and which compile flags each needs by keeping a database of Autotools packages in `[sysroot]/usr/lib/pkgconfig`. For instance, the one for SQLite3 is named `sqlite3.pc` and contains essential information needed by other packages that need to make use of it:

```
$ cat $(arm-cortex_a8-linux-gnueabihf-gcc -print-
sysroot)/usr/lib/pkgconfig/sqlite3.pc
# Package Information for pkg-config

prefix=/usr
exec_prefix=${prefix}
libdir=${exec_prefix}/lib
includedir=${prefix}/include

Name: SQLite
Description: SQL database engine
```

```
Version: 3.8.11.1
Libs: -L${libdir} -lsqlite3
Libs.private: -ldl -lpthread
Cflags: -I${includedir}
```

You can use `pkg-config` to extract information in a form that you can feed straight to `gcc`. In the case of a library like `libsqlite3`, you want to know the library name (`--libs`) and any special C flags (`--cflags`):

```
$ pkg-config sqlite3 --libs --cflags
Package sqlite3 was not found in the pkg-config search path.
Perhaps you should add the directory containing `sqlite3.pc'
to the PKG_CONFIG_PATH environment variable
No package 'sqlite3' found
```

Oops! That failed because it was looking in the host's `sysroot` and the development package for `libsqlite3` has not been installed on the host. You need to point it at the `sysroot` of the target toolchain by setting the shell variable `PKG_CONFIG_LIBDIR`:

```
$ export PKG_CONFIG_LIBDIR=$(arm-cortex_a8-linux-gnueabihf-gcc \
-print-sysroot)/usr/lib/pkgconfig

$ pkg-config sqlite3 --libs --cflags -lsqlite3
```

Now the output is `-lsqlite3`. In this case, you knew that already, but generally you wouldn't, so this is a valuable technique. The final commands to compile would be:

```
$ export PKG_CONFIG_LIBDIR=$(arm-cortex_a8-linux-gnueabihf-gcc \
-print-sysroot)/usr/lib/pkgconfig

$ arm-cortex_a8-linux-gnueabihf-gcc $(pkg-config sqlite3 --cflags --libs) \
sqlite-test.c -o sqlite-test
```

Problems with cross compiling

The sqlite3 is a well-behaved package and cross compiles nicely, but not all packages are the same. Typical pain points include:

- Home-grown build systems; `zlib`, for example, has a configure script, but it does not behave like the Autotools configure described in the previous section
- Configure scripts that read `pkg-config` information, headers, and other files from the host, disregarding the `--host` override
- Scripts that insist on trying to run cross compiled code

Each case requires careful analysis of the error and additional parameters to the configure script to provide the correct information, or patches to the code to avoid the problem altogether. Bear in mind that one package may have many dependencies, especially with programs that have a graphical interface using GTK or QT, or that handle multimedia content. As an example, `mplayer`, which is a popular tool for playing multimedia content, has dependencies on over 100 libraries. It would take weeks of effort to build them all.

Therefore, I would not recommend manually cross compiling components for the target in this way, except when there is no alternative or the number of packages to build is small. A much better approach is to use a build tool such as Buildroot or the Yocto Project, or avoid the problem altogether by setting up a native build environment for your target architecture. Now you can see why distributions like Debian are always compiled natively.

Summary

The toolchain is always your starting point; everything that follows from that is dependent on having a working, reliable toolchain.

Most embedded build environments are based on a cross development toolchain, which creates a clear separation between a powerful host computer building the code and a target computer on which it runs. The toolchain itself consists of the GNU binutils, a C compiler from the GNU compiler collection—and quite likely the C++ compiler as well—plus one of the C libraries I have described. Usually, the GNU debugger, GDB, will be generated at this point, which I describe in `Chapter 14`, *Debugging with GDB*. Also, keep a watch out for the Clang compiler, as it will develop over the next few years.

You may start with nothing but a toolchain—perhaps built using crosstool-NG or downloaded from Linaro—and use it to compile all the packages that you need on your target, accepting the amount of hard work this will entail. Or you may obtain the toolchain as part of a distribution which includes a range of packages. A distribution can be generated from source code using a build system such as Buildroot or the Yocto Project, or it can be a binary distribution from a third party, maybe a commercial enterprise like Mentor Graphics, or an open source project such as the Denx ELDK. Beware of toolchains or distributions that are offered to you for free as part of a hardware package; they are often poorly configured and not maintained. In any case, you should make your choice according to your situation, and then be consistent in its use throughout the project.

Once you have a toolchain, you can use it to build the other components of your embedded Linux system. In the next chapter, you will learn about the bootloader, which brings your device to life and begins the boot process.

3
All About Bootloaders

The bootloader is the second element of embedded Linux. It is the part that starts the system up and loads the operating system kernel. In this chapter, I will look at the role of the bootloader and, in particular, how it passes control from itself to the kernel using a data structure called a **device tree**, also known as a **flattened device tree** or **FDT**. I will cover the basics of device trees, so that you will be able to follow the connections described in a device tree and relate it to real hardware.

I will look at the popular open source bootloader, U-Boot, and show you how to use it to boot a target device, and also how to customize it to run on a new device, using the BeagleBone Black as an example. Finally, I will take a quick look at Barebox, a bootloader that shares its past with U-Boot, but which has, arguably, a cleaner design.

In this chapter, we will cover the following topics:

- What does a bootloader do?
- The boot sequence.
- Booting with UEFI firmware.
- Moving from bootloader to kernel.
- Introducing device trees.
- Choosing a bootloader.
- U-Boot.
- Barebox.

What does a bootloader do?

In an embedded Linux system, the bootloader has two main jobs: to initialize the system to a basic level and to load the kernel. In fact, the first job is somewhat subsidiary to the second, in that it is only necessary to get as much of the system working as is needed to load the kernel.

When the first lines of the bootloader code are executed, following a power-on or a reset, the system is in a very minimal state. The DRAM controller would not have been set up, and so the main memory would not be accessible. Likewise, other interfaces would not have been configured, so storage accessed via NAND flash controllers, MMC controllers, and so on, would also not be usable. Typically, the only resources operational at the beginning are a single CPU core and some on-chip static memory. As a result, system bootstrap consists of several phases of code, each bringing more of the system into operation. The final act of the bootloader is to load the kernel into RAM and create an execution environment for it. The details of the interface between the bootloader and the kernel are architecture-specific, but in each case it has to do two things. First, bootloader has to pass a pointer to a structure containing information about the hardware configuration, and second it has to pass a pointer to the kernel command line. The kernel command line is a text string that controls the behavior of Linux. Once the kernel has begun executing, the bootloader is no longer needed and all the memory it was using can be reclaimed.

A subsidiary job of the bootloader is to provide a maintenance mode for updating boot configurations, loading new boot images into memory, and, maybe, running diagnostics. This is usually controlled by a simple command-line user interface, commonly over a serial interface.

The boot sequence

In simpler times, some years ago, it was only necessary to place the bootloader in non-volatile memory at the reset vector of the processor. **NOR flash** memory was common at that time and, since it can be mapped directly into the address space, it was the ideal method of storage. The following diagram shows such a configuration, with the **Reset vector** at `0xfffffffc` at the top end of an area of flash memory. The bootloader is linked so that there is a jump instruction at that location that points to the start of the bootloader code:

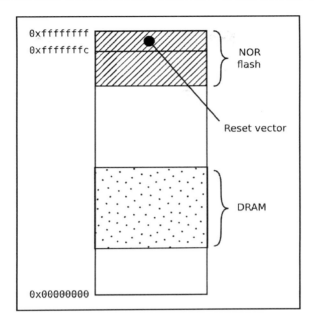

From that point, the bootloader code running in NOR flash memory can initialize the DRAM controller, so that the main memory, the DRAM, becomes available and then it copies itself into the **DRAM**. Once fully operational, the bootloader can load the kernel from flash memory into **DRAM** and transfer control to it.

However, once you move away from a simple linearly addressable storage medium like **NOR flash**, the boot sequence becomes a complex, multi-stage procedure. The details are very specific to each SoC, but they generally follow each of the following phases.

Phase 1 – ROM code

In the absence of reliable external memory, the code that runs immediately after a reset or power-on has to be stored on-chip in the SoC; this is known as **ROM code**. It is loaded into the chip when it is manufactured, and hence the ROM code is proprietary and cannot be replaced by an open source equivalent. Usually, it does not include code to initialize the memory controller, since DRAM configurations are highly device-specific, and so it can only use **Static Random Access Memory (SRAM)**, which does not require a memory controller.

Most embedded SoC designs have a small amount of SRAM on-chip, varying in size from as little as 4 KB to several hundred KB:

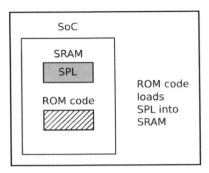

The ROM code is capable of loading a small chunk of code from one of several pre-programmed locations into the SRAM. As an example, TI OMAP and Sitara chips try to load code from the first few pages of NAND flash memory, or from flash memory connected through a **Serial Peripheral Interface** (**SPI**), or from the first sectors of an MMC device (which could be an eMMC chip or an SD card), or from a file named MLO on the first partition of an MMC device. If reading from all of these memory devices fails, then it tries reading a byte stream from Ethernet, USB, or UART; the latter is provided mainly as a means of loading code into flash memory during production, rather than for use in normal operation. Most embedded SoCs have a ROM code that works in a similar way. In SoCs where the SRAM is not large enough to load a full bootloader like U-Boot, there has to be an intermediate loader called the **secondary program loader**, or **SPL**.

At the end of the ROM code phase, the SPL is present in the SRAM and the ROM code jumps to the beginning of that code.

Phase 2 – secondary program loader

The SPL must set up the memory controller and other essential parts of the system preparatory to loading the **Tertiary Program Loader** (**TPL**) into DRAM. The functionality of the SPL is limited by the size of the SRAM. It can read a program from a list of storage devices, as can the ROM code, once again using pre-programmed offsets from the start of a flash device. If the SPL has file system drivers built in, it can read well known file names, such as u-boot.img, from a disk partition. The SPL usually doesn't allow for any user interaction, but it may print version information and progress messages, which you can see on the console. The following diagram explains the phase 2 architecture:

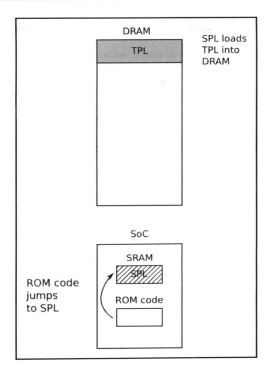

The SPL may be open source, as is the case with the TI x-loader and Atmel AT91Bootstrap, but it is quite common for it to contain proprietary code that is supplied by the manufacturer as a binary blob.

At the end of the second phase, the TPL is present in DRAM, and the SPL can make a jump to that area.

Phase 3 – TPL

Now, at last, we are running a full bootloader, such as U-Boot or BareBox. Usually, there is a simple command-line user interface that lets you perform maintenance tasks, such as loading new boot and kernel images into flash storage, and loading and booting a kernel, and there is a way to load the kernel automatically without user intervention.

The following diagram explains the phase 3 architecture:

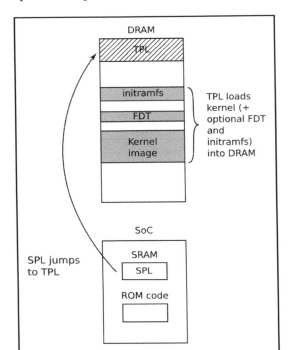

At the end of the third phase, there is a kernel in memory, waiting to be started.

Embedded bootloaders usually disappear from memory once the kernel is running, and perform no further part in the operation of the system.

Booting with UEFI firmware

Most embedded x86/x86_64 designs, and some ARM designs, have firmware based on the **Universal Extensible Firmware Interface (UEFI)** standard. You can take a look at the UEFI website at http://www.uefi.org/ for more information. The boot sequence is fundamentally the same as that described in the preceding section:

- **Phase 1**: The processor loads the platform initialization firmware from flash memory. In some designs, it is loaded directly from NOR flash memory, while in others, there is ROM code on-chip which loads the firmware from SPI flash memory into some on-chip static RAM.

- **Phase 2**: The platform initialization firmware performs the role of SPL. It initializes the DRAM controller and other system interfaces, so as to be able to load an EFI boot manager from the **EFI System Partition** (**ESP**) on a local disk, or from a network server via PXE boot. The ESP must be formatted using FAT16 or FAT32 format and it should have the well-known GUID value of `C12A7328-F81F-11D2-BA4B-00A0C93EC93B`. The path name of the boot manager code must follow the naming convention `<efi_system_partition>/boot/boot<machine_type_short_name>.efi`. For example, the file path to the loader on an x86_64 system would be `/efi/boot/bootx64.efi`.

- **Phase 3**: The UEFI boot manager is the tertiary program loader. The TPL in this case has to be a bootloader that is capable of loading a Linux kernel and an optional RAM disk into memory. Common choices are:
    - `systemd-boot`: This used to be called `gummiboot`. It is a simple UEFI-compatible bootloader, licensed under LGPL v2.1. The website is `https://www.freedesktop.org/wiki/Software/systemd/systemd-boot/`.
    - `Tummiboot`: This is the `gummiboot` with trusted boot support (Intel's **Trusted Execution Technology** (**TEX**)).

Moving from bootloader to kernel

When the bootloader passes control to the kernel it has to pass some basic information, which may include some of the following:

- The *machine number*, which is used on PowerPC, and ARM platforms without support for a device tree, to identify the type of the SoC
- Basic details of the hardware detected so far, including at least the size and location of the physical RAM, and the CPU clock speed
- The kernel command line
- Optionally, the location and size of a device tree binary
- Optionally, the location and size of an initial RAM disk, called the **initial RAM file system** (**initramfs**)

The kernel command line is a plain ASCII string which controls the behavior of Linux by giving, for example, the name of the device that contains the root filesystem. I will look at the details of this in the next chapter. It is common to provide the root filesystem as a RAM disk, in which case it is the responsibility of the bootloader to load the RAM disk image into memory. I will cover the way you create initial RAM disks in Chapter 5, *Building a Root Filesystem*.

The way this information is passed is dependent on the architecture and has changed in recent years. For instance, with PowerPC, the bootloader simply used to pass a pointer to a board information structure, whereas, with ARM, it passed a pointer to a list of *A tags*. There is a good description of the format of A tags in the kernel source in Documentation/arm/Booting.

In both cases, the amount of information passed was very limited, leaving the bulk of it to be discovered at runtime or hard-coded into the kernel as **platform data**. The widespread use of platform data meant that each board had to have a kernel configured and modified for that platform. A better way was needed, and that way is the device tree. In the ARM world, the move away from A tags began in earnest in February 2013 with the release of Linux 3.8. Today, almost all ARM systems use device tree to gather information about the specifics of the hardware platform, allowing a single kernel binary to run on a wide range of those platforms.

Introducing device trees

If you are working with ARM or PowerPC SoCs, you are almost certainly going to encounter device trees at some point. This section aims to give you a quick overview of what they are and how they work, but there are many details that are not discussed.

A device tree is a flexible way to define the hardware components of a computer system. Usually, the device tree is loaded by the bootloader and passed to the kernel, although it is possible to bundle the device tree with the kernel image itself to cater for bootloaders that are not capable of loading them separately.

The format is derived from a Sun Microsystems bootloader known as **OpenBoot**, which was formalized as the Open Firmware specification, which is IEEE standard IEEE1275-1994. It was used in PowerPC-based Macintosh computers and so was a logical choice for the PowerPC Linux port. Since then, it has been adopted on a large scale by the many ARM Linux implementations and, to a lesser extent, by MIPS, MicroBlaze, ARC, and other architectures.

I would recommend visiting https://www.devicetree.org/ for more information.

Device tree basics

The Linux kernel contains a large number of device tree source files in
arch/$ARCH/boot/dts, and this is a good starting point for learning about device trees.
There are also a smaller number of sources in the U-boot source code in arch/$ARCH/dts.
If you acquired your hardware from a third party, the dts file forms part of the board
support package and you should expect to receive one along with the other source files.

The device tree represents a computer system as a collection of components joined together
in a hierarchy, like a tree. The device tree begins with a root node, represented by a forward
slash, /, which contains subsequent nodes representing the hardware of the system. Each
node has a name and contains a number of properties in the form name = "value". Here
is a simple example:

```
/dts-v1/;
/{
    model = "TI AM335x BeagleBone";
    compatible = "ti,am33xx";
    #address-cells = <1>;
    #size-cells = <1>;
    cpus {
        #address-cells = <1>;
        #size-cells = <0>;
        cpu@0 {
            compatible = "arm,cortex-a8";
            device_type = "cpu";
            reg = <0>;
        };
    };
    memory@0x80000000 {
        device_type = "memory";
        reg = <0x80000000 0x20000000>; /* 512 MB */
    };
};
```

Here we have a root node which contains a cpus node and a memory node. The cpus node
contains a single CPU node named cpu@0. It is a common convention that the names of
nodes include an @ followed by an address that distinguishes this node from other nodes of
the same type.

Both the root and CPU nodes have a compatible property. The Linux kernel uses this
property to find a matching device driver by comparing it with the strings exported by each
device driver in a structure of_device_id (more on this in Chapter 9, *Interfacing with
Device Drivers*).

It is a convention that the value is composed of a manufacturer name and a component name, to reduce confusion between similar devices made by different manufacturers; hence, `ti,am33xx` and `arm,cortex-a8`. It is also quite common to have more than one value for the `compatible` property where there is more than one driver that can handle this device. They are listed with the most suitable first.

The CPU node and the memory node have a `device_type` property which describes the class of device. The node name is often derived from `device_type`.

The reg property

The `memory` and `cpu` nodes have a `reg` property, which refers to a range of units in a register space. A reg property consists of two values representing the start address and the size (length) of the range. Both are written as zero or more 32-bit integers, called cells. Hence, the `memory` node refers to a single bank of memory that begins at `0x80000000` and is `0x20000000` bytes long.

Understanding reg properties becomes more complex when the address or size values cannot be represented in 32 bits. For example, on a device with 64-bit addressing, you need two cells for each:

```
/ {
    #address-cells = <2>;
    #size-cells = <2>;
    memory@80000000 {
        device_type = "memory";
        reg = <0x00000000 0x80000000 0 0x80000000>;
    };
};
```

The information about the number of cells required is held in the `#address-cells` and `#size_cells` properties in an ancestor node. In other words, to understand a `reg` property, you have to look backwards down the node hierarchy until you find `#address-cells` and `#size_cells`. If there are none, the default values are 1 for each–but it is bad practice for device tree writers to depend on fall-backs.

Now, let's return to the `cpu` and `cpus` nodes. CPUs have addresses as well; in a quad core device, they might be addressed as 0, 1, 2, and 3. That can be thought of as a one-dimensional array without any depth, so the size is zero. Therefore, you can see that we have `#address-cells = <1>` and `#size-cells = <0>` in the `cpus` node, and in the child node, `cpu@0`, we assign a single value to the reg property, `reg = <0>`.

Labels and interrupts

The structure of the device tree described so far assumes that there is a single hierarchy of components, whereas in fact there are several. As well as the obvious data connection between a component and other parts of the system, it might also be connected to an interrupt controller, to a clock source, and to a voltage regulator. To express these connections, we can add a label to a node and reference the label from other nodes. These labels are sometimes referred to as **phandles**, because when the device tree is compiled, nodes with a reference from another node are assigned a unique numerical value in a property called **phandle**. You can see them if you decompile the device tree binary.

Take as an example a system containing an LCD controller which can generate `interrupts` and an `interrupt-controller`:

```
/dts-v1/;
{
    intc: interrupt-controller@48200000 {
        compatible = "ti,am33xx-intc";
        interrupt-controller;
        #interrupt-cells = <1>;
        reg = <0x48200000 0x1000>;
    };

    lcdc: lcdc@4830e000 {
        compatible = "ti,am33xx-tilcdc";
        reg = <0x4830e000 0x1000>;
        interrupt-parent = <&intc>;
        interrupts = <36>;
        ti,hwmods = "lcdc";
        status = "disabled";
    };
};
```

Here we have node `interrupt-controller@48200000` with the label `intc`. The `interrupt-controller` property identifies it as an interrupt controller. Like all interrupt controllers, it has an `#interrupt-cells` property, which tells us how many cells are needed to represent an interrupt source. In this case, there is only one which represents the **interrupt request (IRQ)** number. Other interrupt controllers may use additional cells to characterize the interrupt, for example to indicate whether it is edge or level triggered. The number of interrupt cells and their meanings is described in the bindings for each interrupt controller. The device tree bindings can be found in the Linux kernel source, in the directory `Documentation/devicetree/bindings/`.

Looking at the `lcdc@4830e000` node, it has an `interrupt-parent` property, which references the interrupt controller it is connected to, using the label. It also has an `interrupts` property, 36 in this case. Note that this node has its own label, lcdc, which is used elsewhere: any node can have a label.

Device tree include files

A lot of hardware is common between SoCs of the same family and between boards using the same SoC. This is reflected in the device tree by splitting out common sections into include files, usually with the extension `.dtsi`. The Open Firmware standard defines `/include/` as the mechanism to be used, as in this snippet from `vexpress-v2p-ca9.dts`:

```
/include/ "vexpress-v2m.dtsi"
```

Look through the `.dts` files in the kernel, though, and you will find an alternative include statement that is borrowed from C, for example in `am335x-boneblack.dts`:

```
#include "am33xx.dtsi"
#include "am335x-bone-common.dtsi"
```

Here is another example from `am33xx.dtsi`:

```
#include <dt-bindings/gpio/gpio.h>
#include <dt-bindings/pinctrl/am33xx.h>
```

Lastly, `include/dt-bindings/pinctrl/am33xx.h` contains normal C macros:

```
#define PULL_DISABLE (1 << 3)
#define INPUT_EN (1 << 5)
#define SLEWCTRL_SLOW (1 << 6)
#define SLEWCTRL_FAST 0
```

All of this is resolved if the device tree sources are built using the Kbuild system, which first runs them through the C pre-processor, CPP, where the `#include` and `#define` statements are processed into text that is suitable for the device tree compiler. The motivation is illustrated in the previous example; it means that the device tree sources can use the same definitions of constants as the kernel code.

When we include files, using either syntax, the nodes are overlaid on top of one another to create a composite tree in which the outer layers extend or modify the inner ones. For example, am33xx.dtsi, which is general to all am33xx SoCs, defines the first MMC controller interface like this:

```
mmc1: mmc@48060000 {
    compatible = "ti,omap4-hsmmc";
    ti,hwmods = "mmc1";
    ti,dual-volt;
    ti,needs-special-reset;
    ti,needs-special-hs-handling;
    dmas = <&edma 24 &edma 25>;
    dma-names = "tx", "rx";
    interrupts = <64>;
    interrupt-parent = <&intc>;
    reg = <0x48060000 0x1000>;
    status = "disabled";
};
```

Note that the status is disabled, meaning that no device driver should be bound to it, and also that it has the label mmc1.

Both the BeagleBone and the BeagleBone Black have a microSD card interface attached to mmc1, hence in am335x-bone-common.dtsi, the same node is referenced by its label, &mmc1:

```
&mmc1 {
    status = "okay";
    bus-width = <0x4>;
    pinctrl-names = "default";
    pinctrl-0 = <&mmc1_pins>;
    cd-gpios = <&gpio0 6 GPIO_ACTIVE_HIGH>;
    cd-inverted;
};
```

The status property is set to okay, which causes the mmc device driver to bind with this interface at runtime on both variants of the BeagleBone. Also, a label is added to the pin control configuration, mmc1_pins. Alas, there is not sufficient space here to describe pin control and pin multiplexing. You will find some information in the Linux kernel source in directory devicetree/bindings/pinctrl.

However, interface `mmc1` is connected to a different voltage regulator on the BeagleBone Black. This is expressed in `am335x-boneblack.dts`, where you will see another reference to `mmc1`, which associates it with the voltage regulator via label `vmmcsd_fixed`:

```
&mmc1 {
    vmmc-supply = <&vmmcsd_fixed>;
};
```

So, layering device tree source files like this gives flexibility and reduces the need for duplicated code.

Compiling a device tree

The bootloader and kernel require a binary representation of the device tree, so it has to be compiled using the device tree compiler, `dtc`. The result is a file ending with `.dtb`, which is referred to as a device tree binary or a device tree blob.

There is a copy of `dtc` in the Linux source, in `scripts/dtc/dtc`, and it is also available as a package on many Linux distributions. You can use it to compile a simple device tree (one that does not use `#include`) like this:

```
$ dtc simpledts-1.dts -o simpledts-1.dtb
DTC: dts->dts on file "simpledts-1.dts"
```

Be wary of the fact that `dtc` does not give helpful error messages and it makes no checks other than on the basic syntax of the language, which means that debugging a typing error in a source file can be a lengthy business.

To build more complex examples, you will have to use the kernel Kbuild, as shown in the next chapter.

Choosing a bootloader

Bootloaders come in all shapes and sizes. The kind of characteristics you want from a bootloader are that they be simple and customizable with lots of sample configurations for common development boards and devices. The following table shows a number of bootloaders that are in general use:

Name	Main architectures supported
Das U-Boot	ARC, ARM, Blackfin, Microblaze, MIPS, Nios2, OpenRiec, PowerPC, SH
Barebox	ARM, Blackfin, MIPS, Nios2, PowerPC
GRUB 2	X86, X86_64
Little Kernel	ARM
RedBoot	ARM, MIPS, PowerPC, SH
CFE	Broadcom MIPS
YAMON	MIPS

We are going to focus on U-Boot because it supports a good number of processor architectures and a large number of individual boards and devices. It has been around for a long time and has a good community for support.

It may be that you received a bootloader along with your SoC or board. As always, take a good look at what you have and ask questions about where you can get the source code from, what the update policy is, how they will support you if you want to make changes, and so on. You may want to consider abandoning the vendor-supplied loader and using the current version of an open source bootloader instead.

U-Boot

U-Boot, or to give its full name, **Das U-Boot**, began life as an open source bootloader for embedded PowerPC boards. Then, it was ported to ARM-based boards and later to other architectures, including MIPS and SH. It is hosted and maintained by Denx Software Engineering. There is plenty of information available, and a good place to start is `http://www.denx.de/wiki/U-Boot`. There is also a mailing list at `u-boot@lists.denx.de`.

Building U-Boot

Begin by getting the source code. As with most projects, the recommended way is to clone the `.git` archive and check out the tag you intend to use, which, in this case, is the version that was current at the time of writing:

```
$ git clone git://git.denx.de/u-boot.git
$ cd u-boot
$ git checkout v2017.01
```

Alternatively, you can get a tarball from `ftp://ftp.denx.de/pub/u-boot.`

There are more than 1,000 configuration files for common development boards and devices in the `configs/` directory. In most cases, you can make a good guess of which to use, based on the filename, but you can get more detailed information by looking through the per-board README files in the `board/` directory, or you can find information in an appropriate web tutorial or forum.

Taking the BeagleBone Black as an example, we find that there is a likely configuration file named `configs/am335x_boneblack_defconfig` and we find the text `The binary produced by this board supports` ... Beaglebone Black in the board README files for the `am335x` chip, `board/ti/am335x/README`. With this knowledge, building U-Boot for a BeagleBone Black is simple. You need to inform U-Boot of the prefix for your cross compiler by setting the make variable `CROSS_COMPILE`, and then selecting the configuration file using a command of the type `make [board]_defconfig`. Therefore, to build U-Boot using the Crosstool-NG compiler we created in `Chapter 2`, *Learning About Toolchains*, you would type:

```
$ source MELP/chapter_02/set-path-arm-cortex_a8-linux-gnueabihf
$ make CROSS_COMPILE=arm-cortex_a8-linux-gnueabihf-
am335x_boneblack_defconfig
$ make CROSS_COMPILE=arm-cortex_a8-linux-gnueabihf-
```

The results of the compilation are:

- `u-boot`: U-Boot in ELF object format, suitable for use with a debugger
- `u-boot.map`: The symbol table
- `u-boot.bin`: U-Boot in raw binary format, suitable for running on your device
- `u-boot.img`: This is `u-boot.bin` with a U-Boot header added, suitable for uploading to a running copy of U-Boot
- `u-boot.srec`: U-Boot in Motorola S-record (**SRECORD** or **SRE**) format, suitable for transferring over a serial connection

The BeagleBone Black also requires a **secondary program loader** (SPL), as described earlier. This is built at the same time and is named `MLO`:

```
$ ls -l MLO u-boot*
-rw-rw-r-- 1 chris chris 78416 Mar 9 10:13 u-boot/MLO
-rwxrwxr-x 1 chris chris 2943940 Mar 9 10:13 u-boot/u-boot
-rwxrwxr-x 1 chris chris 368348 Mar 9 10:13 u-boot/u-boot.bin
-rw-rw-r-- 1 chris chris 368412 Mar 9 10:13 u-boot/u-boot.img
-rw-rw-r-- 1 chris chris 520741 Mar 9 10:13 u-boot/u-boot.map
-rwxrwxr-x 1 chris chris 1105162 Mar 9 10:13 u-boot/u-boot.srec
```

The procedure is similar for other targets.

Installing U-Boot

Installing a bootloader on a board for the first time requires some outside assistance. If the board has a hardware debug interface, such as JTAG, it is usually possible to load a copy of U-Boot directly into RAM and set it running. From that point, you can use U-Boot commands to copy itself into flash memory. The details of this are very board-specific and outside the scope of this book.

Many SoC designs have a boot ROM built in, which can be used to read boot code from various external sources, such as SD cards, serial interfaces, or USB mass storage. This is the case with the am335x chip in the BeagleBone Black, which makes it easy to try out new software.

You will need an SD card reader to write the images to a card. There are two types: external readers that plug into a USB port, and the internal SD readers that are present on many laptops. A device name is assigned by Linux when a card is plugged into the reader. The command lsblk is a useful tool to find out which device has been allocated. For example, this is what I see when I plug a nominal 8 GB microSD card into my card reader:

```
$ lsblk
NAME MAJ:MIN RM SIZE RO TYPE MOUNTPOINT
sda 8:0 0 477G 0 disk
├─sda1 8:1 0 500M 0 part /boot/efi
├─sda2 8:2 0 40M 0 part
├─sda3 8:3 0 3G 0 part
├─sda4 8:4 0 457.6G 0 part /
└─sda5 8:5 0 15.8G 0 part [SWAP]
sdb 8:16 1 7.2G 0 disk
└─sdb1 8:17 1 7.2G 0 part /media/chris/101F-5626
```

In this case, sda is my 512 GB hard drive and sdb is the microSD card. It has a single partition, sdb1, which is mounted as directory /media/chris/101F-5626.

Although the microSD card had 8 GB printed on the outside, it was only 7.2 GB on the inside. In part, this is because of the different units used. The advertised capacity is measured in Gigabytes, 10^9, but the sizes reported by software are in Gibibytes, 2^{30}. Gigabytes are abbreviated GB, Gibibytes as GiB. The same applies for KB and KiB, and MB and MiB. In this book, I have tried to use the right units. In the case of the SD card, it so happens that 8 Gigabytes is approximately 7.4 Gibibytes. The remaining discrepancy is because flash memory always has to reserve some space for bad block handling. This is a topic that I will return to in Chapter 7, *Creating a Storage Strategy*.

If I use the built-in SD card slot, I see this:

```
$ lsblk
NAME MAJ:MIN RM SIZE RO TYPE MOUNTPOINT
sda 8:0 0 477G 0 disk
├─sda1 8:1 0 500M 0 part /boot/efi
├─sda2 8:2 0 40M 0 part
├─sda3 8:3 0 3G 0 part
├─sda4 8:4 0 457.6G 0 part /
└─sda5 8:5 0 15.8G 0 part [SWAP]
mmcblk0 179:0 0 7.2G 0 disk
└─mmcblk0p1 179:1 0 7.2G 0 part /media/chris/101F-5626
```

In this case, the micro SD card appears as mmcblk0 and the partition is mmcblk0p1. Note that the microSD card you use may have been formatted differently to this one and so you may see a different number of partitions with different mount points. When formatting an SD card, it is very important to be sure of its device name. You really don't want to mistake your hard drive for an SD card and format that instead. This has happened to me more than once. So, I have provided a shell script in the book's code archive named MELP/format-sdcard.sh, which has a reasonable number of checks to prevent you (and me) from using the wrong device name. The parameter is the device name of the microSD card, which would be sdb in the first example and mmcblk0 in the second. Here is an example of its use:

```
$ MELP/format-sdcard.sh mmcblk0
```

The script creates two partitions: the first is 64 MiB, formatted as FAT32, and will contain the bootloader, and the second is 1 GiB, formatted as ext4, which you will use in Chapter 5, *Building a Root Filesystem*.

After you have formatted the microSD card, remove it from the card reader and then re-insert it so that the partitions are auto mounted. On current versions of Ubuntu, the two partitions should be mounted as /media/[user]/boot and /media/[user]/rootfs. Now you can copy the SPL and U-Boot to it like this:

```
$ cp MLO u-boot.img /media/chris/boot
```

Finally, unmount it:

```
$ sudo umount /media/chris/boot
```

Now, with no power on the BeagleBone board, insert the micro-SD card into the reader. Plug in the serial cable. A serial port should appear on your PC as /dev/ttyUSB0. Start a suitable terminal program, such as gtkterm, minicom, or picocom, and attach to the port at 115200 bps (bits per second) with no flow control. gtkterm is probably the easiest to setup and use:

```
$ gtkterm -p /dev/ttyUSB0 -s 115200
```

Press and hold the Boot Switch button on the Beaglebone Black, power up the board using the external 5V power connector, and release the button after about 5 seconds. You should see a U-Boot prompt on the serial console:

```
U-Boot#
```

Using U-Boot

In this section, I will describe some of the common tasks that you can use U-Boot to perform.

Usually, U-Boot offers a command-line interface over a serial port. It gives a Command Prompt which is customized for each board. In the examples, I will use U-Boot#. Typing help prints out all the commands configured in this version of U-Boot; typing help <command> prints out more information about a particular command.

The default command interpreter for the BeagleBone Black is quite simple. You cannot do command-line editing by pressing cursor left or right keys; there is no command completion by pressing the *Tab* key; and there is no command history by pressing the cursor up key. Pressing any of these keys will disrupt the command you are currently trying to type, and you will have to type *Ctrl + C* and start over again. The only line editing key you can safely use is the backspace. As an option, you can configure a different command shell called **Hush,** which has more sophisticated interactive support, including command-line editing.

The default number format is hexadecimal. Consider the following command as an example:

```
nand read 82000000 400000 200000
```

This will read 0x200000 bytes from offset 0x400000 from the start of the NAND flash memory into RAM address 0x82000000.

Environment variables

U-Boot uses environment variables extensively to store and pass information between functions and even to create scripts. Environment variables are simple name=value pairs that are stored in an area of memory. The initial population of variables may be coded in the board configuration header file, like this:

```
#define CONFIG_EXTRA_ENV_SETTINGS
"myvar1=value1"
"myvar2=value2"
[...]
```

You can create and modify variables from the U-Boot command line using setenv. For example, setenv foo bar creates the variable foo with the value bar. Note that there is no = sign between the variable name and the value. You can delete a variable by setting it to a null string, setenv foo. You can print all the variables to the console using printenv, or a single variable using printenv foo.

If U-Boot has been configured with space to store the environment, you can use the saveenv command to save it. If there is raw NAND or NOR flash, then an erase block can be reserved for this purpose, often with another used for a redundant copy to guard against corruption. If there is eMMC or SD card storage, it can be stored in a reserved array of sectors, or in a file named uboot.env in a partition of the disk. Other options include storing in a serial EEPROM connected via an I2C or SPI interface or non-volatile RAM.

Boot image format

U-Boot doesn't have a filesystem. Instead, it tags blocks of information with a 64-byte header so that it can track the contents. You prepare files for U-Boot using the mkimage command. Here is a brief summary of its usage:

```
$ mkimage
Usage: mkimage -l image
 -l ==> list image header information
 mkimage [-x] -A arch -O os -T type -C comp -a addr -e ep -n name -d
data_file[:data_file...] image
 -A ==> set architecture to 'arch'
 -O ==> set operating system to 'os'
 -T ==> set image type to 'type'
 -C ==> set compression type 'comp'
 -a ==> set load address to 'addr' (hex)
 -e ==> set entry point to 'ep' (hex)
 -n ==> set image name to 'name'
 -d ==> use image data from 'datafile'
```

```
-x ==> set XIP (execute in place)
mkimage [-D dtc_options] [-f fit-image.its|-F] fit-image
-D => set options for device tree compiler
-f => input filename for FIT source
Signing / verified boot not supported (CONFIG_FIT_SIGNATURE undefined)
mkimage -V ==> print version information and exit
```

For example, to prepare a kernel image for an ARM processor, the command is:

```
$ mkimage -A arm -O linux -T kernel -C gzip -a 0x80008000  -e 0x80008000 \
-n 'Linux' -d zImage uImage
```

Loading images

Usually, you will load images from removable storage, such as an SD card or a network. SD cards are handled in U-Boot by the mmc driver. A typical sequence to load an image into memory would be:

```
U-Boot# mmc rescan
U-Boot# fatload mmc 0:1 82000000 uimage
reading uimage
4605000 bytes read in 254 ms (17.3 MiB/s)
U-Boot# iminfo 82000000

## Checking Image at 82000000 ...
Legacy image found
Image Name: Linux-3.18.0C
reated: 2014-12-23 21:08:07 UTC
Image Type: ARM Linux Kernel Image (uncompressed)
Data Size: 4604936 Bytes = 4.4 MiB
Load Address: 80008000
Entry Point: 80008000
Verifying Checksum ... OK
```

The command mmc rescan re-initializes the mmc driver, perhaps to detect that an SD card has recently been inserted. Next, fatload is used to read a file from a FAT-formatted partition on the SD card. The format is:

```
fatload <interface> [<dev[:part]> [<addr> [<filename> [bytes [pos]]]]]
```

If <interface> is mmc, as in our case, <dev:part> is the device number of the mmc interface counting from zero, and the partition number counting from one. Hence, <0:1> is the first partition on the first device. The memory location, 0x82000000, is chosen to be in an area of RAM that is not being used at this moment. If we intend to boot this kernel, we have to make sure that this area of RAM will not be overwritten when the kernel image is decompressed and located at the runtime location, 0x80008000.

To load image files over a network, you use the Trivial File Transfer Protocol (TFTP). This requires you to install a TFTP daemon, tftpd, on your development system and start it running. You also have to configure any firewalls between your PC and the target board to allow the TFTP protocol on UDP port 69 to pass through. The default configuration of TFTP allows access only to the directory /var/lib/tftpboot. The next step is to copy the files you want to transfer to the target into that directory. Then, assuming that you are using a pair of static IP addresses, which removes the need for further network administration, the sequence of commands to load a set of kernel image files should look like this:

```
U-Boot# setenv ipaddr 192.168.159.42
U-Boot# setenv serverip 192.168.159.99
U-Boot# tftp 82000000 uImage
link up on port 0, speed 100, full duplex
Using cpsw device
TFTP from server 192.168.159.99; our IP address is 192.168.159.42
Filename 'uImage'.
Load address: 0x82000000
Loading:
#################################################################
#################################################################
#################################################################
##########################################################
##########################################################
3 MiB/s
done
Bytes transferred = 4605000 (464448 hex)
```

Finally, let's look at how to program images into NAND flash memory and read them back, which is handled by the nand command. This example loads a kernel image via TFTP and programs it into flash:

```
U-Boot# tftpboot 82000000 uimage
U-Boot# nandecc hw
U-Boot# nand erase 280000 400000

NAND erase: device 0 offset 0x280000, size 0x400000
Erasing at 0x660000 -- 100% complete.
OK
```

```
U-Boot# nand write 82000000 280000 400000

NAND write: device 0 offset 0x280000, size 0x400000
4194304 bytes written: OK
```

Now you can load the kernel from flash memory using the nand read command:

```
U-Boot# nand read 82000000 280000 400000
```

Booting Linux

The bootm command starts a kernel image running. The syntax is:

```
bootm [address of kernel] [address of ramdisk] [address of dtb].
```

The address of the kernel image is necessary, but the address of ramdisk and dtb can be omitted if the kernel configuration does not need them. If there is dtb but no initramfs, the second address can be replaced with a dash (–). That would look like this:

```
U-Boot# bootm 82000000 - 83000000
```

Automating the boot with U-Boot scripts

Plainly, typing a long series of commands to boot your board each time it is turned on is not acceptable. To automate the process, U-Boot stores a sequence of commands in environment variables. If the special variable named bootcmd contains a script, it is run at power-up after a delay of bootdelay seconds. If you watch this on the serial console, you will see the delay counting down to zero. You can press any key during this period to terminate the countdown and enter into an interactive session with U-Boot.

The way that you create scripts is simple, though not easy to read. You simply append commands separated by semicolons, which must be preceded by a *backslash* escape character. So, for example, to load a kernel image from an offset in flash memory and boot it, you might use the following command:

```
setenv bootcmd nand read 82000000 400000 200000\;bootm 82000000
```

Porting U-Boot to a new board

Let's assume that your hardware department has created a new board called **Nova** that is based on the BeagleBone Black and that you need to port U-Boot to it. You will need to understand the layout of the U-Boot code and how the board configuration mechanism works. In this section, I will show you how to create a variant of an existing board—the BeagleBone Black—which you could go on to use as the basis for further customizations. There are quite a few files that need to be changed. I have put them together into a patch file in the code archive in MELP/chapter_03/0001-BSP-for-Nova.patch. You can simply apply that patch to a clean copy of U-Boot version 2017.01 like this:

```
$ cd u-boot
$ patch -p1 < MELP/chapter_03/0001-BSP-for-Nova.patch
```

If you want to use a different version of U-Boot, you will have to make some changes to the patch for it to apply cleanly.

The remainder of this section is a description of how the patch was created. If you want to follow along step-by-step, you will need a clean copy of U-Boot 2017.01 without the Nova BSP patch. The main directories we will be dealing with are:

- arch: Contains code specific to each supported architecture in directories arm, mips, powerpc, and so on. Within each architecture, there is a subdirectory for each member of the family; for example, in arch/arm/cpu/, there are directories for the architecture variants, including amt926ejs, armv7, and armv8.
- board: Contains code specific to a board. Where there are several boards from the same vendor, they can be collected together into a subdirectory. Hence, the support for the am335x evm board, on which the BeagleBone is based, is in board/ti/am335x.
- common: Contains core functions including the command shells and the commands that can be called from them, each in a file named cmd_[command name].c.
- doc: Contains several README files describing various aspects of U-Boot. If you are wondering how to proceed with your U-Boot port, this is a good place to start.
- include: In addition to many shared header files, this contains the very important subdirectory include/configs/ where you will find the majority of the board configuration settings.

The way that Kconfig extracts configuration information from Kconfig files and stores the total system configuration in a file named .config is described in some detail in Chapter 4, *Configuring and Building the Kernel*. Each board has a default configuration stored in configs/[board name]_defconfig. For the Nova board, we can begin by making a copy of the configuration for the BeagleBone Black:

```
$ cp configs/am335x_boneblack_defconfig configs/nova_defconfig
```

Now edit configs/nova_defconfig and change line four from CONFIG_TARGET_AM335X_EVM=y to CONFIG_TARGET_NOVA=y:

```
1 CONFIG_ARM=y
2 CONFIG_AM33XX=y
3 # CONFIG_SPL_NAND_SUPPORT is not set
4 CONFIG_TARGET_NOVA=y
[...]
```

Note that CONFIG_ARM=y causes the contents of arch/arm/Kconfig to be included, and on line two, CONFIG_AM33XX=y causes arch/arm/mach-omap2/am33xx/Kconfig to be included.

Board-specific files

Each board has a subdirectory named board/[board name] or board/[vendor]/[board name], which should contain:

- Kconfig: Contains configuration options for the board
- MAINTAINERS: Contains a record of whether the board is currently maintained and, if so, by whom
- Makefile: Used to build the board-specific code
- README: Contains any useful information about this port of U-Boot; for example, which hardware variants are covered

In addition, there may be source files for board specific functions.

Our Nova board is based on a BeagleBone which, in turn, is based on a TI am335x EVM, so, we should take a copy of the am335x board files:

```
$ mkdir board/ti/nova
$ cp -a board/ti/am335x/* board/ti/nova
```

Next, edit `board/ti/nova/Kconfig` and set `SYS_BOARD` to `"nova"`, so that it will build the files in `board/ti/nova`, and set `SYS_CONFIG_NAME` to `"nova"` also, so that the configuration file used will be `include/configs/nova.h`:

```
 1 if TARGET_NOVA
 2
 3 config SPL_ENV_SUPPORT
 4 default y
 5
 6 config SPL_WATCHDOG_SUPPORT
 7 default y
 8
 9 config SPL_YMODEM_SUPPORT
10 default y
11
12 config SYS_BOARD
13 default "nova"
14
15 config SYS_VENDOR
16 default "ti"
17
18 config SYS_SOC
19 default "am33xx"
20
21 config SYS_CONFIG_NAME
22 default "nova"
[...]
```

There is one other file here that we need to change. The linker script placed at `board/ti/nova/u-boot.lds` has a hard-coded reference to `board/ti/am335x/built-in.o` on line 39. Change it as shown:

```
35      {
36          *(.__image_copy_start)
37          *(.vectors)
38          CPUDIR/start.o (.text*)
39          board/ti/nova/built-in.o (.text*)
40          *(.text*)
41      }
```

Now we need to link the `Kconfig` file for Nova into the chain of `Kconfig` files. First, edit `arch/arm/Kconfig` and add a menu option for Nova, and then source its Kconfig file:

```
[...]
1069 source "board/ti/nova/Kconfig"
[...]
```

Then, edit `arch/arm/mach-omap2/am33xx/Kconfig` and add a configuration option for
`TARGET_NOVA`:

```
[...]
21 config TARGET_NOVA
22         bool "Support the Nova! board"
23         select DM
24         select DM_SERIAL
25         select DM_GPIO
26         select TI_I2C_BOARD_DETECT
27         help
28           The Nova target board
[...]
```

Configuring header files

Each board has a header file in `include/configs/` which contains the majority of the
configuration information. The file is named by the `SYS_CONFIG_NAME` identifier in the
board's `Kconfig`. The format of this file is described in detail in the README file at the top
level of the U-Boot source tree. For the purposes of our Nova board, simply copy
`include/configs/am335c_evm.h` to `include/configs/nova.h` and make a small
number of changes, the most significant of which is to set a new Command Prompt so that
we can identify this bootloader at run-time:

```
[...]
16 #ifndef __CONFIG_NOVA_H
17 #define __CONFIG_NOVA_H
[...]
38 #define CONFIG_SYS_LDSCRIPT          "board/ti/nova/u-boot.lds"
[...]
68 #undef CONFIG_SYS_PROMPT
69 #define CONFIG_SYS_PROMPT "nova!> "
[...]
421 #endif  /* ! __CONFIG_NOVA_H */
```

Building and testing

To build for the Nova board, select the configuration you have just created:

```
$ make CROSS_COMPILE=arm-cortex_a8-linux-gnueabi- distclean
$ make CROSS_COMPILE=arm-cortex_a8-linux-gnueabi- nova_defconfig
$ make CROSS_COMPILE=arm-cortex_a8-linux-gnueabi-
```

Copy MLO and u-boot.img to the boot partition of the microSD card you created earlier and boot the board. You should see output like this (note the Command Prompt):

```
U-Boot SPL 2017.01-dirty (Apr 20 2017 - 16:48:38)
Trying to boot from MMC1MMC partition switch failed
*** Warning - MMC partition switch failed, using default environment

reading u-boot.img
reading u-boot.img


U-Boot 2017.01-dirty (Apr 20 2017 - 16:48:38 +0100)

CPU : AM335X-GP rev 2.0
I2C: ready
DRAM: 512 MiB
MMC: OMAP SD/MMC: 0, OMAP SD/MMC: 1
*** Warning - bad CRC, using default environment

<ethaddr> not set. Validating first E-fuse MAC
Net: cpsw, usb_ether
Press SPACE to abort autoboot in 2 seconds
nova!>
```

You can create a patch for all of these changes by checking them into Git and using the git format-patch command:

```
$ git add .
$ git commit -m "BSP for Nova"
[nova-bsp-2 e160f82] BSP for Nova
 12 files changed, 2272 insertions(+)
 create mode 100644 board/ti/nova/Kconfig
 create mode 100644 board/ti/nova/MAINTAINERS
 create mode 100644 board/ti/nova/Makefile
 create mode 100644 board/ti/nova/README
 create mode 100644 board/ti/nova/board.c
 create mode 100644 board/ti/nova/board.h
 create mode 100644 board/ti/nova/mux.c
 create mode 100644 board/ti/nova/u-boot.lds
 create mode 100644 configs/nova_defconfig
 create mode 100644 include/configs/nova.h
$ git format-patch -1
0001-BSP-for-Nova.patch
```

Falcon mode

We are used to the idea that booting a modern embedded processor involves the CPU boot ROM loading an SPL, which loads u-boot.bin which then loads a Linux kernel. You may be wondering if there is a way to reduce the number of steps, thereby simplifying and speeding up the boot process. The answer is U-Boot **Falcon mode.** The idea is simple: have the SPL load a kernel image directly, missing out u-boot.bin. There is no user interaction and there are no scripts. It just loads a kernel from a known location in flash or eMMC into memory, passes it a pre-prepared parameter block, and starts it running. The details of configuring Falcon mode are beyond the scope of this book. If you would like more information, take a look at doc/README.falcon.

 Falcon mode is named after the Peregrine falcon, which is the fastest bird of all, capable of reaching speeds of more than 200 miles per hour in a dive.

Barebox

I will complete this chapter with a look at another bootloader that has the same roots as U-Boot but takes a new approach to bootloaders. It is derived from U-Boot and was actually called U-Boot v2 in the early days. The barebox developers aimed to combine the best parts of U-Boot and Linux, including a POSIX-like API and mountable filesystems.

The barebox project website is http://barebox.org/ and the developer mailing list is barebox@lists.infradead.org.

Getting barebox

To get barebox, clone the Git repository and check out the version you want to use:

```
$ git clone git://git.pengutronix.de/git/barebox.git
$ cd barebox
$ git checkout v2017.02.0
```

The layout of the code is similar to U-Boot:

- arch: Contains code specific to each supported architecture, which includes all the major embedded architectures. SoC support is in arch/[architecture]/mach-[SoC]. Support for individual boards is in arch/[architecture]/boards.
- common: Contains core functions, including the shell.
- commands: Contains the commands that can be called from the shell.
- Documentation: Contains the templates for documentation files. To build it, type make docs. The results are put in Documentation/html.
- drivers: Contains the code for the device drivers.
- include: Contains header files.

Building barebox

Barebox has used Kconfig/Kbuild for a long time. There are default configuration files in arch/[architecture]/configs. As an example, assume that you want to build barebox for the BeagleBoard C4. You need two configurations, one for the SPL, and one for the main binary. Firstly, build MLO:

```
$ make ARCH=arm CROSS_COMPILE=arm-cortex_a8-linux-gnueabihf- \
am335x_mlo_defconfig
$ make ARCH=arm CROSS_COMPILE=arm-cortex_a8-linux-gnueabihf-
```

The result is the secondary program loader, images/barebox-am33xx-beaglebone-mlo.img.

Next, build barebox:

```
$ make ARCH=arm CROSS_COMPILE=arm-cortex_a8-linux-gnueabihf- \
am335x_defconfig
$ make ARCH=arm CROSS_COMPILE=arm-cortex_a8-linux-gnueabihf-
```

Copy MLO and the barebox binary to an SD card:

```
$ cp images/barebox-am33xx-beaglebone-mlo.img /media/chris/boot/MLO
$ cp images/barebox-am33xx-beaglebone.img /media/chris/boot/barebox.bin
```

Then, boot up the board and you should see messages like these on the console:

```
barebox 2017.02.0 #1 Thu Mar 9 20:27:08 GMT 2017


Board: TI AM335x BeagleBone black
detected 'BeagleBone Black'
[...]
running /env/bin/init...
changing USB current limit to 1300 mA... done

Hit m for menu or any other key to stop autoboot: 3

type exit to get to the menu
barebox@TI AM335x BeagleBone black:/
```

Using barebox

Using barebox at the command line you can see the similarities with Linux. First, you can see that there are filesystem commands such as ls, and there is a /dev directory:

```
# ls /dev
full      mdio0-phy00 mem      mmc0      mmc0.0
mmc0.1    mmc1        mmc1.0   null      ram0      zero
```

The device /dev/mmc0.0 is the first partition on the microSD card, which contains the kernel and initial ramdisk. You can mount it like this:

```
# mount /dev/mmc0.0 /mnt
```

Now you can see the files:

```
# ls /mnt
MLO am335x-boneblack.dtb barebox.bin
u-boot.img uRamdisk zImage
```

Boot from the root partition:

```
# global.bootm.oftree=/mnt/am335x-boneblack.dtb
# global linux.bootargs.root="root=/dev/mmcblk0p2 rootwait"
# bootm /mnt/zImage
```

Summary

Every system needs a bootloader to bring the hardware to life and to load a kernel. U-Boot has found favor with many developers because it supports a useful range of hardware and it is fairly easy to port to a new device. Over the last few years, the complexity and ever increasing variety of embedded hardware has led to the introduction of the device tree as a way of describing hardware. The device tree is simply a textual representation of a system that is compiled into a **device tree binary (dtb)** and which is passed to the kernel when it loads. It is up to the kernel to interpret the device tree and to load and initialize drivers for the devices it finds there.

In use, U-Boot is very flexible, allowing images to be loaded from mass storage, flash memory, or a network, and booted. Likewise, barebox can achieve the same but with a smaller base of hardware support. Despite its cleaner design and POSIX-inspired internal APIs, at the time of writing it does not seem to have been accepted beyond its own small but dedicated community.

Having covered some of the intricacies of booting Linux, in the next chapter you will see the next stage of the process as the third element of your embedded project, the kernel, comes into play.

4
Configuring and Building the Kernel

The kernel is the third element of embedded Linux. It is the component that is responsible for managing resources and interfacing with hardware, and so affects almost every aspect of your final software build. It is usually tailored to your particular hardware configuration, although, as we saw in Chapter 3, *All About Bootloaders*, device trees allow you to create a generic kernel that is tailored to particular hardware by the contents of the device tree.

In this chapter, we will look at how to get a kernel for a board, and how to configure and compile it. We will look again at bootstrap, this time focusing on the part the kernel plays. We will also look at device drivers and how they pick up information from the device tree.

In this chapter, we will cover the following topics:

- What does the kernel do?
- Choosing a kernel.
- Building the kernel.
- Booting the kernel.
- Porting Linux to a new board.

What does the kernel do?

Linux began in 1991, when Linus Torvalds started writing an operating system for Intel 386- and 486-based personal computers. He was inspired by the Minix operating system written by *Andrew S. Tanenbaum* four years earlier. Linux differed in many ways from Minix; the main differences being that it was a 32-bit virtual memory kernel and the code was open source, later released under the GPL v2 license. He announced it on 25th August, 1991, on the `comp.os.minix` newsgroup in a famous post that began with:

> *Hello everybody out there using minix—I'm doing a (free) operating system (just a hobby, won't be big and professional like GNU) for 386(486) AT clones. This has been brewing since April, and is starting to get ready. I'd like any feedback on things people like/dislike in minix, as my OS resembles it somewhat (same physical layout of the filesystem (due to practical reasons) among other things).*

To be strictly accurate, Linus did not write an operating system, rather he wrote a kernel, which is only one component of an operating system. To create a complete operating system with user space commands and a shell command interpreter, he used components from the GNU project, especially the toolchain, the C-library, and basic command-line tools. That distinction remains today, and gives Linux a lot of flexibility in the way it is used. It can be combined with a GNU user space to create a full Linux distribution that runs on desktops and servers, which is sometimes called GNU/Linux; it can be combined with an Android user space to create the well-known mobile operating system, or it can be combined with a small BusyBox-based user space to create a compact embedded system. Contrast this with the BSD operating systems, FreeBSD, OpenBSD, and NetBSD, in which the kernel, the toolchain, and the user space are combined into a single code base.

The kernel has three main jobs: to manage resources, to interface with hardware, and to provide an API that offers a useful level of abstraction to user space programs, as summarized in the following diagram:

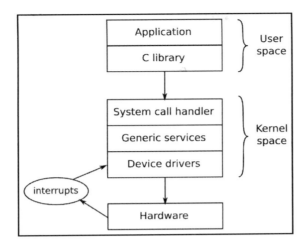

Applications running in **User space** run at a low CPU privilege level. They can do very little other than make library calls. The primary interface between the **User space** and the **Kernel space** is the **C library**, which translates user level functions, such as those defined by POSIX, into kernel system calls. The system call interface uses an architecture-specific method, such as a trap or a software interrupt, to switch the CPU from low privilege user mode to high privilege kernel mode, which allows access to all memory addresses and CPU registers.

The **System call handler** dispatches the call to the appropriate kernel subsystem: memory allocation calls go to the memory manager, filesystem calls to the filesystem code, and so on. Some of those calls require input from the underlying hardware and will be passed down to a device driver. In some cases, the hardware itself invokes a kernel function by raising an interrupt.

The preceding diagram shows that there is a second entry point into kernel code: hardware interrupts. Interrupts can only be handled in a device driver, never by a user space application.

In other words, all the useful things that your application does, it does them through the kernel. The kernel, then, is one of the most important elements in the system.

Choosing a kernel

The next step is to choose the kernel for your project, balancing the desire to always use the latest version of software against the need for vendor-specific additions and an interest in the long term support of the code base.

Kernel development cycle

Linux is developed at a fast pace, with a new version being released every 8 to 12 weeks. The way that the version numbers are constructed has changed a bit in recent years. Before July 2011, there was a three number version scheme with version numbers that looked like 2.6.39. The middle number indicated whether it was a developer or stable release; odd numbers (2.1.x, 2.3.x, 2.5.x) were for developers and even numbers were for end users. From version 2.6 onwards, the idea of a long-lived development branch (the odd numbers) was dropped, as it slowed down the rate at which new features were made available to the users. The change in numbering from 2.6.39 to 3.0 in July 2011 was purely because Linus felt that the numbers were becoming too large; there was no huge leap in the features or architecture of Linux between those two versions. He also took the opportunity to drop the middle number. Since then, in April 2015, he bumped the major from 3 to 4, again purely for neatness, not because of any large architectural shift.

Linus manages the development kernel tree. You can follow him by cloning the Git tree like so:

```
$ git clone
git://git.kernel.org/pub/scm/linux/kernel/git/torvalds/linux.git
```

This will check out into subdirectory `linux`. You can keep up to date by running the command `git pull` in that directory from time to time.

Currently, a full cycle of kernel development begins with a merge window of two weeks, during which Linus will accept patches for new features. At the end of the merge window, a stabilization phase begins, during which Linus will produce weekly release candidates with version numbers ending in `-rc1`, `-rc2`, and so on, usually up to `-rc7` or `-rc8`. During this time, people test the candidates and submit bug reports and fixes. When all significant bugs have been fixed, the kernel is released.

The code incorporated during the merge window has to be fairly mature already. Usually, it is pulled from the repositories of the many subsystem and architecture maintainers of the kernel. By keeping to a short development cycle, features can be merged when they are ready. If a feature is deemed not sufficiently stable or well developed by the kernel maintainers, it can simply be delayed until the next release.

Keeping a track of what has changed from release to release is not easy. You can read the commit log in Linus' Git repository but, with roughly 10,000 or more entries, it is not easy to get an overview. Thankfully, there is the Linux **Kernel Newbies** website, `http://kernelne wbies.org`, where you will find a succinct overview of each version at `http://kernelnewbi es.org/LinuxVersions`.

Stable and long term support releases

The rapid rate of change of Linux is a good thing in that it brings new features into the mainline code base, but it does not fit very well with the longer life cycle of embedded projects. Kernel developers address this in two ways, with **stable** releases and **long term** releases. After the release of a mainline kernel (maintained by Linus Torvalds) it is moved to the **stable** tree (maintained by Greg Kroah-Hartman). Bug fixes are applied to the stable kernel, while the mainline kernel begins the next development cycle. Point releases of the stable kernel are marked by a third number, 3.18.1, 3.18.2, and so on. Before version 3, there were four release numbers, 2.6.29.1, 2.6.39.2, and so on.

You can get the stable tree by using the following command:

```
$ git clone git://git.kernel.org/pub/scm/linux/kernel/git/stable/linux-
stable.git
```

You can use `git checkout` to get a particular version, for example version 4.9.13:

```
$ cd linux-stable
$ git checkout v4.9.13
```

Usually, the stable kernel is updated only until the next mainline release (8 to 12 weeks later), so you will see that there is just one or sometimes two stable kernels at `https://www. kernel.org/`. To cater for those users who would like updates for a longer period of time and be assured that any bugs will be found and fixed, some kernels are labeled **long term** and maintained for two or more years. There is at least one long term kernel release each year. Looking at `https://www.kernel.org/` at the time of writing, there are a total of nine long term kernels: 4.9, 4.4, 4.1, 3.18, 3.14, 3.12, 3.10, 3.4, and 3.2. The latter has been maintained for five years and is at version 3.2.86. If you are building a product that you will have to maintain for this length of time, then the latest long term kernel might well be a good choice.

Vendor support

In an ideal world, you would be able to download a kernel from `https://www.kernel.org` / and configure it for any device that claims to support Linux. However, that is not always possible; in fact mainline Linux has solid support for only a small subset of the many devices that can run Linux. You may find support for your board or SoC from independent open source projects, Linaro or the Yocto Project, for example, or from companies providing third party support for embedded Linux, but in many cases you will be obliged to look to the vendor of your SoC or board for a working kernel. As we know, some are better at supporting Linux than others. My only advice at this point is to choose vendors who give good support or who, even better, take the trouble to get their kernel changes into the mainline.

Licensing

The Linux source code is licensed under GPL v2, which means that you must make the source code of your kernel available in one of the ways specified in the license.

The actual text of the license for the kernel is in the file COPYING. It begins with an addendum written by Linus that states that code calling the kernel from user space via the system call interface is not considered a derivative work of the kernel and so is not covered by the license. Hence, there is no problem with proprietary applications running on top of Linux.

However, there is one area of Linux licensing that causes endless confusion and debate: kernel modules. A kernel module is simply a piece of code that is dynamically linked with the kernel at runtime, thereby extending the functionality of the kernel. The GPL makes no distinction between static and dynamic linking, so it would appear that the source for kernel modules is covered by the GPL. But, in the early days of Linux, there were debates about exceptions to this rule, for example, in connection with the Andrew filesystem. This code predates Linux and therefore (it was argued) is not a derivative work, and so the license does not apply. Similar discussions took place over the years with respect to other pieces of code, with the result that it is now accepted practice that the GPL does not *necessarily* apply to kernel modules. This is codified by the kernel MODULE_LICENSE macro, which may take the value Proprietary to indicate that it is not released under the GPL. If you plan to use the same arguments yourself, you may want to read though an oft-quoted e-mail thread titled *Linux GPL and binary module exception clause?* which is archived at `http ://yarchive.net/comp/linux/gpl_modules.html`.

The GPL should be considered a good thing because it guarantees that when you and I are working on embedded projects, we can always get the source code for the kernel. Without it, embedded Linux would be much harder to use and more fragmented.

Building the kernel

Having decided which kernel to base your build on, the next step is to build it.

Getting the source

Both of the targets used in this book, the BeagleBone Black and the ARM Versatile PB, are well supported by the mainline kernel. Therefore, it makes sense to use the latest long-term kernel available from `https://www.kernel.org/`, which at the time of writing was 4.9.13. When you come to do this for yourself, you should check to see if there is a later version of the 4.9 kernel and use that instead since it will have fixes for bugs found after 4.9.13 was released. If there is a later long-term release, you may want to consider using that one, but be aware that there may have been changes that mean that the following sequence of commands do not work exactly as given.

Use this command to clone the stable kernel and check out version 4.9.13:

```
$ git clone git://git.kernel.org/pub/scm/linux/kernel/git/stable/linux-
stable.git
$ cd linux-stable
$ git checkout v4.9.13
```

Alternatively, you could download the tar file from `https://cdn.kernel.org/pub/linux/kernel/v4.x/linux-4.9.13.tar.xz`.

There is a lot of code here. There are over 57,000 files in the 4.9 kernel containing C-source code, header files, and assembly code, amounting to a total of over 14 million lines of code, as measured by the SLOCCount utility. Nevertheless, it is worth knowing the basic layout of the code and to know, approximately, where to look for a particular component. The main directories of interest are:

- `arch`: Contains architecture-specific files. There is one subdirectory per architecture.
- `Documentation`: Contains kernel documentation. Always look here first if you want to find more information about an aspect of Linux.

- `drivers`: Contains device drivers, thousands of them. There is a subdirectory for each type of driver.
- `fs`: Contains filesystem code.
- `include`: Contains kernel header files, including those required when building the toolchain.
- `init`: Contains the kernel start-up code.
- `kernel`: Contains core functions, including scheduling, locking, timers, power management, and debug/trace code.
- `mm`: Contains memory management.
- `net`: Contains network protocols.
- `scripts`: Contains many useful scripts, including the device tree compiler, DTC, which I described in `Chapter 3`, *All About Bootloaders*.
- `tools`: Contains many useful tools and including the Linux performance counters tool, perf, which I will describe in `Chapter 15`, *Profiling and Tracing*.

Over a period of time, you will become familiar with this structure, and realize that if you are looking for the code for the serial port of a particular SoC, you will find it in `drivers/tty/serial` and not in `arch/$ARCH/mach-foo`, because it is a device driver and not something central to the running of Linux on that SoC.

Understanding kernel configuration – Kconfig

One of the strengths of Linux is the degree to which you can configure the kernel to suit different jobs, from a small dedicated device such as a smart thermostat to a complex mobile handset. In current versions, there are many thousands of configuration options. Getting the configuration right is a task in itself but, before that, I want to show you how it works so that you can better understand what is going on.

The configuration mechanism is called `Kconfig`, and the build system that it integrates with is called `Kbuild`. Both are documented in `Documentation/kbuild`. `Kconfig/Kbuild` is used in a number of other projects as well as the kernel, including Crosstool-NG, U-Boot, Barebox, and BusyBox.

The configuration options are declared in a hierarchy of files named `Kconfig`, using a syntax described in `Documentation/kbuild/kconfig-language.txt`. In Linux, the top level `Kconfig` looks like this:

```
mainmenu "Linux/$ARCH $KERNELVERSION Kernel Configuration"

config SRCARCH
    string
    option env="SRCARCH"

source "arch/$SRCARCH/Kconfig"
```

The last line includes the architecture-dependent configuration file which sources other `Kconfig` files, depending on which options are enabled. Having the architecture play such a role has two implications: firstly, that you must specify an architecture when configuring Linux by setting `ARCH=[architecture]`, otherwise it will default to the local machine architecture, and second, that the layout of the top level menu is different for each architecture.

The value you put into `ARCH` is one of the subdirectories you find in directory arch, with the oddity that `ARCH=i386` and `ARCH=x86_64` both source `arch/x86/Kconfig`.

The `Kconfig` files consist largely of menus, delineated by `menu` and `endmenu` keywords. Menu items are marked by the keyword `config`. Here is an example, taken from `drivers/char/Kconfig`:

```
menu "Character devices"
[...]
config DEVMEM
    bool "/dev/mem virtual device support"
    default y
    help
      Say Y here if you want to support the /dev/mem device.
      The /dev/mem device is used to access areas of physical
      memory.
      When in doubt, say "Y".
[...]
endmenu
```

The parameter following `config` names a variable that, in this case, is `DEVMEM`. Since this option is a `bool` (Boolean), it can only have two values: if it is enabled, it is assigned to `y`, if it is not enabled, the variable is not defined at all. The name of the menu item that is displayed on the screen is the string following the `bool` keyword.

This configuration item, along with all the others, is stored in a file named `.config` (note that the leading dot (`.`) means that it is a hidden file that will not be shown by the `ls` command, unless you type `ls -a` to show all the files). The line corresponding to this configuration item reads:

```
CONFIG_DEVMEM=y
```

There are several other data types in addition to `bool`. Here is the list:

- `bool`: Either `y` or not defined.
- `tristate`: Used where a feature can be built as a kernel module or built into the main kernel image. The values are `m` for a module, `y` to be built in, and not defined if the feature is not enabled.
- `int`: An integer value using decimal notation.
- `hex`: An unsigned integer value using hexadecimal notation.
- `string`: A string value.

There may be dependencies between items, expressed by the `depends on` construct, as shown here:

```
config MTD_CMDLINE_PARTS
    tristate "Command line partition table parsing"
    depends on MTD
```

If `CONFIG_MTD` has not been enabled elsewhere, this menu option is not shown and so cannot be selected.

There are also reverse dependencies; the `select` keyword enables other options if this one is enabled. The `Kconfig` file in `arch/$ARCH` has a large number of `select` statements that enable features specific to the architecture, as can be seen here for `ARM`:

```
config ARM
    bool
    default y
    select ARCH_CLOCKSOURCE_DATA
    select ARCH_HAS_DEVMEM_IS_ALLOWED
[...]
```

There are several configuration utilities that can read the `Kconfig` files and produce a `.config` file. Some of them display the menus on screen and allow you to make choices interactively. `menuconfig` is probably the one most people are familiar with, but there are also `xconfig` and `gconfig`.

You launch each one via the `make` command, remembering that, in the case of the kernel, you have to supply an architecture, as illustrated here:

```
$ make ARCH=arm menuconfig
```

Here, you can see `menuconfig` with the `DEVMEM` config option highlighted in the previous paragraph:

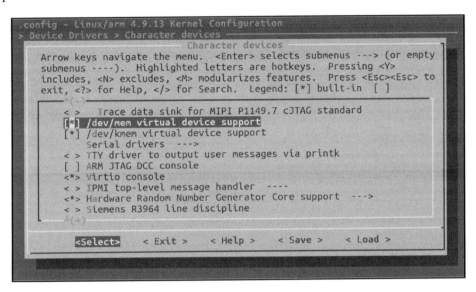

The star (*) to the left of an item means that it is selected (**Y**) or, if it is an **M**, that it has been selected to be built as a kernel module.

> You often see instructions like enable `CONFIG_BLK_DEV_INITRD`, but with so many menus to browse through, it can take a while to find the place where that configuration is set. All configuration editors have a search function. You can access it in `menuconfig` by pressing the forward slash key, `/`. In `xconfig`, it is in the edit menu, but make sure you miss off `CONFIG_` part of the configuration item you are searching for.

With so many things to configure, it is unreasonable to start with a clean sheet each time you want to build a kernel, so there are a set of known working configuration files in `arch/$ARCH/configs`, each containing suitable configuration values for a single SoC or a group of SoCs.

You can select one with the `make [configuration file name]` command. For example, to configure Linux to run on a wide range of SoCs using the `ARMv7-A` architecture, you would type:

```
$ make ARCH=arm multi_v7_defconfig
```

This is a generic kernel that runs on various different boards. For a more specialized application, for example, when using a vendor-supplied kernel, the default configuration file is part of the board support package; you will need to find out which one to use before you can build the kernel.

There is another useful configuration target named `oldconfig`. This takes an existing `.config` file and asks you to supply configuration values for any options that don't have them. You would use it when moving a configuration to a newer kernel version; copy `.config` from the old kernel to the new source directory and run the `make ARCH=arm oldconfig` command to bring it up to date. It can also be used to validate a `.config` file that you have edited manually (ignoring the text "*Automatically generated file; DO NOT EDIT*" that occurs at the top; sometimes it is OK to ignore warnings).

If you do make changes to the configuration, the modified `.config` file becomes part of your board support package and needs to be placed under source code control.

When you start the kernel build, a header file, `include/generated/autoconf.h`, is generated, which contains `#define` for each configuration value so that it can be included in the kernel source.

Using LOCALVERSION to identify your kernel

You can discover the kernel version that you have built using the `make kernelversion` target:

```
$ make ARCH=arm kernelversion
4.9.13
```

This is reported at runtime through the `uname` command, and is also used in naming the directory where kernel modules are stored.

If you change the configuration from the default, it is advisable to append your own version information, which you can configure by setting `CONFIG_LOCALVERSION`. As an example, if I wanted to mark the kernel I am building with the identifier `melp` and version 1.0, I would define the local version in `menuconfig` like this:

```
.config - Linux/arm 4.9.13 Kernel Configuration
 > General setup
                          General setup
  Arrow keys navigate the menu. <Enter> selects submenus ---> (or empty
  submenus ----). Highlighted letters are hotkeys. Pressing <Y>
  includes, <N> excludes, <M> modularizes features. Press <Esc><Esc> to
  exit, <?> for Help, </> for Search. Legend: [*] built-in [ ]

        () Cross-compiler tool prefix
        [ ] Compile also drivers which will not load
        (-melp-v1.0) Local version - append to kernel release
        [*] Automatically append version information to the version strin
            Kernel compression mode (Gzip) --->
        ((none)) Default hostname
        [*] Support for paging of anonymous memory (swap)
        [*] System V IPC
        [ ] POSIX Message Queues
        [*] Enable process_vm_readv/writev syscalls
         (+)

             <Select>    < Exit >    < Help >    < Save >    < Load >
```

Running `make kernelversion` produces the same output as before, but now if I run `make kernelrelease`, I see:

```
$ make ARCH=arm kernelrelease
4.9.13-melp-v1.0
```

Kernel modules

I have mentioned kernel modules several times already. Desktop Linux distributions use them extensively so that the correct device and kernel functions can be loaded at runtime, depending on the hardware detected and features required. Without them, every single driver and feature would have to be statically linked in to the kernel, making it infeasibly large.

On the other hand, with embedded devices, the hardware and kernel configuration is usually known at the time the kernel is built, and therefore modules are not so useful. In fact, they cause a problem because they create a version dependency between the kernel and the root filesystem, which can cause boot failures if one is updated but not the other. Consequently, it is quite common for embedded kernels to be built without any modules at all.

Here are a few cases where kernel modules are a good idea in embedded systems:

- When you have proprietary modules, for the licensing reasons given in the preceding section.
- To reduce boot time by deferring the loading of non-essential drivers.
- When there are a number of drivers that could be loaded and it would take up too much memory to compile them statically. For example, you have a USB interface that supports a range of devices. This is essentially the same argument as is used in desktop distributions.

Compiling – Kbuild

The kernel build system, `Kbuild`, is a set of `make` scripts that take the configuration information from the `.config` file, work out the dependencies, and compile everything that is necessary to produce a kernel image containing all the statically linked components, possibly a device tree binary and possibly one or more kernel modules. The dependencies are expressed in `makefiles` that are in each directory with buildable components. For instance, the following two lines are taken from `drivers/char/Makefile`:

```
obj-y += mem.o random.o
obj-$(CONFIG_TTY_PRINTK) += ttyprintk.o
```

The `obj-y` rule unconditionally compiles a file to produce the target, so `mem.c` and `random.c` are always part of the kernel. In the second line, `ttyprintk.c` is dependent on a configuration parameter. If `CONFIG_TTY_PRINTK` is `y`, it is compiled as a built-in; if it is `m`, it is built as a module; and if the parameter is undefined, it is not compiled at all.

For most targets, just typing `make` (with the appropriate `ARCH` and `CROSS_COMPILE`) will do the job, but it is instructive to take it one step at a time.

Finding out which kernel target to build

To build a kernel image, you need to know what your bootloader expects. This is a rough guide:

- **U-Boot**: Traditionally, U-Boot has required `uImage`, but newer versions can load a `zImage` file using the `bootz` command
- **x86 targets**: Requires a `bzImage` file
- **Most other bootloaders**: Require a `zImage` file

Here is an example of building a zImage file:

```
$ make -j 4 ARCH=arm CROSS_COMPILE=arm-cortex_a8-linux-gnueabihf- zImage
```

The -j 4 option tells make how many jobs to run in parallel, which reduces the time taken to build. A rough guide is to run as many jobs as you have CPU cores.

There is a small issue with building a uImage file for ARM with multi-platform support, which is the norm for the current generation of ARM SoC kernels. Multi-platform support for ARM was introduced in Linux 3.7. It allows a single kernel binary to run on multiple platforms and is a step on the road toward having a small number of kernels for all ARM devices. The kernel selects the correct platform by reading the machine number or the device tree passed to it by the bootloader. The problem occurs because the location of physical memory might be different for each platform, and so the relocation address for the kernel (usually 0x8000 bytes from the start of physical RAM) might also be different. The relocation address is coded into the uImage header by the mkimage command when the kernel is built, but it will fail if there is more than one relocation address to choose from. To put it another way, the uImage format is not compatible with multi-platform images. You can still create a uImage binary from a multi-platform build, so long as you give the LOADADDR of the particular SoC you are hoping to boot this kernel on. You can find the load address by looking in mach -[your SoC]/Makefile.boot and noting the value of zreladdr-y:

```
$ make -j 4 ARCH=arm CROSS_COMPILE=arm-cortex_a8-linux-gnueabihf-
LOADADDR=0x80008000 uImage
```

Build artifacts

A kernel build generates two files in the top level directory: vmlinux and System.map. The first, vmlinux, is the kernel as an ELF binary. If you have compiled your kernel with debug enabled (CONFIG_DEBUG_INFO=y), it will contain debug symbols which can be used with debuggers like kgdb. You can also use other ELF binary tools, such as size:

```
$ arm-cortex_a8-linux-gnueabihf-size vmlinux
   text    data     bss     dec     hex  filename
10605896 5291748  351864 16249508  f7f2a4 vmlinux
```

System.map contains the symbol table in a human readable form.

Most bootloaders cannot handle ELF code directly. There is a further stage of processing which takes `vmlinux` and places those binaries in `arch/$ARCH/boot` that are suitable for the various bootloaders:

- `Image`: `vmlinux` converted to raw binary format.
- `zImage`: For the PowerPC architecture, this is just a compressed version of `Image`, which implies that the bootloader must do the decompression. For all other architectures, the compressed `Image` is piggybacked onto a stub of code that decompresses and relocates it.
- `uImage`: `zImage` plus a 64-byte U-Boot header.

While the build is running, you will see a summary of the commands being executed:

```
$ make -j 4 ARCH=arm CROSS_COMPILE=arm-cortex_a8-linux-gnueabihf- \
zImage
CHK include/config/kernel.release
CHK include/generated/uapi/linux/version.h
HOSTCC scripts/basic/fixdep
HOSTCC scripts/kallsyms
HOSTCC scripts/dtc/dtc.o
[...]
```

Sometimes, when the kernel build fails, it is useful to see the actual commands being executed. To do that, add `V=1` to the command line:

```
$ make -j 4 ARCH=arm CROSS_COMPILE=arm-cortex_a8-linux-gnueabihf- \
V=1 zImage
[...]
  arm-cortex_a8-linux-gnueabihf-gcc -Wp,-MD,arch/arm/kernel/.irq.o.d  -
nostdinc -isystem /home/chris/x-tools/arm-cortex_a8-linux-
gnueabihf/lib/gcc/arm-cortex_a8-linux-gnueabihf/5.2.0/include -
I./arch/arm/include -I./arch/arm/include/generated/uapi -
I./arch/arm/include/generated  -I./include -I./arch/arm/include/uapi -
I./include/uapi -I./include/generated/uapi -include
./include/linux/kconfig.h -D__KERNEL__ -mlittle-endian -Wall -Wundef -
Wstrict-prototypes -Wno-trigraphs -fno-strict-aliasing -fno-common -Werror-
implicit-function-declaration -Wno-format-security -std=gnu89 -fno-PIE -
fno-dwarf2-cfi-asm -fno-ipa-sra -mabi=aapcs-linux -mno-thumb-interwork -
mfpu=vfp -funwind-tables -marm -D__LINUX_ARM_ARCH__=7 -march=armv7-a -
msoft-float -Uarm -fno-delete-null-pointer-checks -O2 --param=allow-store-
data-races=0 -Wframe-larger-than=1024 -fno-stack-protector -Wno-unused-but-
set-variable -fomit-frame-pointer -fno-var-tracking-assignments -
Wdeclaration-after-statement -Wno-pointer-sign -fno-strict-overflow -
fconserve-stack -Werror=implicit-int -Werror=strict-prototypes -
Werror=date-time -Werror=incompatible-pointer-types -DCC_HAVE_ASM_GOTO  -
DKBUILD_BASENAME='"irq"'  -DKBUILD_MODNAME='"irq"' -c -o
```

```
arch/arm/kernel/irq.o arch/arm/kernel/irq.c
[...]
```

Compiling device trees

The next step is to build the device tree, or trees if you have a multi-platform build. The dtbs target builds device trees according to the rules in arch/$ARCH/boot/dts/Makefile, using the device tree source files in that directory. Following is a snippet from building the dtbs target for multi_v7_defconfig:

```
$ make ARCH=arm dtbs
[...]
 DTC arch/arm/boot/dts/alpine-db.dtb
 DTC arch/arm/boot/dts/artpec6-devboard.dtb
 DTC arch/arm/boot/dts/at91-kizbox2.dtb
 DTC arch/arm/boot/dts/at91-sama5d2_xplained.dtb
 DTC arch/arm/boot/dts/at91-sama5d3_xplained.dtb
 DTC arch/arm/boot/dts/sama5d31ek.dtb
[...]
```

The compiled .dtb files are generated in the same directory as the sources.

Compiling modules

If you have configured some features to be built as modules, you can build them separately using the modules target:

```
$ make -j 4 ARCH=arm CROSS_COMPILE=arm-cortex_a8-linux-gnueabihf- \
modules
```

The compiled modules have a .ko suffix and are generated in the same directory as the source code, meaning that they are scattered all around the kernel source tree. Finding them is a little tricky, but you can use the modules_install make target to install them in the right place. The default location is /lib/modules in your development system, which is almost certainly not what you want. To install them into the staging area of your root filesystem (we will talk about root filesystems in the next chapter), provide the path using INSTALL_MOD_PATH:

```
$ make -j4 ARCH=arm CROSS_COMPILE=arm-cortex_a8-linux-gnueabihf- \
  INSTALL_MOD_PATH=$HOME/rootfs modules_install
```

Kernel modules are put into the directory /lib/modules/[kernel version], relative to the root of the filesystem.

Cleaning kernel sources

There are three `make` targets for cleaning the kernel source tree:

- `clean`: Removes object files and most intermediates.
- `mrproper`: Removes all intermediate files, including the `.config` file. Use this target to return the source tree to the state it was in immediately after cloning or extracting the source code. If you are curious about the name, Mr Proper is a cleaning product common in some parts of the world. The meaning of `make mrproper` is to give the kernel sources a really good scrub.
- `distclean`: This is the same as `mrproper`, but also deletes editor backup files, patch files, and other artifacts of software development.

Building a kernel for the BeagleBone Black

In light of the information already given, here is the complete sequence of commands to build a kernel, the modules, and a device tree for the BeagleBone Black, using the Crosstool-NG ARM Cortex A8 cross compiler:

```
$ cd linux-stable
$ make ARCH=arm CROSS_COMPILE=arm-cortex_a8-linux-gnueabihf- mrproper
$ make ARCH=arm multi_v7_defconfig
$ make -j4 ARCH=arm CROSS_COMPILE=arm-cortex_a8-linux-gnueabihf- zImage
$ make -j4 ARCH=arm CROSS_COMPILE=arm-cortex_a8-linux-gnueabihf- modules
$ make ARCH=arm CROSS_COMPILE=arm-cortex_a8-linux-gnueabihf- dtbs
```

These commands are in the script `MELP/chapter_04/build-linux-bbb.sh`.

Building a kernel for QEMU

Here is the sequence of commands to build Linux for the ARM Versatile PB that is emulated by QEMU, using the Crosstool-NG V5te compiler:

```
$ cd linux-stable
$ make ARCH=arm CROSS_COMPILE=arm-unknown-linux-gnueabi- mrproper
$ make -j4 ARCH=arm CROSS_COMPILE=arm-unknown-linux-gnueabi- zImage
$ make -j4 ARCH=arm CROSS_COMPILE=arm-unknown-linux-gnueabi- modules
$ make ARCH=arm CROSS_COMPILE=arm-unknown-linux-gnueabi- dtbs
```

These commands are in the script `MELP/chapter_04/build-linux-versatilepb.sh`.

Booting the kernel

Booting Linux is highly device-dependent. In this section, I will show you how it works for the BeagleBone Black and QEMU. For other target boards, you must consult the information from the vendor or from the community project, if there is one.

At this point, you should have the zImage file and the dtbs targets for the BeagleBone Black or QEMU.

Booting the BeagleBone Black

To begin, you need a microSD card with U-Boot installed, as described in the section *Installing U-Boot*. Plug the microSD card into your card reader and from the linux-stable directory the files arch/arm/boot/zImage and arch/arm/boot/dts/am335x-boneblack.dtb to the boot partition. Unmount the card and plug it into the BeagleBone Black. Start a terminal emulator, such as gtkterm, and be prepared to press the space bar as soon as you see the U-Boot messages appear. Next, power on the BeagleBone Black and press the space bar. You should get a U-Boot prompt, . Now enter the following commands to load Linux and the device tree binary:

```
U-Boot# fatload mmc 0:1 0x80200000 zImage
reading zImage
7062472 bytes read in 447 ms (15.1 MiB/s)
U-Boot# fatload mmc 0:1 0x80f00000 am335x-boneblack.dtb
reading am335x-boneblack.dtb
34184 bytes read in 10 ms (3.3 MiB/s)
U-Boot# setenv bootargs console=ttyO0
U-Boot# bootz 0x80200000 - 0x80f00000
## Flattened Device Tree blob at 80f00000
 Booting using the fdt blob at 0x80f00000
 Loading Device Tree to 8fff4000, end 8ffff587 ... OK

Starting kernel ...

[ 0.000000] Booting Linux on physical CPU 0x0
[...]
```

Note that we set the kernel command line to console=ttyO0. That tells Linux which device to use for console output, which in this case is the first UART on the board, device ttyO0. Without this, we would not see any messages after Starting the kernel..., and therefore would not know if it was working or not. The sequence will end in a kernel panic, for reasons I will explain later on.

Booting QEMU

Assuming that you have already installed `qemu-system-arm`, you can launch with the kernel and the `.dtb` file for the ARM Versatile PB, as follows:

```
$ QEMU_AUDIO_DRV=none \
qemu-system-arm -m 256M -nographic -M versatilepb -kernel zImage \
-append "console=ttyAMA0,115200" -dtb versatile-pb.dtb
```

Note that setting `QEMU_AUDIO_DRV` to `none` is just to suppress error messages from QEMU about missing configurations for the audio drivers, which we do not use. As with the BeagleBone Black, this will end with a kernel panic and the system will halt. To exit from QEMU, type *Ctrl + A* and then *x* (two separate keystrokes).

Kernel panic

While things started off well, they ended badly:

```
[ 1.886379] Kernel panic - not syncing: VFS: Unable to mount root fs on
unknown-block(0,0)
[ 1.895105] ---[ end Kernel panic - not syncing: VFS: Unable to mount root
fs on unknown-block(0, 0)
```

This is a good example of a kernel panic. A panic occurs when the kernel encounters an unrecoverable error. By default, it will print out a message to the console and then halt. You can set the `panic` command-line parameter to allow a few seconds before reboots following a panic. In this case, the unrecoverable error is no root filesystem, illustrating that a kernel is useless without a user space to control it. You can supply a user space by providing a root filesystem, either as a ramdisk or on a mountable mass storage device. We will talk about how to create a root filesystem in the next chapter, but first I want to describe the sequence of events that leads up to `panic`.

Early user space

In order to transition from kernel initialization to user space, the kernel has to mount a root filesystem and execute a program in that root filesystem. This can be achieved via a ramdisk or by mounting a real filesystem on a block device. The code for all of this is in `init/main.c`, starting with the function `rest_init()`, which creates the first thread with PID 1 and runs the code in `kernel_init()`. If there is a ramdisk, it will try to execute the program `/init`, which will take on the task of setting up the user space.

If fails to find and run /init, it tries to mount a filesystem by calling the function
prepare_namespace() in init/do_mounts.c. This requires a root= command line to
give the name of the block device to use for mounting, usually in the form:

```
root=/dev/<disk name><partition number>
```

Or, for SD cards and eMMC:

```
root=/dev/<disk name>p<partition number>
```

For example, for the first partition on an SD card, that would be root=/dev/mmcblk0p1. If
the mount succeeds, it will try to execute /sbin/init, followed by /etc/init,
/bin/init, and then /bin/sh, stopping at the first one that works.

The program can be overridden on the command line. For a ramdisk, use rdinit=, and for
a filesystem, use init=.

Kernel messages

Kernel developers are fond of printing out useful information through liberal use of
printk() and similar functions. The messages are categorized according to importance,
with 0 being the highest:

Level	Value	Meaning
KERN_EMERG	0	The system is unusable
KERN_ALERT	1	Action must be taken immediately
KERN_CRIT	2	Critical conditions
KERN_ERR	3	Error conditions
KERN_WARNING	4	Warning conditions
KERN_NOTICE	5	Normal but significant conditions
KERN_INFO	6	Informational
KERN_DEBUG	7	Debug-level messages

They are first written to a buffer, __log_buf, the size of which is two to the power of
CONFIG_LOG_BUF_SHIFT. For example, if CONFIG_LOG_BUF_SHIFT is 16, then __log_buf
is 64 KiB. You can dump the entire buffer using the command dmesg.

If the level of a message is less than the console log level, it is displayed on the console as well as placed in __log_buf. The default console log level is 7, meaning that messages of level 6 and lower are displayed, filtering out KERN_DEBUG, which is level 7. You can change the console log level in several ways, including by using the kernel parameter loglevel=<level>, or the command dmesg -n <level>.

Kernel command line

The kernel command line is a string that is passed to the kernel by the bootloader, via the bootargs variable in the case of U-Boot; it can also be defined in the device tree, or set as part of the kernel configuration in CONFIG_CMDLINE.

We have seen some examples of the kernel command line already, but there are many more. There is a complete list in Documentation/kernel-parameters.txt. Here is a smaller list of the most useful ones:

Name	Description
debug	Sets the console log level to the highest level, 8, to ensure that you see all the kernel messages on the console.
init=	The init program to run from a mounted root filesystem, which defaults to /sbin/init.
lpj=	Sets loops_per_jiffy to a given constant. There is a description of the significance of this in the paragraph following this table.
panic=	Behavior when the kernel panics: if it is greater than zero, it gives the number of seconds before rebooting; if it is zero, it waits forever (this is the default); or if it is less than zero, it reboots without any delay.
quiet	Sets the console log level to , suppressing all but emergency messages. Since most devices have a serial console, it takes time to output all those strings. Consequently, reducing the number of messages using this option reduces boot time.
rdinit=	The init program to run from a ramdisk. It defaults to /init.
ro	Mounts the root device as read-only. Has no effect on a ramdisk, which is always read/write.
root=	Device to mount the root filesystem.

rootdelay=	The number of seconds to wait before trying to mount the root device; defaults to zero. Useful if the device takes time to probe the hardware, but also see `rootwait`.
rootfstype=	The filesystem type for the root device. In many cases, it is auto-detected during mount, but it is required for `jffs2` filesystems.
rootwait	Waits indefinitely for the root device to be detected. Usually necessary with mmc devices.
rw	Mounts the root device as read-write (default).

The `lpj` parameter is often mentioned in connection with reducing the kernel boot time. During initialization, the kernel loops for approximately 250 ms to calibrate a delay loop. The value is stored in the variable `loops_per_jiffy`, and reported like this:

```
Calibrating delay loop... 996.14 BogoMIPS (lpj=4980736)
```

If the kernel always runs on the same hardware, it will always calculate the same value. You can shave 250 ms off the boot time by adding `lpj=4980736` to the command line.

Porting Linux to a new board

Porting Linux to a new board can be easy or difficult, depending on how similar your board is to an existing development board. In `Chapter 3`, *All About Bootloaders*, we ported U-Boot to a new board, named `Nova`, which is based on the BeagleBone Black. very few changes to be made to the kernel code and so it very easy. If you are porting to completely new and innovative hardware, there will be more to do. I am only going to consider the simple case.

The organization of architecture-specific code in `arch/$ARCH` differs from one system to another. The x86 architecture is pretty clean because most hardware details are detected at runtime. The PowerPC architecture puts SoC and board-specific files into sub directory platforms. The ARM architecture, on the other hand, is quite messy, in part because there is a lot of variability between the many ARM-based SoCs. Platform-dependent code is put in directories named `mach-*`, approximately one per SoC. There are other directories named `plat-*` which contain code common to several versions of an SoC. In the case of the BeagleBone Black, the relevant directory is `arch/arm/mach-omap2`. Don't be fooled by the name though; it contains support for OMAP2, 3, and 4 chips, as well as the AM33xx family of chips that the BeagleBone uses.

In the following sections, I am going to explain how to create a device tree for a new board and how to key that into the initialization code of Linux.

A new device tree

The first thing to do is create a device tree for the board and modify it to describe the additional or changed hardware of the Nova board. In this simple case, we will just copy am335x-boneblack.dts to nova.dts and change the board name in nova.dts, as shown highlighted here:

```
/dts-v1/;

#include "am33xx.dtsi"
#include "am335x-bone-common.dtsi"
#include <dt-bindings/display/tda998x.h>

/ {
    model = "Nova";
    compatible = "ti,am335x-bone-black", "ti,am335x-bone", "ti,am33xx";
};
[...]
```

We can build the Nova device tree binary explicitly like this:

```
$ make ARCH=arm nova.dtb
```

If we want the device tree for Nova to be compiled by make ARCH=arm dtbs whenever an AM33xx target is selected, we could add a dependency in arch/arm/boot/dts/Makefile as follows:

```
[...]
dtb-$(CONFIG_SOC_AM33XX) +=
    nova.dtb
[...
```

We can see the effect of using the Nova device tree by booting the BeagleBone Black, following the same procedure as in the section *Booting the BeagleBone Black*, with the same zImage file as before, but loading nova.dtb in place of am335x-boneblack.dtb. The following highlighted output is the point at which the machine model is printed out:

```
Starting kernel ...

[ 0.000000] Booting Linux on physical CPU 0x0
[ 0.000000] Linux version 4.9.13-melp-v1.0-dirty (chris@chris-xps) (gcc
version 5.2.0 (crosstool-NG crosstool-ng-1.22.0) ) #2 SMP Fri Mar 24
17:51:41 GMT 2017
[ 0.000000] CPU: ARMv7 Processor [413fc082] revision 2 (ARMv7), cr=10c5387d
[ 0.000000] CPU: PIPT / VIPT nonaliasing data cache, VIPT aliasing
instruction cache
```

```
[ 0.000000] OF: fdt:Machine model: Nova
[...]
```

Now that we have a device tree specifically for the Nova board, we could modify it to describe the hardware differences between Nova and the BeagleBone Black. There are quite likely to be changes to the kernel configuration as well, in which case you would create a custom configuration file based on a copy of `arch/arm/configs/multi_v7_defconfig`.

Setting the board compatible property

Creating a new device tree means that we can describe the hardware on the Nova board, selecting device drivers and setting properties to match. But, suppose the Nova board needs different early initialization code than the BeagleBone Black; how can we link that in?

The board setup is controlled by the `compatible` property in the root node. This is what we have for the Nova board at the moment:

```
/ {
    model = "Nova";
    compatible = "ti,am335x-bone-black", "ti,am335x-bone", "ti,am33xx";
};
```

When the kernel parses this node, it will search for a matching machine for each of the values of the compatible property, starting on the left and stopping with the first match found. Each machine is defined in a structure delimited by `DT_MACHINE_START` and `MACHINE_END` macros. In `arch/arm/mach-omap2/board-generic.c`, we find:

```
#ifdef CONFIG_SOC_AM33XX
static const char *const am33xx_boards_compat[] __initconst = {
    "ti,am33xx",
    NULL,
};

DT_MACHINE_START(AM33XX_DT, "Generic AM33XX (Flattened Device Tree)")
    .reserve = omap_reserve,
    .map_io = am33xx_map_io,
    .init_early = am33xx_init_early,
    .init_machine = omap_generic_init,
    .init_late = am33xx_init_late,
    .init_time = omap3_gptimer_timer_init,
    .dt_compat = am33xx_boards_compat,
    .restart = am33xx_restart,
MACHINE_END
#endif
```

Note that the string array, `am33xx_boards_compat`, contains `"ti,am33xx"` which matches one of the machines listed in the compatible property. In fact, it is the only match possible, since there are none for `ti,am335x-bone-black` or `ti,am335x-bone`. The structure between `DT_MACHINE_START` and `MACHINE_END` contains a pointer to the string array, and function pointers for the board setup functions. You may wonder why bother with `ti,am335x-bone-black` and `ti,am335x-bone` if they never match anything? The answer is partly that they are place holders for the future, but also that there are places in the kernel that contain runtime tests for the machine using the function `of_machine_is_compatible()`. For example, in `drivers/net/ethernet/ti/cpsw-common.c`:

```
int ti_cm_get_macid(struct device *dev, int slave, u8 *mac_addr)
{
[...]
    if (of_machine_is_compatible("ti,am33xx"))
        return cpsw_am33xx_cm_get_macid(dev, 0x630, slave, mac_addr);
[...]
```

Thus, we have to look through not just the `mach-*` directories but the entire kernel source code to get a list of all the places that depend on the machine compatible property. In the 4.9 kernel, you will find that there are still no checks for `ti,am335x-bone-black` and `ti,am335x-bone`, but there may be in the future.

Returning to the Nova board, if we want to add machine specific setup, we can add a machine in `arch/arm/mach-omap2/board-generic.c`, like this:

```
#ifdef CONFIG_SOC_AM33XX
[...]
static const char *const nova_compat[] __initconst = {
    "ti,nova",
    NULL,
};

DT_MACHINE_START(NOVA_DT, "Nova board (Flattened Device Tree)")
    .reserve = omap_reserve,
    .map_io = am33xx_map_io,
    .init_early = am33xx_init_early,
    .init_machine = omap_generic_init,
    .init_late = am33xx_init_late,
    .init_time = omap3_gptimer_timer_init,
    .dt_compat = nova_compat,
    .restart = am33xx_restart,
MACHINE_END
#endif
```

Then we could change the device tree root node like this:

```
/ {
    model = "Nova";
    compatible = "ti,nova", "ti,am33xx";
};
```

Now, the machine will match `ti,nova` in `board-generic.c`. We keep `ti,am33xx` because we want the runtime tests, such as the one in `drivers/net/ethernet/ti/cpsw-common.c`, to continue to work.

Additional reading

The following resources have further information about the topics introduced in this chapter:

- *Linux Kernel Development*, 3rd Edition by Robert Love
- Linux weekly news, `https://lwn.net/`

Summary

Linux is a very powerful and complex operating system kernel that can be married to various types of user space, ranging from a simple embedded device, through increasingly complex mobile devices using Android, to a full server operating system. One of its strengths is the degree of configurability. The definitive place to get the source code is `https://www.kernel.org/`, but you will probably need to get the source for a particular SoC or board from the vendor of that device or a third-party that supports that device. The customization of the kernel for a particular target may consist of changes to the core kernel code, additional drivers for devices that are not in mainline Linux, a default kernel configuration file, and a device tree source file.

Normally, you start with the default configuration for your target board, and then tweak it by running one of the configuration tools such as `menuconfig`. One of the things you should consider at this point is whether the kernel features and drivers should be compiled as modules or built-in. Kernel modules are usually no great advantage for embedded systems, where the feature set and hardware are usually well defined. However, modules are often used as a way to import proprietary code into the kernel, and also to reduce boot time by loading non-essential drivers after boot.

Building the kernel produces a compressed kernel image file, named `zImage`, `bzImage`, or `uImage`, depending on the bootloader you will be using and the target architecture. A kernel build will also generate any kernel modules (as `.ko` files) that you have configured, and device tree binaries (as `.dtb` files) if your target requires them.

Porting Linux to a new target board can be quite simple or very difficult, depending on how different the hardware is from that in the mainline or vendor supplied kernel. If your hardware is based on a well-known reference design, then it may be just a question of making changes to the device tree or to the platform data. You may well need to add device drivers, which I discuss in `Chapter 9`, *Interfacing with Device Drivers*. However, if the hardware is radically different to a reference design, you may need additional core support, which is outside the scope of this book.

The kernel is the core of a Linux-based system, but it cannot work by itself. It requires a root filesystem that contains the user space components. The root filesystem can be a ramdisk or a filesystem accessed via a block device, which will be the subject of the next chapter. As we have seen, booting a kernel without a root filesystem results in a kernel panic.

5
Building a Root Filesystem

The root filesystem is the fourth and the final element of embedded Linux. Once you have read this chapter, you will be able build, boot, and run a simple embedded Linux system.

The techniques I will describe here are broadly known as **roll your own** or **RYO**. Back in the earlier days of embedded Linux, this was the only way to create a root filesystem. There are still some use cases where an RYO root filesystem is applicable, for example, when the amount of RAM or storage is very limited, for quick demonstrations, or for any case in which your requirements are not (easily) covered by the standard build system tools. Nevertheless, these cases are quite rare. Let me emphasize that the purpose of this chapter is educational; it is not meant to be a recipe for building everyday embedded systems: use the tools described in the next chapter for this.

The first objective is to create a minimal root filesystem that will give us a shell prompt. Then, using this as a base, we will add scripts to start up other programs and configure a network interface and user permissions. There are worked examples for both the BeagleBone Black and QEMU targets. Knowing how to build the root filesystem from scratch is a useful skill, and it will help you to understand what is going on when we look at more complex examples in later chapters.

In this chapter, we will cover the following topics:

- What should be in the root filesystem?
- Transferring the root filesystem to the target.
- Creating a boot `initramfs`.
- The init program.
- Configuring user accounts.
- A better way of managing device nodes.

- Configuring the network.
- Creating filesystem images with device tables.
- Mounting the root filesystem using NFS.

What should be in the root filesystem?

The kernel will get a root filesystem, either an `initramfs`, passed as a pointer from the bootloader, or by mounting the block device given on the kernel command line by the `root=` parameter. Once it has a root filesystem, the kernel will execute the first program, by default named init, as described in the section *Early user space* in `Chapter 4`, *Configuring and Building the Kernel*. Then, as far as the kernel is concerned, its job is complete. It is up to the init program to begin starting other programs and so bring the system to life.

To make a minimal root filesystem, you need these components:

- **init**: This is the program that starts everything off, usually by running a series of scripts. I will describe how init works in much more detail in `Chapter 10`, *Starting Up – The init Program*
- **Shell**: You need a shell to give you a command prompt but, more importantly, also to run the shell scripts called by init and other programs.
- **Daemons**: A daemon is a background program that provides a service to others. Good examples are the **system log daemon (syslogd)** and the **secure shell daemon (sshd)**. The init program must start the initial population of daemons to support the main system applications. In fact, init is itself a daemon: it is the daemon that provides the service of launching other daemons.
- **Shared libraries**: Most programs are linked with shared libraries, and so they must be present in the root filesystem.
- **Configuration files**: The configuration for init and other daemons is stored in a series of text files, usually in the `/etc` directory.
- **Device nodes**: These are the special files that give access to various device drivers.
- `/proc` and `/sys`: These two pseudo filesystems represent kernel data structures as a hierarchy of directories and files. Many programs and library functions depend on proc and sys.
- **Kernel modules**: If you have configured some parts of your kernel to be modules, they need to be installed in the root filesystem, usually in `/lib/modules/[kernel version]`.

In addition, there are the device-specific applications that make the device do the job it is intended for, and also the run-time data files that they generate.

 In some cases, you could condense most of these components into a single, statically-linked program, and start the program instead of init. For example, if your program was named /myprog, you would add the following command to the kernel command line: init=/myprog. I have come across such a configuration only once, in a secure system in which the fork system call had been disabled, thus making it impossible for any other program to be started. The downside of this approach is that you can't make use of the many tools that normally go into an embedded system; you have to do everything yourself.

The directory layout

Interestingly, the Linux kernel does not care about the layout of files and directories beyond the existence of the program named by init= or rdinit=, so you are free to put things wherever you like. As an example, compare the file layout of a device running Android to that of a desktop Linux distribution: they are almost completely different.

However, many programs expect certain files to be in certain places, and it helps us developers if devices use a similar layout, Android aside. The basic layout of a Linux system is defined in the **Filesystem Hierarchy Standard (FHS)**, which is available at http://refspecs.linuxfoundation.org/fhs.shtml. The FHS covers all the implementations of Linux operating systems from the largest to the smallest. Embedded devices tend to use a subset based on their needs, but it usually includes the following:

- /bin: Programs essential for all users
- /dev: Device nodes and other special files
- /etc: System configuration files
- /lib: Essential shared libraries, for example, those that make up the C-library
- /proc: The proc filesystem
- /sbin: Programs essential to the system administrator
- /sys: The sysfs filesystem
- /tmp: A place to put temporary or volatile files
- /usr: Additional programs, libraries, and system administrator utilities, in the directories /usr/bin, /usr/lib and /usr/sbin, respectively
- /var: A hierarchy of files and directories that may be modified at runtime, for example, log messages, some of which must be retained after boot

There are some subtle distinctions here. The difference between /bin and /sbin is simply that the latter need not be included in the search path for non-root users. Users of Red Hat-derived distributions will be familiar with this. The significance of /usr is that it maybe in a separate partition from the root filesystem, so it cannot contain anything that is needed to boot the system up.

The staging directory

You should begin by creating a **staging** directory on your host computer where you can assemble the files that will eventually be transferred to the target. In the following examples, I have used ~/rootfs. You need to create a *skeleton* directory structure in it, for example, take a look here:

```
$ mkdir ~/rootfs
$ cd ~/rootfs
$ mkdir bin dev etc home lib proc sbin sys tmp usr var
$ mkdir usr/bin usr/lib usr/sbin
$ mkdir -p var/log
```

To see the directory hierarchy more clearly, you can use the handy tree command used in the following example with the -d option to show only the directories:

```
$ tree -d
```

```
.
├── bin
├── dev
├── etc
├── home
├── lib
├── proc
├── sbin
├── sys
├── tmp
├── usr
│   ├── bin
│   ├── lib
│   └── sbin
├── va
└── var
    └── log
```

POSIX file access permissions

Every process, which in the context of this discussion means every running program, belongs to a user and one or more groups. The user is represented by a 32-bit number called the **user ID** or **UID**. Information about users, including the mapping from a UID to a name, is kept in /etc/passwd. Likewise, groups are represented by a **group ID** or **GID** with information kept in /etc/group. There is always a root user with a UID of 0 and a root group with a GID of 0. The root user is also called the **superuser** because; in a default configuration, it bypasses most permission checks and can access all the resources in the system. Security in Linux-based systems is mainly about restricting access to the root account.

Each file and directory also has an owner and belongs to exactly one group. The level of access a process has to a file or directory is controlled by a set of access permission flags, called the **mode** of the file. There are three collections of three bits: the first collection applies to the *owner* of the file, the second to the *members* of the same group as the file, and the last to *everyone else:* the rest of the world. The bits are for **read (r)**, **write (w)**, and **execute (x)** permissions on the file. Since three bits fit neatly into an octal digit, they are usually represented in octal, as shown in the following diagram:

```
400  r--------  ┐
200  -w-------  ├─  Owner permissions
100  --x------  ┘
040  ---r-----  ┐
020  ----w----  ├─  Group permissions
010  -----x---  ┘
004  ------r--  ┐
002  -------w-  ├─  World permissions
001  --------x  ┘
```

There is a further group of three bits that have special meanings:

- **SUID (4)**: If the file is executable, it changes the effective UID of the process to that of the owner of the file when the program is run.
- **SGID (2)**: Similar to SUID, this changes the effective GID of the process to that of the group of the file.
- **Sticky (1)**: In a directory, this restricts deletion so that one user cannot delete files that are owned by another user. This is usually set on /tmp and /var/tmp.

The SUID bit is probably used most often . It gives non-root users a temporary privilege escalation to superuser to perform a task. A good example is the ping program: ping opens a raw socket, which is a privileged operation. In order for normal users to use ping, it is owned by user root and has the SUID bit set so that when you run ping, it executes with UID 0 regardless of your UID.

To set these bits, use the octal numbers, 4, 2, and 1 with the chmod command. For example, to set SUID on /bin/ping in your staging root directory, you could use the following:

```
$ cd ~/rootfs
$ ls -l bin/ping
-rwxr-xr-x 1 root  root  35712 Feb 6 09:15 bin/ping

$ sudo chmod 4755 bin/ping
$ ls -l bin/ping
-rwsr-xr-x 1 root  root  35712 Feb 6 09:15 bin/ping
```

Note that the second ls command shows the first three bits of the mode to be rws, whereas previously, they had been rwx. That 's' indicates that the SUID bit is set.

File ownership permissions in the staging directory

For security and stability reasons, it is vitally important to pay attention to the ownership and permissions of the files that will be placed on the target device. Generally speaking, you want to restrict sensitive resources to be accessible only by the root and wherever possible, to run programs using non-root users so that if they are compromised by an outside attack, they offer as few system resources to the attacker as possible. For example, the device node called /dev/mem gives access to system memory, which is necessary in some programs. But, if it is readable and writeable by everyone, then there is no security because everyone can access everything in memory. So, /dev/mem should be owned by root, belong to the root group, and have a mode of 600, which denies read and write access to all but the owner.

There is a problem with the staging directory though. The files you create there will be owned by you, but when they are installed on the device, they should belong to specific owners and groups, mostly the root user. An obvious fix is to change the ownership to root at this stage with the commands shown here:

```
$ cd ~/rootfs
$ sudo chown -R root:root *
```

The problem is that you need `root` privileges to run the `chown` command, and from that point onward, you will need to be `root` to modify any files in the staging directory. Before you know it, you are doing all your development logged on as `root`, which is not a good idea. This is a problem that we will come back to later.

Programs for the root filesystem

Now, it is time to start populating the `root` filesystem with the essential programs and the supporting libraries, configuration, and data files that they need to operate. I will begin with an overview of the types of programs you will need.

The init program

Init is the first program to be run, and so it is an essential part of the root filesystem. In this chapter, we will be using the simple init program provided by BusyBox.

Shell

We need a shell to run scripts and to give us a command prompt so that we can interact with the system. An interactive shell is probably not necessary in a production device, but it is useful for development, debugging, and maintenance. There are various shells in common use in embedded systems:

- **bash**: This is the big beast that we all know and love from desktop Linux. It is a superset of the Unix Bourne shell with many extensions or *bashisms*.
- **ash**: Also based on the Bourne shell, it has a long history with the BSD variants of Unix. BusyBox has a version of `ash`, which has been extended to make it more compatible with `bash`. It is much smaller than `bash`, and hence it is a very popular choice for embedded systems.
- **hush**: This is a very small shell that we briefly looked at in Chapter 3, *All about Bootloaders*. It is useful on devices with very little memory. There is a version of hush in BusyBox.

 If you are using `ash` or `hush` as the shell on the target, make sure that you test your shell scripts on the target. It is very tempting to test them only on the host, using `bash`, and then be surprised that they don't work when you copy them to the target.

Utilities

The shell is just a way of launching other programs, and a shell script is little more than a list of programs to run, with some flow control and a means of passing information between programs. To make a shell useful, you need the utility programs that the Unix command line is based on. Even for a basic root filesystem, you need approximately 50 utilities, which presents two problems. Firstly, tracking down the source code for each one and cross-compiling it would be quite a big job. Secondly, the resulting collection of programs would take up several tens of megabytes, which was a real problem in the early days of embedded Linux when a few megabytes was all you had. To solve this problem, BusyBox was born.

BusyBox to the rescue!

The genesis of **BusyBox** had nothing to do with embedded Linux. The project was instigated in 1996 by Bruce Perens for the Debian installer so that he could boot Linux from a 1.44 MB floppy disk. Coincidentally, this was about the size of the storage on contemporary devices, and so the embedded Linux community quickly took it up. BusyBox has been at the heart of embedded Linux ever since.

BusyBox was written from scratch to perform the essential functions of those essential Linux utilities. The developers took advantage of the 80:20 rule: the most useful 80% of a program is implemented in 20% of the code. Hence, BusyBox tools implement a subset of the functions of the desktop equivalents, but they do enough of it to be useful in the majority of cases.

Another trick BusyBox employs is to combine all the tools together into a single binary, making it easy to share code between them. It works like this: BusyBox is a collection of applets, each of which exports its main function in the form `[applet]_main`. For example, the `cat` command is implemented in `coreutils/cat.c` and exports `cat_main`. The `main` function of BusyBox itself dispatches the call to the correct applet, based on the command-line arguments.

So, to read a file, you can launch BusyBox with the name of the applet you want to run, followed by any arguments the applet expects, as shown here:

```
$ busybox cat my_file.txt
```

You can also run BusyBox with no arguments to get a list of all the applets that have been compiled.

Using BusyBox in this way is rather clumsy. A better way to get BusyBox to run the `cat` applet is to create a symbolic link from `/bin/cat` to `/bin/busybox`:

```
$ ls -l bin/cat bin/busybox
-rwxr-xr-x 1 root root 892868 Feb 2 11:01 bin/busybox
lrwxrwxrwx 1 root root 7      Feb 2 11:01 bin/cat -> busybox
```

When you type `cat` at the command line, BusyBox is the program that actually runs. BusyBox only has to check the command tail passed in `argv[0]`, which will be `/bin/cat`, extract the application name, `cat`, and do a table look-up to match `cat` with `cat_main`. All this is in `libbb/applet lib.c` in this section of code (slightly simplified):

```
applet_name = argv[0];
applet_name = bb_basename(applet_name);
run_applet_and_exit(applet_name, argv);
```

BusyBox has over three hundred applets including an init program, several shells of varying levels of complexity, and utilities for most admin tasks. There is even a simple version of the `vi` editor, so you can change text files on your device.

To summarize, a typical installation of BusyBox consists of a single program with a symbolic link for each applet, but which behaves exactly as if it were a collection of individual applications.

Building BusyBox

BusyBox uses the same `Kconfig` and `Kbuild` system as the kernel, so cross compiling is straightforward. You can get the source by cloning the Git archive and checking out the version you want (`1_26_2` was the latest at the time of writing), such as follows:

```
$ git clone git://busybox.net/busybox.git
$ cd busybox
$ git checkout 1_26_2
```

You can also download the corresponding TAR file from `http://busybox.net/downloads`.

Then, configure BusyBox by starting with the default configuration, which enables pretty much all of the features of BusyBox:

```
$ make distclean
$ make defconfig
```

At this point, you probably want to run `make menuconfig` to fine tune the configuration. For example, you almost certainly want to set the install path in **Busybox Settings | Installation Options** (`CONFIG_PREFIX`) to point to the staging directory. Then, you can cross compile in the usual way. If your intended target is the BeagleBone Black, use this command:

```
$ make ARCH=arm CROSS_COMPILE=arm-cortex_a8-linux-gnueabihf-
```

If your intended target is the QEMU emulation of a Versatile PB, use this command:

```
$ make ARCH=arm CROSS_COMPILE=arm-unknown-linux-gnueabi-
```

In either case, the result is the executable, `busybox`. For a default configuration build like this, the size is about 900 KiB. If this is too big for you, you can slim it down by changing the configuration to leave out the utilities you don't need.

To install BusyBox into the staging area, use the following command:

```
$ make ARCH=arm CROSS_COMPILE=arm-cortex_a8-linux-gnueabihf- install
```

This will copy the binary to the directory configured in `CONFIG_PREFIX` and create all the symbolic links to it.

ToyBox – an alternative to BusyBox

BusyBox is not the only game in town. In addition, there is **ToyBox**, which you can find at h ttp://landley.net/toybox/. The project was started by Rob Landley, who was previously a maintainer of BusyBox. ToyBox has the same aim as BusyBox, but with more emphasis on complying with standards, especially POSIX-2008 and LSB 4.1, and less on compatibility with GNU extensions to those standards. ToyBox is smaller than BusyBox, partly because it implements fewer applets. However, the main difference is the license, which is BSD rather than GPL v2. This makes it license compatible with operating systems with a BSD-licensed user space, such as Android, and hence it is part of all the new Android devices.

Libraries for the root filesystem

Programs are linked with libraries. You could link them all statically, in which case, there would be no libraries on the target device. But, this takes up an unnecessarily large amount of storage if you have more than two or three programs. So, you need to copy shared libraries from the toolchain to the staging directory. How do you know which libraries?

One option is to copy all of the .so files from the sysroot directory of your toolchain, since they must be of some use otherwise they wouldn't exist! This is certainly logical and, if you are creating a platform to be used by others for a range of applications, it would be the correct approach. Be aware, though, that a full glibc is quite large. In the case of a crosstool-NG build of glibc 2.22, the libraries, locales, and other supporting files come to 33 MiB. Of course, you could cut down on that considerably using musl libc or uClibc-ng.

Another option is to cherry pick only those libraries that you require, for which you need a means of discovering library dependencies. Using some of our knowledge from Chapter 2, *Learning About Toolchains*, we can use the readelf command for this task:

```
$ cd ~/rootfs
$ arm-cortex_a8-linux-gnueabihf-readelf -a bin/busybox | grep "program
interpreter"
[Requesting program interpreter: /lib/ld-linux-armhf.so.3]

$ arm-cortex_a8-linux-gnueabihf-readelf -a bin/busybox | grep "Shared
library"
0x00000001 (NEEDED)     Shared library: [libm.so.6]
0x00000001 (NEEDED)     Shared library: [libc.so.6]
```

Now, you need to find these files in the toolchain sysroot directory and copy them to the staging directory. Remember that you can find sysroot like this:

```
$ arm-cortex_a8-linux-gnueabihf-gcc -print-sysroot
/home/chris/x-tools/arm-cortex_a8-linux-gnueabihf/arm-cortex_a8-linux-
gnueabihf/sysroot
```

To reduce the amount of typing, I am going to keep a copy of that in a shell variable:

```
$ export SYSROOT=$(arm-cortex_a8-linux-gnueabihf-gcc -print-sysroot)
```

If you look at /lib/ld-linux-armhf.so.3 in sysroot, you will see that, it is, in fact, a symbolic link:

```
$ cd $SYSROOT
$ ls -l lib/ld-linux-armhf.so.3
lrwxrwxrwx 1 chris chris 10 Mar 3 15:22 lib/ld-linux-armhf.so.3 ->
ld-2.22.so
```

Repeat the exercise for `libc.so.6` and `libm.so.6,` and you will end up with a list of three files and three symbolic links. Now, you can copy each one using `cp -a`, which will preserve the symbolic link:

```
$ cd ~/rootfs
$ cp -a $SYSROOT/lib/ld-linux-armhf.so.3 lib
$ cp -a $SYSROOT/lib/ld-2.22.so lib
$ cp -a $SYSROOT/lib/libc.so.6 lib
$ cp -a $SYSROOT/lib/libc-2.22.so lib
$ cp -a $SYSROOT/lib/libm.so.6 lib
$ cp -a $SYSROOT/lib/libm-2.22.so lib
```

Repeat this procedure for each program.

It is only worth doing this to get the very smallest embedded footprint possible. There is a danger that you will miss libraries that are loaded through dlopen(3) calls–plugins mostly. We will look at an example with the **name service switch** (**NSS**) libraries when we come to configure network interfaces later on in this chapter.

Reducing the size by stripping

Libraries and programs are often compiled with some information stored in symbol tables to aid debugging and tracing. You seldom need these in a production system. A quick and easy way to save space is to strip the binaries of symbol tables. This example shows `libc` before stripping:

```
$ file rootfs/lib/libc-2.22.so
lib/libc-2.22.so: ELF 32-bit LSB shared object, ARM, EABI5 version 1
(GNU/Linux), dynamically linked (uses shared libs), for GNU/Linux 4.3.0,
not stripped

$ ls -og rootfs/lib/libc-2.22.so
-rwxr-xr-x 1 1542572 Mar 3 15:22 rootfs/lib/libc-2.22.so
```

Now, let's see the result of stripping debug information:

```
$ arm-cortex_a8-linux-gnueabihf-strip rootfs/lib/libc-2.22.so
$ file rootfs/lib/libc-2.22.so
rootfs/lib/libc-2.22.so: ELF 32-bit LSB shared object, ARM, EABI5 version 1
(GNU/Linux), dynamically linked (uses shared libs), for GNU/Linux 4.3.0,
stripped

$ ls -og rootfs/lib/libc-2.22.so
-rwxr-xr-x 1 1218200 Mar 22 19:57 rootfs/lib/libc-2.22.so
```

In this case, we saved 324,372 bytes, or about 20% of the size of the file before stripping.

 Be careful about stripping kernel modules. Some symbols are required by the module loader to relocate the module code, and so the module will fail to load if they are stripped out. Use this command to remove debug symbols while keeping those used for relocation: `strip --strip-unneeded <module name>`.

Device nodes

Most devices in Linux are represented by device nodes, in accordance with the Unix philosophy that *everything is a file* (except network interfaces, which are sockets). A device node may refer to a block device or a character device. Block devices are mass storage devices, such as SD cards or hard drives. A character device is pretty much anything else, once again with the exception of network interfaces. The conventional location for device nodes is the directory called /dev. For example, a serial port maybe represented by the device node called /dev/ttyS0.

Device nodes are created using the program named mknod (short for **make node**):

```
mknod <name> <type> <major> <minor>
```

The parameters to mknod are as follows:

- name is the name of the device node that you want to create.
- type is either c for character devices or b for a block.
- major and minor are a pair of numbers, which are used by the kernel to route file requests to the appropriate device driver code. There is a list of standard major and minor numbers in the kernel source in the file Documentation/devices.txt.

You will need to create device nodes for all the devices you want to access on your system. You can do so manually using the mknod command, as I will illustrate here; or you can create them automatically at runtime using one of the device managers that I will mention later.

In a really minimal root filesystem, you need just two nodes to boot with BusyBox: `console` and `null`. The console only needs to be accessible to `root`, the owner of the device node, so the access permissions are `600`. The null device should be readable and writable by everyone, so the mode is `666`. You can use the `-m` option for `mknod` to set the mode when creating the node. You need to be `root` to create device nodes, as shown here:

```
$ cd ~/rootfs
$ sudo mknod -m 666 dev/null c 1 3
$ sudo mknod -m 600 dev/console c 5 1

$ ls -l dev
total 0
crw------- 1 root root 5, 1 Mar 22 20:01 console
crw-rw-rw- 1 root root 1, 3 Mar 22 20:01 null
```

You can delete device nodes using the standard `rm` command: there is no `rmnod` command because, once created, they are just files.

The proc and sysfs filesystems

`proc` and `sysfs` are two pseudo filesystems that give a window onto the inner workings of the kernel. They both represent kernel data as files in a hierarchy of directories: when you read one of the files, the contents you see do not come from disk storage; it has been formatted on-the-fly by a function in the kernel. Some files are also writable, meaning that a kernel function is called with the new data you have written and, if it is of the correct format and you have sufficient permissions, it will modify the value stored in the kernel's memory. In other words, `proc` and `sysfs` provide another way to interact with device drivers and other kernel code. The `proc` and `sysfs` filesystems should be mounted on the directories called `/proc` and `/sys`:

```
# mount -t proc proc /proc
# mount -t sysfs sysfs /sys
```

Although they are very similar in concept, they perform different functions. `proc` has been part of Linux since the early days. Its original purpose was to expose information about processes to user space, hence the name. To this end, there is a directory for each process named `/proc/<PID>`, which contains information about its state. The process list command, `ps`, reads these files to generate its output. In addition, there are files that give information about other parts of the kernel, for example, `/proc/cpuinfo` tells you about the CPU, `/proc/interrupts` has information about interrupts, and so on.

Finally, in /proc/sys, there are files that display and control the state and behavior of kernel subsystems, especially scheduling, memory management, and networking. The manual page is the best reference for the files you will find in the proc directory, which you can see by typing man 5 proc.

On the other hand, the role of sysfs is to present the kernel *driver model* to user space. It exports a hierarchy of files relating to devices and device drivers and the way they are connected to each other. I will go into more detail on the Linux driver model when I describe the interaction with device drivers in Chapter 9, *Interfacing with Device Drivers*.

Mounting filesystems

The mount command allows us to attach one filesystem to a directory within another, forming a hierarchy of filesystems. The one at the top, which was mounted by the kernel when it booted, is called the **root filesystem**. The format of the mount command is as follows:

```
mount [-t vfstype] [-o options] device directory
```

You need to specify the type of the filesystem, vfstype, the block device node it resides on, and the directory you want to mount it to. There are various options you can give after-o; have a look at the manual page *mount(8)* for more information. As an example, if you want to mount an SD card containing an ext4 filesystem in the first partition onto the directory called /mnt, you would type the following code:

```
# mount -t ext4 /dev/mmcblk0p1 /mnt
```

Assuming the mount succeeds, you would be able to see the files stored on the SD card in the directory: /mnt. In some cases, you can leave out the filesystem type, and let the kernel probe the device to find out what is stored there.

Looking at the example of mounting the proc filesystem, there is something odd: there is no device node, such as /dev/proc, since it is a pseudo filesystem and not a real one. But the mount command requires a device parameter. Consequently, we have to give a string where device should go, but it does not matter much what that string is. These two commands achieve exactly the same result:

```
# mount -t proc procfs /proc
# mount -t proc nodevice /proc
```

The strings "procfs" and "nodevice" are ignored by the mount command. It is fairly common to use the filesystem type in the place of the device when mounting pseudo filesystems.

Kernel modules

If you have kernel modules, they need to be installed into the root filesystem, using the kernel make target `modules_install`, as we saw in the last chapter. This will copy them into the directory called `/lib/modules/<kernel version>` together with the configuration files needed by the `modprobe` command.

Be aware that you have just created a dependency between the kernel and the root filesystem. If you update one, you will have to update the other.

Transferring the root filesystem to the target

After having created a skeleton root filesystem in your staging directory, the next task is to transfer it to the target. In the sections that follow, I will describe three possibilities:

- **initramfs**: Also known as a ramdisk, this is a filesystem image that is loaded into RAM by the bootloader. Ramdisks are easy to create and have no dependencies on mass storage drivers. They can be used in fallback maintenance mode when the main root filesystem needs updating. They can even be used as the main root filesystem in small embedded devices, and they are commonly used as the early user space in mainstream Linux distributions. Remember that the contents of the root filesystem are volatile, and any changes you make in the root filesystem at runtime will be lost when the system next boots. You would need another storage type to store permanent data such as configuration parameters.
- **Disk image**: This is a copy of the root filesystem formatted and ready to be loaded onto a mass storage device on the target. For example, it could be an image in the `ext4` format ready to be copied onto an SD card, or it could be in the `jffs2` format ready to be loaded into flash memory via the bootloader. Creating a disk image is probably the most common option. There is more information about the different types of mass storage in `Chapter 7`, *Creating a Storage Strategy*.
- **Network filesystem**: The staging directory can be exported to the network via an NFS server and mounted by the target at boot time. This is often done during the development phase, in preference to repeated cycles of creating a disk image and reloading it onto the mass storage device, which is quite a slow process.

I will start with ramdisk, and use it to illustrate a few refinements to the root filesystem, such as adding usernames and a device manager to create device nodes automatically. Then, I will show you how to create a disk image and how to use NFS to mount the root filesystem over a network.

Creating a boot initramfs

An initial RAM filesystem, or `initramfs`, is a compressed `cpio` archive. `cpio` is an old Unix archive format, similar to TAR and ZIP but easier to decode and so requiring less code in the kernel. You need to configure your kernel with `CONFIG_BLK_DEV_INITRD` to support `initramfs`.

As it happens, there are three different ways to create a boot ramdisk: as a standalone `cpio` archive, as a `cpio` archive embedded in the kernel image, and as a device table which the kernel build system processes as part of the build. The first option gives the most flexibility, because we can mix and match kernels and ramdisks to our heart's content. However, it means that you have two files to deal with instead of one, and not all bootloaders have the facility to load a separate ramdisk. I will show you how to build one into the kernel later.

Standalone initramfs

The following sequence of instructions creates the archive, compresses it, and adds a U-Boot header ready for loading onto the target:

```
$ cd ~/rootfs
$ find . | cpio -H newc -ov --owner root:root > ../initramfs.cpio
$ cd ..
$ gzip initramfs.cpio
$ mkimage -A arm -O linux -T ramdisk -d initramfs.cpio.gz uRamdisk
```

Note that we run `cpio` with the option: `--owner root:root`. This is a quick fix for the file ownership problem mentioned earlier, making everything in the `cpio` archive have UID and GID of `0`.

The final size of the `uRamdisk` file is about 2.9 MB with no kernel modules. Add to that 4.4 MB for the kernel `zImage` file and 440 KB for U-Boot, and this gives a total of 7.7 MB of storage needed to boot this board. We are a little way off the 1.44 MB floppy that started it all off. If size was a real problem, you could use one of these options:

* Make the kernel smaller by leaving out drivers and functions you don't need
* Make BusyBox smaller by leaving out utilities you don't need
* Use `musl libc` or `uClibc-ng` in place of `glibc`
* Compile BusyBox statically

Booting the initramfs

The simplest thing we can do is to run a shell on the console so that we can interact with the target. We can do that by adding `rdinit=/bin/sh` to the kernel command line. The next two sections show how to do that for both QEMU and the BeagleBone Black.

Booting with QEMU

QEMU has the option called `-initrd` to load `initramfs` into memory. You should already have from Chapter 4, *Configuring and Building the Kernel*, a `zImage` compiled with the `arm-unknown-linux-gnueabi` toolchain and the device tree binary for the Versatile PB. From this chapter, you should have created `initramfs`, which includes BusyBox compiled with the same toolchain. Now, you can launch QEMU using the script in `MELP/chapter_05/run-qemu-initramfs.sh` or using this command:

```
$ QEMU_AUDIO_DRV=none \
qemu-system-arm -m 256M -nographic -M versatilepb -kernel zImage \
-append "console=ttyAMA0 rdinit=/bin/sh" -dtb versatile-pb.dtb \
-initrd initramfs.cpio.gz
```

You should get a root shell with the prompt / #.

Booting the BeagleBone Black

For the BeagleBone Black, we need the microSD card prepared in Chapter 4, *Configuring and Building the Kernel*, plus a root filesystem built using the `arm-cortex_a8-linux-gnueabihf` toolchain. Copy `uRamdisk` you created earlier in this section to the boot partition on the microSD card, and then use it to boot the BeagleBone Black to point that you get a U-Boot prompt. Then enter these commands:

```
fatload mmc 0:1 0x80200000 zImage
fatload mmc 0:1 0x80f00000 am335x-boneblack.dtb
fatload mmc 0:1 0x81000000 uRamdisk
setenv bootargs console=ttyO0,115200 rdinit=/bin/sh
bootz 0x80200000 0x81000000 0x80f00000
```

If all goes well, you will get a root shell with the prompt / # on the serial console.

Mounting proc

You will find that on both platforms the `ps` command doesn't work. This is because the `proc` filesystem has not been mounted yet. Try mounting it:

```
# mount -t proc proc /proc
```

Now, run `ps` again, and you will see the process listing.

A refinement to this setup would be to write a shell script that mounts `proc`, and anything else that needs to be done at boot-up. Then, you could run this script instead of `/bin/sh` at boot. The following snippet gives an idea of how it would work:

```
#!/bin/sh
/bin/mount -t proc proc /proc
# Other boot-time commands go here
/bin/sh
```

The last line, `/bin/sh`, launches a new shell that gives you an interactive root shell prompt. Using a shell as init in this way is very handy for quick hacks, for example, when you want to rescue a system with a broken init program. However, in most cases, you would use an init program, which we will cover later on in this chapter. But, before this, I want to look at two other ways to load `initramfs`.

Building an initramfs into the kernel image

So far, we have created a compressed `initramfs` as a separate file and used the bootloader to load it into memory. Some bootloaders do not have the ability to load an initramfs file in this way. To cope with these situations, Linux can be configured to incorporate `initramfs` into the kernel image. To do this, change the kernel configuration and set `CONFIG_INITRAMFS_SOURCE` to the full path of the `cpio` archive you created earlier. If you are using `menuconfig`, it is in **General setup | Initramfs source file(s)**. Note that it has to be the uncompressed `cpio` file ending in `.cpio`, not the `gzipped` version. Then, build the kernel.

Booting is the same as before, except that there is no ramdisk file. For QEMU, the command is like this:

```
$ QEMU_AUDIO_DRV=none \
qemu-system-arm -m 256M -nographic -M versatilepb -kernel zImage \
-append "console=ttyAMA0 rdinit=/bin/sh" -dtb versatile-pb.dtb
```

For the BeagleBone Black, enter these commands at the U-Boot prompt:

```
fatload mmc 0:1 0x80200000 zImage
fatload mmc 0:1 0x80f00000 am335x-boneblack.dtb
setenv bootargs console=ttyO0,115200 rdinit=/bin/sh
bootz 0x80200000 - 0x80f00000
```

Of course, you must remember to regenerate the cpio file each time you change the contents of the root filesystem, and then rebuild the kernel.

Building an initramfs using a device table

A device table is a text file that lists the files, directories, device nodes, and links that go into an archive or filesystem image. The overwhelming advantage is that it allows you to create entries in the archive file that are owned by the root user, or any other UID, without having root privileges yourself. You can even create device nodes without needing root privileges. All this is possible because the archive is just a data file. It is only when it is expanded by Linux at boot time that real files and directories get created, using the attributes you have specified.

The kernel has a feature that allows us to use a device table when creating an initramfs. You write the device table file, and then point CONFIG_INITRAMFS_SOURCE at it. Then, when you build the kernel, it creates the cpio archive from the instructions in the device table. At no point do you need root access.

Here is a device table for our simple rootfs, but missing most of the symbolic links to BusyBox to make it manageable:

```
dir /bin 775 0 0
dir /sys 775 0 0
dir /tmp 775 0 0
dir /dev 775 0 0
nod /dev/null 666 0 0 c 1 3
nod /dev/console 600 0 0 c 5 1
dir /home 775 0 0
dir /proc 775 0 0
dir /lib 775 0 0
slink /lib/libm.so.6 libm-2.22.so 777 0 0
slink /lib/libc.so.6 libc-2.22.so 777 0 0
slink /lib/ld-linux-armhf.so.3 ld-2.22.so 777 0 0
file /lib/libm-2.22.so /home/chris/rootfs/lib/libm-2.22.so 755 0 0
file /lib/libc-2.22.so /home/chris/rootfs/lib/libc-2.22.so 755 0 0
file /lib/ld-2.22.so /home/chris/rootfs/lib/ld-2.22.so 755 0 0
```

The syntax is fairly obvious:

- `dir <name> <mode> <uid> <gid>`
- `file <name> <location> <mode> <uid> <gid>`
- `nod <name> <mode> <uid> <gid> <dev_type> <maj> <min>`
- `slink <name> <target> <mode> <uid> <gid>`

The commands `dir`, `nod`, and `slink` create a file system object in the `initramfs` cpio archive with the name, mode, user ID and group ID given. The `file` command copies the file from the source location into the archive and sets the mode, the user ID, and the group ID.

The task of creating an `initramfs` device table from scratch is made easier by a script in the kernel source code in `scripts/gen_initramfs_list.sh`, which creates a device table from a given directory. For example, to create the `initramfs` device table for directory `rootfs`, and to change the ownership of all files owned by user ID `1000` and group ID `1000` to user and group ID `0`, you would use this command:

```
$ bash linux-stable/scripts/gen_initramfs_list.sh  -u 1000 -g 1000 \
rootfs > initramfs-device-table
```

Note that the script only works with a `bash` shell. If you have a system with a different default shell, as is the case with most Ubuntu configurations, you will find that the script fails. Hence, in the command given previously, I explicitly used `bash` to run the script.

The old initrd format

There is an older format for a Linux ramdisk, known as `initrd`. It was the only format available before Linux 2.6 and is still needed if you are using the mmu-less variant of Linux, uClinux. It is pretty obscure and I will not cover it here. There is more information in the kernel source in `Documentation/initrd.txt`.

The init program

Running a shell, or even a shell script, at boot time is fine for simple cases, but really you need something more flexible. Normally, Unix systems run a program called init that starts up and monitors other programs. Over the years, there have been many init programs, some of which I will describe in `Chapter 9`, *Interfacing with Device Drivers*. For now, I will briefly introduce the init from BusyBox.

The init program begins by reading the configuration file, /etc/inittab. Here is a simple example, which is adequate for our needs:

```
::sysinit:/etc/init.d/rcS
::askfirst:-/bin/ash
```

The first line runs a shell script, rcS, when init is started. The second line prints the message Please press Enter to activate this console to the console and starts a shell when you press *Enter*. The leading – before /bin/ash means that it will become a login shell, which sources /etc/profile and $HOME/.profile before giving the shell prompt. One of the advantages of launching the shell like this is that job control is *enabled*. The most immediate effect is that you can use *Ctrl + C* to terminate the current program. Maybe you didn't notice it before but, wait until you run the ping program and find you can't stop it!

BusyBox init provides a default inittab if none is present in the root filesystem. It is a little more extensive than the preceding one.

The script called /etc/init.d/rcS is the place to put initialization commands that need to be performed at boot, for example, mounting the proc and sysfs filesystems:

```
#!/bin/sh
mount -t proc proc /proc
mount -t sysfs sysfs /sys
```

Make sure that you make rcS executable like this:

```
$ cd ~/rootfs
$ chmod +x etc/init.d/rcS
```

You can try it out on QEMU by changing the –append parameter like this:

```
-append "console=ttyAMA0 rdinit=/sbin/init"
```

For the BeagleBone Black, you need to set the bootargs variable in U-Boot as shown here:

```
setenv bootargs console=ttyO0,115200 rdinit=/sbin/init
```

Starting a daemon process

Typically, you would want to run certain background processes at startup. Let's take the log daemon, syslogd, as an example. The purpose of syslogd is to accumulate log messages from other programs, mostly other daemons. Naturally, BusyBox has an applet for that!

Starting the daemon is as simple as adding a line like this to `etc/inittab`:

```
::respawn:/sbin/syslogd -n
```

`respawn` means that if the program terminates, it will be automatically restarted; `-n` means that it should run as a foreground process. The log is written to `/var/log/messages`.

 You may also want to start `klogd` in the same way: `klogd` sends kernel log messages to `syslogd` so that they can be logged to permanent storage.

Configuring user accounts

As I have hinted already, it is not good practice to run all programs as root, since if one is compromised by an outside attack, then the whole system is at risk. It is preferable to create unprivileged user accounts and use them where full root is not necessary.

User names are configured in `/etc/passwd`. There is one line per user, with seven fields of information separated by colons, which are in order:

- The login name
- A hash code used to verify the password, or more usually an x to indicate that the password is stored in `/etc/shadow`
- The user ID
- The group ID
- A comment field, often left blank
- The user's `home` directory
- (Optional) the shell this user will use

Here is a simple example in which we have user `root` with UID 0, and user `daemon` with UID 1:

```
root:x:0:0:root:/root:/bin/sh
daemon:x:1:1:daemon:/usr/sbin:/bin/false
```

Setting the shell for user `daemon` to `/bin/false` ensures that any attempt to log on with that name will fail.

Various programs have to read /etc/passwd in order to look up user names and UIDs, and so the file has to be world readable. This is a problem if the password hashes are stored in there as well, because a malicious program would be able to take a copy and discover the actual passwords using a variety of cracker programs. Therefore, to reduce the exposure of this sensitive information, the passwords are stored in /etc/shadow and x is placed in the password field to indicate that this is the case. The file called /etc/shadow only needs to be accessed by root, so as long as the root user is not compromised, the passwords are safe. The shadow password file consists of one entry per user, made up of nine fields. Here is an example that mirrors the password file shown in the preceding paragraph:

```
root::10933:0:99999:7:::
daemon:*:10933:0:99999:7:::
```

The first two fields are the username and the password hash. The remaining seven fields are related to password aging, which is not usually an issue on embedded devices. If you are curious about the full details, refer to the manual page for *shadow(5)*.

In the example, the password for root is empty, meaning that root can log on without giving a password. Having an empty password for root is useful during development but not for production. You can generate or change a password hash by running the passwd command on the target, which will write a new hash to /etc/shadow. If you want all subsequent root filesystems to have this same password, you could copy this file back to the staging directory.

Group names are stored in a similar way in /etc/group. There is one line per group consisting of four fields separated by colons. The fields are here:

- The name of the group
- The group password, usually an x character, indicating that there is no group password
- The GID or group ID
- An optional list of users who belong to this group, separated by commas

Here is an example:

```
root:x:0:
daemon:x:1:
```

Adding user accounts to the root filesystem

Firstly, you have to add to your staging directory the files `etc/passwd`, `etc/shadow`, and `etc/group`, as shown in the preceding section. Make sure that the permissions of shadow are `0600`. Next, you need to initiate the login procedure by starting a program called `getty`. There is a version of `getty` in BusyBox. You launch it from `inittab` using the keyword **respawn**, which restarts `getty` when a login shell is terminated, so `inittab` should read like this:

```
::sysinit:/etc/init.d/rcS
::respawn:/sbin/getty 115200 console
```

Then, rebuild the ramdisk and try it out using QEMU or the BeagleBone Black as before.

A better way of managing device nodes

Creating device nodes statically with `mknod` is quite hard work and inflexible. There are other ways to create device nodes automatically on demand:

- `devtmpfs`: This is a pseudo filesystem that you mount over `/dev` at boot time. The kernel populates it with device nodes for all the devices that the kernel currently knows about, and it creates nodes for new devices as they are detected at runtime. The nodes are owned by `root` and have default permissions of `0600`. Some well-known device nodes, such as `/dev/null` and `/dev/random`, override the default to `0666`. To see exactly how this is done, take a look at the Linux source file: `drivers/char/mem.c` and see how `struct memdev` is initialized.

- `mdev`: This is a BusyBox applet that is used to populate a directory with device nodes and to create new nodes as needed. There is a configuration file, `/etc/mdev.conf`, which contains rules for ownership and the mode of the nodes.

- `udev`: This is the mainstream equivalent of mdev. You will find it on desktop Linux and in some embedded devices. It is very flexible and a good choice for higher end embedded devices. It is now part of `systemd`.

 Although both `mdev` and `udev` create the device nodes themselves, it is more usual to let `devtmpfs` do the job and use `mdev`/`udev` as a layer on top to implement the policy for setting ownership and permissions.

An example using devtmpfs

Support for the `devtmpfs` filesystem is controlled by kernel configuration variable: `CONFIG_DEVTMPFS`. It is not enabled in the default configuration of the ARM Versatile PB, so if you want to try out the following using this target, you will have to go back and enable this option. Trying out `devtmpfs` is as simple as entering this command:

```
# mount -t devtmpfs devtmpfs /dev
```

You will notice that afterward, there are many more device nodes in `/dev`. For a permanent fix, add this to `/etc/init.d/rcS`:

```
#!/bin/sh
mount -t proc proc /proc
mount -t sysfs sysfs /sys
mount -t devtmpfs devtmpfs /dev
```

If you enable `CONFIG_DEVTMPFS_MOUNT` in your kernel configuration, the kernel will automatically mount `devtmpfs` just after mounting the root filesystem. However, this option has no effect when booting `initramfs`, as we are doing here.

An example using mdev

While `mdev` is a bit more complex to set up, it does allow you to modify the permissions of device nodes as they are created. You begin by running `mdev` with the `-s` option, which causes it to scan the `/sys` directory looking for information about current devices. From this information, it populates the `/dev` directory with the corresponding nodes. If you want to keep track of new devices coming online and create nodes for them as well, you need to make `mdev` a hot plug client by writing to `/proc/sys/kernel/hotplug`. These additions to `/etc/init.d/rcS` will achieve all of this:

```
#!/bin/sh
mount -t proc proc /proc
mount -t sysfs sysfs /sys
mount -t devtmpfs devtmpfs /dev
echo /sbin/mdev > /proc/sys/kernel/hotplug
mdev -s
```

The default mode is `660` and the ownership is `root:root`. You can change this by adding rules in `/etc/mdev.conf`. For example, to give the `null`, `random`, and `urandom` devices their correct modes, you would add this to `/etc/mdev.conf`:

```
null root:root 666
random root:root 444
urandom root:root 444
```

The format is documented in the BusyBox source code in `docs/mdev.txt`, and there are more examples in the directory named `examples`.

Are static device nodes so bad after all?

Statically created device nodes do have one advantage over running a device manager: they don't take any time during boot to create. If minimizing boot time is a priority, using statically-created device nodes will save a measurable amount of time.

Configuring the network

Next, let's look at some basic network configurations so that we can communicate with the outside world. I am assuming that there is an Ethernet interface, `eth0`, and that we only need a simple IPv4 configuration.

These examples use the network utilities that are part of BusyBox, and they are sufficient for a simple use case, using the old-but-reliable `ifup` and `ifdown` programs. You can read the manual pages for both to get the details. The main network configuration is stored in `/etc/network/interfaces`. You will need to create these directories in the staging directory:

```
etc/network
etc/network/if-pre-up.d
etc/network/if-up.d
var/run
```

For a static IP address, `/etc/network/interfaces` would look like this:

```
auto lo
iface lo inet loopback

auto eth0
iface eth0 inet static
    address 192.168.1.101
```

```
netmask 255.255.255.0
network 192.168.1.0
```

For a dynamic IP address allocated using DHCP, `/etc/network/interfaces` would look like this:

```
auto lo
iface lo inet loopback

auto eth0
iface eth0 inet dhcp
```

You will also have to configure a DHCP client program. BusyBox has one named `udchpcd`. It needs a shell script that should go in `/usr/share/udhcpc/default.script`. There is a suitable default in the BusyBox source code in the directory `examples/udhcp/simple.script`.

Network components for glibc

`glibc` uses a mechanism known as the **name service switch (NSS)** to control the way that names are resolved to numbers for networking and users. Usernames, for example, maybe resolved to UIDs via the file `/etc/passwd`, and network services such as HTTP can be resolved to the service port number via `/etc/services`. All this is configured by `/etc/nsswitch.conf`; see the manual page, *nss(5)*, for full details. Here is a simple example that will suffice for most embedded Linux implementations:

```
passwd:     files
group:      files
shadow:     files
hosts:      files dns
networks:   files
protocols:  files
services:   files
```

Everything is resolved by the correspondingly named file in `/etc`, except for the host names, which may additionally be resolved by a DNS lookup.

To make this work, you need to populate `/etc` with those files. Networks, protocols, and services are the same across all Linux systems, so they can be copied from `/etc` in your development PC. `/etc/hosts` should, at least, contain the loopback address:

```
127.0.0.1 localhost
```

The other files, `passwd`, `group`, and `shadow`, have been described earlier in the section *Configuring user accounts*.

The last piece of the jigsaw is the libraries that perform the name resolution. They are plugins that are loaded as needed based on the contents of `nsswitch.conf`, meaning that they do not show up as dependencies if you use `readelf` or `ldd`. You will simply have to copy them from the toolchain's `sysroot`:

```
$ cd ~/rootfs
$ cp -a $SYSROOT/lib/libnss* lib
$ cp -a $SYSROOT/lib/libresolv* lib
```

Creating filesystem images with device tables

We saw earlier in the section *Creating a boot initramfs* that the kernel has an option to create `initramfs` using a device table. Device tables are really useful because they allow a non-root user to create device nodes and to allocate arbitrary UID and GID values to any file or directory. The same concept has been applied to tools that create other filesystem image formats, as shown in this table:

Filesystem format	Tool
jffs2	mkfs.jffs2
ubifs	mkfs.ubifs
ext2	genext2fs

We will look at `jffs2` and `ubifs` in `Chapter 7`, *Creating a Storage Strategy*, when we look at filesystems for flash memory. The third, `ext2`, is a format commonly used for managed flash memory, including SD cards. The example that follows uses `ext2` to create a disk image that can be copied to an SD card.

They each take a device table file with the format <name> <type> <mode> <uid> <gid> <major> <minor> <start> <inc> <count>, where the meanings of the fields is as follows:

- name:
- type: One of the following:
    - f: A regular file
    - d: A directory
    - c: A character special device file
    - b: A block special device file
    - p: A FIFO (named pipe)
- uid The UID of the file
- gid: The GID of the file
- major and minor: The device numbers (device nodes only)
- start, inc, and count: Allow you to create a group of device nodes starting from the minor number in start (device nodes only)

You do not have to specify every file, as you do with the kernel initramfs table. You just have to point at a directory—the staging directory—and list the changes and exceptions you need to make in the final filesystem image.

A simple example which populates static device nodes for us is as follows:

```
/dev d 755 0 0 - - - - -
/dev/null c 666 0 0 1 3 0 0 -
/dev/console c 600 0 0 5 1 0 0 -
/dev/ttyO0 c 600 0 0 252 0 0 0 -
```

Then, you can use genext2fs to generate a filesystem image of 4 MB (that is 4,096 blocks of the default size, 1,024 bytes):

```
$ genext2fs -b 4096 -d rootfs -D device-table.txt -U rootfs.ext2
```

Now, you can copy the resulting image, rootfs.ext2, to an SD card or similar, which we will do next.

Booting the BeagleBone Black

The script called `MELP/format-sdcard.sh` creates two partitions on the micro SD card: one for the boot files and one for the root filesystem. Assuming that you have created the root filesystem image as shown in the previous section, you can use the `dd` command to write it to the second partition. As always, when copying files directly to storage devices like this, make absolutely sure that you know which is the micro SD card. In this case, I am using a built-in card reader, which is the device called `/dev/mmcblk0`, so the command is as follows:

```
$ sudo dd if=rootfs.ext2 of=/dev/mmcblk0p2
```

Then, slot the micro SD card into the BeagleBone Black, and set the kernel command line to `root=/dev/mmcblk0p2`. The complete sequence of U-Boot commands is as follows:

```
fatload mmc 0:1 0x80200000 zImage
fatload mmc 0:1 0x80f00000 am335x-boneblack.dtb
setenv bootargs console=ttyO0,115200 root=/dev/mmcblk0p2
bootz 0x80200000 - 0x80f00000
```

This is an example of mounting a filesystem from a normal block device, such as an SD card. The same principles apply to other filesystem types and we will look at them in more detail in `Chapter 7`, *Creating a Storage Strategy*.

Mounting the root filesystem using NFS

If your device has a network interface, it is often useful to mount the root filesystem over the network during development. It gives you access to the almost unlimited storage on your host machine, so you can add in debug tools and executables with large symbol tables. As an added bonus, updates made to the root filesystem on the development machine are made available on the target immediately. You can also access all the target's log files from the host.

To begin with, you need to install and configure an NFS server on your host. On Ubuntu, the package to install is named `nfs-kernel-server`:

```
$ sudo apt-get install nfs-kernel-server
```

The NFS server needs to be told which directories are being exported to the network, which is controlled by /etc/exports. There is one line for each export. The format is described in the manual page *exports(5)*. As an example, to export the root filesystem on my host, I have this:

```
/home/chris/rootfs *(rw,sync,no_subtree_check,no_root_squash)
```

* exports the directory to any address on my local network. If you wish, you can give a single IP address or a range at this point. There follows a list of options enclosed in parentheses. There must not be any spaces between * and the opening parenthesis. The options are here:

- rw: This exports the directory as read-write.
- sync: This option selects the synchronous version of the NFS protocol, which is more robust but a little slower than the async option.
- no_subtree_check: This option disables subtree checking, which has mild security implications, but can improve reliability in some circumstances.
- no_root_squash: This option allows requests from user ID 0 to be processed without *squashing* to a different user ID. It is necessary to allow the target to access correctly the files owned by root.

Having made changes to /etc/exports, restart the NFS server to pick them up.

Now, you need to set up the target to mount the root filesystem over NFS. For this to work, your kernel has to be configured with CONFIG_ROOT_NFS. Then, you can configure Linux to do the mount at boot time by adding the following to the kernel command line:

```
root=/dev/nfs rw nfsroot=<host-ip>:<root-dir> ip=<target-ip>
```

The options are as follows:

- rw: This mounts the root filesystem read-write.
- nfsroot: This specifies the IP address of the host, followed by the path to the exported root filesystem.
- ip: This is the IP address to be assigned to the target. Usually, network addresses are assigned at runtime, as we have seen in the section *Configuring the network*. However, in this case, the interface has to be configured before the root filesystem is mounted and init has been started. Hence it is configured on the kernel command line.

There is more information about NFS root mounts in the kernel source in
`Documentation/filesystems/nfs/nfsroot.txt`.

Testing with QEMU

The following script creates a virtual network between the network device called `tap0` on
the host and `eth0` on the target using a pair of static IPv4 addresses, and then launches
QEMU with the parameters to use `tap0` as the emulated interface.

You will need to change the path to the root filesystem to be the full path to your staging
directory and maybe the IP addresses if they conflict with your network configuration:

```
#!/bin/bash

KERNEL=zImage
DTB=versatile-pb.dtb
ROOTDIR=/home/chris/rootfs
HOST_IP=192.168.1.1
TARGET_IP=192.168.1.101
NET_NUMBER=192.168.1.0
NET_MASK=255.255.255.0

sudo tunctl -u $(whoami) -t tap0
sudo ifconfig tap0 ${HOST_IP}
sudo route add -net ${NET_NUMBER} netmask ${NET_MASK} dev tap0
sudo sh -c "echo 1 > /proc/sys/net/ipv4/ip_forward"

QEMU_AUDIO_DRV=none
qemu-system-arm -m 256M -nographic -M versatilepb -kernel ${KERNEL} -append
"console=ttyAMA0,115200 root=/dev/nfs rw nfsroot=${HOST_IP}:${ROOTDIR}
ip=${TARGET_IP}" -dtb ${DTB} -net nic -net tap,ifname=tap0,script=no
```

 The script is available in `MELP/chapter_05/run-qemu-nfsroot.sh`.

It should boot up as before, now using the staging directory directly via the NFS export.
Any files that you create in that directory will be immediately visible to the target device,
and any files created in the device will be visible to the development PC.

Testing with the BeagleBone Black

In a similar way, you can enter these commands at the U-Boot prompt of the BeagleBone Black:

```
setenv serverip 192.168.1.1
setenv ipaddr 192.168.1.101
setenv npath [path to staging directory]
setenv bootargs console=ttyO0,115200 root=/dev/nfs rw
nfsroot=${serverip}:${npath} ip=${ipaddr}
fatload mmc 0:1 0x80200000 zImage
fatload mmc 0:1 0x80f00000 am335x-boneblack.dtb
bootz 0x80200000 - 0x80f00000
```

There is a U-Boot environment file in `chapter_05/uEnv.txt`, which contains all these commands. Just copy it to the boot partition of the microSD card and U-Boot will do the rest.

Problems with file permissions

The files that you copied into the staging directory will be owned by the UID of the user you are logged on as, typically `1000`. However, the target has no knowledge of this user. What is more, any files created by the target will be owned by users configured by the target, often the `root` user. The whole thing is a mess. Unfortunately, there is no simple way out. The best solution is to make a copy of the staging directory and change ownership to UID and GID to 0, using the command `sudo chown -R 0:0 *`. Then, export this directory as the NFS mount. It removes the convenience of having just one copy of the root filesystem shared between development and target systems, but, at least, the file ownership will be correct.

Using TFTP to load the kernel

Now that we know how to mount the root filesystem over a network using NFS, you may be wondering if there is a way to load the kernel, device tree, and `initramfs` over the network as well. If we could do this, the only component that needs to be written to storage on the target is the bootloader. Everything else could be loaded from the host machine. It would save time since you would not need to keep reflashing the target, and you could even get work done while the flash storage drivers are still being developed (it happens).

The **Trivial File Transfer Protocol (TFTP)** is the answer to the problem. TFTP is a very simple file transfer protocol, designed to be easy to implement in bootloaders such as U-Boot.

But, firstly, you need to install a TFTP daemon on your development machine. On Ubuntu, you could install the `tftpd-hpa` package, which, by default, grants read-only access to files in the directory `/var/lib/tftpboot`. With `tftpd-hpa` installed and running, copy the files that you want to copy to the target into `/var/lib/tftpboot`, which, for the BeagleBone Black, would be `zImage` and `am335x-boneblack.dtb`. Then enter these commands at the U-Boot Command Prompt:

```
setenv serverip 192.168.1.1
setenv ipaddr 192.168.1.101
tftpboot 0x80200000 zImage
tftpboot 0x80f00000 am335x-boneblack.dtb
setenv npath [path to staging]
setenv bootargs console=ttyO0,115200 root=/dev/nfs rw
nfsroot=${serverip}:${npath} ip=${ipaddr}
bootz 0x80200000 - 0x80f00000
```

You may find that the `tftpboot` command hangs, endlessly printing out the letter `T`, which means that the TFTP requests are timing out. There are a number of reasons why this happens, the most common ones being:

- There is an incorrect IP address for `serverip`.
- The TFTP daemon is not running on the server.
- There is a firewall on the server which is blocking the TFTP protocol. Most firewalls do indeed block the TFTP port, `69`, by default.

Once you have resolved the problem, U-Boot can load the files from the host machine and boot in the usual way. You can automate the process by putting the commands into a `uEnv.txt` file.

Additional reading

Filesystem Hierarchy Standard, Version 3.0, `http://refspecs.linuxfoundation.org/fhs.shtml`

ramfs, rootfs and initramfs , Rob Landley, October 17, 2005, which is part of the Linux source in `Documentation/filesystems/ramfs-rootfs-initramfs.txt`.

Summary

One of the strengths of Linux is that it can support a wide range of root filesystems, and so it can be tailored to suit a wide range of needs. We have seen that it is possible to construct a simple root filesystem manually with a small number of components and that BusyBox is especially useful in this regard. By going through the process one step at a time, it has given us insight into some of the basic workings of Linux systems, including network configuration and user accounts. However, the task rapidly becomes unmanageable as devices get more complex. And, there is the ever-present worry that there may be a security hole in the implementation, which we have not noticed.

In the next chapter, I will show you how using an embedded build system can make the process of creating an embedded Linux system much easier and more reliable. I will start by looking at Buildroot, and then go onto look at the more complex, but powerful, Yocto Project.

6
Selecting a Build System

In the preceding chapters, we covered the four elements of embedded Linux and showed you step-by-step how to build a toolchain, a bootloader, a kernel, a root filesystem, and then combined them into a basic embedded Linux system. And there are a lot of steps! Now, it is time to look at ways to simplify the process by automating it as much as possible. I will look at how embedded build systems can help and look at two of them in particular: Buildroot and the Yocto Project. Both are complex and flexible tools, which would require an entire book to describe fully how they work. In this chapter, I only want to show you the general ideas behind build systems. I will show you how to build a simple device image to get an overall feel of the system, and then how to make some useful changes using the Nova board example from the previous chapters.

In this chapter, we will cover the following topics:

- Build systems
- Package formats and package managers
- Buildroot
- The Yocto Project

Build systems

I have described the process of creating a system manually, as described in Chapter 5, *Building a Root Filesystem*, as the **Roll Your Own (RYO)** process. It has the advantage that you are in complete control of the software, and you can tailor it to do anything you like. If you want it to do something truly odd but innovative, or if you want to reduce the memory footprint to the smallest size possible, RYO is the way to go. But, in the vast majority of situations, building manually is a waste of time and produces inferior, unmaintainable systems.

The idea of a build system is to automate all the steps I have described up to this point. A build system should be able to build, from upstream source code, some or all of the following:

- A toolchain
- A bootloader
- A kernel
- A root filesystem

Building from upstream source code is important for a number of reasons. It means that you have peace of mind that you can rebuild at any time, without external dependencies. It also means that you have the source code for debugging and also that you can meet your license requirements to distribute the code to users where necessary.

Therefore, to do its job, a build system has to be able to do the following:

1. Download the source code from upstream, either directly from the source code control system or as an archive, and cache it locally.
2. Apply patches to enable cross compilation, fix architecture-dependent bugs, apply local configuration policies, and so on.
3. Build the various components.
4. Create a staging area and assemble a root filesystem.
5. Create image files in various formats ready to be loaded onto the target.

Other things that are useful are as follows:

1. Add your own packages containing, for example, applications or kernel changes.
2. Select various root filesystem profiles: large or small, with and without graphics or other features.
3. Create a standalone SDK that you can distribute to other developers so that they don't have to install the complete build system.
4. Track which open source licenses are used by the various packages you have selected.
5. Have a user-friendly user interface.

In all cases, they encapsulate the components of a system into packages, some for the host and some for the target. Each package is defined by a set of rules to get the source, build it, and install the results in the correct location. There are dependencies between the packages and a build mechanism to resolve the dependencies and build the set of packages required.

Open source build systems have matured considerably over the last few years. There are many around, including the following:

- **Buildroot**: This is an easy-to-use system using GNU make and Kconfig (`https://buildroot.org/`)
- **EmbToolkit:** This is a simple system for generating root filesystems; the only one so far that supports LLVM/Clang out of the box (`https://www.embtoolkit.org`)
- **OpenEmbedded:** This is a powerful system, which is also a core component of the Yocto Project and others (`http://openembedded.org`)
- **OpenWrt:** This is a build tool oriented towards building firmware for wireless routers (`https://openwrt.org`)
- **PTXdist:** This is an open source build system sponsored by Pengutronix (`http://www.pengutronix.de/software/ptxdist/index_en.html`)
- **The Yocto Project:** This extends the OpenEmbedded core with metadata, tools and documentation: probably the most popular system (`http://www.yoctoproject.org`)

I will concentrate on two of these: Buildroot and the Yocto Project. They approach the problem in different ways and with different objectives.

Buildroot has the primary aim of building root filesystem images, hence the name, although it can build bootloader and kernel images as well. It is easy to install and configure and generates target images quickly.

The Yocto Project, on the other hand, is more general in the way it defines the target system, and so it can build fairly complex embedded devices. Every component is generated as a binary package, by default, using the RPM format, and then the packages are combined together to make the filesystem image. Furthermore, you can install a package manager in the filesystem image, which allows you to update packages at runtime. In other words, when you build with the Yocto Project, you are, in effect, creating your own custom Linux distribution.

Package formats and package managers

Mainstream Linux distributions are, in most cases, constructed from collections of binary (precompiled) packages in either RPM or DEB format. RPM stands for the Red Hat package manager and is used in Red Hat, Suse, Fedora, and other distributions based on them. Debian and Debian-derived distributions, including Ubuntu and Mint, use the Debian package manager format, DEB. In addition, there is a light-weight format specific to embedded devices known as the **Itsy package format** or **IPK**, which is based on DEB.

The ability to include a package manager on the device is one of the big differentiators between build systems. Once you have a package manager on the target device, you have an easy path to deploy new packages to it and to update the existing ones. I will talk about the implications of this in Chapter 8, *Updating Software in the Field*.

Buildroot

The Buildroot project website is at http://buildroot.org.

The current versions of Buildroot are capable of building a toolchain, a bootloader, a kernel, and a root filesystem. It uses GNU make as the principal build tool. There is good online documentation at http://buildroot.org/docs.html, including *The Buildroot user manual* at https://buildroot.org/downloads/manual/manual.html.

Background

Buildroot was one of the first build systems. It began as part of the uClinux and uClibc projects as a way of generating a small root filesystem for testing. It became a separate project in late 2001 and continued to evolve through to 2006, after which it went into a rather dormant phase. However, since 2009, when Peter Korsgaard took over stewardship, it has been developing rapidly, adding support for glibc based toolchains and a greatly increased number of packages and target boards.

As a matter of interest, Buildroot is also the ancestor of another popular build system, **OpenWrt** (http://wiki.openwrt.org), which forked from Buildroot around 2004. The primary focus of OpenWrt is to produce software for wireless routers, and so the package mix is oriented toward the networking infrastructure. It also has a runtime package manager using the IPK format so that a device can be updated or upgraded without a complete reflash of the image. However, Buildroot and OpenWrt have diverged to such an extent that they are now almost completely different build systems. Packages built with one are not compatible with the other.

Stable releases and long-term support

The Buildroot developers produce stable releases four times a year, in February, May, August, and November. They are marked by git tags of the form: <year>.02, <year>.05, <year>.08, and <year>.11. From time to time, a release is marked for **Long Term Support (LTS)**, which means that there will be point releases to fix security and other important bugs for 12 months after the initial release. The 2017.02 release is the first to receive the LTS label.

Installing

As usual, you can install Buildroot either by cloning the repository or downloading an archive. Here is an example of obtaining version 2017.02.1, which was the latest stable version at the time of writing:

```
$ git clone git://git.buildroot.net/buildroot -b 2017.02.1
$ cd buildroot
```

The equivalent TAR archive is available at http://buildroot.org/downloads.

Next, you should read the section titled **System requirement** from The Buildroot user manual available at http://buildroot.org/downloads/manual/manual.html, and make sure that you have installed all the packages listed there.

Configuring

Buildroot uses the kernel Kconfig/Kbuild mechanism, which I described in the section *Understanding kernel configuration* in Chapter 4, *Configuring and Building the Kernel*. You can configure Buildroot from scratch directly using make menuconfig (xconfig or gconfig), or you can choose one of the 100+ configurations for various development boards and the QEMU emulator, which you can find stored in the directory, configs/. Typing make list-defconfigs lists all the default configurations.

Let's begin by building a default configuration that you can run on the ARM QEMU emulator:

```
$ cd buildroot
$ make qemu_arm_versatile_defconfig
$ make
```

You do not tell `make` how many parallel jobs to run with a `-j` option: Buildroot will make optimum use of your CPUs all by itself. If you want to limit the number of jobs, you can run `make menuconfig` and look under the **Build** options.

The build will take half an hour to an hour or more depending on the capabilities of your host system and the speed of your link to the internet. It will download approximately 220 MiB of code and will consume about 3.5 GiB of disk space. When it is complete, you will find that two new directories have been created:

- `dl/`: This contains archives of the upstream projects that Buildroot has built
- `output/`: This contains all the intermediate and final compiled resources

You will see the following in `output/`:

- `build/`: Here, you will find the build directory for each component.
- `host/`: This contains various tools required by Buildroot that run on the host, including the executables of the toolchain (in `output/host/usr/bin`).
- `images/`: This is the most important of all since it contains the results of the build. Depending on what you selected when configuring, you will find a bootloader, a kernel, and one or more root filesystem images.
- `staging/`: This is a symbolic link to the `sysroot` of the toolchain. The name of the link is a little confusing, because it does not point to a staging area as I defined it in Chapter 5, *Building a Root Filesystem*.
- `target/`: This is the staging area for the `root` directory. Note that you cannot use it as a root filesystem as it stands because the file ownership and the permissions are not set correctly. Buildroot uses a device table, as described in the previous chapter, to set ownership and permissions when the filesystem image is created in the `image/` directory.

Running

Some of the sample configurations have a corresponding entry in the directory `board/`, which contains custom configuration files and information about installing the results on the target. In the case of the system you have just built, the relevant file is `board/qemu/arm-versatile/readme.txt`, which tells you how to start QEMU with this target. Assuming that you have already installed `qemu-system-arm` as described in Chapter 1, *Starting Out*, you can run it using this command:

```
$ qemu-system-arm -M versatilepb -m 256 \
-kernel output/images/zImage \
-dtb output/images/versatile-pb.dtb \
-drive file=output/images/rootfs.ext2,if=scsi,format=raw \
-append "root=/dev/sda console=ttyAMA0,115200" \
-serial stdio -net nic,model=rtl8139 -net user
```

There is a script named MELP/chapter_06/run-qemu-buildroot.sh in the book code archive, which includes that command. When QEMU boots up, you should see the kernel boot messages appear in the same terminal window where you started QEMU, followed by a login prompt:

```
Booting Linux on physical CPU 0x0
Linux version 4.9.6 (chris@chris-xps) (gcc version 5.4.0
(Buildroot 2017.02.1) ) #1 Tue Apr 18 10:30:03 BST 2017
CPU: ARM926EJ-S [41069265] revision 5 (ARMv5TEJ), cr=00093177
[...]
VFS: Mounted root (ext2 filesystem) readonly on device 8:0.
devtmpfs: mounted
Freeing unused kernel memory: 132K (c042f000 - c0450000)
This architecture does not have kernel memory protection.
EXT4-fs (sda): warning: mounting unchecked fs, running e2fsck is
recommended
EXT4-fs (sda): re-mounted. Opts:
block_validity,barrier,user_xattr,errors=remount-ro
Starting logging: OK
Initializing random number generator... done.
Starting network: 8139cp 0000:00:0c.0 eth0: link up, 100Mbps, full-duplex,
lpa 0x05E1
udhcpc: started, v1.26.2
udhcpc: sending discover
udhcpc: sending select for 10.0.2.15
udhcpc: lease of 10.0.2.15 obtained, lease time 86400
deleting routers
adding dns 10.0.2.3
OK

Welcome to Buildroot
buildroot login:
```

Log in as root, no password.

You will see that QEMU launches a black window in addition to the one with the kernel boot messages. It is there to display the graphics frame buffer of the target. In this case, the target never writes to the framebuffer, which is why it appears black. To close QEMU, either type Ctrl-Alt-2 to get to the QEMU console and then type quit, or just close the framebuffer window.

Creating a custom BSP

Next, let's use Buildroot to create a BSP for our Nova board using the same versions of U-Boot and Linux from earlier chapters. You can see the changes I made to Buildroot during this section in the book code archive in MELP/chapter_06/buildroot.
The recommended places to store your changes are here:

- board/<organization>/<device>: This contains any patches, binary blobs, extra build steps, configuration files for Linux, U-Boot, and other components
- configs/<device>_defconfig: This contains the default configuration for the board
- package/<organization>/<package_name>: This is the place to put any additional packages for this board

Let's begin by creating a directory to store changes for the Nova board:

```
$ mkdir -p board/melp/nova
```

Next, clean the artifacts from any previous build, which you should always do when changing configurations:

```
$ make clean
```

Now, select the configuration for the BeagleBone, which we are going to use as the basis of the Nova configuration.

```
$ make beaglebone_defconfig
```

U-Boot

In Chapter 3, *All About Bootloaders*, we created a custom bootloader for Nova, based on the 2017.01 version of U-Boot and created a patch file for it, which you will find in MELP/chapter_03/0001-BSP-for-Nova.patch. We can configure Buildroot to select the same version and apply our patch. Begin by copying the patch file into board/melp/nova, and then use make menuconfig to set the U-Boot version to 2017.01, the patch file to board/melp/nova/0001-BSP-for-Nova.patch, and the board name to Nova, as shown in this screenshot:

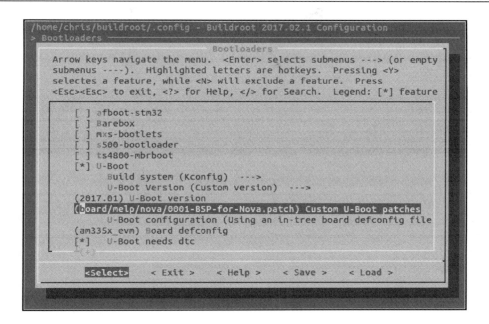

We also need a U-Boot script to load the Nova device tree and the kernel from the SD card. We can put the file into `board/melp/nova/uEnv.txt`. It should contain these commands:

```
bootpart=0:1
bootdir=

bootargs=console=ttyO0,115200n8 root=/dev/mmcblk0p2 rw rootfstype=ext4
rootwait

uenvcmd=fatload mmc 0:1 88000000 nova.dtb;fatload mmc 0:1 82000000 zImage;
bootz 82000000 - 88000000
```

Linux

In Chapter 4, *Configuring and Building the Kernel*, we based the kernel on Linux 4.9.13 and supplied a new device tree, which is in MELP/chapter_04/nova.dts. Copy the device tree to board/melp/nova, change the Buildroot kernel configuration to select Linux version 4.9.13, and the device tree source to board/melp/nova/nova.dts, as shown in the following screenshot:

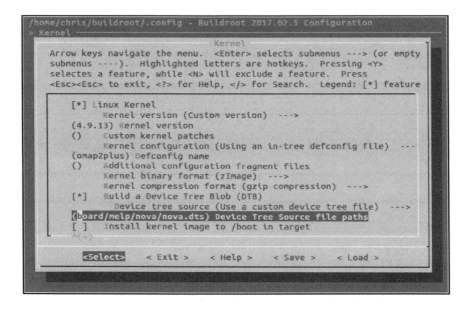

We will also have to change the kernel series to be used for kernel headers to match the kernel being built:

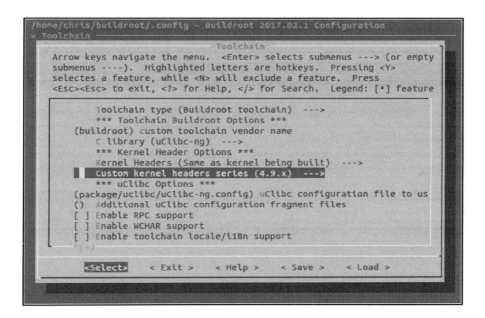

Build

In the last stage of the build, Buildroot uses a tool named `genimage` to create an image for the SD card that we can copy directory to the card. We need a configuration file to layout the image in the right way. We will name the file `board/melp/nova/genimage.cfg` and populate it as shown here:

```
image boot.vfat {
    vfat {
        files = {
            "MLO",
            "u-boot.img",
            "zImage",
            "uEnv.txt",
            "nova.dtb",
        }
    }
    size = 16M
```

```
}

image sdcard.img {
    hdimage {
    }

    partition u-boot {
        partition-type = 0xC
        bootable = "true"
        image = "boot.vfat"
    }

    partition rootfs {
        partition-type = 0x83
        image = "rootfs.ext4"
        size = 512M
    }
}
```

This will create a file named `sdcard.img`, which contains two partitions named `u-boot` and `rootfs`. The first contains the boot files listed in `boot.vfat`, and the second contains the root filesystem image named `rootfs.ext4`, which will be generated by Buildroot.

Finally, we need to create a `post image` script that will call `genimage`, and so create the SD card image. We will put it in `board/melp/nova/post-image.sh`:

```
#!/bin/sh
BOARD_DIR="$(dirname $0)"

cp ${BOARD_DIR}/uEnv.txt $BINARIES_DIR/uEnv.txt

GENIMAGE_CFG="${BOARD_DIR}/genimage.cfg"
GENIMAGE_TMP="${BUILD_DIR}/genimage.tmp"

rm -rf "${GENIMAGE_TMP}"

genimage \
 --rootpath "${TARGET_DIR}" \
 --tmppath "${GENIMAGE_TMP}" \
 --inputpath "${BINARIES_DIR}" \
 --outputpath "${BINARIES_DIR}" \
 --config "${GENIMAGE_CFG}"
```

This copies the `uEnv.txt` script into the `output/images` directory and runs `genimage` with our configuration file.

Now, we can run `menuconfig` again and to change the **System configuration** option, **Custom scripts to run before creating filesystem images**, to run our `post-image.sh` script, as shown in this screenshot:

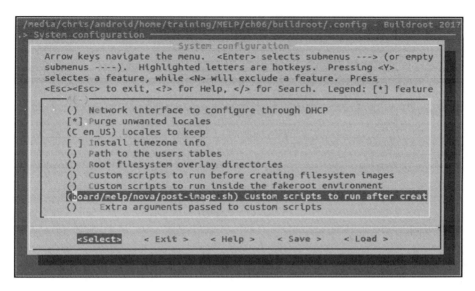

Finally, you can build Linux for the Nova board just by typing `make`. When it has finished, you will see these files in the directory, `output/images/`:

```
boot.vfat    rootfs.ext2    sdcard.img         uEnv.txt
MLO          rootfs.ext4    u-boot.img         zImage
nova.dtb     rootfs.tar     u-boot-spl.bin
```

To test it, put a microSD card in the card reader, unmount any partitions that are auto mounted, and then copy `sdcard.img` to the root of the SD card. There is no need to format it beforehand, as we did in the previous chapter, because `genimage` has created the exact disk layout required. In the following example, my SD card reader is `/dev/mmcblk0`:

```
$ sudo umount /dev/mmcblk0*
$ sudo dd if=output/images/sdcard.img of=/dev/mmcblk0 bs=1M
```

Put the SD card into the BeagleBone Black and power on while pressing the boot button to force it to load from the SD card. You should see that it boots up with our selected versions of U-Boot, Linux, and with the Nova device tree.

Having shown that our custom configuration for the Nova board works, it would be nice to keep a copy of the configuration so that you and others can use it again, which you can do with this command:

```
$ make savedefconfig BR2_DEFCONFIG=configs/nova_defconfig
```

Now, you have a Buildroot configuration for the Nova board. Subsequently, you can retrieve this configuration by typing the following command:

```
$ make nova_defconfig
```

Adding your own code

Suppose there is a program that you have developed and that you want to include it in the build. You have two options: firstly to build it separately using its own build system, and then roll the binary into the final build as an overlay. Secondly, you could create a Buildroot package that can be selected from the menu and built like any other.

Overlays

An overlay is simply a directory structure that is copied over the top of the Buildroot root filesystem at a late stage in the build process. It can contain executables, libraries, and anything else you may want to include. Note that any compiled code must be compatible with the libraries deployed at runtime, which, in turn, means that it must be compiled with the same toolchain that Buildroot uses. Using the Buildroot toolchain is quite easy. Just add it to PATH:

```
$ PATH=<path_to_buildroot>/output/host/usr/bin:$PATH
```

The prefix for the toolchain is <ARCH>-linux-. So, to compile a simple program, you would do something like this:

```
$ PATH=/home/chris/buildroot/output/host/usr/bin:$PATH
$ arm-linux-gcc helloworld.c -o helloworld
```

Once you have compiled your program with the correct toolchain, you just need to install the executables and other supporting files into a staging area, and mark it as an overlay for Buildroot. For the helloworld example, you might put it in the board/melp/nova directory:

```
$ mkdir -p board/melp/nova/overlay/usr/bin
$ cp helloworld board/melp/nova/overlay/usr/bin
```

Finally, you set BR2_ROOTFS_OVERLAY to the path to the overlay. It can be configured in menuconfig with the option, **System configuration | Root filesystem overlay directories**.

Adding a package

Buildroot packages are stored in the package directory, over 2,000 of them, each in its own subdirectory. A package consists of at least two files: Config.in, containing the snippet of Kconfig code required to make the package visible in the configuration menu, and a makefile named <package_name>.mk. Note that the package does not contain the code, just the instructions to get the code by downloading a tarball, doing git pull or whatever is necessary to obtain the upstream source.

The makefile is written in a format expected by Buildroot and contains directives that allow Buildroot to download, configure, compile, and install the program. Writing a new package makefile is a complex operation, which is covered in detail in the Buildroot user manual. Here is an example which shows you how to create a package for a simple program stored locally, such as our helloworld program.

Begin by creating the package/helloworld/ subdirectory with a configuration file, Config.in, which looks like this:

```
config BR2_PACKAGE_HELLOWORLD
    bool "helloworld"
    help
       A friendly program that prints Hello World! every 10s
```

The first line must be of the format, BR2_PACKAGE_<uppercase package name>. This is followed by a Boolean and the package name, as it will appear in the **configuration** menu, which will allow a user to select this package. The help section is optional (but hopefully useful).

Next, link the new package into the **Target Packages** menu by editing package/Config.in and sourcing the configuration file as mentioned in the preceding section. You could append this to an existing submenu but, in this case, it seems neater to create a new submenu, which only contains our package:

```
menu "My programs"
   source "package/helloworld/Config.in"
endmenu
```

Then, create a makefile, `package/helloworld/helloworld.mk`, to supply the data needed by Buildroot:

```
HELLOWORLD_VERSION = 1.0.0
HELLOWORLD_SITE = /home/chris/MELP/helloworld
HELLOWORLD_SITE_METHOD = local

define HELLOWORLD_BUILD_CMDS
    $(MAKE) CC="$(TARGET_CC)" LD="$(TARGET_LD)" -C $(@D) all
endef

define HELLOWORLD_INSTALL_TARGET_CMDS
    $(INSTALL) -D -m 0755 $(@D)/helloworld $(TARGET_DIR)/usr/bin/helloworld
endef

$(eval $(generic-package))
```

You can find my helloworld package in the book code archive in `MELP/chapter_06/buildroot/package/helloworld` and the source code for the program in `MELP/chapter_06/helloworld`. The location of the code is hard coded to a local pathname. In a more realistic case, you would get the code from a source code system or from a central server of some kind: there are details of how to do this in the Buildroot user manual and plenty of examples in other packages.

License compliance

Buildroot is based on an open source software as are the packages it compiles. At some point during the project, you should check the licenses, which you can do by running:

```
$ make legal-info
```

The information is gathered into `output/legal-info/`. There are summaries of the licenses used to compile the host tools in `host-manifest.csv` and, on the target, in `manifest.csv`. There is more information in the README file and in the Buildroot user manual.

The Yocto Project

The Yocto Project is a more complex beast than Buildroot. Not only can it build toolchains, bootloaders, kernels, and root filesystems as Buildroot can, but it can generate an entire Linux distribution for you with binary packages that can be installed at runtime. The Yocto Project is primarily a group of recipes, similar to Buildroot packages but written using a combination of Python and shell script, together with a task scheduler called **BitBake** that produces whatever you have configured, from the recipes.

There is plenty of online documentation at `https://www.yoctoproject.org/`.

Background

The structure of the Yocto Project makes more sense if you look at the background first. It's roots are in **OpenEmbedded**, `http://openembedded.org/`, which, in turn, grew out of a number of projects to port Linux to various hand-held computers, including the Sharp Zaurus and the Compaq iPaq. OpenEmbedded, which came to life in 2003 as the build system for those hand-held computers. Soon after, other developers began to use it as a general build asystem for devices running embedded Linux. It was developed, and continues to be developed, by an enthusiastic community of programmers.

The OpenEmbedded project is set out to create a set of binary packages using the compact IPK format, which could then be combined in various ways to create a target system and be installed on the target at runtime. It did this by creating recipes for each package and using BitBake as the task scheduler. It was, and is, very flexible. By supplying the right metadata, you can create an entire Linux distribution to your own specification. One that, which is fairly well-known is the **Ångström Distribution**, `http://www.angstrom-distribution.or g`, but there are many others as well.

At some time in 2005, Richard Purdie, then a developer at OpenedHand, created a fork of OpenEmbedded, which had a more conservative choice of packages and created releases that were stable over a period of time. He named it **Poky** after the Japanese snack (if you are worried about these things, Poky is pronounced to rhyme with hockey). Although Poky was a fork, OpenEmbedded and Poky continued to run alongside each other, sharing updates and keeping the architectures more or less in step. Intel brought out OpenedHand in 2008, and they transferred Poky Linux to the Linux Foundation in 2010 when they formed the Yocto Project.

Since 2010, the common components of OpenEmbedded and Poky have been combined into a separate project known as **OpenEmbedded Core** or just **OE-Core**.

Therefore, the Yocto Project collects together several components, the most important of which are the following:

- **OE-Core:** This is the core metadata, which is shared with OpenEmbedded
- **BitBake:** This is the task scheduler, which is shared with OpenEmbedded and other projects
- **Poky:** This is the reference distribution
- **Documentation:** This is the user's manuals and developer's guides for each component
- **Toaster:** This is a web-based interface to BitBake and its metadata
- **ADT Eclipse:** This is a plugin for Eclipse

The Yocto Project provides a stable base, which can be used as it is or can be extended using **meta layers**, which I will discuss later in this chapter. Many SoC vendors provide BSPs for their devices in this way. Meta layers can also be used to create extended or just different build systems. Some are open source, such as the Ångström Distribution, and others are commercial, such as MontaVista Carrier Grade Edition, Mentor Embedded Linux, and Wind River Linux. The Yocto Project has a branding and compatibility testing scheme to ensure that there is interoperability between components. You will see statements like **Yocto Project compatible** on various web pages.

Consequently, you should think of the Yocto Project as the foundation of a whole sector of embedded Linux, as well as being a complete build system in its own right.

You maybe wondering about the name, Yocto. yocto is the SI prefix for 10^{-24}, in the same way that micro is 10^{-6}. Why name the project Yocto? It was partly to indicate that it could build very small Linux systems (although, to be fair, so can other build systems), but also to steal a march on the Ångström Distribution, which is based on OpenEmbedded. An Ångström is 10^{-10}. That's huge, compared to a yocto!

Stable releases and supports

Usually, there is a release of the Yocto Project every six months: in April and October. They are principally known by the code name, but it is useful to know the version numbers of the Yocto Project and Poky as well. Here is a table of the six most recent releases at the time of writing:

Code name	Release date	Yocto version	Poky version
Morty	October 2016	2.2	16
Krogoth	April 2016	2.1	15
Jethro	October 2015	2.0	14
Fido	April 2015	1.8	13
Dizzy	October 2014	1.7	12
Daisy	April 2014	1.6	11

The stable releases are supported with security and critical bug fixes for the current release cycle and the next cycle. In other words, each version is supported for approximately 12 months after the release. As with Buildroot, if you want continued support, you can update to the next stable release, or you can backport changes to your version. You also have the option of commercial support for periods of several years with the Yocto Project from operating system vendors, such as Mentor Graphics, Wind River, and many others.

Installing the Yocto Project

To get a copy of the Yocto Project, you can either clone the repository, choosing the code name as the branch, which is morty in this case:

```
$ git clone -b morty git://git.yoctoproject.org/poky.git
```

You can also download the archive from http://downloads.yoctoproject.org/releases/yocto/yocto-2.2/poky-morty-16.0.0.tar.bz2. In the first case, you will find everything in the directory, poky/, in the second case, poky-morty-16.0.0/.

In addition, you should read the section titled **System Requirements** from the *Yocto Project Reference Manual* (http://www.yoctoproject.org/docs/current/ref-manual/ref-manual.html#detailed-supported-distros); and, in particular, you should make sure that the packages listed there are installed on your host computer.

Configuring

As with Buildroot, let's begin with a build for the QEMU ARM emulator. Begin by sourcing a script to set up the environment:

```
$ cd poky
$ source oe-init-build-env
```

This creates a working directory for you named `build/` and makes it the current directory. All of the configuration, intermediate, and target image files will be put in this directory. You must source this script each time you want to work on this project.

You can choose a different working directory by adding it as a parameter to `oe-init-build-env`, for example:

```
$ source oe-init-build-env build-qemuarm
```

This will put you into the directory: `build-qemuarm/`. This way you can have several build directories, each for a different project: you choose which one you want to work with through the parameter to `oe-init-build-env`.

Initially, the build directory contains only one subdirectory named `conf/`, which contains the configuration files for this project:

- `local.conf`: This contains a specification of the device you are going to build and the build environment.
- `bblayers.conf`: This contains paths of the meta layers you are going to use. I will describe layers later on.
- `templateconf.cfg`: This contains the name of a directory, which contains various `conf` files. By default, it points to `meta-poky/conf/`.

For now, we just need to set the `MACHINE` variable in `local.conf` to qemuarm by removing the comment character (#) at the start of this line:

```
MACHINE ?= "qemuarm"
```

Building

To actually perform the build, you need to run BitBake, telling it which root filesystem image you want to create. Some common images are as follows:

- `core-image-minimal`: This is a small console-based system which is useful for tests and as the basis for custom images.
- `core-image-minimal-initramfs`: This is similar to core-image-minimal, but built as a ramdisk.
- `core-image-x11`: This is a basic image with support for graphics through an X11 server and the xterminal terminal app.
- `core-image-sato`: This is a full graphical system based on Sato, which is a mobile graphical environment built on X11, and GNOME. The image includes several apps including a Terminal, an editor, and a file manager.

By giving BitBake the final target, it will work backwards and build all the dependencies first, beginning with the toolchain. For now, we just want to create a minimal image to see how it works:

```
$ bitbake core-image-minimal
```

The build is likely to take some time, probably more than an hour. It will download about 4 GiB of source code, and it will consume about about 24 GiB of disk space. When it is complete, you will find several new directories in the build directory including `downloads/`, which contains all the source downloaded for the build, and `tmp/`, which contains most of the build artifacts. You should see the following in `tmp/`:

- `work/`: This contains the build directory and the staging area for the root filesystem.
- `deploy/`: This contains the final binaries to be deployed on the target:
    - `deploy/images/[machine name]/`: Contains the bootloader, the kernel, and the root filesystem images ready to be run on the target
    - `deploy/rpm/`: This contains the RPM packages that went to make up the images
    - `deploy/licenses/`: This contains the license files extracted from each package

Running the QEMU target

When you build a QEMU target, an internal version of QEMU is generated, which removes the need to install the QEMU package for your distribution, and thus avoids version dependencies. There is a wrapper script named `runqemu` to run this version of QEMU.

To run the QEMU emulation, make sure that you have sourced `oe-init-build-env`, and then just type this:

```
$ runqemu qemuarm
```

In this case, QEMU has been configured with a graphic console so that the boot messages and login prompt appear in the black framebuffer, as shown in the following screenshot:

```
[    8.179808] md: If you don't use raid, use raid=noautodetect
[    8.193152] md: Autodetecting RAID arrays.
[    8.197292] md: Scanned 0 and added 0 devices.
[    8.201323] md: autorun ...
[    8.204339] md: ... autorun DONE.
[    8.214568] EXT4-fs (vda): couldn't mount as ext3 due to feature incompatibil
ities
[    8.224943] EXT4-fs (vda): couldn't mount as ext2 due to feature incompatibil
ities
[    8.267365] EXT4-fs (vda): mounted filesystem with ordered data mode. Opts: (
null)
[    8.276284] VFS: Mounted root (ext4 filesystem) on device 253:0.
[    8.283072] devtmpfs: mounted
[    8.305016] Freeing unused kernel memory: 412K (c0945000 - c09ac000)
[    8.310417] This architecture does not have kernel memory protection.
INIT: version 2.88 booting

Please wait: booting...
Starting udev
[    9.316513] udevd[115]: starting version 3.2
[    9.436544] udevd[116]: starting eudev-3.2
[   12.073243] EXT4-fs (vda): re-mounted. Opts: data=ordered
Populating dev cache
INIT: Entering runlevel: 5
Configuring network interfaces... done.
Starting syslogd/klogd: done

Poky (Yocto Project Reference Distro) 2.2.1 qemuarm /dev/tty1

qemuarm login:
```

You can login as `root`, without a password. You can close down QEMU by closing the framebuffer window.

You can launch QEMU without the graphic window by adding `nographic` to the command line:

```
$ runqemu qemuarm nographic
```

In this case, you close QEMU using the key sequence *Ctrl + A* and then *x*.

The `runqemu` script has many other options. Type `runqemu help` for more information.

Layers

The metadata for the Yocto Project is structured into layers. By convention, each layer has a name beginning with `meta`. The core layers of the Yocto Project are as follows:

- `meta`: This is the OpenEmbedded core with some changes for Poky
- `meta-poky`: This is the metadata specific to the Poky distribution
- `meta-yocto-bsp`: This contains the board support packages for the machines that the Yocto Project supports

The list of layers in which BitBake searches for recipes is stored in `<your build directory>/conf/bblayers.conf` and, by default, includes all three layers mentioned in the preceding list.

By structuring the recipes and other configuration data in this way, it is very easy to extend the Yocto Project by adding new layers. Additional layers are available from SoC manufacturers, the Yocto Project itself, and a wide range of people wishing to add value to the Yocto Project and OpenEmbedded. There is a useful list of layers at `http://layers.ope nembedded.org/layerindex/branch/master/layers/`. Here are some examples:

- `meta-angstrom`: The Ångström distribution
- `meta-qt5`: Qt 5 libraries and utilities
- `meta-intel`: BSPs for Intel CPUs and SoCs
- `meta-ti`: BSPs for TI ARM-based SoCs

Adding a layer is as simple as copying the `meta` directory into a suitable location, usually alongside the default meta layers and adding it to `bblayers.conf`. Make sure that you read the `REAMDE` file that should accompany each layer to see what dependencies it has on other layers and which versions of the Yocto Project it is compatible with.

To illustrate the way that layers work, let's create a layer for our Nova board, which we can use for the remainder of the chapter as we add features. You can see the complete implementation of the layer in the code archive in `MELP/chapter_06/poky/meta-nova`.

Each `meta` layer has to have at least one configuration file, named `conf/layer.conf`, and it should also have the README file and a license. There is a handy helper script that does the basics for us:

```
$ cd poky
$ scripts/yocto-layer create nova
```

The script asks for a priority, and whether you want to create sample recipes. In the example here, I just accepted the defaults:

```
Please enter the layer priority you'd like to use for the layer:
 [default: 6]
Would you like to have an example recipe created? (y/n) [default: n]
Would you like to have an example bbappend file created? (y/n)
 [default: n]
New layer created in meta-nova.
Don't forget to add it to your BBLAYERS (for details see
 meta-nova/README).
```

This will create a layer named `meta-nova` with a `conf/layer.conf`, an outline README and an MIT LICENSE in COPYING.MIT. The `layer.conf` file looks like this:

```
# We have a conf and classes directory, add to BBPATH
BBPATH .= ":${LAYERDIR}"

# We have recipes-* directories, add to BBFILES
BBFILES += "${LAYERDIR}/recipes-*/*/*.bb
${LAYERDIR}/recipes-*/*/*.bbappend"

BBFILE_COLLECTIONS += "nova"
BBFILE_PATTERN_nova = "^${LAYERDIR}/"
BBFILE_PRIORITY_nova = "6"
```

It adds itself to BBPATH and the recipes it contains to BBFILES. From looking at the code, you can see that the recipes are found in the directories with names beginning `recipes-` and have filenames ending in `.bb` (for normal BitBake recipes) or `.bbappend` (for recipes that extend existing recipes by overriding or adding to the instructions). This layer has the name `nova` added to the list of layers in BBFILE_COLLECTIONS and has a priority of 6. The layer priority is used if the same recipe appears in several layers: the one in the layer with the highest priority wins.

Since you are about to build a new configuration, it is best to begin by creating a new build directory named `build-nova`:

```
$ cd ~/poky
$ source oe-init-build-env build-nova
```

Now, you need to add this layer to your build configuration using the command:

```
$ bitbake-layers add-layer ../meta-nova
```

You can confirm that it is set up correctly like this:

```
$ bitbake-layers show-layers
layer                   path                              priority
================================================================
meta                    /home/chris/poky/meta                5
meta-yocto              /home/chris/poky/meta-yocto          5
meta-yocto-bsp          /home/chris/poky/meta-poky-bsp       5
meta-nova               /home/chris/poky/meta-nova           6
```

There you can see the new layer. It has a priority 6, which means that we could override recipes in the other layers, which all have a lower priority.

At this point, it would be a good idea to run a build, using this empty layer. The final target will be the Nova board but, for now, build for a BeagleBone Black by removing the comment before MACHINE ?= "beaglebone" in conf/local.conf. Then, build a small image using bitbake core-image-minimal as before.

As well as recipes, layers may contain BitBake classes, configuration files for machines, distributions, and more. I will look at recipes next and show you how to create a customized image and how to create a package.

BitBake and recipes

BitBake processes metadata of several different types, which include the following:

- **Recipes**: Files ending in .bb. These contain information about building a unit of software, including how to get a copy of the source code, the dependencies on other components, and how to build and install it.
- **Append**: Files ending in .bbappend. These allow some details of a recipe to be overridden or extended. A bbappend file simply appends its instructions to the end of a recipe (.bb) file of the same root name.
- **Include**: Files ending in .inc. These contain information that is common to several recipes, allowing information to be shared among them. The files maybe included using the **include** or **require** keywords. The difference is that **require** produces an error if the file does not exist, whereas **include** does not.

- **Classes**: Files ending in `.bbclass`. These contain common build information, for example, how to build a kernel or how to build an autotools project. The classes are inherited and extended in recipes and other classes using the **inherit** keyword. The class `classes/base.bbclass` is implicitly inherited in every recipe.
- **Configuration**: Files ending in `.conf`. They define various configuration variables that govern the project's build process.

A recipe is a collection of tasks written in a combination of Python and shell script. The tasks have names such as `do_fetch`, `do_unpack`, `do_patch`, `do_configure`, `do_compile`, and `do_install`. You use BitBake to execute these tasks. The default task is `do_build`, which performs all the subtasks required to build the recipe. You can list the tasks available in a recipe using `bitbake -c listtasks [recipe]`. For example, you can list the tasks in `core-image-minimal` like this:

```
$ bitbake -c listtasks core-image-minimal
[...]
core-image-minimal-1.0-r0 do_listtasks: do_build
core-image-minimal-1.0-r0 do_listtasks: do_bundle_initramfs
core-image-minimal-1.0-r0 do_listtasks: do_checkuri
core-image-minimal-1.0-r0 do_listtasks: do_checkuriall
core-image-minimal-1.0-r0 do_listtasks: do_clean
[...]
```

In fact, `-c` is the option that tells BitBake to run a specific task in a recipe with the task being named with the `do_` part stripped off. The task `do_listtasks` is simply a special task that lists all the tasks defined within a recipe. Another example is the `fetch` task, which downloads the source code for a recipe:

```
$ bitbake -c fetch busybox
```

You can also use the `fetchall` task to get the code for the target and all the dependencies, which is useful if you want to make sure you have downloaded all the code for the image you are about to build:

```
$ bitbake -c fetchall core-image-minimal
```

The recipe files are are usually named `<package-name>_<version>.bb`. They may have dependencies on other recipes, which would allow BitBake to work out all the subtasks that need to be executed to complete the top level job.

As an example, to create a recipe for our `helloworld` program in `meta-nova`, you would create a directory structure like this:

```
meta-nova/recipes-local/helloworld
├── files
│   └── helloworld.c
└── helloworld_1.0.bb
```

The recipe is `helloworld_1.0.bb` and the source is local to the recipe directory in the subdirectory `files/`. The recipe contains these instructions:

```
DESCRIPTION = "A friendly program that prints Hello World!"
PRIORITY = "optional"
SECTION = "examples"

LICENSE = "GPLv2"
LIC_FILES_CHKSUM = "file://${COMMON_LICENSE_DIR}/GPL-2.0;
md5=801f80980d171dd6425610833a22dbe6"

SRC_URI = "file://helloworld.c"

S = "${WORKDIR}"

do_compile() {
    ${CC} ${CFLAGS} ${LDFLAGS} helloworld.c -o helloworld
}

do_install() {
    install -d ${D}${bindir}
    install -m 0755 helloworld ${D}${bindir}
}
```

The location of the source code is set by `SRC_URI:`. In this case, the `file://` URI means that the code is local to the `recipe` directory. BitBake will search directories, `files/`, `helloworld/`, and `helloworld-1.0/` relative to the directory that contains the recipe. The tasks that need to be defined are `do_compile` and `do_install`, which compile the one source file and install it into the target root filesystem: `${D}` expands to the staging area of the recipe and `${bindir}` to the default binary directory, `/usr/bin`.

Every recipe has a license, defined by **LICENSE**, which is set to **GPL V2** here. The file containing the text of the license and a checksum is defined by `LIC_FILES_CHKSUM`. BitBake will terminate the build if the checksum does not match, indicating that the license has changed in some way. The license file may be part of the package or it may point to one of the standard license texts in `meta/files/common-licenses/`, as is the case here.

By default, commercial licenses are disallowed, but it is easy to enable them. You need to specify the license in the recipe, as shown here:

```
LICENSE_FLAGS = "commercial"
```

Then, in your `conf/local.conf`, you would explicitly allow this license, like so:

```
LICENSE_FLAGS_WHITELIST = "commercial"
```

Now, to make sure that our `helloworld` recipe compiles correctly, you can ask BitBake to build it, like so:

```
$ bitbake helloworld
```

If all goes well, you should see that it has created a working directory for it in `tmp/work/cortexa8hf-vfp-neon-poky-linux-gnueabi/helloworld/`. You should also see there is an RPM package for it in `tmp/deploy/rpm/cortexa8hf_vfp_neon/helloworld-1.0-r0.cortexa8hf_vfp_neon.rpm`.

It is not part of the target image yet, though. The list of packages to be installed is held in a variable named `IMAGE_INSTALL`. You can append to the end of that list by adding this line to `conf/local.conf`:

```
IMAGE_INSTALL_append = " helloworld"
```

Note that there has to be a space between the opening double quote and the first package name. Now, the package will be added to any image that you `bitbake`:

```
$ bitbake core-image-minimal
```

If you look in `tmp/deploy/images/beaglebone/core-image-minimal-beaglebone.tar.bz2`, you will see that `/usr/bin/helloworld` has indeed been installed.

Customizing images via local.conf

You may often want to add a package to an image during development or tweak it in other ways. As shown previously, you can simply append to the list of packages to be installed by adding a statement like this:

```
IMAGE_INSTALL_append = " strace helloworld"
```

You can make more sweeping changes via EXTRA_IMAGE_FEATURES. Here is a short list which should give you an idea of the features you can enable:

- dbg-pkgs: This installs debug symbol packages for all the packages installed in the image.
- debug-tweaks: This allows root logins without passwords and other changes that make development easier.
- package-management: This installs package management tools and preserves the package manager database.
- read-only-rootfs: This makes the root filesystem read-only. We will cover this in more detail in Chapter 7, *Creating a Storage Strategy*.
- x11: This installs the X server.
- x11-base: This installs the X server with a minimal environment.
- x11-sato: This installs the OpenedHand Sato environment.

There are many more features that you can add in this way. I recommend you look at the **Image Features** section of the *Yocto Project Reference Manual* and also read through the code in meta/classes/core-image.bbclass.

Writing an image recipe

The problem with making changes to local.conf is that they are, well, local. If you want to create an image that is to be shared with other developers or to be loaded onto a production system, then you should put the changes into an **image recipe**.

An image recipe contains instructions about how to create the image files for a target, including the bootloader, the kernel, and the root filesystem images. By convention, image recipes are put into a directory named images, so you can get a list of all the images that are available by using this command:

```
$ ls meta*/recipes*/images/*.bb
```

You will find that the recipe for core-image-minimal is in meta/recipes-core/images/core-image-minimal.bb.

A simple approach is to take an existing image recipe and modify it using statements similar to those you used in local.conf.

For example, imagine that you want an image that is the same as `core-image-minimal` but includes your `helloworld` program and the strace utility. You can do that with a two-line recipe file, which includes (using the `require` keyword) the base image and adds the packages you want. It is conventional to put the image in a directory named images, so add the recipe `nova-image.bb` with this content in `meta-nova/recipes-local/images`:

```
require recipes-core/images/core-image-minimal.bb
IMAGE_INSTALL += "helloworld strace"
```

Now, you can remove the `IMAGE_INSTALL_append` line from your `local.conf` and build it using this:

```
$ bitbake nova-image
```

Creating an SDK

It is very useful to be able to create a standalone toolchain that other developers can install, avoiding the need for everyone in the team to have a full installation of the Yocto Project. Ideally, you want the toolchain to include development libraries and header files for all the libraries installed on the target. You can do that for any image using the `populate_sdk` task, as shown here:

```
$ bitbake -c populate_sdk nova-image
```

The result is a self-installing shell script in `tmp/deploy/sdk`:

```
poky-<c_library>-<host_machine>-<target_image><target_machine>
-toolchain-<version>.sh
```

For the SDK built with the `nova-image` recipe, it is this:

```
poky-glibc-x86_64-nova-image-cortexa8hf-neon-toolchain-2.2.1.sh
```

If you only want a basic toolchain with just C and C++ cross compilers, the C-library and header files, you can instead run this:

```
$ bitbake meta-toolchain
```

To install the SDK, just run the shell script. The default install directory is /opt/poky, but the install script allows you to change this:

```
$ tmp/deploy/sdk/poky-glibc-x86_64-nova-image-cortexa8hf-neon-
toolchain-2.2.1.sh
Poky (Yocto Project Reference Distro) SDK installer version 2.2.1
================================================================
Enter target directory for SDK (default: /opt/poky/2.2.1):
You are about to install the SDK to "/opt/poky/2.2.1". Proceed[Y/n]?
[sudo] password for chris:
Extracting SDK..........................done
Setting it up...done
```

To make use of the toolchain, first source the environment and set up the script:

```
$ source /opt/poky/2.2.1/environment-setup-cortexa8hf-neon-poky
-linux-gnueabi
```

> The environment-setup-* script that sets things up for the SDK is not compatible with the oe-init-build-env script that you source when working in the Yocto Project build directory. It is a good rule to always start a new terminal session before you source either script.

The toolchain generated by Yocto Project does not have a valid sysroot directory:

```
$ arm-poky-linux-gnueabi-gcc -print-sysroot
/not/exist
```

Consequently, if you try to cross compile, as I have shown in previous chapters, it will fail like this:

```
$ arm-poky-linux-gnueabi-gcc helloworld.c -o helloworld
helloworld.c:1:19: fatal error: stdio.h: No such file or directory
#include <stdio.h>
                  ^
compilation terminated.
```

This is because the compiler has been configured to work for a wide range of ARM processors, and the fine tuning is done when you launch it using the right set of flags. Instead, you should use the shell variables that are created when you source the environment-setup script for cross compiling. They include these:

- CC: The C compiler
- CXX: The C++ compiler
- CPP: The C preprocessor

- `AS`: The assembler
- `LD`: The linker

As an example, this is what we find that `CC` has been set to this:

```
$ echo $CC
arm-poky-linux-gnueabi-gcc -march=armv7-a -mfpu=neon
-mfloat-abi=hard -mcpu=cortex-a8 --sysroot=/opt/poky/
2.2.1/sysroots/cortexa8hf-neon-poky-linux-gnueabi
```

So long as you use `$CC` to compile, everything should work fine:

```
$ $CC helloworld.c -o helloworld
```

The license audit

The Yocto Project insists that each package has a license. A copy of the license is placed in `tmp/deploy/licenses/[package name]` for each package as it is built. In addition, a summary of the packages and licenses used in an image are put into the directory: `<image name>-<machine name>-<date stamp>/`. For `nova-image` we just built, the directory would be named something like this:

```
tmp/deploy/licenses/nova-image-beaglebone-20170417192546/
```

Further reading

You may want to look at the following documentation for more information:

- *The Buildroot User Manual*, `http://buildroot.org/downloads/manual/manual.html`
- *Instant Buildroot*, by Daniel Manchón Vizuete, *Packt Publishing*, 2013
- *Yocto Project documentation*: There are nine reference guides plus a tenth which is a composite of the others (the so-called **Mega-manual**) at `https://www.yoctoproject.org/documentation`
- *Embedded Linux Systems with the Yocto Project*, by Rudolf J. Streif, *Prentice Hall*, 2016
- *Embedded Linux Projects Using Yocto Project Cookbook*, by Alex Gonzalez, *Packt Publishing*, 2015

Summary

Using a build system takes the hard work out of creating an embedded Linux system, and it is almost always better than hand crafting a roll-your-own system. There is a range of open source build systems available these days: Buildroot and the Yocto Project represent two different approaches. Buildroot is simple and quick, making it a good choice for fairly simple single-purpose devices: traditional embedded Linux as I like to think of them. The Yocto Project is more complex and flexible. It is package based, meaning that you have the option to install a package manager and perform updates of individual packages in the field. The meta layer structure makes it easy to extend the metadata, and indeed there is good support throughout the community and industry for the Yocto Project. The downside is that there is a very steep learning curve: you should expect it to take several months to become proficient with it, and even then it will sometimes do things that you don't expect, or at least that is my experience.

Don't forget that any devices you create using these tools will need to be maintained in the field for a period of time, often many years. Both Yocto Project and Buildroot provide point releases for about one year after the initial release. In either case, you will find yourself having to maintain your release yourself or else paying for commercial support. The third possibility, ignoring the problem, should not be considered an option!

In the next chapter, I will look at file storage and filesystems, and at the way that the choices you make there will affect the stability and maintainability of your embedded Linux.

7
Creating a Storage Strategy

The mass-storage options for embedded devices have a great impact on the rest of the system in terms of robustness, speed, and methods of in-field updates. Most devices employ flash memory in some form or other. Flash memory has become much less expensive over the past few years as storage capacities have increased from tens of megabytes to tens of gigabytes.

In this chapter, I will begin with a detailed look at the technology behind flash memory and how different memory organization affects the low-level driver software that has to manage it, including the Linux memory technology device layer, MTD.

For each flash technology, there are different choices of filesystem. I will describe those most commonly found on embedded devices and complete the survey with a section giving a summary of choices for each type of flash memory. The final sections consider techniques to make the best use of flash memory and draw everything together into a coherent storage strategy.

We will cover the following topics:

- Storage options
- Accessing flash memory from the bootloader
- Accessing flash memory from Linux
- Filesystems for flash memory
- Filesystems for NOR and NAND flash memory
- Filesystems for managed flash
- Read-only compressed filesystems
- Temporary filesystems
- Making the root filesystem read-only
- Filesystem choices

Storage options

Embedded devices need storage that takes little power and is physically compact, robust, and reliable over a lifetime of perhaps tens of years. In almost all cases, this means solid-state storage. Solid-state storage was introduced many years ago with **read-only memory (ROM)**, but for the past 20 years, it has been flash memory of some kind. There have been several generations of flash memory in that time, progressing from NOR to NAND to managed flash such as eMMC.

NOR flash is expensive but reliable and can be mapped into the CPU address space, which allows you to execute code directly from flash. NOR flash chips are low capacity, ranging from a few megabytes to a gigabyte or so.

NAND flash memory is much cheaper than NOR and is available in higher capacities, in the range of tens of megabytes to tens of gigabytes. However, it needs a lot of hardware and software support to turn it into a useful storage medium.

Managed flash memory consists of one or more NAND flash chips packaged with a controller that handles the complexities of flash memory and presents a hardware interface similar to that of a hard disk. The attraction is that it removes complexity from the driver software and insulates the system designer from the frequent changes in flash technology. SD cards, eMMC chips, and USB flash drives fit into this category. Almost all of the current generation of smartphones and tablets have eMMC storage, and this trend is likely to progress with other categories of embedded devices.

Hard drives are seldom found in embedded systems. One exception is digital video recording in set-top boxes and smart TVs, in which a large amount of storage is needed with fast write times.

In all cases, robustness is of prime importance: you want the device to boot and reach a functional state despite power failures and unexpected resets. You should choose filesystems that behave well under such circumstances.

NOR flash

The memory cells in NOR flash chips are arranged into erase blocks of, for example, 128 KiB. Erasing a block sets all the bits to 1. It can be programmed one word at a time (8, 16, or 32 bits, depending on the data bus width). Each erase cycle damages the memory cells slightly, and after a number of cycles, the erase block becomes unreliable and cannot be used anymore. The maximum number of erase cycles should be given in the data sheet for the chip but is usually in the range of 100K to 1M.

The data can be read word by word. The chip is usually mapped into the CPU address space, which means that you can execute code directly from NOR flash. This makes it a convenient place to put the bootloader code as it needs no initialization beyond hardwiring the address mapping. SoCs that support NOR flash in this way have configurations that provide a default memory mapping such that it encompasses the reset vector of the CPU.

The kernel, and even the root filesystem, can also be located in flash memory, avoiding the need for copying them into RAM, and thus creating devices with small memory footprints. The technique is known as **eXecute In Place**, or **XIP**. It is very specialized and I will not examine it further here. I have included some references at the end of the chapter.

There is a standard register-level interface for NOR flash chips called the **Common Flash Interface** or **CFI**, which all modern chips support. The CFI is described in standard JESD68, which you can get from `https://www.jedec.org/`.

NAND flash

NAND flash is much cheaper than NOR flash and has a higher capacity. First-generation NAND chips stored one bit per memory cell in what is now known as an **SLC** or **single-level cell** organization. Later generations moved on to two bits per cell in **multi-level cell (MLC)** chips and now to three bits per cell in **tri-level cell (TLC)** chips. As the number of bits per cell has increased, the reliability of the storage has decreased, requiring more complex controller hardware and software to compensate. Where reliability is a concern, you should make sure you are using SLC NAND flash chips.

As with NOR flash, NAND flash is organized into erase blocks ranging in size from 16 KiB to 512 KiB and, once again, erasing a block sets all the bits to 1. However, the number of erase cycles before the block becomes unreliable is lower, typically as few as 1K cycles for TLC chips and up to 100K for SLC. NAND flash can only be read and written in pages, usually of 2 or 4 KiB. Since they cannot be accessed byte-by-byte, they cannot be mapped into the address space and so code and data have to be copied into RAM before they can be accessed.

Data transfers to and from the chip are prone to bit flips, which can be detected and corrected using **error-correction codes (ECCs)**. SLC chips generally use a simple **Hamming code**, which can be implemented efficiently in software and can correct a single-bit error in a page read. MLC and TLC chips need more sophisticated codes, such as **Bose-Chaudhuri-Hocquenghem (BCH)**, which can correct up to 8-bit errors per page. These need hardware support.

The ECCs have to be stored somewhere, and so there is an extra area of memory per page known as the **out-of-band (OOB)** area, or the spare area. SLC designs usually have 1 byte of OOB per 32 bytes of main storage, so for a 2 KiB page device, the OOB is 64 bytes per page, and for a 4 KiB page, it is 128 bytes. MLC and TLC chips have proportionally larger OOB areas to accommodate more complex ECCs. The following diagram shows the organization of a chip with a 128 KiB erase block and 2 KiB pages:

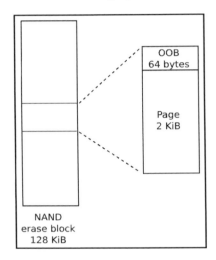

During production, the manufacturer tests all the blocks and marks any that fail by setting a flag in the OOB area of each page in the block. It is not uncommon to find that brand new chips have up to 2% of their blocks marked bad in this way. Furthermore, it is within the specification for a similar proportion of blocks to give errors on erase before the erase cycle limit is reached. The NAND flash driver should detect this and mark it as bad.

After space has been taken in the OOB area for a bad block flag and ECC bytes, there are still some bytes left. Some flash filesystems make use of these free bytes to store filesystem metadata. Consequently, many parts of the system are interested in the layout of the OOB area: the SoC ROM boot code, the bootloader, the kernel MTD driver, the filesystem code, and the tools to create filesystem images. There is not much standardization, so it is easy to get into a situation in which the bootloader writes data using an OOB format that cannot be read by the kernel MTD driver. It is up to you to make sure that they all agree.

Access to NAND flash chips requires a NAND flash controller, which is usually part of the SoC. You will need the corresponding driver in the bootloader and kernel. The NAND flash controller handles the hardware interface to the chip, transferring data to and from pages, and may include hardware for error correction.

There is a standard register-level interface for NAND flash chips known as the **Open NAND Flash Interface** or **ONFi**, which most modern chips adhere to. See `http://www.onf i.org/`.

Managed flash

The burden of supporting flash memory in the operating system, NAND in particular, becomes less if there is a well-defined hardware interface and a standard flash controller that hides the complexities of the memory. This is managed flash memory, and it is becoming more and more common. In essence, it means combining one or more flash chips with a microcontroller that offers an ideal storage device with a small sector size that is compatible with conventional filesystems. The most important types of chips for embedded systems are **Secure Digital (SD)** cards and the embedded variant known as **eMMC**.

MultiMediaCard and Secure Digital cards

The **MultiMediaCard** (**MMC**) was introduced in 1997 by SanDisk and Siemens as a form of packaged storage using flash memory. Shortly after, in 1999, SanDisk, Matsushita, and Toshiba created the **Secure Digital** (**SD**) card, which is based on MMC but adds encryption and DRM (the *secure* in the name). Both were intended for consumer electronics such as digital cameras, music players, and similar devices. Currently, SD cards are the dominant form of managed flash for consumer and embedded electronics, even though the encryption features are seldom used. Newer versions of the SD specification allow smaller packaging (mini SD and microSD, which is often written as uSD) and larger capacities: high capacity SDHC up to 32 GB and extended capacity SDXC up to 2TB.

The hardware interface for MMC and SD cards is very similar, and it is possible to use full-sized MMC cards in full-sized SD card slots (but not the other way round). Early incarnations used a 1-bit **Serial Peripheral Interface** (**SPI**); more recent cards use a 4-bit interface.

There is a command set for reading and writing memory in sectors of 512 bytes. Inside the package is a microcontroller and one or more NAND flash chips, as shown in the following diagram:

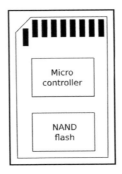

The microcontroller implements the command set and manages the flash memory, performing the function of a flash translation layer, as described later on in this chapter. They are preformatted with a FAT filesystem: FAT16 on *SDSC* cards, FAT32 on *SDHC*, and exFAT on *SDXC*. The quality of the NAND flash chips and the software on the microcontroller varies greatly between cards. It is questionable whether any of them are sufficiently reliable for deep embedded use, and certainly not with a FAT filesystem, which is prone to file corruption. Remember that the prime use case for MMC and SD cards is for removable storage on cameras, tablets, and phones.

eMMC

eMMC or **Embedded MMC** is simply MMC memory packaged so that it can be soldered on to the motherboard, using a 4- or 8-bit interface for data transfer. However, they are intended to be used as storage for an operating system so the components are capable of performing that task. The chips are usually not preformatted with any filesystem.

Other types of managed flash

One of the first managed flash technologies was **CompactFlash (CF)**, which uses a subset of the **Personal Computer Memory Card International Association (PCMCIA)** hardware interface. CF exposes the memory through a parallel ATA interface and appears to the operating system as a standard hard disk. They are common in x86-based single board computers and professional video and camera equipment.

One other format that we use every day is the **USB flash drive**. In this case, the memory is accessed through a USB interface and the controller implements the USB mass storage specification as well as the flash translation layer and interface to the flash chip, or chips. The USB mass storage protocol, in turn, is based on the SCSI disk command set. As with MMC and SD cards, they are usually preformatted with a FAT filesystem. Their main use case in embedded systems is to exchange data with PCs.

A recent addition to the list of options for managed flash storage is **Universal Flash Storage (UFS)**. Like eMMC, it is packaged in a chip that is mounted on the motherboard. It has a high-speed serial interface and can achieve data rates greater than eMMC. It supports a SCSI disk command set.

Accessing flash memory from the bootloader

In Chapter 3, *All About Bootloaders*, I mentioned the need for the bootloader to load kernel binaries and other images from various flash devices, and to perform system maintenance tasks such as erasing and reprogramming flash memory. It follows that the bootloader must have the drivers and infrastructure needed to support read, erase, and write operations on the type of memory you have, whether it be NOR, NAND, or managed. I will use U-Boot in the following examples; other bootloaders follow a similar pattern.

U-Boot and NOR flash

U-Boot has drivers for NOR CFI chips in drivers/mtd and has the commands erase to erase memory and cp.b to copy data byte by byte, programming the flash cells. Suppose that you have NOR flash memory mapped from 0x40000000 to 0x48000000, of which 4 MiB starting at 0x40040000 is a kernel image, then you would load a new kernel into flash using these U-Boot commands:

```
U-Boot# tftpboot 100000 uImage
U-Boot# erase 40040000 403fffff
U-Boot# cp.b 100000 40040000 $(filesize)
```

The variable filesize in the preceding example is set by the tftpboot command to the size of the file just downloaded.

U-Boot and NAND flash

For NAND flash, you need a driver for the NAND flash controller on your SoC, which you can find in the U-Boot source code in the directory `drivers/mtd/nand`. You use the `nand` command to manage the memory using the sub-commands `erase`, `write`, and `read`. This example shows a kernel image being loaded into RAM at `0x82000000` and then placed into flash starting at offset `0x280000`:

```
U-Boot# tftpboot 82000000 uImage
U-Boot# nand erase 280000 400000
U-Boot# nand write 82000000 280000 $(filesize)
```

U-Boot can also read files stored in the `JFFS2`, `YAFFS2`, and `UBIFS` filesystems.

U-Boot and MMC, SD, and eMMC

U-Boot has drivers for several MMC controllers in `drivers/mmc`. You can access the raw data using `mmc read` and `mmc write` at the user interface level, which allows you to handle raw kernel and filesystem images.

U-boot can also read files from the `FAT32` and `ext4` filesystems on `MMC` storage.

Accessing flash memory from Linux

Raw NOR and NAND flash memory is handled by the **Memory Technology Device** subsystem, or **MTD**, which provides basic interfaces to read, erase, and write blocks of flash memory. In the case of NAND flash, there are also functions to handle the OOB area and to identify bad blocks.

For managed flash, you need drivers to handle the particular hardware interface. MMC/SD cards and eMMC use the `mmcblk` driver; **CompactFlash** and hard drives use the SCSI disk driver, `sd`. USB flash drives use the `usb_storage` driver together with the `sd` driver.

Memory technology devices

The MTD subsystem was started by David Woodhouse in 1999 and has been extensively developed over the intervening years. In this section, I will concentrate on the way it handles the two main technologies, NOR and NAND flash.

MTD consists of three layers: a core set of functions, a set of drivers for various types of chips, and user-level drivers that present the flash memory as a character device or a block device, as shown in the following diagram:

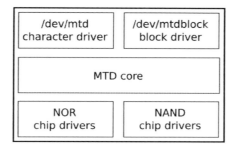

The chip drivers are at the lowest level and interface with flash chips. Only a small number of drivers are needed for NOR flash chips, enough to cover the CFI standard and variations plus a few non-compliant chips, which are now mostly obsolete. For NAND flash, you will need a driver for the NAND flash controller you are using; this is usually supplied as part of the board support package. There are drivers for about 40 of them in the current mainline kernel in the directory `drivers/mtd/nand`.

MTD partitions

In most cases, you will want to partition the flash memory into a number of areas, for example, to provide space for a bootloader, a kernel image, or a root filesystem. In MTD, there are several ways to specify the size and location of partitions, the main ones being:

- Through the kernel command line using CONFIG_MTD_CMDLINE_PARTS
- Via the device tree using CONFIG_MTD_OF_PARTS
- With a platform-mapping driver

In the case of the first option, the kernel command-line option to use is `mtdparts`, which is defined as follows in the Linux source code in `drivers/mtd/cmdlinepart.c`:

```
mtdparts=<mtddef>[;<mtddef]
<mtddef>   := <mtd-id>:<partdef>[,<partdef>]
<mtd-id>   := unique name for the chip
<partdef>  := <size>[@<offset>][<name>][ro][lk]
<size>     := size of partition OR "-" to denote all remaining
              space
<offset>   := offset to the start of the partition; leave blank
              to follow the previous partition without any gap
<name>     := '(' NAME ')'
```

Perhaps an example will help. Imagine that you have one flash chip of 128 MiB that is to be divided into five partitions. A typical command line would be this:

```
mtdparts=:512k(SPL)ro,780k(U-Boot)ro,128k(U-BootEnv),
4m(Kernel),-(Filesystem)
```

The first element, before the colon, is `mtd-id`, which identifies the flash chip, either by number or by the name assigned by the board support package. If there is only one chip, as here, it can be left empty. If there is more than one chip, the information for each is separated by a semicolon. Then, for each chip, there is a comma-separated list of partitions, each with a size in bytes, KiB (`k`) or MiB (`m`) and a name in parentheses. The `ro` suffix makes the partition read-only to MTD and is often used to prevent accidental overwriting of the bootloader. The size of the last partition for the chip may be replaced by a dash (-), indicating that it should take up all the remaining space.

You can see a summary of the configuration at runtime by reading `/proc/mtd`:

```
# cat /proc/mtd
dev:    size    erasesize    name
mtd0: 00080000 00020000    "SPL"
mtd1: 000C3000 00020000    "U-Boot"
mtd2: 00020000 00020000    "U-BootEnv"
mtd3: 00400000 00020000    "Kernel"
mtd4: 07A9D000 00020000    "Filesystem"
```

There is more detailed information for each partition in `/sys/class/mtd`, including the erase block size and the page size, and it is nicely summarized using `mtdinfo`:

```
# mtdinfo /dev/mtd0
mtd0
Name:                            SPL
Type:                            nand
Eraseblock size:                 131072 bytes, 128.0 KiB
Amount of eraseblocks:           4 (524288 bytes, 512.0 KiB)
Minimum input/output unit size:  2048 bytes
Sub-page size:                   512 bytes
OOB size:                        64 bytes
Character device major/minor:    90:0
Bad blocks are allowed:          true
Device is writable:              false
```

Another way of specifying MTD partitions is through the device tree. Here is an example that creates the same partitions as the command-line example:

```
nand@0,0 {
  #address-cells = <1>;
  #size-cells = <1>;
```

```
partition@0 {
  label = "SPL";
  reg = <0 0x80000>;
};
partition@80000 {
  label = "U-Boot";
  reg = <0x80000 0xc3000>;
};
partition@143000 {
  label = "U-BootEnv";
  reg = <0x143000 0x20000>;
};
partition@163000 {
  label = "Kernel";
  reg = <0x163000 0x400000>;
};
partition@563000 {
  label = "Filesystem";
  reg = <0x563000 0x7a9d000>;
};
};
```

A third alternative is to code the partition information as platform data in an
`mtd_partition` structure, as shown in this example taken from `arch/arm/mach-omap2/board-omap3beagle.c` (`NAND_BLOCK_SIZE` is defined elsewhere to
be 128 KiB):

```
static struct mtd_partition omap3beagle_nand_partitions[] = {
  {
    .name           = "X-Loader",
    .offset         = 0,
    .size           = 4 * NAND_BLOCK_SIZE,
    .mask_flags     = MTD_WRITEABLE,   /* force read-only */
  },
  {
    .name           = "U-Boot",
    .offset         = 0x80000;
    .size           = 15 * NAND_BLOCK_SIZE,
    .mask_flags     = MTD_WRITEABLE,   /* force read-only */
  },
  {
    .name           = "U-Boot Env",
    .offset         = 0x260000;
    .size           = 1 * NAND_BLOCK_SIZE,
  },
  {
    .name           = "Kernel",
    .offset         = 0x280000;
```

```
    .size             = 32 * NAND_BLOCK_SIZE,
},
{
    .name             = "File System",
    .offset           = 0x680000;
    .size             = MTDPART_SIZ_FULL,
},
};
```

Platform data is deprecated: you will only find it used in BSPs for old SoCs that have not been updated to use a device tree.

MTD device drivers

The upper level of the MTD subsystem is a pair of device drivers:

- A character device, with a major number of 90. There are two device nodes per MTD partition number, N: /dev/mtdN (*minor number=N*2*) and /dev/mtdNro (*minor number=(N*2 + 1)*). The latter is just a read-only version of the former.
- A block device, with a major number of 31 and a minor number of N. The device nodes are in the form /dev/mtdblockN.

The MTD character device, mtd

The character devices are the most important: they allow you to access the underlying flash memory as an array of bytes so that you can read and write (program) the flash. It also implements a number of ioctl functions that allow you to erase blocks and to manage the OOB area on NAND chips. The following list is taken from include/uapi/mtd/mtd-abi.h:

IOCTL	Description
MEMGETINFO	Gets basic MTD characteristic information
MEMERASE	Erases blocks in the MTD partition
MEMWRITEOOB	Writes out-of-band data for the page
MEMREADOOB	Reads out-of-band data for the page
MEMLOCK	Locks the chip (if supported)
MEMUNLOCK	Unlocks the chip (if supported)

IOCTL	Description
MEMGETREGIONCOUNT	Gets the number of erase regions: non-zero if there are erase blocks of differing sizes in the partition, which is common for NOR flash, rare on NAND
MEMGETREGIONINFO	If MEMGETREGIONCOUNT is non-zero, this can be used to get the offset, size, and block count of each region
MEMGETOOBSEL	Deprecated
MEMGETBADBLOCK	This gets the bad block flag
MEMSETBADBLOCK	This sets the bad block flag
OTPSELECT	This sets OTP (one-time programmable) mode, if the chip supports it
OTPGETREGIONCOUNT	This gets the number of OTP regions
OTPGETREGIONINFO	This gets information about an OTP region
ECCGETLAYOUT	Deprecated

There is a set of utility programs known as **mtd-utils** for manipulating flash memory that makes use of these ioctl functions. The source is available from `git://git.infradead.org/mtd-utils.git` and is available as a package in the Yocto Project and Buildroot. The essential tools are shown in the following list. The package also contains utilities for the JFFS2 and UBI/UBIFS filesystems, which I will cover later. For each of these tools, the MTD character device is one of the parameters:

- **flash_erase**: Erases a range of blocks.
- **flash_lock**: Locks a range of blocks.
- **flash_unlock**: Unlocks a range of blocks.
- **nanddump**: Dumps memory from NAND flash, optionally including the OOB area. Skips bad blocks.
- **nandtest**: Tests and diagnostics for NAND flash.
- **nandwrite**: Writes (programs) data from a file in to NAND flash, skipping bad blocks.

 You must always erase flash memory before writing new contents to it: `flash_erase` is the command to do that.

To program NOR flash, you simply copy bytes to the MTD device node using a file copy command such as `cp`.

Unfortunately, this doesn't work with NAND memory as the copy will fail at the first bad block. Instead, use `nandwrite`, which skips over any bad blocks. To read back NAND memory, you should use `nanddump`, which also skips bad blocks.

The MTD block device, mtdblock

The mtdblock driver is little used. Its purpose is to present flash memory as a block device you can use to format and mount as a filesystem. However, it has severe limitations because it does not handle bad blocks in NAND flash, it does not do wear leveling, and it does not handle the mismatch in size between filesystem blocks and flash erase blocks. In other words, it does not have a flash translation layer, which is essential for reliable file storage. The only case where the mtdblock device is useful is to mount read-only file systems such as Squashfs on top of reliable flash memory such as NOR.

 If you want a read-only filesystem on NAND flash, you should use the UBI driver, as described later in this chapter.

Logging kernel oops to MTD

A kernel error, or oops, is normally logged via the klogd and syslogd daemons to a circular memory buffer or a file. Following a reboot, the log will be lost in the case of a ring buffer, and even in the case of a file, it may not have been properly written to before the system crashed. A more reliable method is to write oops and kernel panics to an MTD partition as a circular log buffer. You enable it with `CONFIG_MTD_OOPS` and add `console=ttyMTDN` to the kernel command line, N being the MTD device number to write the messages to.

Simulating NAND memory

The NAND simulator emulates a NAND chip using system RAM. The main use is for testing code that has to be NAND-aware without access to physical NAND memory. In particular, the ability to simulate bad blocks, bit flips, and other errors allows you to test code paths that are difficult to exercise using real flash memory. For more information, the best place to look is in the code itself, which has a comprehensive description of the ways you can configure the driver. The code is in `drivers/mtd/nand/nandsim.c`. Enable it with the kernel configuration `CONFIG_MTD_NAND_NANDSIM`.

The MMC block driver

MMC/SD cards and eMMC chips are accessed using the mmcblk block driver. You need a host controller to match the MMC adapter you are using, which is part of the board support package. The drivers are located in the Linux source code in `drivers/mmc/host`.

MMC storage is partitioned using a partition table in exactly the same way you would for hard disks, using `fdisk` or a similar utility.

Filesystems for flash memory

There are several challenges when making efficient use of flash memory for mass storage: the mismatch between the size of an erase block and a disk sector, the limited number of erase cycles per erase block, and the need for bad block handling on NAND chips. These differences are resolved by a **Flash translation layer**, or **FTL**.

Flash translation layers

A flash translation layer has the following features:

- **Sub allocation**: Filesystems work best with a small allocation unit, traditionally a 512-byte sector. This is much smaller than a flash erase block of 128 KiB or more. Therefore, erase blocks have to be subdivided into smaller units to avoid wasting large amounts of space.
- **Garbage collection**: A consequence of suballocation is that an erase block will contain a mixture of good data and stale data after the filesystem has been in use for a while. Since we can only free up whole erase blocks, the only way to reclaim the free space is to coalesce the good data into one place and return the now empty erase block to the free list: this is garbage collection, and is usually implemented as a background thread.
- **Wear leveling**: There is a limit on the number of erase cycles for each block. To maximize the lifespan of a chip, it is important to move data around so that each block is erased roughly the same number of times.
- **Bad block handling**: On NAND flash chips, you have to avoid using any block marked bad and also mark good blocks as bad if they cannot be erased.
- **Robustness**: Embedded devices may be powered off or reset without warning, so any filesystem should be able to cope without corruption, usually by incorporating a journal or log of transactions.

There are several ways to deploy the flash translation layer:

- **In the filesystem**: as with JFFS2, YAFFS2, and UBIFS
- **In the block device driver**: the UBI driver, on which UBIFS depends, implements some aspects of a flash translation layer
- **In the device controller**: as with managed flash devices

When the flash translation layer is in the filesystem or the block driver, the code is part of the kernel and so it is open source, meaning that we can see how it works and we can expect that it will be improved over time. On the other hand, if the FTL is inside a managed flash device, it is hidden from view and we cannot verify whether or not it works as we would want. Not only that, but putting the FTL into the disk controller means that it misses out on information that is held at the filesystem layer, such as which sectors belong to files that have been deleted and so do not contain useful data anymore. The latter problem is solved by adding commands that pass this information between the filesystem and the device. I will describe how this works in the section on the TRIM command later on. However, the question of code visibility remains. If you are using managed flash, you just have to choose a manufacturer you can trust.

Filesystems for NOR and NAND flash memory

To use raw flash chips for mass storage, you have to use a filesystem that understands the peculiarities of the underlying technology. There are three such filesystems:

- **JFFS2 (Journaling Flash File System 2)**: This was the first flash filesystem for Linux, and is still in use today. It works for NOR and NAND memory, but is notoriously slow during mount.
- **YAFFS2 (Yet Another Flash File System 2)**: This is similar to JFFS2, but specifically for NAND flash memory. It was adopted by Google as the preferred raw flash filesystem on Android devices.
- **UBIFS (Unsorted Block Image File System)**: This works in conjunction with the UBI block driver to create a reliable flash filesystem. It works well with both NOR and NAND memory, and since it generally offers better performance than JFFS2 or YAFFS2, it should be the preferred solution for new designs.

All of these use MTD as the common interface to flash memory.

JFFS2

The **Journaling Flash File System** had its beginnings in the software for the Axis 2100 network camera in 1999. For many years, it was the only flash filesystem for Linux and has been deployed on many thousands of different types of devices. Today, it is not the best choice, but I will cover it first because it shows the beginning of the evolutionary path.

JFFS2 is a log-structured filesystem that uses MTD to access flash memory. In a log-structured filesystem, changes are written sequentially as nodes to the flash memory. A node may contain changes to a directory, such as the names of files created and deleted, or it may contain changes to file data. After a while, a node may be superseded by information contained in subsequent nodes and becomes an obsolete node.

Erase blocks are categorized into three types:

- **Free**: This contains no nodes at all
- **Clean**: This contains only valid nodes
- **Dirty**: This contains at least one obsolete node

At any one time, there is one block receiving updates, which is called the open block. If power is lost or the system is reset, the only data that can be lost is the last write to the open block. In addition, nodes are compressed as they are written, increasing the effective storage capacity of the flash chip, which is important if you are using expensive NOR flash memory.

When the number of free blocks falls below a threshold, a garbage-collector kernel thread is started, which scans for dirty blocks, copies the valid nodes into the open block, and then frees up the dirty block.

At the same time, the garbage collector provides a crude form of wear leveling because it cycles valid data from one block to another. The way that the open block is chosen means that each block is erased roughly the same number of times so long as it contains data that changes from time to time. Sometimes a clean block is chosen for garbage collection to make sure that blocks containing static data that is seldom written are also wear-leveled.

JFFS2 filesystems have a write-through cache, meaning that writes are written to the flash memory synchronously as if they have been mounted with the -o sync option. While improving reliability, it does increase the time to write data. There is a further problem with small writes: if the length of a write is comparable to the size of the node header (40 bytes) the overhead becomes high. A well-known corner case is log files, produced, for example, by syslogd.

Summary nodes

There is one overriding disadvantage to JFFS2: since there is no on-chip index, the directory structure has to be deduced at mount-time by reading the log from start to finish. At the end of the scan, you have a complete picture of the directory structure of the valid nodes, but the time taken is proportional to the size of the partition. It is not uncommon to see mount times of the order of one second per megabyte, leading to total mount times of tens or hundreds of seconds.

To reduce the time to scan during mount, summary nodes became an option in Linux 2.6.15. A summary node is written at the end of the open erase block just before it is closed. The summary node contains all of the information needed for the mount-time scan, thereby reducing the amount of data to process during the scan. Summary nodes can reduce mount times by a factor of between two and five, at the expense of an overhead of about 5% of the storage space. They are enabled with the kernel configuration CONFIG_JFFS2_SUMMARY.

Clean markers

An erased block with all bits set to 1 is indistinguishable from a block that has been written with 1's, but the latter has not had its memory cells refreshed and cannot be programmed again until it is erased. JFFS2 uses a mechanism called **clean markers** to distinguish between these two situations. After a successful block erase, a clean marker is written, either to the beginning of the block or to the OOB area of the first page of the block. If the clean marker exists, then it must be a clean block.

Creating a JFFS2 filesystem

Creating an empty JFFS2 filesystem at runtime is as simple as erasing an MTD partition with clean markers and then mounting it. There is no formatting step because a blank JFFS2 filesystem consists entirely of free blocks. For example, to format MTD partition 6, you would enter these commands on the device:

```
# flash_erase -j /dev/mtd6 0 0
# mount -t jffs2 mtd6 /mnt
```

The -j option to flash_erase adds the clean markers, and mounting with type jffs2 presents the partition as an empty filesystem. Note that the device to be mounted is given as mtd6, not /dev/mtd6. Alternatively, you can give the block device node /dev/mtdblock6. This is just a peculiarity of JFFS2. Once mounted, you can treat it like any other filesystem.

You can create a filesystem image directly from the staging area of your development system using `mkfs.jffs2` to write out the files in JFFS2 format, and `sumtool` to add the summary nodes. Both of these are part of the `mtd-utils` package.

As an example, to create an image of the files in `rootfs` for a NAND flash device with an erase block size of 128 KiB (`0x20000`) and with summary nodes, you would use these two commands:

```
$ mkfs.jffs2 -n -e 0x20000 -p -d ~/rootfs -o ~/rootfs.jffs2
$ sumtool -n -e 0x20000 -p -i ~/rootfs.jffs2 -o ~/rootfs-sum.jffs2
```

The `-p` option adds padding at the end of the image file to make it a whole number of erase blocks. The `-n` option suppresses the creation of clean markers in the image, which is normal for NAND devices, as the clean marker is in the OOB area. For NOR devices, you would leave out the `-n` option. You can use a device table with `mkfs.jffs2` to set the permissions and the ownership of files by adding `-D [device table]`. Of course, Buildroot and the Yocto Project will do all this for you.

You can program the image into flash memory from your bootloader. For example, if you have loaded a filesytem image into RAM at address `0x82000000` and you want to load it into a flash partition that begins at `0x163000` bytes from the start of the flash chip and is `0x7a9d000` bytes long, the U-Boot commands would be:

```
nand erase clean 163000 7a9d000
nand write 82000000 163000 7a9d000
```

You can do the same thing from Linux using the mtd driver like this:

```
# flash_erase -j /dev/mtd6 0 0
# nandwrite /dev/mtd6 rootfs-sum.jffs2
```

To boot with a JFFS2 root filesystem, you need to pass the mtdblock device on the kernel command line for the partition and a `rootfstype` because JFFS2 cannot be auto-detected:

```
root=/dev/mtdblock6 rootfstype=jffs2
```

YAFFS2

The YAFFS filesystem was written by Charles Manning, beginning in 2001, specifically to handle NAND flash chips at a time when JFFS2 did not. Subsequent changes to handle larger (2 KiB) page sizes resulted in YAFFS2. The website for YAFFS is `http://www.yaffs.net`.

YAFFS is also a log-structured filesystem following the same design principles as JFFS2. The different design decisions mean that it has a faster mount-time scan, simpler and faster garbage collection, and has no compression, which speeds up reads and writes at the expense of less efficient use of storage.

YAFFS is not limited to Linux; it has been ported to a wide range of operating systems. It has a dual license: GPLv2 to be compatible with Linux, and a commercial license for other operating systems. Unfortunately, the YAFFS code has never been merged into mainline Linux, so you will have to patch your kernel.

To get YAFFS2 and patch a kernel, you would use this:

```
$ git clone git://www.aleph1.co.uk/yaffs2
$ cd yaffs2
$ ./patch-ker.sh c m <path to your link source>
```

Then, configure the kernel with CONFIG_YAFFS_YAFFS2.

Creating a YAFFS2 filesystem

As with JFFS2, to create a YAFFS2 filesystem at runtime, you only need to erase the partition and mount it, but note that in this case, you do not enable clean markers:

```
# flash_erase /dev/mtd/mtd6 0 0
# mount -t yaffs2 /dev/mtdblock6 /mnt
```

To create a filesystem image, the simplest thing to do is use the mkyaffs2 tool from https://code.google.com/p/yaffs2utils using the following command:

```
$ mkyaffs2 -c 2048 -s 64 rootfs rootfs.yaffs2
```

Here, -c is the page size and -s the OOB size. There is a tool named mkyaffs2image that is part of the YAFFS code, but it has a couple of drawbacks. Firstly, the page and OOB size are hard-coded in the source: you will have to edit and recompile if you have memory that does not match the defaults of 2,048 and 64. Secondly, the OOB layout is incompatible with MTD, which uses the first two bytes as a bad block marker, whereas mkyaffs2image uses those bytes to store part of the YAFFS metadata.

To copy the image to the MTD partition from a Linux shell prompt on the target, follow these steps:

```
# flash_erase /dev/mtd6 0 0
# nandwrite -a /dev/mtd6 rootfs.yaffs2
```

To boot with a YAFFS2 root filesystem, add the following to the kernel command line:

```
root=/dev/mtdblock6 rootfstype=yaffs2
```

UBI and UBIFS

The **Unsorted Block Image (UBI)** driver is a volume manager for flash memory that takes care of bad block handling and wear leveling. It was implemented by Artem Bityutskiy and first appeared in Linux 2.6.22. In parallel with that, engineers at Nokia were working on a filesystem that would take advantage of the features of UBI, which they called **UBIFS**; it appeared in Linux 2.6.27. Splitting the flash translation layer in this way makes the code more modular and also allows other filesystems to take advantage of the UBI driver, as we shall see later on.

UBI

UBI provides an idealized, reliable view of a flash chip by mapping **physical erase blocks (PEB)** to **logical erase blocks (LEB)**. Bad blocks are not mapped to LEBs and so are never used. If a block cannot be erased, it is marked as bad and dropped from the mapping. UBI keeps a count of the number of times each PEB has been erased in the header of the LEB and changes the mapping to ensure that each PEB is erased the same number of times.

UBI accesses the flash memory through the MTD layer. As an extra feature, it can divide an MTD partition into a number of UBI volumes, which improves wear leveling in the following way: Imagine that you have two filesystems, one containing fairly static data, for example a root filesystem, and the other containing data that is constantly changing.

If they are stored in separate MTD partitions, the wear leveling only has an effect on the second one, whereas if you choose to store them in two UBI volumes in a single MTD partition, the wear leveling takes place over both areas of the storage, and the lifetime of the flash memory is increased. The following diagram illustrates this situation:

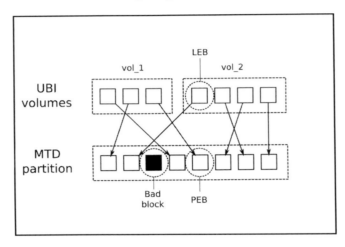

In this way, UBI fulfills two of the requirements of a flash translation layer: wear leveling and bad-block handling.

To prepare an MTD partition for UBI, you don't use `flash_erase` as with JFFS2 and YAFFS2. Instead, you use the `ubiformat` utility, which preserves the erase counts that are stored in the PEB headers. `ubiformat` needs to know the minimum unit of I/O, which for most NAND flash chips is the page size, but some chips allow reading and writing in sub pages that are a half or a quarter of the page size. Consult the chip data sheet for details and, if in doubt, use the page size. This example prepares `mtd6` using a page size of 2048 bytes:

```
# ubiformat /dev/mtd6 -s 2048
ubiformat: mtd0 (nand), size 134217728 bytes (128.0 MiB),
1024 eraseblocks of 131072 bytes (128.0 KiB),
min. I/O size 2048 bytes
```

Then you can use the `ubiattach` command to load the UBI driver on an MTD partition that has been prepared in this way:

```
# ubiattach -p /dev/mtd6 -O 2048
UBI device number 0, total 1024 LEBs (130023424 bytes, 124.0 MiB),
available 998 LEBs (126722048 bytes, 120.9 MiB),
LEB size 126976 bytes (124.0 KiB)
```

This creates the device node /dev/ubi0 through which you can access the UBI volumes. You can use ubiattach on several MTD partitions, in which case they can be accessed through /dev/ubi1, /dev/ubi2, and so on. Note that since each LEB has a header containing the meta information used by UBI, the LEB is smaller than the PEB by two pages. For example, a chip with a PEB size of 128 KiB and 2 KiB pages would have an LEB of 124 KiB. This is important information that you will need when creating a UBIFS image.

The PEB-to-LEB mapping is loaded into memory during the attach phase, a process that takes time proportional to the number of PEBs, typically a few seconds. A new feature was added in Linux 3.7 called the UBI fastmap, which checkpoints the mapping to flash from time to time and so reduces the attach time. The kernel configuration option is CONFIG_MTD_UBI_FASTMAP.

The first time you attach to an MTD partition after a ubiformat, there will be no volumes. You can create volumes using ubimkvol. For example, suppose you have a 128 MiB MTD partition and you want to split it into two volumes; the first is to be 32 MiB in size and the second will take up the remaining space:

```
# ubimkvol /dev/ubi0 -N vol_1 -s 32MiB
Volume ID 0, size 265 LEBs (33648640 bytes, 32.1 MiB),
LEB size 126976 bytes (124.0 KiB), dynamic, name "vol_1", alignment 1
# ubimkvol /dev/ubi0 -N vol_2 -m
Volume ID 1, size 733 LEBs (93073408 bytes, 88.8 MiB),
LEB size 126976 bytes (124.0 KiB), dynamic, name "vol_2", alignment 1
```

Now, you have a device with the nodes /dev/ubi0_0 and /dev/ubi0_1. You can confirm the situation using ubinfo:

```
# ubinfo -a /dev/ubi0
ubi0
Volumes count: 2
Logical eraseblock size: 126976 bytes, 124.0 KiB
Total amount of logical eraseblocks: 1024 (130023424 bytes, 124.0 MiB)
Amount of available logical eraseblocks: 0 (0 bytes)
Maximum count of volumes 128
Count of bad physical eraseblocks: 0
Count of reserved physical eraseblocks: 20
Current maximum erase counter value: 1
Minimum input/output unit size: 2048 bytes
Character device major/minor: 250:0
Present volumes: 0, 1

Volume ID: 0 (on ubi0)
Type: dynamic
Alignment: 1
Size: 265 LEBs (33648640 bytes, 32.1 MiB)
```

```
State: OK
Name: vol_1
Character device major/minor: 250:1
-----------------------------------
Volume ID: 1 (on ubi0)
Type: dynamic
Alignment: 1
Size: 733 LEBs (93073408 bytes, 88.8 MiB)
State: OK
Name: vol_2
Character device major/minor: 250:2
```

At this point, you have a 128 MiB MTD partition containing two UBI volumes of sizes 32 MiB and 88.8 MiB. The total storage available is 32 MiB plus 88.8 MiB, which equals 120.8 MiB. The remaining space, 7.2 MiB, is taken up by the UBI headers at the start of each PEB and space reserved for mapping out blocks that go bad during the lifetime of the chip.

UBIFS

UBIFS uses a UBI volume to create a robust filesystem. It adds sub-allocation and garbage collection to create a complete flash translation layer. Unlike JFFS2 and YAFFS2, it stores index information on-chip, and so mounting is fast, although don't forget that attaching the UBI volume beforehand may take a significant amount of time. It also allows write-back caching as in a normal disk filesystem, which means that writes are much faster, but with the usual problem of potential loss of data that has not been flushed from the cache to flash memory in the event of power down. You can resolve the problem by making careful use of the fsync(2) and fdatasync(2) functions to force a flush of file data at crucial points.

UBIFS has a journal for fast recovery in the event of power down. The minimum size of the journal is 4 MiB, so UBIFS is not suitable for very small flash devices.

Once you have created the UBI volumes, you can mount them using the device node for the volume, such as /dev/ubi0_0, or by using the device node for the whole partition plus the volume name, as shown here:

```
# mount -t ubifs ubi0:vol_1 /mnt
```

Creating a filesystem image for UBIFS is a two-stage process: first you create a UBIFS image using mkfs.ubifs, and then embed it into a UBI volume using ubinize.

For the first stage, `mkfs.ubifs` needs to be informed of the page size with `-m`, the size of the UBI LEB with `-e`, and the maximum number of erase blocks in the volume with `-c`. If the first volume is 32 MiB and an erase block is 128 KiB, then the number of erase blocks is 256. So, to take the contents of the directory rootfs and create a UBIFS image named rootfs.ubi, you would type the following:

```
$ mkfs.ubifs -r rootfs -m 2048 -e 124KiB -c 256 -o rootfs.ubi
```

The second stage requires you to create a configuration file for `ubinize`, which describes the characteristics of each volume in the image. The help page (`ubinize -h`) gives details of the format. This example creates two volumes, `vol_1` and `vol_2`:

```
[ubifsi_vol_1]
mode=ubi
image=rootfs.ubi
vol_id=0
vol_name=vol_1
vol_size=32MiB
vol_type=dynamic

[ubifsi_vol_2]
mode=ubi
image=data.ubi
vol_id=1
vol_name=vol_2
vol_type=dynamic
vol_flags=autoresize
```

The second volume has an `auto-resize` flag and so will expand to fill the remaining space on the MTD partition. Only one volume can have this flag. From this information, `ubinize` will create an image file named by the `-o` parameter, with the PEB size `-p`, the page size `-m`, and the sub-page size `-s`:

```
$ ubinize -o ~/ubi.img -p 128KiB -m 2048 -s 512 ubinize.cfg
```

To install this image on the target, you would enter these commands on the target:

```
# ubiformat /dev/mtd6 -s 2048
# nandwrite /dev/mtd6 /ubi.img
# ubiattach -p /dev/mtd6 -O 2048
```

If you want to boot with a UBIFS root filesystem, you would provide these kernel command-line parameters:

```
ubi.mtd=6 root=ubi0:vol_1 rootfstype=ubifs
```

Filesystems for managed flash

As the trend towards managed flash technologies continues, particularly eMMC, we need to consider how to use it effectively. While they appear to have the same characteristics as hard disk drives, the underlying NAND flash chips have the limitations of large erase blocks with limited erase cycles and bad block handling. And, of course, we need robustness in the event of losing power.

It is possible to use any of the normal disk filesystems, but we should try to choose one that reduces disk writes and has a fast restart after an unscheduled shutdown.

Flashbench

To make optimum use of the underlying flash memory, you need to know the erase block size and page size. Manufacturers do not publish these numbers as a rule, but it is possible to deduce them by observing the behavior of the chip or card.

Flashbench is one such tool. It was initially written by Arnd Bergman, as described in the LWN article available at `http://lwn.net/Articles/428584`. You can get the code from `https://github.com/bradfa/flashbench`.

Here is a typical run on a SanDisk 4GB SDHC card:

```
$ sudo ./flashbench -a  /dev/mmcblk0 --blocksize=1024
align 536870912 pre 4.38ms  on 4.48ms    post 3.92ms  diff 332µs
align 268435456 pre 4.86ms  on 4.9ms     post 4.48ms  diff 227µs
align 134217728 pre 4.57ms  on 5.99ms    post 5.12ms  diff 1.15ms
align 67108864  pre 4.95ms  on 5.03ms    post 4.54ms  diff 292µs
align 33554432  pre 5.46ms  on 5.48ms    post 4.58ms  diff 462µs
align 16777216  pre 3.16ms  on 3.28ms    post 2.52ms  diff 446µs
align 8388608   pre 3.89ms  on 4.1ms     post 3.07ms  diff 622µs
align 4194304   pre 4.01ms  on 4.89ms    post 3.9ms   diff 940µs
align 2097152   pre 3.55ms  on 4.42ms    post 3.46ms  diff 917µs
align 1048576   pre 4.19ms  on 5.02ms    post 4.09ms  diff 876µs
align 524288    pre 3.83ms  on 4.55ms    post 3.65ms  diff 805µs
align 262144    pre 3.95ms  on 4.25ms    post 3.57ms  diff 485µs
align 131072    pre 4.2ms   on 4.25ms    post 3.58ms  diff 362µs
align 65536     pre 3.89ms  on 4.24ms    post 3.57ms  diff 511µs
align 32768     pre 3.94ms  on 4.28ms    post 3.6ms   diff 502µs
align 16384     pre 4.82ms  on 4.86ms    post 4.17ms  diff 372µs
align 8192      pre 4.81ms  on 4.83ms    post 4.16ms  diff 349µs
align 4096      pre 4.16ms  on 4.21ms    post 4.16ms  diff 52.4µs
align 2048      pre 4.16ms  on 4.16ms    post 4.17ms  diff 9ns
```

The `flashbench` reads blocks of, in this case, 1,024 bytes just before and just after various power-of-two boundaries. As you cross a page or erase block boundary, the reads after the boundary take longer. The rightmost column shows the difference and is the one that is most interesting. Reading from the bottom, there is a big jump at 4 KiB, which is the most likely size of a page. There is a second jump from 52.4µs to 349µs at 8 KiB. This is fairly common and indicates that the card can use multi-plane accesses to read two 4 KiB pages at the same time. Beyond that, the differences are less well marked, but there is a clear jump from 485µs to 805µs at 512 KiB, which is probably the erase block size. Given that the card being tested is quite old, these are the sort of numbers you would expect.

Discard and TRIM

Usually, when you delete a file, only the modified directory node is written to storage, while the sectors containing the file's contents remain unchanged. When the flash translation layer is in the disk controller, as with managed flash, it does not know that this group of disk sectors no longer contains useful data and so it ends up copying stale data.

In the last few years, the addition of transactions that pass information about deleted sectors down to the disk controller has improved the situation. The SCSI and SATA specifications have a TRIM command and MMC has a similar command named ERASE. In Linux, this feature is known as **discard**.

To make use of discard, you need a storage device that supports it—most current eMMC chips do—and a Linux device driver to match. You can check by looking at the block system queue parameters in `/sys/block/<block device>/queue/`. The ones of interest are as follows:

- `discard_granularity`: The size of the internal allocation unit of the device
- `discard_max_bytes`: The maximum number of bytes that can be discarded in one go
- `discard_zeroes_data`: If 1, discarded data will be set to 0

If the device or the device driver do not support discard, these values are all set to 0. As an example, these are the parameters you will see from the 2 GiB eMMC chip on my BeagleBone Black:

```
# grep -s "" /sys/block/mmcblk0/queue/discard_*
/sys/block/mmcblk0/queue/discard_granularity:2097152
/sys/block/mmcblk0/queue/discard_max_bytes:2199023255040
/sys/block/mmcblk0/queue/discard_zeroes_data:1
```

There is more information in the kernel documentation file,
`Documentation/block/queue-sysfs.txt`.

You can enable discard when mounting a filesystem by adding the option `-o discard` to
the `mount` command. Both `ext4` and `F2FS` support it.

 Make sure that the storage device supports discard before using the `-o`
`discard` mount option, or data loss can occur.

It is also possible to force discard from the command line independently of how the
partition is mounted using the `fstrim` command, which is part of the `util-linux`
package. Typically, you would run this command periodically to free up unused space.
`fstrim` operates on a mounted filesystem, so to trim the root filesystem, /, you would type
the following:

```
# fstrim -v /
/: 2061000704 bytes were trimmed
```

The preceding example uses the verbose option, `-v`, so that it prints out the number of bytes
potentially freed up. In this case, 2,061,000,704 is the approximate amount of free space in
the filesystem, so it is the maximum amount of storage that could have been trimmed.

Ext4

The **extended filesystem, ext**, has been the main filesystem for Linux desktops since 1992.
The current version, **ext4**, is very stable and well tested and has a journal that makes
recovery from an unscheduled shutdown fast and mostly painless. It is a good choice for
managed flash devices and you will find that it is the preferred filesystem for Android
devices that have eMMC storage. If the device supports discard, you can mount with the
option `-o discard`.

To format and create an `ext4` filesystem at runtime, you would type the following:

```
# mkfs.ext4 /dev/mmcblk0p2
# mount -t ext4 -o discard /dev/mmcblk0p1 /mnt
```

To create a filesystem image at build time, you can use the `genext2fs` utility, available
from `http://genext2fs.sourceforge.net`. In this example, I have specified the block size
with `-B` and the number of blocks in the image with `-b`:

```
$ genext2fs -B 1024 -b 10000 -d rootfs rootfs.ext4
```

The `genext2fs` can make use of a device table to set the file permissions and ownership, as described in `Chapter 5`, *Building a Root Filesystem*, with `-D [file table]`.

As the name implies, this will actually generate an image in `Ext2` format. You can upgrade to `Ext4` using `tune2fs` as follows (details of the command options can be found in the manual page `tune2fs(8)`):

```
$ tune2fs -j -J size=1 -O filetype,extents,uninit_bg,dir_index \
  rootfs.ext4
$ e2fsck -pDf rootfs.ext4
```

Both the Yocto Project and Buildroot use exactly these steps when creating images in `Ext4` format.

While a journal is an asset for devices that may power down without warning, it does add extra write cycles to each write transaction, wearing out the flash memory. If the device is battery powered, especially if the battery is not removable, the chances of an unscheduled power down are small and so you may want to leave the journal out.

F2FS

The **Flash-Friendly File System**, known as **F2FS**, is a log-structured filesystem designed for managed flash devices, especially eMMC chips and SD cards. It was written by Samsung and was merged into mainline Linux in 3.8. It is marked experimental, indicating that it has not been extensively deployed as yet, but it seems that some Android devices are using it.

F2FS takes into account the page and erase block sizes and tries to align data on these boundaries. The log format provides resilience in the face of power down and also provides good write performance, in some tests showing a twofold improvement over `ext4`. There is a good description of the design of F2FS in the kernel documentation in `Documentation/filesystems/f2fs.txt`, and there are references at the end of the chapter.

The `mkfs.f2fs` utility creates an empty F2FS filesystem with the label `-l`:

```
# mkfs.f2fs -l rootfs /dev/mmcblock0p1
# mount -t f2fs /dev/mmcblock0p1 /mnt
```

There isn't (yet) a tool to create F2FS filesystem images offline.

FAT16/32

The old Microsoft filesystems, FAT16 and FAT32, continue to be important as a common format understood by most operating systems. When you buy an SD card or USB flash drive, it is almost certain to be formatted as FAT32 and, in some cases, the on-card microcontroller is optimized for FAT32 access patterns. Also, some boot ROMs require a FAT partition for the second-stage bootloader, the TI OMAP-based chips for example. However, FAT formats are definitely not suitable for storing critical files because they are prone to corruption and make poor use of the storage space.

Linux supports FAT16 through the msdos filesystem and both FAT32 and FAT16 through the vfat filesystem. To mount a device, say an SD card, on the second mmc hardware adapter, you would type this:

```
# mount -t vfat /dev/mmcblock1p1 /mnt
```

In the past, there have been licensing issues with the vfat driver, which may (or may not) infringe a patent held by Microsoft.

FAT32 has a limitation of 32 GiB on the device size. Devices of a larger capacity may be formatted using the Microsoft exFAT format, and it is a requirement for SDXC cards. There is no kernel driver for exFAT, but it can be supported by means of a userspace FUSE driver. Since exFAT is proprietary to Microsoft, there are bound to be licensing implications if you support this format on your device.

Read-only compressed filesystems

Compressing data is useful if you don't have quite enough storage to fit everything in. Both JFFS2 and UBIFS do on-the-fly data compression by default. However, if the files are never going to be written, as is usually the case with the root filesystem, you can achieve better compression ratios by using a read-only compressed filesystem. Linux supports several of these: romfs, cramfs, and squashfs. The first two are obsolete now, so I will describe only squashfs.

squashfs

The `squashfs` filesystem was written by Phillip Lougher in 2002 as a replacement for `cramfs`. It existed as a kernel patch for a long time, eventually being merged into mainline Linux in version 2.6.29 in 2009. It is very easy to use: you create a filesystem image using `mksquashfs` and install it to the flash memory:

```
$ mksquashfs rootfs rootfs.squashfs
```

The resulting filesystem is read-only, so there is no mechanism to modify any of the files at runtime. The only way to update a `squashfs` filesystem is to erase the whole partition and program in a new image.

`squashfs` is not bad-block aware and so must be used with reliable flash memory such as NOR flash. However, it can be used on NAND flash as long as you use UBI to create an emulated, reliable MTD. You have to enable the kernel configuration `CONFIG_MTD_UBI_BLOCK`, which will create a read-only MTD block device for each UBI volume. The following diagram shows two MTD partitions, each with accompanying `mtdblock` devices. The second partition is also used to create a UBI volume that is exposed as a third, reliable `mtdblock` device, which you can use for any read-only filesystem that is not bad-block aware:

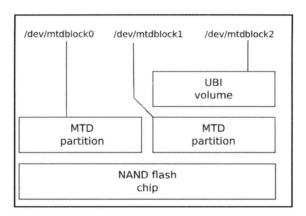

Temporary filesystems

There are always some files that have a short lifetime or have no significance after a reboot. Many such files are put into /tmp, and so it makes sense to keep these files from reaching permanent storage.

The temporary filesystem, tmpfs, is ideal for this purpose. You can create a temporary RAM-based filesystem by simply mounting tmpfs:

```
# mount -t tmpfs tmp_files /tmp
```

As with procfs and sysfs, there is no device node associated with tmpfs, so you have to supply a place-keeper string, tmp_files in the preceding example.

The amount of memory used will grow and shrink as files are created and deleted. The default maximum size is half the physical RAM. In most cases, it would be a disaster if tmpfs grew to be that large, so it is a very good idea to cap it with a -o size parameter. The parameter can be given in bytes, KiB (k), MiB (m), or GiB (g), like this, for example:

```
# mount -t tmpfs -o size=1m tmp_files /tmp
```

In addition to /tmp, some subdirectories of /var contain volatile data, and it is good practice to use tmpfs for them as well, either by creating a separate filesystem for each or, more economically, using symbolic links. Buildroot does it this way:

```
/var/cache -> /tmp
/var/lock ->  /tmp
/var/log ->   /tmp
/var/run ->   /tmp
/var/spool -> /tmp
/var/tmp ->   /tmp
```

In the Yocto Project, /run and /var/volatile are tmpfs mounts with symbolic links pointing to them, as shown here:

```
/tmp ->       /var/tmp
/var/lock ->  /run/lock
/var/log ->   /var/volatile/log
/var/run ->   /run
/var/tmp ->   /var/volatile/tmp
```

Making the root filesystem read-only

You need to make your target device able to survive unexpected events, including file corruption, and still be able to boot and achieve at least a minimum level of function. Making the root filesystem read-only is a key part of achieving this ambition because it eliminates accidental overwrites. Making it read-only is easy: replace rw with ro on the kernel command line or use an inherently read-only filesystem such as squashfs. However, you will find that there are a few files and directories that are traditionally writable:

- /etc/resolv.conf: This file is written by network configuration scripts to record the addresses of DNS name servers. The information is volatile, so you simply have to make it a symlink to a temporary directory, for example, /etc/resolv.conf -> /var/run/resolv.conf.

- /etc/passwd: This file, along with /etc/group, /etc/shadow, and /etc/gshadow, stores user and group names and passwords. They need to be symbolically linked to an area of persistent storage.

- /var/lib: Many applications expect to be able to write to this directory and to keep permanent data here as well. One solution is to copy a base set of files to a tmpfs filesystem at boot time and then bind mount /var/lib to the new location by putting a sequence of commands such as these into one of the boot scripts:

```
$ mkdir -p /var/volatile/lib
$ cp -a /var/lib/* /var/volatile/lib
$ mount --bind /var/volatile/lib /var/lib
```

- /var/log: This is the place where syslog and other daemons keep their logs. Generally, logging to flash memory is not desirable because of the many small write cycles it generates. A simple solution is to mount /var/log using tmpfs, making all log messages volatile. In the case of syslogd, BusyBox has a version that can log to a circular ring buffer.

If you are using the Yocto Project, you can create a read-only root filesystem by adding IMAGE_FEATURES = "read-only-rootfs" to conf/local.conf or to your image recipe.

Filesystem choices

So far we have looked at the technology behind solid-state memory and at the many types of filesystems. Now it is time to summarize the options. In most cases, you will be able to divide your storage requirements into these three categories:

- **Permanent, read-write data**: Runtime configuration, network parameters, passwords, data logs, and user data
- **Permanent, read-only data**: Programs, libraries, and configurations files that are constant, for example, the root filesystem
- **Volatile data**: Temporary storage, for example, /tmp

The choices for read-write storage are as follows:

- NOR: UBIFS or JFFS2
- NAND: UBIFS, JFFS2, or YAFFS2
- eMMC: ext4 or F2FS

For read-only storage, you can use any of these, mounted with the ro attribute. Additionally, if you want to save space, you could use squashfs. Finally, for volatile storage, there is only one choice, tmpfs.

Further reading

The following resources have further information about the topics introduced in this chapter:

- *XIP: The past, the present... the future?*, Vitaly Wool, presentation at FOSDEM 2007: https://archive.fosdem.org/2007/slides/devrooms/embedded/Vitaly_Wool _XIP.pdf
- *General MTD documentation*, http://www.linux-mtd.infradead.org/doc/gener al.html
- *Optimizing Linux with cheap flash drives*, Arnd Bergmann: http://lwn.net/Articl es/428584/
- *Flash memory card design*: https://wiki.linaro.org/WorkingGroups/KernelArc hived/Projects/FlashCardSurvey

- *eMMC/SSD File System Tuning Methodology*: `http://elinux.org/images/b/b6/E` `MMC-SSD_File_System_Tuning_Methodology_v1.0.pdf`
- *Flash-Friendly File System (F2FS)*: `http://elinux.org/images/1/12/Elc2013_Hwa` `ng.pdf`
- *An f2fS teardown*: `http://lwn.net/Articles/518988/`

Summary

Flash memory has been the storage technology of choice for embedded Linux from the beginning, and over the years, Linux has gained very good support, from low-level drivers up to flash-aware filesystems, the latest being UBIFS.

As the rate at which new flash technologies are introduced increases, it is becoming harder to keep pace with the changes at the high end. System designers are increasingly turning to managed flash in the form of eMMC to provide a stable hardware and software interface that is independent of the memory chips inside. Embedded Linux developers are beginning to get to grips with these new chips. Support for TRIM in ext4 and F2FS is well established, and it is slowly finding its way into the chips themselves. Also, the appearance of new filesystems that are optimized to manage flash, such as F2FS, is a welcome step forward.

However, the fact remains that flash memory is not the same as a hard disk drive. You have to be careful to minimize the number of filesystem writes—especially as the higher density TLC chips may be able to support as few as 1,000 erase cycles.

In the next chapter, I will continue on the theme of storage options as I consider different ways to keep the software up to date on devices that may be deployed to remote locations.

8
Updating Software in the Field

In previous chapters, we discussed various ways to build the software for a Linux device and also how to create system images for various types of mass storage. When you go into production, you just need to copy the system image to the flash memory and it is ready to be deployed. Now, I want to consider the life of the device beyond the first shipment.

As we move into the era of the *Internet of Things*, the devices that we create are very likely to be connected together by the internet. At the same time, the software is becoming exponentially more complex. More software means more bugs. Connection to the internet means those bugs can be exploited from afar. Consequentially, we have a common requirement to be able to update the software *in the field*. Software update brings more advantages than fixing bugs, however. It opens the door to adding value to existing hardware by improving system performance over time or enabling features.

There are many approaches to software update. Broadly, I characterize them as:

- Local update, often performed by a technician who carries the update on a portable medium such as a USB flash drive or an SD card, and has to access each system individually
- Remote update, where the update is initiated by the user or a technician locally, but it is downloaded from a remote server
- **Over-the-air (OTA)** update, where the update is pushed and managed entirely remotely, without any need for local input

I will begin by describing several approaches to software update, and then I will show an example using Mender (`https://mender.io`).

In this chapter, we will cover these topics:

- What to update?
- The basics of software update.
- Types of update mechanism.
- OTA updates.
- Using Mender for local updates.
- Using Mender for OTA updates.

What to update?

Embedded Linux devices are very diverse in their design and implementation. However, they all have these basic components:

- Bootloader
- Kernel
- Root filesystem
- System applications
- Device-specific data

Some components are harder to update than others, as summarized in this diagram:

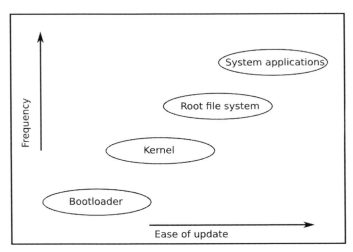

Let's look at each component in turn.

Bootloader

The bootloader is the first piece of code to run when the processor is powered up. The way the processor locates the bootloader is very device specific, but in most cases there is only one such location, and so there can only be one bootloader. If there is no backup, updating the bootloader is risky: what happens if the system powers down midway? Consequently, most update solutions leave the bootloader alone. This is not a big problem, because the bootloader only runs for a short time at power-on and is not normally a great source of run-time bugs.

Kernel

The Linux kernel is a critical component that will certainly need updating from time to time. There are several parts to the kernel:

- A binary image loaded by the bootloader, often stored in the root filesystem.
- Many devices also have a **Device Tree Binary** (**DTB**) that describes hardware to the kernel, and so has to be updated in tandem. The DTB is usually stored alongside the kernel binary.
- There may be kernel modules in the root filesystem.

The kernel and DTB may be stored in the root filesystem, so long as the bootloader has the ability to read that filesystem format, or it may be in a dedicated partition. In either case, it is possible to have redundant copies.

Root filesystem

The root filesystem contains the essential system libraries, utilities, and scripts needed to make the system work. It is very desirable to be able to replace and upgrade all of these. The mechanism depends on the implementation. Common formats for embedded root file systems are:

- Ramdisk, loaded from raw flash memory or a disk image at boot. To update it, you just need to overwrite the ramdisk image and reboot.
- Read-only compressed filesystems, such as `squashfs`, stored in a flash partition. Since these types of filesystem do not implement a write function, the only way to update them is to write a complete filesystem image to the partition.

- Normal filesystem types. For raw flash memory, JFFS2 and UBIFS formats are common, and for managed flash memory, such as eMMC and SD cards, the format is likely to be ext4 or F2FS. Since these are writable at runtime, it is possible to update them file by file.

System applications

The system applications are the main payload of the device; they implement its primary function. As such, they are likely to be updated frequently to fix bugs and to add features. They may be bundled with the root filesystem, but it is also common for them to be placed in a separate filesystem to make updating easier and to maintain separation between the system files, which are usually open source, and the application files, which are often proprietary.

Device-specific data

This is the combination of files that are modified at runtime, and includes configuration settings, logs, user-supplied data, and the like. It is not often that they need to be updated, but they do need to be preserved during an update. Such data needs to be stored in a partition of its own.

Components that need to be updated

In summary, then, an update may include new versions of the kernel, root filesystem, and system applications. The device will have other partitions that should not be disturbed by an update, as is the case with the device runtime data.

The basics of software update

Updating software seems, at first sight, to be a simple task: you just need to overwrite some files with new copies. But then your engineer's training kicks in as you begin to realize all the things that could go wrong. What if the power goes down during the update? What if a bug, not seen while testing the update, renders a percentage of the devices unbootable? What if a third party sends a fake update that enlists your device as part of a botnet? At the very least the software update mechanism must be:

- Robust, so that an update does not render the device unusable
- Fail-safe, so that there is a fall-back mode if all else fails
- Secure, to prevent the device from being hijacked by people installing unauthorized updates

In other words, we need a system that is not susceptible to Murphy's law, which states that if something can go wrong, then it will go wrong, eventually. Some of these problems are non-trivial, however.

Making updates robust

You might think that the problem of updating Linux systems was solved a long time ago-- we all have Linux desktops that we update regularly (don't we?). Also, there are vast numbers of Linux servers running in data centers that are similarly kept up to date. However, there is a difference between a server and a device. The former is operating in a protected environment. It is unlikely to suffer a sudden loss of power or network connectivity. In the unlikely event that an update does fail, it is always possible to get access to the server and use external mechanisms to repeat the install. Devices, on the other hand, are often deployed at remote sites with intermittent power and a poor network connections, which makes it much more likely that an update will be interrupted. Then, consider that it may be very expensive to get access to a device to take remedial action over a failed update if, for example, the device is an environmental monitoring station at the top of a mountain or controlling the valves of an oil well at the bottom of the sea. In consequence, it is much more important for embedded devices to have a robust update mechanism that will not result in the system becoming unusable.

The key word here is **atomicity**. The update as a whole must be atomic: there should be no stage at which part of the system is updated but not other parts. There must be a single, uninterruptible change to the system that switches to the new version of software.

This removes the most obvious update mechanism from consideration: that of simply updating individual files, for example, by extracting an archive over parts of the filesystem. There is just no way to ensure that there will be a consistent set of files if the system is reset during the update. Even using a package manager such as `apt`, `yum`, or `zypper` does not help. If you look at the internals of all these package mangers, you will see that they do indeed work by extracting an archive over the filesystem and running scripts to configure the package both before and after the update. Package managers are fine for the protected world of the data center, or even your desktop, but not for a device.

To achieve atomicity, the update must be installed alongside the running system, and then a switch thrown to move from the old to the new. In later sections, will describe two different approaches to achieving atomicity. The first is to have two copies of the root filesystem and other major components. One is live, while the other can receive updates. When the update is complete, the switch is thrown so that on reboot, the bootloader selects the updated copy. This is known as **symmetric image update**, or **A/B image update**. A variant of this theme is to use a special **recovery mode** operating system that is responsible for updating the main operating system. The guarantee of atomicity is shared between the bootloader and the recovery operating system. This is known as **asymmetric image update**. It is the approach taken in Android prior to the Nougat 7.x version.

The second approach is to have two or more copies of the root filesystem in different subdirectories of the system partition, and then use chroot(8) at boot time to select one of them. Once Linux is running, the update client can install updates into the other root filesystem, and then when everything is complete and checked, it can throw the switch and reboot. This is known as **atomic file update**, and is exemplified by **OSTree**.

Making updates fail-safe

The next problem to consider is that of recovering from an update that was installed correctly, but which contains code that stops the system from booting. Ideally, we want the system to detect this case and to revert to a previous working image.

There are several failure modes that can lead to a non-operational system. The first is a kernel panic, caused for example by a bug in a kernel device driver, or being unable to run the init program. A sensible place to start is by configuring the kernel to reboot a number of seconds after a panic. You can do this either when you build the kernel by setting CONFIG_PANIC_TIMEOUT or by setting the kernel command line to panic. For example, to reboot 5 seconds after a panic, you would add panic=5 to the kernel command line.

You may want to go further and configure the kernel to panic on an Oops. Remember that an Oops is generated when the kernel encounters a fatal error. In some cases, it will be able to recover from the error, in other cases not, but in all cases, something has gone wrong and the system is not working as it should. To enable panic on Oops in the kernel configuration, set CONFIG_PANIC_ON_OOPS=y or, on the kernel command line, oops=panic.

A second failure mode occurs when the kernel launches init successfully but for some reason the main application fails to run. For this, you need a watchdog. A watchdog is a hardware or software timer that restarts the system if the timer is not reset before it expires. If you are using systemd, you can use the inbuilt watchdog function, which I'll describe in `Chapter 10`, *Starting Up – The init Program*. If not, you may want to enable the watchdog support built into Linux, as described in the kernel source code in `Documentation/watchdog`.

Both failures result in **boot loops**: either a kernel panic or a watchdog timeout causes the system to reboot. If the problem is persistent, the system will reboot continually. To break out of the boot loop, we need some code in the bootloader to detect the case and to revert to the previous, known good, version. A typical approach is to use a **boot count** that is incremented by the bootloader on each boot, and which is reset to zero in user space once the system is up and running. If the system enters a boot loop, the counter is not reset and so continues to increase. Then, the bootloader is configured to take remedial action if the counter exceeds a threshold.

In U-Boot, this is handled by three variables:

- `bootcount`: This variable is incremented each time the processor boots

- `bootlimit`: If the `bootcount` exceeds the `bootlimit`, U-Boot runs the commands in `altbootcmd` instead of `bootcmd`

- `altbootcmd`: This contains the alternative boot commands, for example to roll back to a previous version of software or to start the recovery-mode operating system

For this to work, there must be a way for a user space program to reset the boot count. We can do that using U-Boot utilities that allow the U-Boot environment to be accessed at runtime:

- `fw_printenv`: Prints the value of a U-Boot variable
- `fw_setenv`: Sets the value of a U-Boot variable

These two commands need to know where the U-Boot environment block is stored, for which there is a configuration file in /etc/fw_env.config. For example, if the U-Boot environment is stored at offset 0x800000 from the start of the eMMC memory, with a backup copy at 0x1000000, then the configuration would look like this:

```
# cat /etc/fw_env.config
/dev/mmcblk0 0x800000 0x40000
/dev/mmcblk0 0x1000000 0x40000
```

There is one final thing to cover in this section. Incrementing the boot count on each boot and then resetting it when the application begins to run leads to unnecessary writes to the environment block, wearing out the flash memory and slowing down system initialization. To prevent having to do this on all reboots, U-Boot has a further variable named upgrade_available. If upgrade_available is 0, then bootcount is not incremented. upgrade_available is set to 1 after an update has been installed so that the boot count protection is in use only when it is needed.

Making updates secure

The final problem relates to the potential misuse of the update mechanism itself. Your prime intention when implementing an update mechanism is to provide a reliable, automated or semi-automated method to install security patches and new features. However, others may use the same mechanism to install unauthorized versions of software and so *hijack* the device. We need to look at how we can ensure that this cannot happen.

The biggest vulnerability is that of a fake remote update. To prevent this, we need to authenticate the update server before starting the download. We also need a secure transfer channel, such as HTTPS, to guard against tampering with the download stream. I will return to this when describing OTA updates later on.

There is also the question of the authenticity of updates supplied locally. One way to detect a bogus update is to use a secure boot protocol in the bootloader. If the kernel image is signed at the factory with a digital key, the bootloader can check the key before it loads the kernel and refuse to load it if the keys do not match. So long as the keys are kept private by the manufacturer, it will not be possible to load a kernel that is not authorized. U-Boot implements such a mechanism, which is described in the U-Boot source code in doc/uImage.FIT/verified-boot.txt.

Secure boot: good or bad?
If I have purchased a device that has a software update feature, then I am trusting the vendor of that device to deliver useful updates. I definitely do not want a malicious third party to install software without my knowledge. But should I be allowed to install software myself? If I own the device outright, should I not be entitled to modify it, including loading new software? Recall the TiVo set-top box, which ultimately led to the creation of the GPL v3 license. Remember also the Lynksys WRT54G Wi-Fi router: when access to the hardware became easy, it spawned a whole new industry, including the OpenWrt project. See, for example, `http://www.wi-fiplanet.com/tutorials/article.php/3562391` for more details. This is a complex issue that sits at the crossroads between freedom and control. It is my opinion that some device manufacturers use security as an excuse to protect their, sometimes shoddy, software.

Types of update mechanism

In this section, I will describe three approaches to applying software updates: symmetric, or A/B, image update; asymmetric image update, also known as **recovery mode update**; and finally, atomic file update.

Symmetric image update

In this scheme, there are two copies of the operating system, each comprising the Linux kernel, root filesystem, and system applications. They are labelled as **A** and **B** in the following diagram:

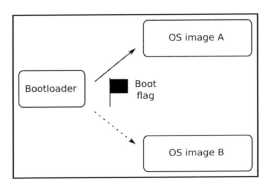

The bootloader has a flag that indicates which it should load. Initially, the flag is set to **A**, so the bootloader, loads **OS image A**. To install an update, the updater application, which is part of the operating system, overwrites **OS image B**. When complete, it changes the **Boot flag** to B and reboots. Now the bootloader will load the new operating system. When a further update is installed, the updater overwrites **image A** and changes the **Boot flag** to **A**, and so you ping-pong between the two copies. If an update fails before the **Boot flag** is changed, the bootloader continues to load the good operating system.

There are several open source projects that implement symmetric image update. One is the **Mender** client operating in standalone mode, which I will describe later on in this chapter. Another is **SWUpdate** (`https://github.com/sbabic/swupdate`). SWUpdate can receive multiple image updates in a CPIO format package and then deploy those updates to different parts of the system. It allows you to write plugins in the LUA language to do custom processing. It has filesystem support for raw flash memory that is accessed as MTD flash partitions, for storage organized into UBI volumes, and for SD/eMMC storage with a disk partition table. A third example is **RAUC**, the **Robust Auto-Update Controller**, (`https://github.com/rauc/rauc`). It too has support for raw flash storage, UBI volumes, and SD/eMMC devices. The images can be signed and verified using OpenSSL keys.

There are some drawbacks with this scheme. One is that by updating an entire filesystem image, the size of the update package is large, which can put a strain on the network infrastructure connecting the devices. This can be mitigated by sending only the filesystem blocks that have changed by performing a binary `diff` of the new filesystem with the previous version, although none of the previously mentioned projects implement this at the time of writing.

A second drawback is the need to keep storage space for a redundant copy of the root filesystem and other components. If the root filesystem is the largest component, it comes close to doubling the amount of flash memory you need to fit. It is for this reason that the asymmetric update scheme is used, which I describe next.

Asymmetric image update

You can reduce storage requirements by keeping a minimal *recovery* operating system purely for updating the main one, as shown here:

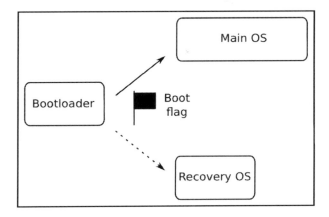

When you want to install an update, set the **Boot flag** to point to the **Recovery OS** and reboot. Once the **Recovery OS** is running, it can stream updates to the main operating system image. If the update is interrupted, the **Bootloader** will again boot into the **Recovery OS**, which can resume the update. Only when the update is complete and verified will the **Recovery OS** clear the **Boot flag** and reboot again, this time loading the new main operating system. Fallback in the case of a correct but buggy update is to drop the system back into recovery mode, which can attempt remedial actions, possibly by requesting an earlier update version.

The **Recovery OS** is usually a lot smaller than the main operating system, maybe only a few megabytes, and so the storage overhead is not great. As a matter of interest, this is the scheme that was adopted by Android prior to the Nougat release. For open source implementations of asymmetric image update, you could consider **SWUpdate** or **RAUC**, both of which I mentioned in the previous section.

The major drawback of this scheme is that while the **Recovery OS** is running, the device it not operational.

Atomic file updates

Another approach is to have redundant copies of a root filesystem present in multiple directories of a single filesystem and then use the chroot(8) command to choose one of them at boot time. This allows one directory tree to be updated while another is mounted as the root directory. Furthermore, rather than making copies of files that have not changed between versions of the root filesystem, you could use links. That would save a lot of disk spacew2 and reduce the amount of data to be downloaded in an update package. These are the basic ideas behind atomic file update.

The `chroot` command runs a program in an existing directory. The program sees this directory as its `root` directory, and so cannot access any files or directories at a higher level. It is often used to run a program in a constrained environment, which is sometimes refereed to a **chroot jail**.

The *OSTree* project (`https://ostree.readthedocs.org/en/latest/`), now renamed **libOSTree**, is the most popular implementation of this idea. OSTree started around 2011 as a means of deploying updates to the GNOME desktop developers, and to improve their continuous integration testing (`https://wiki.gnome.org/Projects/GnomeContinuous`). It has since been adopted as an update solution for embedded devices. It is one of the update methods available in **Automotive Grade Linux** (**AGL**), and it is available in the Yocto Project through the `meta-update` layer, which is supported by **Advanced Telematic Systems** (**ATS**).

With OSTree, the files are stored on the target in directory `/ostree/repo/objects`. They are given names such that several version of the same file can exist in the repository. Then, a given set of files are linked into a deployment directory, which has a name such as `/ostree/deploy/os/29ff9.../`. This is refereed to as *checking out*, since it has some similarities to the way a branch is checked out of a Git repository. Each deploy directory contains the files that make up a root filesystem. There can be any number of them, but by default there are only two. For example, here are two deploy directories, each with links back into the `repo` directory.

```
/ostree/repo/objects/...
/ostree/deploy/os/a3c83.../
   /usr/bin/bash
   /usr/bin/echo
/ostree/deploy/os/29ff9.../
   /usr/bin/bash
   /usr/bin/echo
```

The bootloader boots the kernel with an `initramfs`, passing on the kernel command-line the path of the deployment to use:

```
bootargs=ostree=/ostree/deploy/os/deploy/29ff9...
```

The `initramfs` contains an `init` program, `ostree-init`, which reads the command line and executes the `chroot` to the path given.

When a system update is installed, the files that have changed are downloaded into the `repo` directory by the OSTree install agent. When complete, a new deploy directory is created, with links to the collection of files that will make up the new root filesystem. Some of these will be new files, some will be the same as before.

Finally, it will change the bootloader's boot flag so that on the next reboot it will `chroot` to the new deploy directory. The bootloader implements the check on boot count and falls back to the previous root if a boot loop is detected.

OTA updates

Updating OTA means having the ability to push software to a device or group of devices via a network, usually without any end user interaction with the device. For this to happen we need a central server to control the update process and a protocol for downloading the update to the update client. In a typical implementation, the client polls the update server from time to time to check if there are any updates pending. The polling interval needs to be long enough that the poll traffic does not take a significant portion of the network bandwidth, but short enough that the updates can be delivered in a timely fashion. An interval of tens of minutes to several hours is often a good compromise. The poll messages from the device contain some sort of unique identifier, such a serial number or MAC address, and the current software version. From this the update server can see if an update is needed. The poll messages may also contain other status information, such as up time, environmental parameters or anything that would be useful for central management of the devices.

The update server it usually linked to a management system that will assign new versions of software to the various populations of devices under its control. If the device population is large it may send updates in batches to avoid overloading the network. There will be some soft of status display where the current state of the devices can be shown and problems highlighted.

Of course, the update mechanism must be secure so that fake updates cannot be sent to the end devices. This involves the client and server being able to authenticate each other by an exchange of certificates. Then the client can validate the packages downloaded are signed by the key that is expected.

Here are two examples of open source projects that you can use for OTA update:

- Mender in managed mode
- The hawkBit (`https://projects.eclipse.org/proposals/hawkbit`) in conjunction with an updater client such as SWUpdate or RAUC

Using Mender for local updates

So much for the theory. In the last two sections of this chapter I want to demonstrate the principles I have talked about so far with examples of software update working in practice. As the basis of the example I will be using Mender. Mender uses a symmetric **A/B** image update mechanism, with fall-back in the case of a failed update. It can operate in a *standalone mode* for local updates, or in *managed mode* for OTA updates. I will begin with the standalone mode.

Mender is written and supported by `mender.io` (`https://mender.io`). There is much more information about the software in the documentation section of the web site. I will not delve deeply into the configuration of the software here, since my aim is to illustrate the principles of software update.

Building the Mender client

The Mender client is available as a Yocto Project meta layer. These examples use the Morty release of the Yocto Project, which is the same one that we used in `Chapter 6`, *Selecting a Build System*. We begin by getting the `meta-mender` layer, and also `oe-meta-go` because the Mender client is written in the Go language:

```
$ cd poky
$ git clone git://github.com/mem/oe-meta-go
$ git clone -b morty git://github.com/mendersoftware/meta-mender
```

The Mender client requires some changes to the configuration of U-Boot to handle the boot flag and boot count variables. The stock Mender client layer has sub-layers for three sample implementations of this U-Boot integration that we can use straight out of the box: `meta-mender-beaglebone`, `meta-mender-qemu`, `meta-mender-raspberrypi`. We will be using QEMU. The next step, therefore, is to create a build directory and add the layers for this configuration:

```
$ source oe-init-build-env build-mender-qemu
$ bitbake-layers add-layer ../oe-meta-go
$ bitbake-layers add-layer ../meta-mender/meta-mender-core
$ bitbake-layers add-layer ../meta-mender/meta-mender-demo
$ bitbake-layers add-layer ../meta-mender/meta-mender-qemu
```

We need to set up the environment by adding some settings to `conf/local.conf`:

```
1   MENDER_ARTIFACT_NAME = "release-1"
2   INHERIT += "mender-full"
3   MACHINE = "vexpress-qemu"
4   DISTRO_FEATURES_append = " systemd"
5   VIRTUAL-RUNTIME_init_manager = "systemd"
6   DISTRO_FEATURES_BACKFILL_CONSIDERED = "sysvinit"
7   VIRTUAL-RUNTIME_initscripts = ""
8   IMAGE_FSTYPES = "ext4"
```

Line 2 includes a BitBake class, named `mender-full`, which is responsible for the special processing of the image required to create the **A/B** image format. Line 3 selects a machine named `vexpress-qemu`, which uses QEMU to emulate an ARM Versatile Express board, rather than the Versatile PB that is the default in the Yocto Project. Lines 4 to 7 select systemd as the init daemon in place of the default System V `init`. I describe init daemons in more detail in `Chapter 10`, *Starting Up – The init Program*. Line 8 causes the root filesystem images to be generated in `ext4` format.

Now we can build an image:

```
$ bitbake core-image-full-cmdline
```

As usual, the results of the build are in `tmp/deploy/images/vexpress-qemu`. You will notice some new things in here compared to the Yocto Project builds we have done previously. There is a file named `core-image-full-cmdline-vexpress-qemu-[time stamp].mender`, and another similarly named file that ends with `sdimg`. The `mender` file will be required when we perform an update later on: I will talk more about it then. The `sdimg` file is created using a tool from the Yocto Project known as `wic`. The output is an image that contains a partition table and which is ready to be copied directly to an SD card or eMMC chip.

We can run the QEMU target using the script provided by the Mender layer, which will first boot U-Boot and then load the Linux kernel:

```
$ ../meta-mender/meta-mender-qemu/scripts/mender-qemu
[...]
[  OK  ] Started Mender OTA update service.
[  OK  ] Reached target Multi-User System.
Poky (Yocto Project Reference Distro) 2.2.1 vexpress-qemu ttyAMA0

vexpress-qemu login:
```

Log on as `root`, no password. Looking at the layout of the partitions on the target, we can see this:

```
# fdisk -l /dev/mmcblk0
Disk /dev/mmcblk0: 384 MiB, 402653184 bytes, 786432 sectors
[...]

Device         Boot   Start    End  Sectors  Size Id Type
/dev/mmcblk0p1 *      49152  81919    32768   16M  c W95 FAT32 (LBA)
/dev/mmcblk0p2        81920 294911   212992  104M 83 Linux
/dev/mmcblk0p3       294912 507903   212992  104M 83 Linux
/dev/mmcblk0p4       524287 786431   262145  128M  f W95 Ext'd (LBA)
/dev/mmcblk0p5       524288 786431   262144  128M 83 Linux
```

There are 5 partitions in all:

- **Partition 1**: This contains the U-Boot boot files
- **Partitions 2 and 3**: This contain the A/B root filesystems: at this stage, they are identical
- **Partition 4**: This is just an extension partition that contains the remaining partitions
- **Partition 5**: This contains a writable partition that stores the device-specific data that must not be overwritten during an image update

Running the `mount` command shows that the second partition is being used as the root filesystem, leaving the third to receive updates:

```
# mount
/dev/mmcblk0p2 on / type ext4 (rw,relatime,data=ordered)
[...]
```

Installing an update

Now we want make a change to the root filesystem and then install it as an update.

We will begin by taking a copy of the image we just built. This will be the live image that we are going to update. If we don't do this, the QEMU script will just load the latest image generated by BitBake, including updates, which defeats the object of the demonstration:

```
$ cd tmp/deploy/images/vexpress-qemu
$ cp core-image-full-cmdline-vexpress-qemu.sdimg \
core-image-live-vexpress-qemu.sdimg
$ cd -
```

We are just going to change the hostname of the target, which will be easy to see when it is installed. To do this, edit `conf/local.conf` and add this line:

```
hostname_pn-base-files = "vexpress-qemu-release2"
```

We can build it in the same way as before:

```
$ bitbake core-image-full-cmdline
```

This time we are not interested in the `sdimg` file, which contains a complete new image. Instead we want to take only the new root filesystem, which is in `core-image-full-cmdline-vexpress-qemu.mender`. The `mender` file is in a format that is recognized by the Mender client. The `mender` file format consists of version information, a header, and the root filesystem image put together in a compressed `.tar` archive.

The next step is to deploy the new artifact to the target, initiating the update locally on the device, but receiving the update from a server. So, boot QEMU using the original image:

```
$ ../meta-mender/meta-mender-qemu/scripts/mender-qemu \
core-image-live
```

Check that the network is configured, with QEMU at `10.0.2.15`, and the host at `10.0.2.2`:

```
# ping -c1 10.0.2.2
PING 10.0.2.2 (10.0.2.2) 56(84) bytes of data.
64 bytes from 10.0.2.2: icmp_seq=1 ttl=255 time=0.326 ms
--- 10.0.2.2 ping statistics ---
1 packets transmitted, 1 received, 0% packet loss, time 0ms
rtt min/avg/max/mdev = 0.326/0.326/0.326/0.000 ms
```

Now, in another Terminal session, start a web server on the host that can serve up the update:

```
$ cd  tmp/deploy/images/vexpress-qemu
$ python -m SimpleHTTPServer
Serving HTTP on 0.0.0.0 port 8000 ...
```

 It is listening on port `8000`. When you are done with the web server, type `Ctrl-C` to terminate it.

Back on the target, issue this command to get the update:

```
# mender -log-level info -rootfs \
http://10.0.2.2:8000/core-image-full-cmdline-vexpress-qemu.mender
[...]
INFO[0104] wrote 109051904/109051904 bytes of update to device
/dev/mmcblk0p3  module=device 100% 37132 KiB
INFO[0106] Enabling partition with new image installed to be a
boot candidate: 3 module=device
```

 The update was written to the third partition, /dev/mmcblk0p3, while our root filesystem is still on partition 2, mmcblk0p2.

Reboot QEMU. Note that now the root filesystem is mounted on partition 3, and that the hostname has changed:

```
# mount
/dev/mmcblk0p3 on / type ext4 (rw,relatime,data=ordered)
[...]
# hostname
vexpress-qemu-release2
```

Success!

There is one more thing to do. We need to consider the issue of boot loops. Using fw-printenv to look at the U-Boot variables, we see:

```
# fw_printenv upgrade_available
upgrade_available=1
# fw_printenv bootcount
bootcount=1
# fw_printenv bootlimit
bootlimit=1
```

If the system reboots without clearing the boot count, U-Boot should detect it and fall-back to the previous installation. Let's try it out by rebooting the target right away.

When the target comes up again, we see that has indeed happened:

```
# mount
/dev/mmcblk0p2 on / type ext4 (rw,relatime,data=ordered)
[...]
# hostname
vexpress-qemu
```

Now, let's repeat the update procedure, but this time, after the reboot, `commit` the change:

```
# mender -commit
[...]
# fw_printenv upgrade_available
upgrade_available=0
# fw_printenv bootcount
bootcount=1
# fw_printenv bootlimit
bootlimit=1
```

Once `upgrade_available` is cleared, U-Boot will no longer check bootcount, and so the device will continue to mount this updated root filesystem. When a further update is loaded, the Mender client will clear `bootcount` and set `upgrade_available` once again.

This example uses the Mender client from the command line to initiate an update locally. The update itself came from a server, but could just as easily have been provided on a USB flash drive or an SD card. In place of Mender, we could have used the other image update clients mentioned: SWUpdate or RAUC. They each have their advantages, but the basic technique is the same.

Using Mender for OTA updates

The next stage is to see how OTA updates work in practice. Once again we will be using the Mender client on the device, but this time operating it in *managed mode*, and in addition we will be configuring a server to deploy the update, so that no local interaction is needed. Mender provide an open source server for this.

The installation requires Docker Engine version 17.0.3 or later to be installed. Refer to the Docker website at `https://docs.docker.com/engine/installation`. It also requires Docker Compose version 1.6, as described here: `https://docs.docker.com/compose/install/`. Once they are installed, you can install Mender integration environment:

```
$ curl -L \
https://github.com/mendersoftware/integration/archive/1.0.1.tar.gz | tar xz
$ cd integration-1.0.1
$ ./up
```

Once you run the `up` script you will see that it downloads several hundreds of megabytes of Docker images, which may take some time, depending on your internet connection speed. After a while, you will see that it boots a copy of the Mender client running in a QEMU emulation.

This means that the server is up and running. Do not be mislead by the rather verbose message logging, which makes it appear to be busy downloading still when it has in fact finished.

The Mender web interface is now running on `https://localhost/`. Copy that URL into a web browser and accept the certificate warning that pops up. This is because the web service is using a self-signed certificate that the browser will not recognize. Then create a test user account:

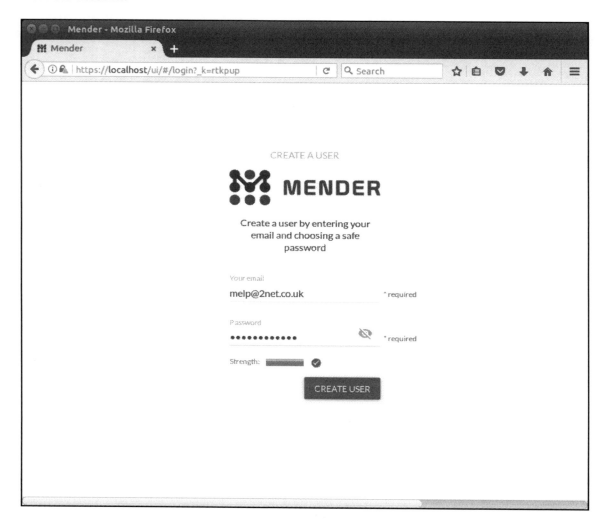

On the Dashboard, you will see that there is one device waiting for authorization. This is the QEMU client that is started by the `./up` script, not the one we created. Click on the *green* arrow to authorize it.

We need to make a change to the configuration of the target so that it will poll our local server for updates. For this demonstration, the server URL is going to be `s3.docker.mender.io`, which we map to the address `localhost` by appending a line to the hosts file. They way to do this with the Yocto Project is to create a layer with a file that appends to the recipe that creates the hosts file, which is `meta/recipes-core/netbase/netbase_5.3.bb`. There is a suitable layer in `MELP/chapter_08/meta-ota`:

```
$ cd poky
$ cp -a MELP/chapter_08/meta-ota
$ source oe-init-build-env build-mender-qemu
$ bitbake-layers add-layer ../meta-ota
```

Build the new image using the following command:

```
$ bitbake core-image-full-cmdline
```

Then take a copy. This will become our live image for this section:

```
$ cd tmp/deploy/images/vexpress-qemu
$ cp core-image-full-cmdline-vexpress-qemu.sdimg \
core-image-live-ota-vexpress-qemu.sdimg
$ cd -
```

Boot up the QEMU build that we created earlier in this section:

```
$ ../meta-mender/meta-mender-qemu/scripts/mender-qemu \
core-image-live-ota
```

After a few seconds, you will see a new device appear in the dashboard of the web interface. This happens so quickly because for the purposes of demonstrating the system, the Mender client has been configured to poll the server every 5 seconds. A much longer polling interval would be used in production: 30 minutes is suggested. You can see how this is configured by looking at the file `/etc/mender/mender.conf` on the target:

```
{
  "ClientProtocol": "http",
  "HttpsClient": {
    "Certificate": "",
    "Key": ""
  },
  "RootfsPartA": "/dev/mmcblk0p2",
```

```
    "RootfsPartB": "/dev/mmcblk0p3",
    "UpdatePollIntervalSeconds": 5,
    "InventoryPollIntervalSeconds": 5,
    "RetryPollIntervalSeconds": 1,
    "ServerURL": "https://docker.mender.io",
    "ServerCertificate": "/etc/mender/server.crt"
}
```

Also in there you can see the server URL, and that the server certificate has been set to the default, `server.crt`.

In the web user interface, click the *green* icon to authorize the new device, and then click on the entry for the device to see the details:

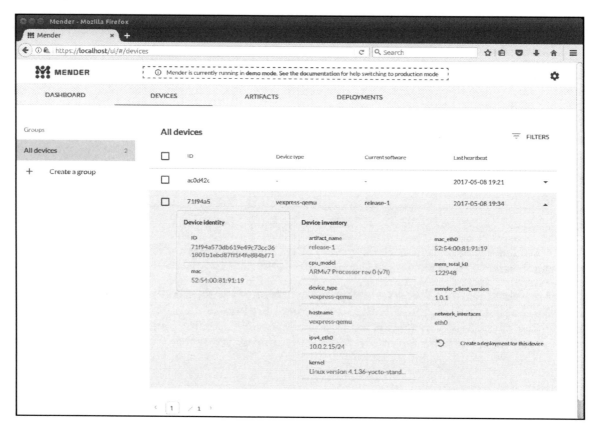

Now, we can once again create an update and deploy it, this time OTA. `conf/local.conf`:

```
MENDER_ARTIFACT_NAME = "OTA-update1"
```

Build it once again, producing a new `core-image-full-cmdline-vexpress-qemu.mender` in `tmp/deploy/images`. Then import this into the web interface by clicking on the **Artifacts** tab and navigating to the directory containing the update. It should copy it into the server data store, and it should appear as a new artifact with the name `OTA-update1`.

To deploy the update to our QEMU device. Click on the **Devices** tab, and select the device. Click on the **Create a deployment for this device** option at the bottom right of the device information, and select the `OTA-update1` artifact. It should become a **Pending** deployment, and then an **In progress** deployment. After a while the QEMU client should have written the update to the spare file system image and then it will reboot and commit the update. The web UI should now report it as a **Past deployment**, and now the client is running `OTA-update1`.

After a few experiments with the server you may want to clear the state and start all over again. You can do that with these three commands, entered in the directory `integration-1.0.1/`:

- `./stop`
- `./reset`
- `./up`

Summary

Being able to update the software on devices in the field is at the very least a useful attribute, and if the device is connected to the internet, it becomes an absolute must. And yet, all too often it is a feature that is left until the last part of a project, on the assumption that it is not a hard problem to solve. In this chapter, I hope that I have illustrated the problems that are associated with designing an effective and robust update mechanism, and also that there are several open-source options readily available. You do not have to reinvent the wheel any more.

The approach used most often, and also the one with most real-world testing, is the symmetric image (**A/B**) update, or its cousin the asymmetric (recovery) image update. Here, you have the choice of SWUpdate, RAUC, and Mender. A more recent innovation is the atomic file update, in the form of OSTree. This has good characteristics in reducing the amount of data that needs to be downloaded and of redundant storage that needs to be fitted on the target.

It is quite common to deploy updates on a small scale by visiting each site and applying the update from a USB memory stick or SD card. But, if you want to deploy to remote locations, or deploy at scale, an Over The Air update option will be needed.

The next chapter describes how you control the hardware components of your system through the use of device drivers, both in the conventional sense of drivers that are part of the kernel, and also the extent to which you can control hardware from the user space.

Interfacing with Device Drivers

9

Kernel device drivers are the mechanism through which the underlying hardware is exposed to the rest of the system. As a developer of embedded systems, you need to know how these device drivers fit into the overall architecture and how to access them from user space programs. Your system will probably have some novel pieces of hardware, and you will have to work out a way of accessing them. In many cases, you will find that there are device drivers provided for you, and you can achieve everything you want without writing any kernel code. For example, you can manipulate GPIO pins and LEDs using files in sysfs, and there are libraries to access serial buses, including **SPI (Serial Peripheral Interface)** and **I²C (Inter-Integrated Circuit)**.

There are many places to find out how to write a device driver, but few to tell you why you would want to and the choices you have in doing so. This is what I want to cover here. However, remember that this is not a book dedicated to writing kernel device drivers and that the information given here is to help you navigate the territory but not necessarily to set up home there. There are many good books and articles that will help you to write device drivers, some of which are listed at the end of this chapter.

In this chapter we will cover the following topics:

- The role of device drivers
- Character devices
- Block devices
- Network devices
- Finding out about drivers at runtime
- Finding the right device driver
- Device drivers in user space
- Writing a kernel device driver
- Discovering the hardware configuration

The role of device drivers

As I mentioned in Chapter 4, *Configuring and Building the Kernel*, one of the functions of the kernel is to encapsulate the many hardware interfaces of a computer system and present them in a consistent manner to user space programs. The kernel has frameworks designed to make it easy to write a device driver, which is the piece of code that mediates between the kernel above and the hardware below. A device driver maybe written to control physical devices such as a UART or an MMC controller, or it may represent a virtual device such as the null device (/dev/null) or a ramdisk. One driver may control multiple devices of the same kind.

Kernel device driver code runs at a high privilege level, as does the rest of the kernel. It has full access to the processor address space and hardware registers. It can handle interrupts and DMA transfers. It can make use of the sophisticated kernel infrastructure for synchronization and memory management. However, you should be aware that there is a downside to this; if something goes wrong in a buggy driver, it can go really wrong and bring the system down. Consequently, there is a principle that device drivers should be as simple as possible by just providing information to applications where the real decisions are made. You often hear this being expressed as *no policy in the kernel*. It is the responsibility of user space to set the policy that governs the overall behavior of the system. For example, the loading of kernel modules in response to external events, such as plugging in a new USB device, is the responsibility of the user space program, udev, not the kernel. The kernel just supplies a means of loading a kernel module.

In Linux, there are three main types of device driver:

- **Character**: This is for an unbuffered I/O with a rich range of functions and a thin layer between the application code and the driver. It is the first choice when implementing custom device drivers.
- **Block**: This has an interface tailored for block I/O to and from mass storage devices. There is a thick layer of buffering designed to make disk reads and writes as fast as possible, which makes it unsuitable for anything else.
- **Network**: This is similar to a block device but is used for transmitting and receiving network packets rather than disk blocks.

There is also a fourth type that presents itself as a group of files in one of the pseudo file systems. For example, you might access the GPIO driver through a group of files in /sys/class/gpio, as I will describe later on in this chapter. Let's begin by looking in more detail at the three basic device types.

Character devices

Character devices are identified in user space by a special file called a **device node**. This file name is mapped to a device driver using the major and minor numbers associated with it. Broadly speaking, the **major number** maps the device node to a particular device driver, and the **minor number** tells the driver which interface is being accessed. For example, the device node of the first serial port on the ARM Versatile PB is named /dev/ttyAMA0, and it has major number 204 and minor number 64. The device node for the second serial port has the same major number, since it is handled by the same device driver, but the minor number is 65. We can see the numbers for all four serial ports from the directory listing here:

```
# ls -l /dev/ttyAMA*
crw-rw----    1 root     root      204,  64 Jan  1  1970 /dev/ttyAMA0
crw-rw----    1 root     root      204,  65 Jan  1  1970 /dev/ttyAMA1
crw-rw----    1 root     root      204,  66 Jan  1  1970 /dev/ttyAMA2
crw-rw----    1 root     root      204,  67 Jan  1  1970 /dev/ttyAMA3
```

The list of standard major and minor numbers can be found in the kernel documentation in Documentation/devices.txt. The list does not get updated very often and does not include the ttyAMA device described in the preceding paragraph. Nevertheless, if you look at the kernel source code in drivers/tty/serial/amba-pl011.c, you will see where the major and minor numbers are declared:

```
#define SERIAL_AMBA_MAJOR        204
#define SERIAL_AMBA_MINOR        64
```

Where there is more than one instance of a device, as with the ttyAMA driver, the convention for forming the name of the device node is to take a base name, ttyAMA, and append the instance number from 0 to 3 in this example.

As I mentioned in Chapter 5, *Building a Root Filesystem*, the device nodes can be created in several ways:

- devtmpfs: The device node is created when the device driver registers a new device interface using a base name supplied by the driver (ttyAMA) and an instance number.
- udev or mdev (without devtmpfs): Essentially the same as with devtmpfs, except that a user space daemon program has to extract the device name from sysfs and create the node. I will talk about sysfs later.
- mknod: If you are using static device nodes, they are created manually using mknod.

You may have the impression from the numbers I have used above that both major and minor numbers are 8-bit numbers in the range 0 to 255. In fact, from Linux 2.6 onwards, the major number is 12 bits long, which gives valid numbers from 1 to 4,095, and the minor number is 20 bits, from 0 to 1,048,575.

When you open a character device node, the kernel checks to see whether the major and minor numbers fall into a range registered by a character device driver . If so, it passes the call to the driver, otherwise the open call fails. The device driver can extract the minor number to find out which hardware interface to use.

To write a program that accesses a device driver, you have to have some knowledge of how it works. In other words, a device driver is not the same as a file: the things you do with it change the state of the device. A simple example is the pseudo random number generator, urandom, which returns bytes of random data every time you read it. Here is a program that does just this (you will find the code in MELP/chapter_09/read-urandom):

```c
#include <stdio.h>
#include <sys/types.h>
#include <sys/stat.h>
#include <fcntl.h>
#include <unistd.h>

int main(void)
{
  int f;
  unsigned int rnd;
  int n;
  f = open("/dev/urandom", O_RDONLY);
  if (f < 0) {
    perror("Failed to open urandom");
    return 1;
  }
  n = read(f, &rnd, sizeof(rnd));
  if (n != sizeof(rnd)) {
    perror("Problem reading urandom");
    return 1;
  }
  printf("Random number = 0x%x\n", rnd);
  close(f);
  return 0;
}
```

The nice thing about the Unix driver model is that once we know that there is a device named urandom and that every time we read from it, it returns a fresh set of pseudo random data, we don't need to know anything else about it. We can just use standard functions such as *open(2)*, *read(2)*, and *close(2)*.

You could use the stream I/O functions, *fopen(3)*, *fread(3)*, and *fclose(3)* instead, but the buffering implicit in these functions often causes unexpected behavior. For example, *fwrite(3)* usually only writes to the user space buffer, not to the device. You would need to call *fflush(3)* to force the buffer to be written out. Therefore, it is best to not use stream I/O functions when calling device drivers.

Block devices

Block devices are also associated with a device node, which also has major and minor numbers.

Although character and block devices are identified using major and minor numbers, they are in different namespaces. A character driver with a major number 4 is in no way related to a block driver with a major number 4.

With block devices, the major number is used to identify the device driver and the minor number is used to identify the partition. Let's look at the MMC driver on the BeagleBone Black as an example:

```
# ls -l /dev/mmcblk*
brw-rw---- 1 root disk 179, 0    Jan 1 2000 /dev/mmcblk0
brw-rw---- 1 root disk 179, 1    Jan 1 2000 /dev/mmcblk0p1
brw-rw---- 1 root disk 179, 2    Jan 1 2000 /dev/mmcblk0p2
brw-rw---- 1 root disk 179, 8    Jan 1 2000 /dev/mmcblk1
brw-rw---- 1 root disk 179, 16   Jan 1 2000 /dev/mmcblk1boot0
brw-rw---- 1 root disk 179, 24   Jan 1 2000 /dev/mmcblk1boot1
brw-rw---- 1 root disk 179, 9    Jan 1 2000 /dev/mmcblk1p1
brw-rw---- 1 root disk 179, 10   Jan 1 2000 /dev/mmcblk1p2
```

Here, mmcblk0 is the microSD card slot, which has a card that has two partitions, and mmcblk1 is the eMMC chip that also has two partitions. The major number for the MMC block driver is 179 (you can look it up in devices.txt). The minor numbers are used in ranges to identify different physical MMC devices, and the partitions of the storage medium that are on that device. In the case of the MMC driver, the ranges are eight minor numbers per device: the minor numbers from 0 to 7 are for the first device, the numbers from 8 to 15 are for the second, and so on. Within each range, the first minor number represents the entire device as raw sectors, and the others represent up to seven partitions. On eMMC chips, there are two 128 KiB areas of memory reserved for use by a bootloader. These are represented as devices: mmcblk1boot0 and mmcblk1boot1, and they have minor numbers 16 and 24.

As another example, you are probably aware of the SCSI disk driver, known as sd, which is used to control a range of disks that use the SCSI command set, which includes SCSI, SATA, USB mass storage, and universal flash storage (UFS). It has the major number 8 and ranges of 16 minor numbers per interface (or disk). The minor numbers from 0 to 15 are for the first interface with device nodes named sda up to sda15, the numbers from 16 to 31 are for the second disk with device nodes sdb up to sdb15, and so on. This continues up to the 16 disk from 240 to 255 with the node name sdp. There are other major numbers reserved for them because SCSI disks are so popular, but we needn't worry about that here.

Both the MMC and SCSI block drivers expect to find a partiton table at the start of the disk. The partition table is created using utilities such as fdisk, sfidsk, or parted.

A user space program can open and interact with a block device directly via the device node. This is not a common thing to do, though, and is usually only done to perform administrative operations such as creating partitions, formatting a partition with a filesystem, and mounting. Once the filesystem is mounted, you interact with the block device indirectly through the files in that filesystem.

Network devices

Network devices are not accessed through device nodes, and they do not have major and minor numbers. Instead, a network device is allocated a name by the kernel, based on a string and an instance number. Here is an example of the way a network driver registers an interface:

```
my_netdev = alloc_netdev(0, "net%d", NET_NAME_UNKNOWN, netdev_setup);
ret = register_netdev(my_netdev);
```

This creates a network device named net0 the first time it is called, net1 the second time, and so on. More common names are lo, eth0, and wlan0. Note that this is the name it starts off with; device managers, such as udev, may change it to something different later on.

Usually, the network interface name is only used when configuring the network using utilities, such as ip and ifconfig, to establish a network address and route. Thereafter, you interact with the network driver indirectly by opening sockets, and letting the network layer decide how to route them to the right interface.

However, it is possible to access network devices directly from user space by creating a socket and using the `ioctl` commands listed in `include/linux/sockios.h`. For example, this program uses `SIOCGIFHWADDR` to query the driver for the hardware (MAC) address (the code is in `MELP/chapter_09/show-mac-addresses`):

```c
#include <stdio.h>
#include <stdlib.h>
#include <string.h>
#include <unistd.h>
#include <sys/ioctl.h>
#include <linux/sockios.h>
#include <net/if.h>
int main (int argc, char *argv[])
{
  int s;
  int ret;
  struct ifreq ifr;
  int i;
  if (argc != 2) {
    printf("Usage %s [network interface]\n", argv[0]);
    return 1;
  }
  s = socket(PF_INET, SOCK_DGRAM, 0);
  if (s < 0) {
    perror("socket");
    return 1;
  }
  strcpy(ifr.ifr_name, argv[1]);
  ret = ioctl(s, SIOCGIFHWADDR, &ifr);
  if (ret < 0) {
    perror("ioctl");
    return 1;
  }
  for (i = 0; i < 6; i++)
  printf("%02x:", (unsigned char)ifr.ifr_hwaddr.sa_data[i]);
  printf("\n");
  close(s);
  return 0;
}
```

Finding out about drivers at runtime

Once you have a running Linux system, it is useful to know which device drivers are loaded and what state they are in. You can find out a lot by reading the files in `/proc` and `/sys`.

First of all, you can list the character and block device drivers currently loaded and active by reading /proc/devices:

```
# cat /proc/devices
Character devices:
  1 mem
  2 pty
  3 ttyp
  4 /dev/vc/0
  4 tty
  4 ttyS
  5 /dev/tty
  5 /dev/console
  5 /dev/ptmx
  7 vcs
 10 misc
 13 input
 29 fb
 81 video4linux
 89 i2c
 90 mtd
116 alsa
128 ptm
136 pts
153 spi
180 usb
189 usb_device
204 ttySC
204 ttyAMA
207 ttymxc
226 drm
239 ttyLP
240 ttyTHS
241 ttySiRF
242 ttyPS
243 ttyWMT
244 ttyAS
245 ttyO
246 ttyMSM
247 ttyAML
248 bsg
249 iio
250 watchdog
251 ptp
252 pps
253 media
254 rtc
```

```
Block devices:
259 blkext
  7 loop
  8 sd
 11 sr
 31 mtdblock
 65 sd
 66 sd
 67 sd
 68 sd
 69 sd
 70 sd
 71 sd
128 sd
129 sd
130 sd
131 sd
132 sd
133 sd
134 sd
135 sd
179 mmc
```

For each driver, you can see the major number and the base name. However, this does not tell you how many devices each driver is attached to. It only shows `ttyAMA` but gives you no clue that it is attached to four real serial ports. I will come back to that later when I look at `sysfs`.

Of course, network devices do not appear in this list, because they do not have device nodes. Instead, you can use tools such as `ifconfig` or `ip` to get a list of network devices:

```
# ip link show
1: lo: <LOOPBACK,UP,LOWER_UP> mtu 65536 qdisc noqueue state
 UNKNOWN mode DEFAULT
    link/loopback 00:00:00:00:00:00 brd 00:00:00:00:00:00
2: eth0: <NO-CARRIER,BROADCAST,MULTICAST,UP> mtu 1500 qdisc
 pfifo_fast state DOWN mode DEFAULT qlen 1000
    link/ether 54:4a:16:bb:b7:03 brd ff:ff:ff:ff:ff:ff
3: usb0: <BROADCAST,MULTICAST,UP,LOWER_UP> mtu 1500 qdisc
 pfifo_fast state UP mode DEFAULT qlen 1000
    link/ether aa:fb:7f:5e:a8:d5 brd ff:ff:ff:ff:ff:ff
```

You can also find out about devices attached to USB or PCI buses using the well-known commands: `lsusb` and `lspci`. There is information about them in the respective manual pages and plenty of online guides, so I will not describe them any further here.

The really interesting information is in `sysfs`, which is the next topic.

Getting information from sysfs

You can define `sysfs` in a pedantic way as a representation of kernel objects, attributes, and relationships. A kernel object is a **directory**, an attribute is a **file**, and a relationship is a **symbolic link** from one object to another. From a more practical point of view, since the Linux device driver model represents all devices and drivers as kernel objects, you can see the kernel's view of the system laid out before you by looking in `/sys`, as shown here:

```
# ls /sys
block      class      devices    fs        module
bus        dev        firmware   kernel    power
```

In the context of discovering information about devices and drivers, I will look at three of these directories: `devices`, `class`, and `block`.

The devices: /sys/devices

This is the kernel's view of the devices discovered since boot and how they are connected to each other. It is organized at the top level by the system bus, so what you see varies from one system to another. This is the QEMU emulation of the ARM Versatile:

```
# ls /sys/devices
platform    software    system      tracepoint    virtual
```

There are three directories that are present on all systems:

- `system/`: This contains devices at the heart of the system, including CPUs and clocks.
- `virtual/`: This contains devices that are memory-based. You will find the memory devices that appear as `/dev/null`, `/dev/random`, and `/dev/zero` in `virtual/mem`. You will find the loopback device, `lo`, in `virtual/net`.
- `platform/`: This is a catch-all for devices that are not connected via a conventional hardware bus. This maybe almost everything on an embedded device.

The other devices appear in directories that correspond to actual system buses. For example, the PCI root bus, if there is one, appears as `pci0000:00`.

Navigating this hierarchy is quite hard, because it requires some knowledge of the topology of your system, and the path-names become quite long and hard to remember. To make life easier, `/sys/class` and `/sys/block` offer two different views of the devices.

The drivers: /sys/class

This is a view of the device drivers presented by their type. In other words, it is a software view rather than a hardware view. Each of the subdirectories represents a class of driver and is implemented by a component of the driver framework. For example, UART devices are managed by the `tty` layer, and you will find them in `/sys/class/tty`. Likewise, you will find network devices in `/sys/class/net`, input devices such as the keyboard, the touchscreen, and the mouse in `/sys/class/input`, and so on.

There is a symbolic link in each subdirectory for each instance of that type of device pointing to its representation in `/sys/device`.

To take a concrete example, let's look at the serial ports on the Versatile PB. First of all, we can see that there are four of them:

```
# ls -d /sys/class/tty/ttyAMA*
/sys/class/tty/ttyAMA0    /sys/class/tty/ttyAMA2
/sys/class/tty/ttyAMA1    /sys/class/tty/ttyAMA3
```

Each directory is a representation of the kernel object that is associated with an instance of a device interface. Looking within one of these directories, we can see the attributes of the object, represented as files, and the relationships with other objects, represented by links:

```
# ls /sys/class/tty/ttyAMA0
close_delay      flags            line             uartclk
closing_wait     io_type          port             uevent
custom_divisor   iomem_base       power            xmit_fifo_size
dev              iomem_reg_shift  subsystem
device           irq              type
```

The link called `device` points to the hardware object for the device. The link named `subsystem` points back to the parent subsystem, `/sys/class/tty`. The remaining directory entries are attributes. Some are specific to a serial port, such as `xmit_fifo_size`, and others apply to many types of device such as the interrupt number, `irq`, and the device number, `dev`. Some attribute files are writable and allow you to tune parameters in the driver at runtime.

The `dev` attribute is particularly interesting. If you look at its value, you will find the following:

```
# cat /sys/class/tty/ttyAMA0/dev
204:64
```

These are the major and minor numbers of this device. This attribute is created when the driver registered this interface. It is from this file that `udev` and `mdev` find the major and minor numbers of the device driver.

The block drivers: /sys/block

There is one more view of the device model that is important to this discussion: the block driver view that you will find in `/sys/block`. There is a subdirectory for each block device. This example is taken from a BeagleBone Black:

```
# ls /sys/block
loop0   loop4   mmcblk0        ram0   ram12   ram2   ram6
loop1   loop5   mmcblk1        ram1   ram13   ram3   ram7
loop2   loop6   mmcblk1boot0   ram10  ram14   ram4   ram8
loop3   loop7   mmcblk1boot1   ram11  ram15   ram5   ram9
```

If you look into `mmcblk1`, which is the eMMC chip on this board, you can see the attributes of the interface and the partitions within it:

```
# ls /sys/block/mmcblk1
alignment_offset   ext_range       mmcblk1p1   ro
bdi                force_ro        mmcblk1p2   size
capability         holders         power       slaves
dev                inflight        queue       stat
device             mmcblk1boot0    range       subsystem
discard_alignment  mmcblk1boot1    removable   uevent
```

The conclusion, then, is that you can learn a lot about the devices (the hardware) and the drivers (the software) that are present on a system by reading `sysfs`.

Finding the right device driver

A typical embedded board is based on a reference design from the manufacturer with changes to make it suitable for a particular application. The BSP that comes with the reference board should support all of the peripherals on that board. But, then you customize the design, perhaps by adding a temperature sensor attached via I^{2}C, some lights and buttons connected via GPIO pins, a display panel via a MIPI interface, or many other things. Your job is to create a custom kernel to control all of these, but where do you start to look for device drivers to support all of these peripherals?

The most obvious place to look is the driver support page on the manufacturer's website, or you could ask them directly. In my experience, this seldom gets the result you want; hardware manufacturers are not particularly Linux-savvy, and they often give you misleading information. They may have proprietary drivers as binary blobs or they may have source code but for a different version of the kernel than the one you have. So, by all means try this route. Personally, I will always try to find an open source driver for the task in hand.

There maybe support in your kernel already: there are many thousands of drivers in mainline Linux and there are many vendor-specific drivers in the vendor kernels. Begin by running `make menuconfig` (or `xconfig`) and search for the product name or number. If you do not find an exact match, try more generic searches, allowing for the fact that most drivers handle a range of products from the same family. Next, try searching through the code in the drivers directory (`grep` is you friend here).

If you still don't have a driver, you can try searching online and asking in the relevant forums to see if there is a driver for a later version of Linux. If you find one, you should seriously consider updating the BSP to use the later kernel. Sometimes this is not practical, and so it may have to think of backporting the driver to your kernel. If the kernel versions are similar, it maybe easy, but if they are more than 12 to 18 months apart, the chances are that the code will have changed to the extent that you will have to rewrite a chunk of the driver to integrate it with your kernel. If all of the above fail, you will have to find a solution yourself by writing the missing kernel driver. But, this is not always necessary, I will show in the next section.

Device drivers in user space

Before you start writing a device driver, pause for a moment to consider whether it is really necessary. There are generic device drivers for many common types of device that allow you to interact with hardware directly from user space without having to write a line of kernel code. User space code is certainly easier to write and debug. It is also not covered by the GPL, although I don't feel that is a good reason in itself to do it this way.

These drivers fall into two broad categories: those that you control through files in `sysfs`, including GPIO and LEDs, and serial buses that expose a generic interface through a device node, such as I^2C.

GPIO

General-Purpose Input/Output (**GPIO**) is the simplest form of digital interface since it gives you direct access to individual hardware pins, each of which can be in one of two states: either high or low. In most cases you can configure the GPIO pin to be either an input or an output. You can even use a group of GPIO pins to create higher level interfaces such as I²C or SPI by manipulating each bit in software, a technique that is called **bit banging**. The main limitation is the speed and accuracy of the software loops and the number of CPU cycles you want to dedicate to them. Generally speaking, it is hard to achieve timer accuracy better than a millisecond unless you configure a real-time kernel, as we shall see in Chapter 16, *Real-Time Programming*. More common use cases for GPIO are for reading push buttons and digital sensors and controlling LEDs, motors, and relays.

Most SoCs have a lot of GPIO bits, which are grouped together in GPIO registers, usually 32 bits per register. On-chip GPIO bits are routed through to GPIO pins on the chip package via a multiplexer, known as a **pin mux**. There maybe additional GPIO pins available off-chip in the power management chip, and in dedicated GPIO extenders, connected through I²C or SPI buses. All this diversity is handled by a kernel subsystem known as gpiolib, which is not actually a library but the infrastructure GPIO drivers use to expose I/O in a consistent way. There are details about the implementation of gpiolib in the kernel source in Documentation/gpio and the code for the drivers themselves is in drivers/gpio.

Applications can interact with gpiolib through files in the /sys/class/gpio directory. Here is an example of what you will see in there on a typical embedded board (a BeagleBone Black):

```
# ls /sys/class/gpio
export  gpiochip0   gpiochip32  gpiochip64  gpiochip96  unexport
```

The directories named gpiochip0 through to gpiochip96 represent four GPIO registers, each with 32 GPIO bits. If you look in one of the gpiochip directories, you will see the following:

```
# ls /sys/class/gpio/gpiochip96
base  label  ngpio  power  subsystem  uevent
```

The file named base contains the number of the first GPIO pin in the register and ngpio contains the number of bits in the register. In this case, gpiochip96/base is 96 and gpiochip96/ngpio is 32, which tells you that it contains GPIO bits 96 to 127. It is possible for there to be a gap between the last GPIO in one register and the first GPIO in the next.

To control a GPIO bit from user space, you first have to export it from kernel space, which you do by writing the GPIO number to /sys/class/gpio/export. This example shows the process for GPIO 53, which is wired to user LED 0 on the BeagleBone Black:

```
# echo 53 > /sys/class/gpio/export
# ls /sys/class/gpio
export gpio53 gpiochip0 gpiochip32 gpiochip64 gpiochip96 unexport
```

Now, there is a new directory, gpio53, which contains the files you need to control the pin.

If the GPIO bit is already claimed by the kernel, you will not be able to export it in this way.

The directory gpio53 contains these files:

```
# ls /sys/class/gpio/gpio53
active_low    direction    power       uevent
device        edge         subsystem   value
```

The pin begins as an input. To change it to an output, write out to the direction file. The file value contains the current state of the pin, which is 0 for low and 1 for high. If it is an output; you can change the state by writing 0 or 1 to value. Sometimes, the meaning of low and high is reversed in hardware (hardware engineers enjoy doing that sort of thing), so writing 1 to active_low inverts the meaning of value such that a low voltage is reported as 1 and a high voltage as 0.

You can remove a GPIO from user space control by writing the GPIO number to /sys/class/gpio/unexport.

Handling interrupts from GPIO

In many cases, a GPIO input can be configured to generate an interrupt when it changes state, which allows you to wait for the interrupt rather than polling in an inefficient software loop. If the GPIO bit can generate interrupts, the file called edge exists. Initially, it has the value called none, meaning that it does not generate interrupts. To enable interrupts, you can set it to one of these values:

- rising: Interrupt on rising edge
- falling: Interrupt on falling edge

- both: Interrupt on both rising and falling edges
- none: No interrupts (default)

You can wait for an interrupt using the poll() function with POLLPRI as the event. If you want to wait for a rising edge on GPIO 48, you first enable the interrupts:

```
# echo 48 > /sys/class/gpio/export
# echo falling > /sys/class/gpio/gpio48/edge
```

Then, you use *poll(2)* to wait for the change, as shown in this code example, which you can see in the book code archive in MELP/chapter_09/gpio-int/gpio-int.c:

```
#include <stdio.h>
#include <unistd.h>
#include <sys/types.h>
#include <sys/stat.h>
#include <fcntl.h>
#include <poll.h>
int main(int argc, char *argv[])
{
    int f;
    struct pollfd poll_fds[1];
    int ret;
    char value[4];
    int n;

    f = open("/sys/class/gpio/gpio48/value", O_RDONLY);
    if (f == -1) {
        perror("Can't open gpio48");
        return 1;
    }
    n = read(f, &value, sizeof(value));
    if (n > 0) {
        printf("Initial value=%c\n",
                value[0]);
        lseek(f, 0, SEEK_SET);
    }
    poll_fds[0].fd = f;
    poll_fds[0].events = POLLPRI | POLLERR;
    while (1) {
        printf("Waiting\n");
        ret = poll(poll_fds, 1, -1);
        if (ret > 0) {
            n = read(f, &value, sizeof(value));
            printf("Button pressed: value=%c\n",
                    value[0]);
            lseek(f, 0, SEEK_SET);
```

```
        }
    }
    return 0;
}
```

LEDs

LEDs are often controlled though a GPIO pin, but there is another kernel subsystem that offers more specialized control specific to the purpose. The `leds` kernel subsystem adds the ability to set brightness, should the LED have that ability, and it can handle LEDs connected in other ways than a simple GPIO pin. It can be configured to trigger the LED on an event such as block device access or just a heartbeat to show that the device is working. You will have to configure your kernel with the option, `CONFIG_LEDS_CLASS`, and with the LED trigger actions that are appropriate to you. There is more information on `Documentation/leds/`, and the drivers are in `drivers/leds/`.

As with GPIOs, LEDs are controlled through an interface in `sysfs` in the directory `/sys/class/leds`. In the case of the BeagleBone Black, the names of the LEDs are encoded in the device tree in the form `devicename:colour:function`, as shown here:

```
# ls /sys/class/leds
beaglebone:green:heartbeat    beaglebone:green:usr2
beaglebone:green:mmc0         beaglebone:green:usr3
```

Now, we can look at the attributes of one of the LEDs, noting that the shell requires that the colon characters, ':', in the path name have to be preceded by a backslash escape character, '\':

```
# cd /sys/class/leds/beaglebone\:green\:usr2
# ls
brightness     max_brightness    subsystem     uevent
device         power             trigger
```

The `brightness` file controls the brightness of the LED and can be a number between 0 (**off**) and `max_brightness` (**fully on**). If the LED doesn't support intermediate brightness, any non-zero value turns it on. The file called `trigger` lists the events that trigger the LED to turn on. The list of triggers is implementation dependent. Here is an example:

```
# cat trigger
none mmc0 mmc1 timer oneshot heartbeat backlight gpio [cpu0]
default-on
```

The trigger currently selected is shown in *square* brackets. You can change it by writing one of the other triggers to the file. If you want to control the LED entirely through brightness, select none. If you set the trigger to timer, two extra files appear that allow you to set the on and off times in milliseconds:

```
# echo timer > trigger
# ls
brightness    delay_on       max_brightness subsystem uevent
delay_off     device         power                     trigger
# cat delay_on
500
# cat /sys/class/leds/beaglebone:green:heartbeat/delay_off
500
```

If the LED has on-chip timer hardware, the blinking takes place without interrupting the CPU.

I2C

I²C is a simple low speed 2-wire bus that is common on embedded boards, typically used to access peripherals that are not on the SoC, such as display controllers, camera sensors, GPIO extenders, and so on. There is a related standard known as **system management bus (SMBus)** that is found on PCs, which is used to access temperature and voltage sensors. SMBus is a subset of I²C.

I²C is a master-slave protocol with the master being one or more host controllers on the SoC. Slaves have a 7-bit address assigned by the manufacturer (read the data sheet), allowing up to 128 nodes per bus, but 16 are reserved, so only 112 nodes are allowed in practice. The master may initiate a read or write transactions with one of the slaves. Frequently, the first byte is used to specify a register on the slave, and the remaining bytes are the data read from or written to that register.

There is one device node for each host controller, for example, this SoC has four:

```
# ls -l /dev/i2c*
crw-rw---- 1 root i2c 89, 0 Jan  1 00:18 /dev/i2c-0
crw-rw---- 1 root i2c 89, 1 Jan  1 00:18 /dev/i2c-1
crw-rw---- 1 root i2c 89, 2 Jan  1 00:18 /dev/i2c-2
crw-rw---- 1 root i2c 89, 3 Jan  1 00:18 /dev/i2c-3
```

The device interface provides a series of `ioctl` commands that query the host controller and send the `read` and `write` commands to I²C slaves. There is a package named `i2c-tools`, which uses this interface to provide basic command-line tools to interact with I²C devices. The tools are as follows:

- `i2cdetect`: This lists the I²C adapters, and probes the bus
- `i2cdump`: This dumps data from all the registers of an I²C peripheral
- `i2cget`: This reads data from an I²C slave
- `i2cset`: This writes data to an I²C slave

The `i2c-tools` package is available in Buildroot and the Yocto Project as well as most mainstream distributions. So, long as you know the address and protocol of the slave, writing a user space program to talk to the device is straightforward. The example that follows shows how to read the first four bytes from the `AT24C512B` EEPROM that is mounted on the BeagleBone Black on I²C bus 0, slave address 0x50 (the code is in `MELP/chapter_09/i2c-example`):

```c
#include <stdio.h>
#include <unistd.h>
#include <fcntl.h>
#include <sys/ioctl.h>
#include <linux/i2c-dev.h>

#define I2C_ADDRESS 0x50

int main(void)
{
  int f;
  int n;
  char buf[10];

  f = open("/dev/i2c-0", O_RDWR);

  /* Set the address of the i2c slave device */
  ioctl(f, I2C_SLAVE, I2C_ADDRESS);

  /* Set the 16-bit address to read from to 0 */
  buf[0] = 0; /* address byte 1 */
  buf[1] = 0; /* address byte 2 */
  n = write(f, buf, 2);

  /* Now read 4 bytes from that address */
  n = read(f, buf, 4);
  printf("0x%x 0x%x0 0x%x 0x%x\n",
```

```
    buf[0], buf[1], buf[2], buf[3]);

    close(f);
    return 0;
}
```

 There is more information about the Linux implementation of I²C in `Documentation/i2c/dev-interface`. The host controller drivers are in `drivers/i2c/busses`.

Serial Peripheral Interface (SPI)

The SPI bus is similar to I²C, but is a lot faster, up to tens of MHz. The interface uses four wires with separate send and receive lines, which allow it to operate in full duplex. Each chip on the bus is selected with a dedicated chip select line. It is commonly used to connect to touchscreen sensors, display controllers, and serial NOR flash devices.

As with I²C, it is a master-slave protocol with most SoCs implementing one or more master host controllers. There is a generic SPI device driver, which you can enable through the kernel configuration `CONFIG_SPI_SPIDEV`. It creates a device node for each SPI controller, which allows you to access SPI chips from user space. The device nodes are named `spidev[bus].[chip select]`:

```
# ls -l /dev/spi*
crw-rw---- 1 root root 153, 0 Jan  1 00:29 /dev/spidev1.0
```

For examples of using the `spidev` interface, refer to the example code in `Documentation/spi`.

Writing a kernel device driver

Eventually, when you have exhausted all the previous user space options, you will find yourself having to write a device driver to access a piece of hardware attached to your device. Character drivers are the most flexible and should cover 90% of all your needs; network drivers apply if you are working with a network interface and block drivers are for mass storage. The task of writing a kernel driver is complex and beyond the scope of this book. There are some references at the end that will help you on your way. In this section, I want to outline the options available for interacting with a driver—a topic not normally covered—and show you the bare bones of a character device driver.

Designing a character driver interface

The main character driver interface is based on a stream of bytes, as you would have with a serial port. However, many devices don't fit this description: a controller for a robot arm needs functions to move and rotate each joint, for example. Luckily, there are other ways to communicate with device drivers than just `read` and `write`:

- `ioctl`: The `ioctl` function allows you to pass two arguments to your driver which can have any meaning you like. By convention, the first argument is a command, which selects one of several functions in your driver, and the second is a pointer to a structure, which serves as a container for the input and output parameters. This is a blank canvas that allows you to design any program interface you like. It is pretty common when the driver and application are closely linked and written by the same team. However, `ioctl` is deprecated in the kernel, and you will find it hard to get any drivers with new uses of `ioctl` accepted upstream. The kernel maintainers dislike `ioctl` because it makes kernel code and application code too interdependent, and it is hard to keep both of them in step across kernel versions and architectures.

- `sysfs`: This is the preferred way now, a good example being the GPIO interface described earlier. The advantages are that it is somewhat self-documenting, so long as you choose descriptive names for the files. It is also scriptable because the file contents are usually text strings. On the other hand, the requirement for each file to contain a single value makes it hard to achieve atomicity if you need to change more than one value at a time. Conversely, `ioctl` passes all its arguments in a structure in a single function call.

- `mmap`: You can get direct access to kernel buffers and hardware registers by mapping kernel memory into user space, bypassing the kernel. You may still need some kernel code to handle interrupts and DMA. There is a subsystem that encapsulates this idea, known as `uio`, which is short for user I/O. There is more documentation in `Documentation/DocBook/uio-howto`, and there are example drivers in `drivers/uio`.

- `sigio`: You can send a signal from a driver using the kernel function named `kill_fasync()` to notify applications of an event such as input becoming ready or an interrupt being received. By convention, the signal called `SIGIO` is used, but it could be any. You can see some examples in the UIO driver, `drivers/uio/uio.c`, and in the RTC driver, `drivers/char/rtc.c`. The main problem is that it is difficult to write reliable signal handlers in user space, and so it remains a little-used facility.

- debugfs: This is another pseudo filesystem that represents kernel data as files and directories, similar to proc and sysfs. The main distinction is that debugfs must not contain information that is needed for the normal operation of the system; it is for the debug and trace information only. It is mounted as mount -t debugfs debug /sys/kernel/debug. There is a good description of debugfs in the kernel documentation, Documentation/filesystems/debugfs.txt.

- proc: The proc filesystem is deprecated for all new code unless it relates to processes, which was the original intended purpose for the filesystem. However, you can use proc to publish any information you choose. And, unlike sysfs and debugfs, it is available to non-GPL modules.

- netlink: This is a socket protocol family. AF_NETLINK creates a socket that links kernel space to user space. It was originally created so that network tools could communicate with the Linux network code to access the routing tables and other details. It is also used by udev to pass events from the kernel to the udev daemon. It is very rarely used in general device drivers.

There are many examples of all of the preceding filesystem in the kernel source code, and you can design really interesting interfaces to your driver code. The only universal rule is the *principle of least astonishment*. In other words, application writers using your driver should find that everything works in a logical way without any quirks or oddities.

The anatomy of a device driver

It's time to draw some threads together by looking at the code for a simple device driver. Here is a device driver named dummy, which creates four devices that are accessed through dev/dummy0 to /dev/dummy3. The complete source code for the driver follows: you will find the code in MELP/chapter_09/dummy-driver:

```
#include <linux/kernel.h>
#include <linux/module.h>
#include <linux/init.h>
#include <linux/fs.h>
#include <linux/device.h>

#define DEVICE_NAME "dummy"
#define MAJOR_NUM 42
#define NUM_DEVICES 4

static struct class *dummy_class;
static int dummy_open(struct inode *inode, struct file *file)
{
  pr_info("%s\n", __func__);
```

```
    return 0;
}

static int dummy_release(struct inode *inode, struct file *file)
{
  pr_info("%s\n", __func__);
  return 0;
}

static ssize_t dummy_read(struct file *file,
  char *buffer, size_t length, loff_t * offset)
{
  pr_info("%s %u\n", __func__, length);
  return 0;
}

static ssize_t dummy_write(struct file *file,
  const char *buffer, size_t length, loff_t * offset)
{
  pr_info("%s %u\n", __func__, length);
  return length;
}

struct file_operations dummy_fops = {
  .owner = THIS_MODULE,
  .open = dummy_open,
  .release = dummy_release,
  .read = dummy_read,
  .write = dummy_write,
};

int __init dummy_init(void)
{
  int ret;
  int i;
  printk("Dummy loaded\n");
  ret = register_chrdev(MAJOR_NUM, DEVICE_NAME, &dummy_fops);
  if (ret != 0)
    return ret;
  dummy_class = class_create(THIS_MODULE, DEVICE_NAME);
  for (i = 0; i < NUM_DEVICES; i++) {
    device_create(dummy_class, NULL,
    MKDEV(MAJOR_NUM, i), NULL, "dummy%d", i);
  }
  return 0;
}

void __exit dummy_exit(void)
```

```
{
  int i;
  for (i = 0; i < NUM_DEVICES; i++) {
    device_destroy(dummy_class, MKDEV(MAJOR_NUM, i));
  }
  class_destroy(dummy_class);
  unregister_chrdev(MAJOR_NUM, DEVICE_NAME);
  printk("Dummy unloaded\n");
}

module_init(dummy_init);
module_exit(dummy_exit);
MODULE_LICENSE("GPL");
MODULE_AUTHOR("Chris Simmonds");
MODULE_DESCRIPTION("A dummy driver");
```

At the end of the code, the macros called `module_init` and `module_exit` specify the functions to be called when the module is loaded and unloaded. The three macros named `MODULE_*` add some basic information about the module, which can be retrieved from the compiled kernel module using the `modinfo` command.

When the module is loaded, the `dummy_init()` function is called. You can see the point at which it becomes a character device when is makes the call to `register_chrdev`, passing a pointer to `struct file_operations`, which contains pointers to the four functions that the driver implements. While `register_chrdev` tells the kernel that there is a driver with a major number of 42, it doesn't say anything about the class of driver, and so it will not create an entry in `/sys/class`. Without an entry in `/sys/class`, the device manager cannot create device nodes. So, the next few lines of code create a device class, dummy and four devices of that class called dummy0 to dummy3. The result is that the `/sys/class/dummy` directory is created when the driver is initialized, containing subdirectories dummy0 to dummy3. Each of the subdirectories contains a file, dev, with the major and minor numbers of the device. This is all that a device manager needs to create device nodes: `/dev/dummy0` to `/dev/dummy3`.

The `dummy_exit` function has to release the resources claimed by `dummy_init`, which here means freeing up the device class and major number.

The file operations for this driver are implemented by `dummy_open()`, `dummy_read()`, `dummy_write()`, and `dummy_release()` and are called when a user space program calls `open(2)`, `read(2)`, `write(2)`, and `close(2)`. They just print a kernel message so that you can see that they were called. You can demonstrate this from the command line using the `echo` command:

```
# echo hello > /dev/dummy0
dummy_open
dummy_write 6
dummy_release
```

In this case, the messages appear because I was logged on to the console, and kernel messages are printed to the console by default. If you are not logged onto the console, you can still see the kernel messages using the command `dmesg`.

The full source code for this driver is less than 100 lines, but it is enough to illustrate how the linkage between a device node and driver code works, how the device class is created, allowing a device manager to create device nodes automatically when the driver is loaded, and how the data is moved between user and kernel spaces. Next, you need to build it.

Compiling kernel modules

At this point, you have some driver code that you want to compile and test on your target system. You can copy it into the kernel source tree and modify makefiles to build it, or you can compile it as a module out of tree. Let's start by building out of tree.

You need a simple makefile which uses the kernel build system to do the hard work:

```
LINUXDIR := $(HOME)/MELP/build/linux

obj-m := dummy.o
all:
        make ARCH=arm CROSS_COMPILE=arm-cortex_a8-linux-gnueabihf- \
          -C $(LINUXDIR) M=$(shell pwd)
clean:
        make -C $(LINUXDIR) M=$(shell pwd) clean
```

Set `LINUXDIR` to the directory of the kernel for your target device that you will be running the module on. The `obj-m := dummy.o` code will invoke the kernel build rule to take the source file, `dummy.c`, and create kernel module, `dummy.ko`. I will show you how to load kernel modules in the next section.

Kernel modules are not binary compatible between kernel releases and configurations: the module will only load on the kernel it was compiled with.

If you want to build a driver in the kernel source tree, the procedure is quite simple. Choose a directory appropriate to the type of driver you have. The driver is a basic character device, so I would put dummy.c in drivers/char. Then, edit the makefile in the directory, and add a line to build the driver unconditionally as a module, as follows:

```
obj-m   += dummy.o
```

Or add the following line to build it unconditionally as a built-in:

```
obj-y   += dummy.o
```

If you want to make the driver optional, you can add a menu option to the Kconfig file and make the compilation conditional on the configuration option, as I described in Chapter 4, *Configuring and Building the Kernel*, in the section, *Understanding kernel configuration*.

Loading kernel modules

You can load, unload, and list modules using the simple insmod, lsmod, and rmmod commands. Here they are shown loading the dummy driver:

```
# insmod /lib/modules/4.8.12-yocto-standard/kernel/drivers/dummy.ko
# lsmod
 Tainted: G
dummy 2062 0 - Live 0xbf004000 (O)
# rmmod dummy
```

If the module is placed in a subdirectory in /lib/modules/<kernel release>, you can create a **modules dependency database** using the command, depmod -a:

```
# depmod -a
# ls /lib/modules/4.8.12-yocto-standard
kernel   modules.alias   modules.dep   modules.symbols
```

The information in the module.* files is used by the modprobe command to locate a module by name rather than the full path. modprobe has many other features, which are described on the manual page *modprobe(8)*.

Discovering the hardware configuration

The dummy driver demonstrates the structure of a device driver, but it lacks interaction with real hardware since it only manipulates memory structures. Device drivers are usually written to interact with hardware. Part of that is being able to discover the hardware in the first place, bearing in mind that it maybe at different addresses in different configurations.

In some cases, the hardware provides the information itself. Devices on a discoverable bus such as PCI or USB have a query mode, which returns resource requirements and a unique identifier. The kernel matches the identifier and possibly other characteristics with the device drivers, and marries them up.

However, most of the hardware blocks on an embedded board do not have such identifiers. You have to provide the information yourself in the form of a **device tree** or as C structures known as **platform data**.

In the standard driver model for Linux, device drivers register themselves with the appropriate subsystem: PCI, USB, open firmware (device tree), platform device, and so on. The registration includes an identifier and a callback function called a `probe` function that is called if there is a match between the ID of the hardware and the ID of the driver. For PCI and USB, the ID is based on the vendor and the product IDs of the devices; for device tree and platform devices, it is a name (an text string).

Device trees

I gave you an introduction to device trees in `Chapter 3`, *All About Bootloaders*. Here, I want to show you how the Linux device drivers hook up with this information.

As an example, I will use the ARM Versatile board, `arch/arm/boot/dts/versatile-ab.dts`, for which the Ethernet adapter is defined here:

```
net@10010000 {
  compatible = "smsc,lan91c111";
  reg = <0x10010000 0x10000>;
  interrupts = <25>;
};
```

The platform data

In the absence of device tree support, there is a fallback method of describing hardware using C structures, known as the platform data.

Each piece of hardware is described by struct platform_device, which has a name and a pointer to an array of resources. The type of the resource is determined by flags, which include the following:

- IORESOURCE_MEM: This is the physical address of a region of memory
- IORESOURCE_IO: This is the physical address or port number of IO registers
- IORESOURCE_IRQ: This is the interrupt number

Here is an example of the platform data for an Ethernet controller taken from arch/arm/mach-versatile/core.c, which has been edited for clarity:

```
#define VERSATILE_ETH_BASE      0x10010000
#define IRQ_ETH                 25
static struct resource smc91x_resources[] = {
  [0] = {
    .start           = VERSATILE_ETH_BASE,
    .end             = VERSATILE_ETH_BASE + SZ_64K - 1,
    .flags           = IORESOURCE_MEM,
  },
  [1] = {
    .start           = IRQ_ETH,
    .end             = IRQ_ETH,
    .flags           = IORESOURCE_IRQ,
  },
};
static struct platform_device smc91x_device = {
  .name            = "smc91x",
  .id              = 0,
  .num_resources   = ARRAY_SIZE(smc91x_resources),
  .resource        = smc91x_resources,
};
```

It has a memory area of 64 KB and an interrupt. The platform data has to be registered with the kernel, usually when the board is initialized:

```
void __init versatile_init(void)
{
  platform_device_register(&versatile_flash_device);
  platform_device_register(&versatile_i2c_device);
  platform_device_register(&smc91x_device);
  [ ...]
```

Linking hardware with device drivers

You have seen in the preceding section how an Ethernet adapter is described using a device tree and using platform data. The corresponding driver code is in `drivers/net/ethernet/smsc/smc91x.c`, and it works with both the device tree and platform data. Here is the initialization code, once again edited for clarity:

```
static const struct of_device_id smc91x_match[] = {
   { .compatible = "smsc,lan91c94", },
   { .compatible = "smsc,lan91c111", },
   {},
};
MODULE_DEVICE_TABLE(of, smc91x_match);
static struct platform_driver smc_driver = {
   .probe          = smc_drv_probe,
   .remove         = smc_drv_remove,
   .driver         = {
     .name   = "smc91x",
     .of_match_table = of_match_ptr(smc91x_match),
   },
};
static int __init smc_driver_init(void)
{
   return platform_driver_register(&smc_driver);
}
static void __exit smc_driver_exit(void)
{
   platform_driver_unregister(&smc_driver);
}
module_init(smc_driver_init);
module_exit(smc_driver_exit);
```

When the driver is initialized, it calls `platform_driver_register()`, pointing to `struct platform_driver`, in which there is a callback to a `probe` function, a driver name, `smc91x`, and a pointer to `struct of_device_id`.

If this driver has been configured by the device tree, the kernel will look for a match between the `compatible` property in the device tree node and the string pointed to by the compatible structure element. For each match, it calls the `probe` function.

On the other hand, if it was configured through platform data, the `probe` function will be called for each match on the string pointed to by `driver.name`.

The `probe` function extracts information about the interface:

```
static int smc_drv_probe(struct platform_device *pdev)
{
   struct smc91x_platdata *pd = dev_get_platdata(&pdev->dev);
   const struct of_device_id *match = NULL;
   struct resource *res, *ires;
   int irq;

   res = platform_get_resource(pdev, IORESOURCE_MEM, 0);
   ires = platform_get_resource(pdev, IORESOURCE_IRQ, 0);
   [...]
   addr = ioremap(res->start, SMC_IO_EXTENT);
   irq = ires->start;
   [...]
}
```

The calls to `platform_get_resource()` extract the memory and `irq` information from either the device tree or the platform data. It is up to the driver to map the memory and install the interrupt handler. The third parameter, which is zero in both of the previous cases, comes into play if there is more than one resource of that particular type.

Device trees allow you to configure more than just basic memory ranges and interrupts. There is a section of code in the `probe` function that extracts optional parameters from the device tree. In this snippet, it gets the `register-io-width` property:

```
match = of_match_device(of_match_ptr(smc91x_match), &pdev->dev);
if (match) {
   struct device_node *np = pdev->dev.of_node;
   u32 val;
   [...]
   of_property_read_u32(np, "reg-io-width", &val);
   [...]
}
```

For most drivers, specific bindings are documented in `Documentation/devicetree/bindings`. For this particular driver, the information is in `Documentation/devicetree/bindings/net/smsc911x.txt`.

The main thing to remember here is that drivers should register a `probe` function and enough information for the kernel to call the `probe` , as it finds matches with the hardware it knows about. The linkage between the hardware described by the device tree and the device driver is through the `compatible` property. The linkage between platform data and a driver is through the name.

Additional reading

The following resources have further information about the topics introduced in this chapter:

- *Linux Kernel Development, 3rd edition* by Robert Love.
- *Linux Weekly News,* `https://lwn.net/`, especially the kernel news section.
- *Essential Linux Device Drivers, 1st edition (27 Mar. 2008),* by Sreekrishnan Venkateswaran

Summary

Device drivers have the job of handling devices, usually physical hardware but sometimes virtual interfaces, and presenting them to user space in a consistent and useful way. Linux device drivers fall into three broad categories: character, block, and network. Of the three, the character driver interface is the most flexible and therefore, the most common. Linux drivers fit into a framework known as the driver model, which is exposed through `sysfs`. Pretty much the entire state of the devices and drivers is visible in `/sys`.

Each embedded system has its own unique set of hardware interfaces and requirements. Linux provides drivers for most standard interfaces, and by selecting the right kernel configuration, you can get a working target board very quickly. This leaves you with the non-standard components for which you will have to add your own device support.

In some cases, you can sidestep the issue by using generic drivers for GPIO, I^{2}C, and so on, and write user space code to do the work. I recommend this as a starting point, as it gives you the chance to get familiar with the hardware without writing kernel code. Writing kernel drivers is not particularly difficult, but if you do you need to code carefully so as not to compromise the stability of the system.

I have talked about writing the kernel driver code: if you go down this route, you will inevitably want to know how to check whether or not it is working correctly and detect any bugs. I will cover that topic in `Chapter 14`, *Debugging with GDB.*

The next chapter is all about user space initialization and the different options you have for the `init` program, from the simple BusyBox to the complex systems.

10
Starting Up – The init Program

We looked at how the kernel boots up to the point that it launches the first program, init, in Chapter 4, *Configuring and Building the Kernel*. In Chapter 5, *Building a Root Filesystem*, and Chapter 6, *Selecting a Build System*, we looked at creating root filesystems of varying complexity, all of which contained an init program. Now, it is time to look at the init program in more detail and discover why it is so important to the rest of the system.

There are many possible implementations of init. I will describe the three main ones in this chapter: BusyBox init, System V init, and systemd. For each one, I will give an overview of how it works and the types of system it suits best. Part of this is balancing the trade off between complexity and flexibility.

In this chapter we will cover the following topics:

- After the kernel has booted
- Introducing the init programs
- System V init
- The systemd

After the kernel has booted

We saw in Chapter 4, *Configuring and Building the Kernel*, how the kernel bootstrap code seeks to find a root filesystem, either initramfs or a filesystem specified by root= on the kernel command line, and then to execute a program which, by default, is /init for initramfs and /sbin/init for a regular filesystem. The init program has root privilege, and since it is the first process to run, it has a process ID (PID) of 1. If, for some reason, init cannot be started, the kernel will panic.

The `init` program is the ancestor of all other processes, as shown here by the `pstree` command running on a simple embedded Linux system:

```
# pstree -gn
init(1)-+-syslogd(63)
        |-klogd(66)
        |-dropbear(99)
        `-sh(100)---pstree(109)
```

The job of the `init` program is to take control of the system and set it running. It maybe as simple as a `shell` command running a shell script—there is an example at the start of `Chapter 5`, *Building a Root Filesystem*—but, in the majority of cases, you will be using a dedicated `init` daemon. The tasks it has to perform are as follows:

- At boot, it starts daemon programs and configures system parameters and the other things needed to get the system into a working state.
- Optionally, it launches a login daemon, such as `getty`, on Terminals that allow a login shell.
- It adopts processes that become orphaned as a result of their immediate parent terminating and there being no other processes in the thread group.
- It responds to any of the `init`'s immediate children terminating by catching the signal `SIGCHLD` and collecting the return value to prevent them becoming zombie processes. I will talk more about zombies in `Chapter 12`, *Learning About Processes and Threads*.
- Optionally, it restarts those daemons that have terminated.
- It handles the system shutdown.

In other words, `init` manages the lifecycle of the system from boot up to shutdown. The current thinking is that `init` is well placed to handle other runtime events, such as a new hardware and the loading and unloading of modules. This is what `systemd` does.

Introducing the init programs

The three `init` programs that you are most likely to encounter in embedded devices are BusyBox `init`, System V `init`, and `systemd`. Buildroot has options to build all three with the `init` BusyBox as the default. The Yocto Project allows you to choose between the System V called `init` and `systemd` with System `V` `init` as the default.

The following table gives some metrics to compare the three:

Metric	BusyBox init	System V init	systemd
Complexity	Low	Medium	High
Boot-up speed	Fast	Slow	Medium
Required shell	ash	ash or bash	None
Number of executables	0	4	50(*)
libc	Any	Any	glibc
Size (MiB)	0	0.1	34(*)

(*) Based on the Buildroot configuration of `systemd`.

Broadly speaking, there is an increase in flexibility and complexity as you go from BusyBox `init` to `systemd`.

BusyBox init

BusyBox has a minimal `init` program that uses a configuration file, `/etc/inittab`, to define rules to start programs at boot up and to stop them at shutdown. Usually, the actual work is done by shell scripts, which, by convention, are placed in the `/etc/init.d` directory.

`init` begins by reading `/etc/inittab`. This contains a list of programs to run, one per line, with this format:

```
<id>::<action>:<program>
```

The role of these parameter is as follows:

- `id`: This is the controlling Terminal for the command
- `action`: This is the conditions to run this command, as shown in the following paragraph
- `program`: This is the program to run

The actions are as follows:

- sysinit: Runs the program when init starts before any of the other types of actions.
- respawn: Runs the program and restarts it if it terminates. It is typically used to run a program as a daemon.
- askfirst: This is the same as respawn, but it prints the message *Please press Enter to activate this console* to the console, and it runs the program after *Enter* has been pressed. It is used to start an interactive shell on a Terminal without prompting for a username or password.
- once: Runs the program once but does not attempt to restart it if it terminates.
- wait: Runs the program and waits for it to complete.
- restart: Runs the program when init receives the signal SIGHUP, indicating that it should reload the inittab file.
- ctrlaltdel: Runs the program when init receives the signal, SIGINT, usually as a result of pressing *Ctrl + Alt + Del* on the console.
- shutdown: Runs the program when init shuts down.

Here is a small example that mounts proc and sysfs and runs a shell on a serial interface:

```
null::sysinit:/bin/mount -t proc proc /proc
null::sysinit:/bin/mount -t sysfs sysfs /sys
console::askfirst:-/bin/sh
```

For simple projects in which you want to launch a small number of daemons, and perhaps start a login shell on a serial Terminal, it is easy to write the scripts manually. This would be appropriate if you are creating a **roll your own** (**RYO**) embedded Linux. However, you will find that hand-written init scripts rapidly become unmaintainable as the number of things to be configured increases. They tend not to be very modular and so need updating each time a new component is added.

Buildroot init scripts

Buildroot has been making effective use of the BusyBox init for many years. Buildroot has two scripts in /etc/init.d/ named rcS and rcK. The first one runs at boot up and iterates over all the scripts in /etc/init.d/ with names that begin with a capital S followed by two digits, and runs them in numerical order. These are the start scripts. The rcK script is run at shutdown and iterates over all the scripts beginning with a capital K followed by two digits, and runs them in numerical order. These are the kill scripts.

With this in place, it becomes easy for Buildroot packages to supply their own start and kill scripts, using the two digit number to impose the order in which they should be run, and so the system becomes extensible. If you are using Buildroot, this is transparent. If not, you could use it as a model for writing your own BusyBox init scripts.

System V init

This init program was inspired by the one from Unix System V and so dates back to the mid 1980s. The version most often found in Linux distributions was written initially by Miquel van Smoorenburg. Until recently, it was the init daemon for almost all desktop and server distributions and a fair number of embedded systems as well. However, in recent years, it has been replaced by systemd, which I will describe in the next section.

The BusyBox init daemon I have just described is just a trimmed down version of System V init. Compared to the BusyBox init, System V init has two advantages. Firstly, the boot scripts are written in a well-known, modular format, making it easy to add new packages at build time or runtime. Secondly, it has the concept of **runlevels**, which allow a collection of programs to be started or stopped in one go when switching from one runlevel to another.

There are 8 runlevels numbered from 0 to 6, plus S:

- S: Runs startup tasks
- 0: Halts the system
- 1 to 5: Available for general use
- 6: Reboots the system

Levels 1 to 5 can be used as you please. On the desktop Linux distributions, they are conventionally assigned as follows:

- 1: Single user
- 2: Multi-user with no network configuration
- 3: Multi-user with network configuration
- 4: Not used
- 5: Multi-user with graphical login

The `init` program starts the default `runlevel` given by the `initdefault` line in `/etc/inittab`. You can change the runlevel at runtime using the command `telinit [runlevel]`, which sends a message to `init`. You can find the current runlevel and the previous one using the `runlevel` command. Here is an example:

```
# runlevel
N 5
# telinit 3
INIT: Switching to runlevel: 3
# runlevel
5 3
```

Initially, the output from the `runlevel` command is `N 5`, indicating that there is no previous runlevel, because the runlevel has not changed since booting and the current runlevel is 5. After changing the runlevel, the output is `5 3`, showing that there has been a transition from 5 to 3.

The `halt` and `reboot` commands switch to runlevels called 0 and 6 respectively. You can override the default runlevel by giving a different one on the kernel command line as a single digit from 0 to 6. For example, to force the runlevel to be single user, you would append 1 to the kernel command line, and it would look something like this:

```
console=ttyAMA0 root=/dev/mmcblk1p2 1
```

Each runlevel has a number of scripts that stop things, called `kill` scripts, and another group that start things, the `start` scripts. When entering a new runlevel, `init` first runs the `kill` scripts in the new level, and then the `start` scripts in the new level. Daemons that are currently running and which have neither a `start` script nor a `kill` script in the new runlevel are sent a `SIGTERM` signal. In other words, the default action on the switching runlevel is to terminate daemons unless told to do otherwise.

In truth, runlevels are not used that much in embedded Linux: most devices simply boot to the default runlevel and stay there. I have a feeling that it is partly because most people are not aware of them.

Runlevels are a simple and convenient way to switch between modes, for example, from production to maintenance mode.

System V `init` is an option in Buildroot and the Yocto Project. In both cases, the `init` scripts have been stripped of any `bash` shell specifics, so they will work with the BusyBox `ash` shell. However, Buildroot cheats somewhat by replacing the BusyBox `init` program with SystemV `init` and adding `inittab` that mimics the behavior of BusyBox. Buildroot does not implement runlevels, except that switching to levels 0 or 6 halts or reboots the system.

Next, let's look at some of the details. The following examples are taken from the **Morty** version of the Yocto Project. Other distributions may implement the `init` scripts a little differently.

inittab

The `init` program begins by reading `/etc/inttab`, which contains entries that define what happens at each runlevel. The format is an extended version of BusyBox `inittab` that I described in the preceding section, which is not surprising because BusyBox borrowed it from System V in the first place.

The format of each line in `inittab` is as follows:

```
id:runlevels:action:process
```

The fields are shown here:

- `id`: A unique identifier of up to four characters.
- `runlevels`: The runlevels for which this entry should be executed. This was left blank in the BusyBox `inittab`
- `action`: One of the keywords given in the following paragraph.
- `process`: The command to run.

The actions are the same as for BusyBox `init`: `sysinit`, `respawn`, `once`, `wait`, `restart`, `ctrlaltdel`, and `shutdown`. However, System V `init` does not have `askfirst`, which is specific to BusyBox.

As an example, this is the complete `inittab` supplied by the Yocto Project target `core-image-minimal` for the qemuarm machine:

```
# /etc/inittab: init(8) configuration.
# $Id: inittab,v 1.91 2002/01/25 13:35:21 miquels Exp $

# The default runlevel.
id:5:initdefault:
```

```
# Boot-time system configuration/initialization script.
# This is run first except when booting in emergency (-b) mode.
si::sysinit:/etc/init.d/rcS

# What to do in single-user mode.
~~:S:wait:/sbin/sulogin
# /etc/init.d executes the S and K scripts upon change
# of runlevel.
#
# Runlevel 0 is halt.
# Runlevel 1 is single-user.
# Runlevels 2-5 are multi-user.
# Runlevel 6 is reboot.

l0:0:wait:/etc/init.d/rc 0
l1:1:wait:/etc/init.d/rc 1
l2:2:wait:/etc/init.d/rc 2
l3:3:wait:/etc/init.d/rc 3
l4:4:wait:/etc/init.d/rc 4
l5:5:wait:/etc/init.d/rc 5
l6:6:wait:/etc/init.d/rc 6
# Normally not reached, but fallthrough in case of emergency.
z6:6:respawn:/sbin/sulogin
AMA0:12345:respawn:/sbin/getty 115200 ttyAMA0
# /sbin/getty invocations for the runlevels.
#
# The "id" field MUST be the same as the last
# characters of the device (after "tty").
#
# Format:
#   <id>:<runlevels>:<action>:<process>
#

1:2345:respawn:/sbin/getty 38400 tty1
```

The fist entry, `id:5:initdefault`, sets the default `runlevel` to 5. The next entry, `si::sysinit:/etc/init.d/rcS`, runs the script `rcS` at boot up. There will be more about this later. A little further on, there is a group of six entries beginning with `l0:0:wait:/etc/init.d/rc 0`. They run the `/etc/init.d/rc` script each time there is a change in the runlevel: this script is responsible for processing the `start` and `kill` scripts.

Toward the end of `inittab`, there is an entry that runs a `getty` daemon to generate a login prompt on `/dev/ttyAMA0` when entering runlevels 1 through to 5, thereby allowing you to log on and get an interactive shell:

```
AMA0:12345:respawn:/sbin/getty 115200 ttyAMA0
```

The `ttyAMA0` device is the serial console on the ARM Versatile board we are emulating with QEMU; it will be different for other development boards. There is also an entry to run a `getty` on `tty1`, which is triggered when entering runlevels 2 through 5. This is a virtual console, which is often mapped to a graphical screen if you have built your kernel with `CONFIG_FRAMEBUFFER_CONSOLE` or `VGA_CONSOLE`. Desktop Linux distributions usually spawn six `getty` daemons on virtual Terminals 1 to 6, which you can select with the key combination *Ctrl + Alt + F1* through *CTRL + Alt + F6*, with virtual Terminal 7 reserved for the graphical screen. Virtual Terminals are seldom used on embedded devices.

The `/etc/init.d/rcS` script that is run by the `sysinit` entry does little more than enter the runlevel, `S`:

```
#!/bin/sh
[...]
exec /etc/init.d/rc S
```

Hence, the first runlevel entered is `S`, followed by the default `runlevel` of 5. Note that runlevel `S` is not recorded and is never displayed as a prior runlevel by the `runlevel` command.

The init.d scripts

Each component that needs to respond to a runlevel change has a script in `/etc/init.d` to perform the change. The script should expect two parameters: `start` and `stop`. I will give an example of this later.

The runlevel handling script, `/etc/init.d/rc`, takes the runlevel it is switching to as a parameter. For each runlevel, there is a directory named `rc<runlevel>.d`:

```
# ls -d /etc/rc*
/etc/rc0.d  /etc/rc2.d  /etc/rc4.d  /etc/rc6.d
/etc/rc1.d  /etc/rc3.d  /etc/rc5.d  /etc/rcS.d
```

There you will find a set of scripts beginning with a capital `S` followed by two digits, and you may also find scripts beginning with a capital `K`. These are the `start` and `kill` scripts. Here is an example of the scripts for runlevel 5:

```
# ls /etc/rc5.d
S01networking    S20hwclock.sh    S99rmnologin.sh S99stop-bootlogd
S15mountnfs.sh   S20syslog
```

These are in fact symbolic links back to the appropriate script in init.d. The rc script runs all the scripts beginning with a K first, adding the stop parameter, and then runs those beginning with an S adding the start parameter. Once again, the two digit code is there to impart the order in which the scripts should run.

Adding a new daemon

Imagine that you have a program named simpleserver, which is written as a traditional Unix daemon, in other words, it forks and runs in the background: the code for such a program is in MELP/chapter_10/simpleserver. You will need an init.d script like this, which you will find in MELP/chapter_10/simpleserver-sysvinit:

```
#! /bin/sh

case "$1" in
  start)
    echo "Starting simpelserver"
    start-stop-daemon -S -n simpleserver -a /usr/bin/simpleserver
    ;;
  stop)
    echo "Stopping simpleserver"
    start-stop-daemon -K -n simpleserver
    ;;
  *)
    echo "Usage: $0 {start|stop}"
  exit 1
esac

exit 0
```

start-stop-daemon is a helper function that makes it easier to manipulate background processes such as this. It originally came from the Debian installer package, dpkg, but most embedded systems use the one from BusyBox. It starts the daemon with the -S parameter, making sure that there is never more than one instance running at any one time. To stop a daemon, you use the -K parameter, which causes it to send a signal, SIGTERM by default, to indicate to the daemon that it is time to terminate.

To make `simpleserver` operational, copy the script to the target directory called `/etc/init.d/simpleserver` and make it executable. Then, add links from each of the runlevels that you want to run this program from; in this case, only the default `runlevel`, 5:

```
# cd /etc/init.d/rc5.d
# ln -s ../init.d/simpleserver S99simpleserver
```

The number `99` means that this will be one of the last programs to be started. Bear in mind that there maybe other links beginning `S99`, in which case the `rc` script will just run them in lexical order.

It is rare in embedded devices to have to worry too much about shutdown operations, but if there is something that needs to be done, add `kill` links to levels 0 and 6:

```
# cd /etc/init.d/rc0.d
# ln -s ../init.d/simpleserver K01simpleserver
# cd /etc/init.d/rc6.d
# ln -s ../init.d/simpleserver K01simpleserver
```

Starting and stopping services

You can interact with the scripts in `/etc/init.d` by calling them directly. Here is an example using the `syslog` script, which controls the `syslogd` and `klogd` daemons:

```
# /etc/init.d/syslog --help
Usage: syslog { start | stop | restart }

# /etc/init.d/syslog stop
Stopping syslogd/klogd: stopped syslogd (pid 198)
stopped klogd (pid 201)
done

# /etc/init.d/syslog start
Starting syslogd/klogd: done
```

All scripts implement `start` and `stop`, and they should also implement `help`. Some implement `status` as well, which will tell you whether the service is running or not. Mainstream distributions that still use System V `init` have a command named `service` to start and stop services, which hide the details of calling the scripts directly.

systemd

systemd, https://www.freedesktop.org/wiki/Software/systemd/, defines itself as a *system and service manager*. The project was initiated in 2010 by Lennart Poettering and Kay Sievers to create an integrated set of tools for managing a Linux system based around an init daemon. It also includes device management (udev) and logging, among other things. systemd is state of the art and is still evolving rapidly. It is common on desktop and server Linux distributions and is becoming popular on embedded Linux systems too, especially on more complex devices. So, how is it better than System V init for embedded systems?

- The configuration is simpler and more logical (once you understand it). Rather than the sometimes convoluted shell scripts of System V init, systemd has unit configuration files, which are written in a well-defined format.
- There are explicit dependencies between services rather than a two digit code that merely sets the sequence in which the scripts are run.
- It is easy to set the permissions and resource limits for each service, which is important for the security.
- It can monitor services and restart them if needed.
- There are watchdogs for each service and for systemd itself.
- Services are started in parallel, potentially reducing boot time.

A complete description of systemd is neither possible nor appropriate here. As with System V init, I will focus on the embedded use cases with examples based on the configuration produced by the Morty release of the Yocto Project, which has the systemd version 230. I will give a quick overview, and then show you some specific examples.

Building systemd with the Yocto Project and Buildroot

The default init daemon in the Yocto Project is System V. To select systemd, add these lines to your conf/local.conf:

```
DISTRO_FEATURES_append = " systemd"
VIRTUAL-RUNTIME_init_manager = "systemd"
```

If you build with just those two lines in your local configuration, you will find that some components of System V `init` are still present, for example, the `init` scripts in `/etc/init.d` and commands such as `runlevel` and `start-stop-daemon`. If you want to strip those out as well, add this to your local configuration:

```
DISTRO_FEATURES_BACKFILL_CONSIDERED = "sysvinit"
VIRTUAL-RUNTIME_initscripts = ""
```

Buildroot uses BusyBox `init` by default. You can select `systemd` though menuconfig by looking in the menu **System configuration -> Init system**. You will also have to configure the toolchain to use `glibc` for the C-library, since systemd does not support `uClibc-ng` or `musl libc`. In addition, there are restrictions on the version and configuration of the kernel. There is a complete list of library and kernel dependencies in the README file in the top level of the systemd source code.

Introducing targets, services, and units

Before I describe how systemd `init` works, I need to introduce these three key concepts:

- **Unit**, which is a configuration file that describes a target, a service, and several other things. Units are text files that contain properties and values.
- **Service**, which is a daemon that can be started and stopped, very much like a System V `init` service.
- **Target**, which is a group of services, similar to, but more general than, a System V `init` runlevel. There is a default target which is the group of services that are started at boot time.

You can change states and find out what is going on using the `systemctl` command.

Units

The basic item of configuration is the unit file. Unit files are found in three different places:

- `/etc/systemd/system`: Local configuration
- `/run/systemd/system`: Runtime configuration
- `/lib/systemd/system`: Distribution-wide configuration

When looking for a unit, `systemd` searches the directories in that order, stopping as soon as it finds a match, and allowing you to override the behavior of a distribution-wide unit by placing a unit of the same name in `/etc/systemd/system`. You can disable a unit completely by creating a local file that is empty or linked to `/dev/null`.

All unit files begin with a section marked `[Unit]`, which contains basic information and dependencies. As an example, here is the *Unit* section of the D-Bus service, `/lib/systemd/system/dbus.service`:

```
[Unit]
Description=D-Bus System Message Bus
Documentation=man:dbus-daemon(1)
Requires=dbus.socket
```

In addition to the description and a reference to the documentation, there is a dependency on the `dbus.socket` unit expressed through the `Requires` keyword. This tells `systemd` to create a local socket when the D-Bus service is started.

Dependencies in the *Unit* section are expressed though the keywords `Requires`, `Wants`, and `Conflicts`:

- `Requires`: This is a list of units that this unit depends on, which are started when this unit is started
- `Wants`: This is a weaker form of `Requires`; the units listed are started but the current unit is not stopped if any of them fail
- `Conflicts`: This is a negative dependency; the units listed are stopped when this one is started and, conversely, if one of them is started, this one is stopped

These three keywords define **outgoing dependencies**. They are used mostly to create dependencies between targets. There is another sort of dependency called an **incoming dependency**, which is used to create a link between a *service* and a *target*. In other words, outgoing dependencies are used to create the list of targets that need to be started as the system goes from one state to another, and incoming dependencies are used to determine the services that should be started or stopped in any particular state. Incoming dependencies are created by the **WantedBy** keyword, which I will describe in the section on installing your own service.

Processing the dependencies produces a list of units that should be started or stopped. The keywords **Before** and **After** determine the order in which they are started. The order of stopping is just the reverse of the start order:

- **Before**: This unit should be started before the units listed
- **After**: This unit should be started after the units listed

In the following example, the `After` directive makes sure that the web server is started after the network:

```
[Unit]
Description=Lighttpd Web Server
After=network.target
```

In the absence of the `Before` or `After` directive, the units will be started or stopped in parallel with no particular ordering.

Services

A service is a daemon that can be started and stopped, equivalent to a System V `init` service. A service is a type of unit file with a name ending in `.service`, for example, `lighttpd.service`.

A service unit has a `[Service]` section that describes how it should be run. Here is the relevant section from `lighttpd.service`:

```
[Service]
ExecStart=/usr/sbin/lighttpd -f /etc/lighttpd/lighttpd.conf -D
ExecReload=/bin/kill -HUP $MAINPID
```

These are the commands to run when starting the service and restarting it. There are many more configuration points you can add in here, so refer to the manual page for *systemd.service(5)*.

Targets

A target is another type of unit, which groups services (or other types of unit). It is a type of unit that only has dependencies. Targets have names ending in `.target`, for example, `multi-user.target`. A target is a desired state, which performs the same role as System V `init` runlevels. For example, this is the complete unit for `muti-user.target`:

```
[Unit]
Description=Multi-User System
Documentation=man:systemd.special(7)
Requires=basic.target
Conflicts=rescue.service rescue.target
After=basic.target rescue.service rescue.target
AllowIsolate=yes
```

This says that the basic target must be started before the multi-user target. It also says that since it conflicts with the rescue target, starting the rescue target will cause the multi-user target to be stopped first.

How systemd boots the system

Now, we can see how `systemd` implements the bootstrap. `systemd` is run by the kernel as a result of `/sbin/init` being symbolically linked to `/lib/systemd/systemd`. It runs the default target, `default.target`, which is always a link to a desired target such as `multi-user.target` for a text login or `graphical.target` for a graphical environment. For example, if the default target is `multi-user.target`, you will find this symbolic link:

```
/etc/systemd/system/default.target ->
    /lib/systemd/system/multi-user.target
```

The default target maybe overridden by passing `system.unit=<new target>` on the kernel command line. You can use `systemctl` to find out the default target, as shown here:

```
# systemctl get-default
multi-user.target
```

Starting a target such as `multi-user.target` creates a tree of dependencies that bring the system into a working state. In a typical system, `multi-user.target` depends on `basic.target`, which depends on `sysinit.target`, which depends on the services that need to be started early. You can print a graph using `systemctl list-dependencies`.

You can also list all the services and their current state using:

```
# systemctl list-units --type service
```

And the same for targets using:

```
# systemctl list-units --type target
```

Adding your own service

Using the same `simpleserver` example as before, here is a service unit, which you will find in `MELP/chapter_10/simpleserver-systemd`:

```
[Unit]
Description=Simple server

[Service]
```

```
Type=forking
ExecStart=/usr/bin/simpleserver

[Install]
WantedBy=multi-user.target
```

The [Unit] section only contains a description so that it shows up correctly when listed using systemctl and other commands. There are no dependencies; as I said, it is very simple.

The [Service] section points to the executable and has a flag to indicate that it forks. If it were even simpler and ran in the foreground, systemd would do the daemonizing for us and Type=forking would not be needed.

The [Install] section creates an incoming dependency on multi-user.target so that our server is started when the system goes into the multi-user mode.

Once the unit is saved in /etc/systemd/system/simpleserver.service, you can start and stop it using the commands: systemctl start simpleserver and sytemctl stop simpleserver. You can also use systemctl to find its current status:

```
# systemctl status simpleserver
   simpleserver.service - Simple server
   Loaded: loaded (/etc/systemd/system/simpleserver.service;
     disabled)  Active: active (running) since Thu 1970-01-01 02:20:50 UTC;
8s
     ago
   Main PID: 180 (simpleserver)
   CGroup: /system.slice/simpleserver.service
           └─180 /usr/bin/simpleserver -n

Jan 01 02:20:50 qemuarm systemd[1]: Started Simple server.
```

At this point, it will only start and stop on command, as shown here. To make it persistent, you need to add a permanent dependency to a target. This is the purpose of the [Install] section in the unit; it says that when this service is enabled it will become dependent on multi-user.target, and so will be started at boot time. You enable it using systemctl enable, like this:

```
# systemctl enable simpleserver
Created symlink from /etc/systemd/system/multi-
user.target.wants/simpleserver.service to
 /etc/systemd/system/simpleserver.service.
```

Now, you can see how services add dependencies without having to keep on editing target unit files. A target can have a directory named `<target_name>.target.wants`, which can contain links to services. This is exactly the same as adding the dependent unit to the [Wants] list in the target. In this case, you will find that this link has been created:

```
/etc/systemd/system/multi-user.target.wants/simpleserver.service ->
    /etc/systemd/system/simpleserver.service
```

If this is were an important service you might want to restart it if it failed. You can accomplish that by adding this flag to the [Service] section:

```
Restart=on-abort
```

Other options for `Restart` are `on-success`, `on-failure`, `on-abnormal`, `on-watchdog`, `on-abort`, or `always`.

Adding a watchdog

Watchdogs are a common requirement in embedded devices: you need to take action if a critical service stops working, usually by resetting the system. On most embedded SoCs, there is a hardware watchdog, which can be accessed via the `/dev/watchdog` device node. The watchdog is initialized with a timeout at boot, and then must be reset within that period, otherwise the watchdog will be triggered and the system will reboot. The interface with the watchdog driver is described in the kernel source in `Documentation/watchdog` and the code for the drivers is in `drivers/watchdog`.

A problem arises if there are two or more critical services that need to be protected by a watchdog. `systemd` has a useful feature that distributes the watchdog between multiple services.

`systemd` can be configured to expect a regular `keepalive` call from a service and take action if it is not received, creating a per-service software watchdog. For this to work, you have to add code to the daemon to send the `keepalive` messages. It needs to check for a non-zero value in the `WATCHDOG_USEC` environment variable, and then call `sd_notify(false, "WATCHDOG=1")` within this time (a period of half of the watchdog timeout is recommended). There are examples in the `systemd` source code.

To enable the watchdog in the service unit, add something like this to the `[Service]` section:

```
WatchdogSec=30s
Restart=on-watchdog
StartLimitInterval=5min
StartLimitBurst=4
StartLimitAction=reboot-force
```

In this example, the service expects `keepalive` every 30 seconds. If it fails to be delivered, the service will be restarted, but if it is restarted more than four times in five minutes, systemd will force an immediate reboot. Once again, there is a full description of these settings in the `systemd.service(5)` manual page.

A watchdog like this takes care of individual services, but what if systemd itself fails, the kernel crashes, or the hardware locks up. In those cases, we need to tell `systemd` to use the watchdog driver: just add `RuntimeWatchdogSec=NN` to `/etc/systemd/system.conf`. `systemd` will reset the watchdog within that period, and so the system will reset if `systemd` fails for some reason.

Implications for embedded Linux

Systemd has a lot of features that are useful in embedded Linux, including many that I have not mentioned in this brief description, such as resource control using slices (which are described in the manual pages for `systemd.slice(5)` and `systemd.resource-control(5)`), device management (`udev(7)`), and system logging facilities (`journald(5)`).

You have to balance that with its size: even with a minimal build of just the core components, `systemd`, `udevd`, and `journald`, it is approaching 10 MiB of storage, including the shared libraries.

You also have to keep in mind that systemd development follows the kernel closely, so it will not work on a kernel more than a year or two older than the release of systemd.

Further reading

systemd System and Service Manager:
`http://www.freedesktop.org/wiki/Software/systemd/`. There are a lot of useful links at the bottom of that page.

Summary

Every Linux device needs an `init` program of some kind. If you are designing a system, which only has to launch a small number of daemons at startup and remains fairly static after that, then BusyBox init is sufficient for your needs. It is usually a good choice if you are using Buildroot as the build system.

If, on the other hand, you have a system that has complex dependencies between services at boot time or runtime, and you have the storage space, then `systemd` would be the best choice. Even without the complexity, systemd has some useful features in the way it handles watchdogs, remote logging, and so on, so you should certainly give it serious thought.

Meanwhile, System V `init` lives on. It is well understood, and there are `init` scripts already in existence for every component that is important to us. It remains the default `init` for the Poky distribution of the Yocto Project.

In terms of reducing boot time, `systemd` is faster than System V `init` for a similar workload. However, if you are looking for a very fast boot, nothing can beat a simple BusyBox `init` with minimal boot scripts.

In the next chapter, I will turn my attention to the power management of Linux systems with the aim of showing how to reduce energy consumption. This will be especially useful if you are designing devices that run on battery power.

11
Managing Power

For devices operating on battery power, power management is a critical issue: anything we can do to reduce power usage will increase battery life. Even for devices running on mains power, reducing power usage has benefits in reducing the need for cooling and energy costs. In this chapter, I will introduce the four principles of power management:

- Don't rush if you don't have to
- Don't be ashamed of being idle
- Turn off things you are not using
- Sleep when there is nothing else to do

Putting these into more technical terms, the principles mean that the power management system should endeavor to reduce the CPU clock frequency; during idle periods, it should choose the deepest sleep state possible; it should reduce the load by powering down unused peripherals; and it should be able to put the whole system into a suspend state.

Linux has features that address each of these points. I will describe each one in turn, with examples and advice on how to apply them to an embedded system in order to make optimum use of power.

Some of the terminologies of system power management are taken from the **Advanced Configuration and Power Interface (ACPI)** specification: terms such as **C-states** and **P-states**. I will describe these as we get to them. The full reference to the specification is given in the *Further reading* section.

In this chapter, we will specifically cover the following topics:

- Measuring power usage
- Scaling the clock frequency
- Selecting the best idle state

- Powering down peripherals
- Putting the system to sleep

Measuring power usage

For the examples in this chapter, we need to use real hardware rather than virtual. This means that we need a BeagleBone Black with working power management. Unfortunately, the BSP for the BeagleBone that comes with the meta-yocto-bsp layer does not include the necessary firmware for the **Power Management IC (PMIC)**, so we will have to build an image with a customized kernel. The procedure is the same as we covered in Chapter 6, *Selecting a Build System*.

First, get a copy of the Yocto Project Morty release, and add the meta-bbb-pm layer from the code archive:

```
$ git clone -b morty git://git.yoctoproject.org/poky.git
$ cd poky
$ cp -a MELP/chapter_11/poky/meta-bbb-pm
$ source oe-init-build-env build-bbb
$ bitbake-layers add-layer ../meta-bbb-pm
```

Next, edit conf/local.conf and add these lines at the beginning of the file:

```
MACHINE = "beaglebone"
PREFERRED_PROVIDER_virtual/kernel = "ti-linux-kernel"
IMAGE_INSTALL_append = " powertop dropbear rt-tests amx3-cm3 kernel-
vmlinux"
```

Then, build an image, for example, core-image-minimal:

```
$ bitbake core-image-minimal
```

Next, format a microSD card and copy the image to it using the scripts in the MELP archive:

```
$ MELP/format-sdcard.sh [your sdcard reader]
$ MELP/copy-yoctoproject-image-to-sdcard.sh \
beaglebone core-image-minimal
```

Finally, boot the BeagleBone Black and check whether the power management is working:

```
# cat /sys/power/state
freeze standby mem disk
```

If you see all four states, everything is working fine. If you see only `freeze`, the power management subsystem is not working. Go back and double-check the previous steps.

Now we can move on to measuring power usage. There are two approaches: **external** and **internal**. Measuring power externally, from outside the system, we just need an ammeter to measure the current and a voltmeter to measure the voltage, and then multiply the two together in order to get the wattage. You can use basic meters that give a readout, which you then note down. Or, they can be much more sophisticated and combine data logging so that you can see the change in power as the load changes millisecond by millisecond. For the purposes of this chapter, I powered the BeagleBone from the mini USB port and used a cheap USB power monitor of the type that costs a few dollars.

The other approach is to use the monitoring systems that are built into Linux. You will find that plenty of information is reported to you via `sysfs`. There is also a very useful program called **PowerTOP**, which gathers information together from various sources and presents it in a single place. PowerTOP is a package for both Yocto Project and Buildroot. You may notice that I have included `powertop` as an additional package in the Yocto Project configuration I provided at the beginning of this section. Here is an example of PowerTOP running on the BeagleBone Black:

```
PowerTOP 2.8      Overview  Idle stats  Frequency stats  Device stats   Tunables

Summary: 4.2 wakeups/second,  0.0 GPU ops/seconds, 0.0 VFS ops/sec and 0.4% CPU use

          Usage        Events/s    Category    Description
       257.0 us/s        1.0       kWork       phy_state_machine
         2.3 ms/s        0.15      Process     powertop
        72.0 us/s        0.6       Timer       tick_sched_timer
        54.7 us/s        0.6       Process     [rcu_preempt]
        35.0 us/s        0.5       kWork       cache_reap
         8.1 us/s        0.5       kWork       vmstat_shepherd
         0.9 ms/s        0.05      Process     [irq/159-44e0b00]
         6.2 us/s        0.25      Process     [watchdog/0]
        24.4 us/s        0.20      Process     init [5]
         1.4 us/s        0.15      kWork       neigh_periodic_work
        50.7 us/s        0.10      Interrupt   [3] net_rx(softirq)
         1.4 us/s        0.10      kWork       cpts_overflow_check
       189.8 us/s        0.00      Interrupt   [159] 44e0b000.i2c
        41.2 us/s        0.05      kWork       rb_free_work
         6.8 us/s        0.05      kWork       flush_to_ldisc
         0.3 us/s        0.05      Timer       sched_clock_poll
        77.8 us/s        0.00      Process     /usr/sbin/dropbear  -r /etc/dropbear/d
        62.5 us/s        0.00      Process     [kworker/0:1]

<ESC> Exit | <TAB> / <Shift + TAB> Navigate |
```

In this screenshot, we can see that the system is quiet, with only **0.4%** of CPU usage. I will show more interesting examples later on.

Scaling the clock frequency

Running for a kilometer takes more energy than walking. In a similar way, maybe running the CPU at a lower frequency can save energy. Let's see.

The power consumption of a CPU when executing code is the sum of a static component, caused by gate leakage current, among other things, and a dynamic component, caused by switching of the gates:

$$P_{cpu} = P_{static} + P_{dyn}$$

The dynamic power component is dependent on the total capacitance of the logic gates being switched, the clock frequency, and the square of the voltage:

$$P_{dyn} = CfV^2$$

From this, we can see that changing the frequency by itself is not going to save any power because the same number of CPU cycles have to be completed in order to execute a given subroutine. If we reduce the frequency by half, it will take twice as long to complete the calculation, but the total power consumed due to the dynamic power component will be the same. In fact, reducing the frequency may actually increase the power budget because it takes longer for the CPU to enter an idle state. So, in these conditions, it is best to use the highest frequency possible so that the CPU can go back to idle quickly. This is called the **race to idle**.

 There is another motivation to reduce frequency: **thermal management**. It may become necessary to operate at a lower frequency just to keep the temperature of the package within bounds. But that is not our focus here.

Therefore, if we want to save power, we have to be able to change the voltage that the CPU core operates at. But for any given voltage, there is a maximum frequency beyond which the switching of the gates become unreliable. Higher frequencies need higher voltages, and so the two need to be adjusted together. Many SoCs implement such a feature: it is called **Dynamic Voltage and Frequency Scaling**, or **DVFS**. Manufacturers calculate optimum combinations of core frequency and voltage. Each combination is called **Operating Performance Point**, or **OPP**. The ACPI specification refers to them as P-states, with P0 being the OPP with the highest frequency. Although an OPP is a combination of a frequency and a voltage, they are most often referred to by the frequency component alone.

The CPUFreq driver

Linux has a component named CPUFreq that manages the transitions between OPPs. It is part of the board support for the package for each SoC. CPUFreq consists of drivers in drivers/cpufreq/, which make the transition from one OPP to another, and a set of governors that implement the policy of when to switch. It is controlled per-CPU via the /sys/devices/system/cpu/cpuN/cpufreq directory, with N being the CPU number. In there, we find a number of files, the most interesting of which are as follows:

- cpuinfo_cur_freq, cpuinfo_max_freq and cpuinfo_min_freq: The current frequency for this CPU, together with the maximum and minimum, measured in KHz.
- cpuinfo_transition_latency: The time, in nanoseconds, to switch from one OPP to another. If the value is unknown, it is set to −1.
- scaling_available_frequencies: A list of OPP frequencies available on this CPU.
- scaling_available_governors: A list of governors available on this CPU, which are described as follows:
  - scaling_governor: The CPUFreq governor currently being used.
  - scaling_max_freq and scaling_min_freq: The range of frequencies available to the governor in KHz.
  - scaling_setspeed: A file that allows you to manually set the frequency when the governor is userspace, which I will describe in the following section.

The governor sets the policy to change the OPP. It can set the frequency between the limits of scaling_min_freq and scaling_max_freq. The governors are named as follows:

- powersave: Always selects the lowest frequency.
- performance: Always selects the highest frequency.
- ondemand: Changes frequency based on the CPU utilization. If the CPU is idle less than 20% of the time, it sets the frequency to the maximum; if it is idle more than 30% of the time, it decrements the frequency by 5%.
- conservative: As ondemand, but switches to higher frequencies in 5% steps rather than going immediately to the maximum.
- userspace: Frequency is set by a user space program.

The parameters the `ondemand` governor uses to decide when to change OPP can be viewed and modified via `/sys/devices/system/cpu/cpufreq/ondemand/`. Both `ondemand` and `conservative` governors take into account the effort required to change frequency and voltage. This parameter is in `cpuinfo_transition_latency`. These calculations are for threads with a normal scheduling policy; if the thread is being scheduled in real-time, they will both immediately select the highest OPP so that the thread can meet its scheduling deadline.

The `userspace` governor allows the logic of selecting the OPP to be performed by a user space daemon. Examples include `cpudyn` and `powernowd`, although both are orientated toward x86-based laptops rather than embedded devices.

Using CPUFreq

Looking at the BeagleBone Black, we find that the OPPs are coded in the device tree. Here is an extract from `am33xx.dtsi`:

```
cpu0_opp_table: opp-table {
  compatible = "operating-points-v2-ti-cpu";
  syscon = <&scm_conf>;

  opp50@300000000 {
    opp-hz = /bits/ 64 <300000000>;
    opp-microvolt = <950000 931000 969000>;
    opp-supported-hw = <0x06 0x0010>;
    opp-suspend;
  };
  opp100@600000000 {
    opp-hz = /bits/ 64 <600000000>;
    opp-microvolt = <1100000 1078000 1122000>;
    opp-supported-hw = <0x06 0x0040>;
  };
  opp120@720000000 {
    opp-hz = /bits/ 64 <720000000>;
    opp-microvolt = <1200000 1176000 1224000>;
    opp-supported-hw = <0x06 0x0080>;
  };
  oppturbo@800000000 {
    opp-hz = /bits/ 64 <800000000>;
    opp-microvolt = <1260000 1234800 1285200>;
    opp-supported-hw = <0x06 0x0100>;
  };
  oppnitro@1000000000 {
    opp-hz = /bits/ 64 <1000000000>;
```

```
opp-microvolt = <1325000 1298500 1351500>;
opp-supported-hw = <0x04 0x0200>;
};
};
```

We can confirm that these are the OPPs in use at runtime by viewing the available frequencies:

```
# cd /sys/devices/system/cpu/cpu0/cpufreq
# cat scaling_available_frequencies
300000 600000 720000 800000 1000000
```

By selecting the user space governor, we can set the frequency by writing to `scaling_setspeed`, and so we can measure the power consumed at each OPP. These measurements are not very accurate, so do not take them too seriously.

First, with an idle system, the result is 70mA @ 4.6V = 320 mW. This is independent of the frequency, which is what we would expect since this is the static component of the power consumption of this particular system.

Now, I want to know the maximum power consumed at each OPP by running a compute-bound load such as this:

```
# dd if=/dev/urandom of=/dev/null bs=1
```

The results are shown in the following table, with **Delta power** being the additional power usage above the idle system:

OPP	Freq, KHz	Power, mW	Delta power, mW
OPP50	300,000	370	50
OPP100	600,000	505	185
OPP120	720,000	600	280
Turbo	800,000	640	320
Nitro	1,000,000	780	460

These measurements show the maximum power at the various OPPs. But it is not a fair test because the CPU is running at 100%, and so it is executing more instructions at higher frequencies. If we keep the load constant but vary the frequency, then we find the following:

OPP	Freq, KHz	CPU utilization, %	Power, mW
OPP50	300,000	94	320
OPP100	600,000	48	345
OPP120	720,000	40	370
Turbo	800,000	34	370
Nitro	1,000,000	28	370

This shows a definite power saving at the lowest frequency, in the order of 15%.

Using **PowerTOP**, we can see the percentage of time spent in each OPP. The following screenshot shows the BeagleBone Black running a light load and using the ondemand governor:

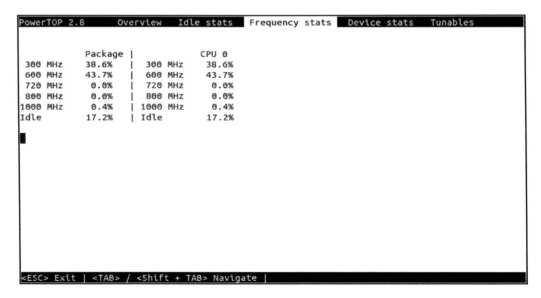

In most cases, the `ondemand` governor is the best one to use. To select a particular governor, you can either configure the kernel with a default governor, for example, `CPU_FREQ_DEFAULT_GOV_ONDEMAND`, or you can use a boot script to change the governor at boot time. There is an example **System V (SysV)** init script in `MELP/chapter_11/sysvinit-ondemand.sh`, taken from Ubuntu 14.04.

For more information on the CPU-freq driver, take a look at the kernel source code in the `Documentation/cpu-freq` directory.

Selecting the best idle state

In the preceding section, we were concerned about the power used when the CPU is busy. In this section, we will look at how to save power when the CPU is idle.

When a processor has no more work to do, it executes a halt instruction and enters an idle state. While idle, the CPU uses less power. It exits the idle state when an event such as a hardware interruption occurs. Most CPUs have multiple idle states that use varying amounts of power. Usually, there is a trade-off between the power usage and the latency, or the length of time, it takes to exit the state. In the ACPI specification, they are called **C-states**.

In the deeper C-states, more circuitry is turned off at the expense of losing some state, and so it takes longer to return to normal operation. For example, in some C-states the CPU caches may be powered off, and so when the CPU runs again, it may have to reload some information from the main memory. This is expensive, and so you only want to do this if there is a good chance that the CPU will remain in this state for some time. The number of states varies from one system to another. Each takes some time to recover from sleeping to being fully active.

The key to selecting the right idle state is to have a good idea of how long the CPU is going to be quiescent. Predicting the future is always tricky, but there are some things that can help. One is the current CPU load: if it is high now, it is likely to continue to be so in the immediate future, so a deep sleep would not be beneficial. Even if the load is low, it is worth looking to see whether there is a timer event that expires soon. If there is no load and no timer, then a deeper idle state is justified.

The part of Linux that selects the best idle state is the CPUIdle driver. There is a good deal of information about it in the kernel source code in the `Documentation/cpuidle` directory.

The CPUIdle driver

As with the CPUFreq subsystem, **CPUIdle** consists of a driver that is part of the BSP and a governor that determines the policy. Unlike CPUFreq, however, the governor cannot be changed at runtime and there is no interface for user space governors.

CPUIdle exposes information about each of the idle states in the `/sys/devices/system/cpu/cpu0/cpuidle` directory, in which there is a subdirectory for each of the sleep states, named `state0` to `stateN`. `state0` is the *lightest* sleep and `stateN` the *deepest*. Note that the numbering does not match that of the C-states and that CPUIdle does not have a state equivalent to `C0` (running). For each state, there are these files:

- `desc`: A short description of the state
- `disable`: An option to disable this state by writing 1 to this file
- `latency`: The time the CPU core takes to resume normal operation when exiting this state, in microseconds
- `name`: The name of this state
- `power`: The power consumed while in this idle state, in milliwatts
- `time`: The total time spent in this idle state, in microseconds
- `usage`: The count of the number of times this state was entered

In the case of the AM335x SoC on the BeagleBone Black, there are two idle states. This is the first:

```
# cd /sys/devices/system/cpu/cpu0/cpuidle
# grep "" state0/*
state0/desc:ARM WFI
state0/disable:0
state0/latency:1
state0/name:WFI
state0/power:4294967295
state0/residency:1
state0/time:1780015
state0/usage:2159
```

This state is named WFI, which refers to the ARM halt instruction, **Wait For Interrupt**. The latency is 1 microsecond because it is just a halt instruction, and the power consumed is given as −1, which means that the power budget is not known (by CPUIdle at least). Now this is the second state:

```
# cd /sys/devices/system/cpu/cpu0/cpuidle
# grep "" state1/*
state1/desc:Bypass MPU PLL
state1/disable:0
state1/latency:100
state1/name:C1
state1/power:497
state1/residency:200
state1/time:8763012731
state1/usage:345285
```

This one is named C1. It has a higher latency of 100 microseconds, but a real power level is given of 497 milliwatts, which seems a little high to me. The idle states may be hardcoded into the CPUIdle driver or presented in the device tree. The AM335x does the former, so here is an example from a different SoC:

```
cpus {
  cpu: cpu0 {
     compatible = "arm,cortex-a9";
     enable-method = "ti,am4372";
     device-type = "cpu";
     reg = <0>;

     cpu-idle-states = <&mpu_gate>;
  };

  idle-states {
     compatible = "arm,idle-state";
     entry-latency-us = <40>;
     exit-latency-us = <100>;
     min-residency-us = <300>;
     local-timer-stop;
  };
};
```

CPUIdle has two governors:

- `ladder`: This steps idle states down or up, one at a time, depending on the time spent in the last idle period. It works well with a regular timer tick but not with a dynamic tick.
- `menu`: This selects an idle state based on the expected idle time. It works well with dynamic tick systems.

You should choose one or the other depending on your configuration of NOHZ, which I will describe at the end of this section.

Once again, user interaction is via the `sysfs` filesystem. In the `/sys/devices/system/cpu/cpuidle` directory, you will find two files:

- `current_driver`: This is the name of the `cpuidle` driver
- `current_governor_ro`: This is the name of the governor

These show which driver and which governor are being used. The idle states can be shown in PowerTOP on the **Idle stats** tab. The following screenshot shows a BeagleBone Black using the `menu` governor:

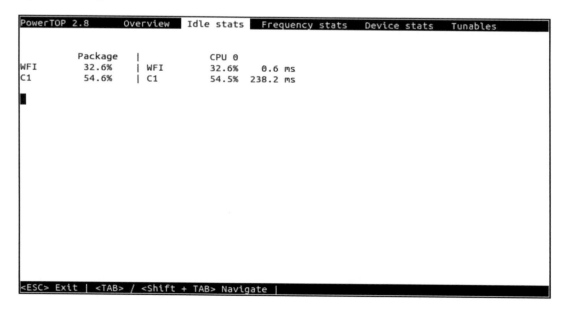

This shows that when the system is idle, it is mostly going to the deeper idle state, C1, which is what we would want.

Tickless operation

A related topic is the tickles, or NOHZ, option. If the system is truly idle, the most likely source of interruptions will be the system timer, which is programmed to generate a regular time tick at a rate of HZ per second, where HZ is typically 100. Historically, Linux uses the timer tick as the main time base for measuring time-outs.

And yet it is plainly wasteful to wake the CPU up to process a timer interruption if no timer events are registered for that particular moment. The dynamic tick kernel configuration option, CONFIG_NO_HZ, looks at the timer queue at the end of the timer processing routine and schedules the next interruption at the time of the next event, avoiding unnecessary wake-ups and allowing the CPU to be idle for longer periods. In any power-sensitive application, the kernel should be configured with this option enabled.

Powering down peripherals

The discussion up to now has been about CPUs and how to reduce power consumption when they are running or idling. Now it is time to focus on other parts of the system peripherals and see whether we can achieve power savings here.

In the Linux kernel, this is managed by the **runtime power management** system, or **runtime pm** for short. It works with drivers that support runtime pm, shutting down those that are not in use and waking them again when they are next needed. It is dynamic and should be transparent to user space. It is up to the device driver to implement the management of the hardware, but typically, it would include turning off the clock to the subsystem, also known as clock gating, and turning off core circuitry where possible.

The runtime power management is exposed via a sysfs interface. Each device has a subdirectory named power, in which you will find these files:

- control: This allows userspace to determine whether runtime pm is used on this device. If it is set to auto, then runtime pm is enabled, but by setting it to on, the device is always on and does not use runtime pm.
- runtime_enabled: This reports that runtime pm is enabled, disabled, or, if control is on, it reports forbidden.
- runtime_status: This reports the current state of the device. It may be active, suspended, or unsupported
- autosuspend_delay_ms: This is the time before the device is suspended. -1 means waiting forever. Some drivers implement this if there is a significant cost to suspending the device hardware since it prevents rapid suspend/resume cycles.

To give a concrete example, I will look at the MMC driver on the BeagleBone Black:

```
# cd /sys/devices/platform/ocp/481d8000.mmc/
mmc_host/mmc1/mmc1:0001/power
# grep "" *
async:disabled
autosuspend_delay_ms:3000
control:auto
runtime_active_kids:0
runtime_active_time:5170
runtime_enabled:enabled
runtime_status:suspended
runtime_suspended_time:137560
runtime_usage:0
```

So, runtime pm is enabled, the device is currently suspended, and there is a delay of 3000 milliseconds after it was last used before it will be suspended again. Now I read a block from the device and see whether it has changed:

```
# dd if=/dev/mmcblk1p3 of=/dev/null count=1
1+0 records in
1+0 records out
# grep "" *
async:disabled
autosuspend_delay_ms:3000
control:auto
runtime_active_kids:0
runtime_active_time:7630
```

```
runtime_enabled:enabled
runtime_status:active
runtime_suspended_time:200680
runtime_usage:0
```

Now MMC driver is active and the power to the board has increased from 320 mW to 500 mW. If I repeat it again after 3 seconds, it is once more suspended and the power has returned to 320 mW.

For more information on runtime pm, look in the kernel source code at `Documentation/power/runtime_pm.txt`.

Putting the system to sleep

There is one more power management technique to consider: putting the whole system into sleep mode with the expectation that it will not be used again for a while. In the Linux kernel, this is known as **system sleep**. It is usually user-initiated: the user decides that the device should be shut down for a while. For example, I shut the lid of my laptop and put it in my bag when it is time to go home. Much of the support for system sleep in Linux comes from the support for laptops. In the laptop world, there are usually two options: suspend or hibernate. The first, also known as **suspend to RAM**, shuts everything down except the system memory, so the machine is still consuming a little power. When the system wakes up, the memory retains all the previous state, and my laptop is operational within a few seconds. If I select the **hibernate** option, the contents of memory are saved to the hard drive. The system consumes no power at all, and so it can stay in this state indefinitely, but on wake-up, it takes some time to restore the memory from disk. Hibernate is very seldom used in embedded systems, mostly because the flash storage tends to be quite slow on read/write but also because it is intrusive to the flow of work.

For more information, look at the kernel source code in the `Documentation/power` directory.

Power states

In the ACPI specification, the sleep states are called **S-states**. Linux supports four sleep states, which are shown in the following table, along with the corresponding ACPI S-state:

Linux system sleep state	ACPI S-state	Description
freeze	[S0]	Stops (freezes) all activity in user space, but otherwise the CPU and memory are operating as normal. The power saving results from the fact that no user space code is being run. ACPI doesn't have an equivalent state: S0 is the closest match. S0 is the state for a running system.
standby	S1	Just like freeze, but additionally takes all CPUs offline except the boot CPU.
mem	S3	Powers down the system and put the memory in the self-refresh mode. Also known as **suspend to RAM**.
disk	S4	Saves the memory to the hard disk and powers down. Also known as **suspend to disk**.

Not all systems have support for all states. You can find out which are available by reading the /sys/power/state file, for example:

```
# cat /sys/power/state
freeze standby mem disk
```

To enter one of the system sleep states, you just have to write the desired state to /sys/power/state.

For embedded devices, the most common need is to suspend to RAM using the mem option. For example, I can suspend the BeagleBone Black like this:

```
# echo mem > /sys/power/state
[ 1646.158274] PM: Syncing filesystems ...done.
[ 1646.178387] Freezing user space processes ...(elapsed 0.001 seconds)
done.
[ 1646.188098] Freezing remaining freezable tasks ...
(elapsed 0.001 seconds) done.
[ 1646.197017] Suspending console(s) (use
no_console_suspend to debug)
[ 1646.338657] PM: suspend of devices complete
after 134.322 msecs
[ 1646.343428] PM: late suspend of devices
```

```
complete after 4.716 msecs
[ 1646.348234] PM: noirq suspend of devices
complete after 4.755 msecs
[ 1646.348251] Disabling non-boot CPUs ...
[ 1646.348264] PM: Successfully put all
powerdomains to target state
```

The device powers down in less than a second and then power usage drops down to below 10 milliwatts, which is the limit of measurement of my simple multimeter. But how do I wake it up again? That is the next topic.

Wakeup events

Before you suspend a device, you must have a method of waking it again. The kernel tries to help you here: if there is not at least one wakeup source, the system will refuse to suspend with the message:

```
No sources enabled to wake-up! Sleep abort.
```

Of course, this means that some parts of the system have to remain powered on even during the deepest sleep. This usually involves the **Power Management IC (PMIC)**, the **real-time clock (RTC)**, and may additionally include interfaces such as GPIO, UART, and Ethernet.

Wakeup events are controlled through sysfs. Each device in /sys/device has a subdirectory power containing a wakeup file that will contain one of these strings:

- enabled: This device will generate wakeup events
- disabled: This device will not generate wakeup events
- (empty): This device is not capable of generating wakeup events

To get a list of devices that can generate wakeups, we can search for all devices where wakeup contains either enabled or disabled:

```
$ find /sys/devices -name wakeup | xargs grep "abled"
```

In the case of the BeagleBone Black, the UARTs are wakeup sources, so pressing a key on the console wakes the BeagleBone:

```
[ 1646.348264] PM: Wakeup source UART
[ 1646.368482] PM: noirq resume of devices complete after 19.963 msecs
[ 1646.372482] PM: early resume of devices
complete after 3.192 msecs
[ 1646.795109] net eth0: initializing cpsw
version 1.12 (0)
[ 1646.798229] net eth0: phy found : id is :
0x7c0f1
[ 1646.798447] libphy: PHY 4a101000.mdio:01 not
found
[ 1646.798469] net eth0: phy 4a101000.mdio:01
not found on slave 1
[ 1646.927874] PM: resume of devices complete
after 555.337 msecs
[ 1647.003829] Restarting tasks ... done.
```

Timed wakeups from the real-time clock

Most systems have an RTC that can generate alarm interruptions up to 24 hours in the future. If so, the directory `/sys/class/rtc/rtc0` will exist. It should contain the `wakealarm` file. Writing a number to `wakealarm` will cause it to generate an alarm that number of seconds later. If you also enable wake up events from `rtc`, it will resume a suspended device. For example, this would wake the system up in 30 seconds:

```
# cd /sys/devices/platform/pmic_rtc.1/rtc/rtc0
# echo "+30" > wakealarm
# echo "enabled" > power/wakeup
```

Further reading

Advanced Configuration and Power Interface Specification, version 6.1, January 2016, `http://ww w.uefi.org/sites/default/files/resources/ACPI_6_1.pdf`.

Summary

Linux has sophisticated power management functions. I have described four main components:

- **CPU-freq** changes the Operating Performance Point of each processor core to reduce power on those that are busy but have some bandwidth to spare, and so allow the opportunity to scale the frequency back. OPPs are known as P-States in the ACPI specification.
- **CPI-Idle** selects deeper idle states when the CPU is not expected to be woken up for a while. Idle states are known as C-States in the ACPI specification.
- **Runtime power management** will shut down peripherals that are not needed.
- **System sleep** modes will put the whole system into a low power state. They are usually under end user control, for example, by pressing a standby button. System sleep states are known as S-States in the ACPI specification.

The majority of the power management is done for you by the BSP. Your main task is to make sure that it is configured correctly for your intended use cases. Only the last component, selecting a system sleep state, requires you to write some code that will allow the end user to enter and exit the state.

In the next chapter, we will look in detail at the Linux process model and describe what a process really is, how it relates to threads, how they cooperate, and how they are scheduled. Understanding these things is important if you want to create a robust and maintainable embedded system.

12
Learning About Processes and Threads

In the preceding chapters, we considered the various aspects of creating an embedded Linux platform. Now it is time to start looking at how you can use the platform to create a working device. In this chapter, I will talk about the implications of the Linux process model and how it encompasses multithreaded programs. I will look at the pros and cons of using single-threaded and multithreaded processes. I will also look at scheduling and differentiate between timeshare and real-time scheduling policies.

While these topics are not specific to embedded computing, it is important for a designer of an embedded device to have an overview of these topics. There are many good references on the subject, some of which I list at the end of the chapter, but in general, they do not consider the embedded use cases. In consequence, I will be concentrating on the concepts and design decisions rather than on the function calls and code.

In this chapter, we will cover the following topics:

- Process or thread?
- Processes.
- Threads.
- Scheduling.

Process or thread?

Many embedded developers who are familiar with **real-time operating systems (RTOS)** consider the Unix process model to be cumbersome. On the other hand, they see a similarity between an RTOS task and a Linux thread and they have a tendency to transfer an existing design using a one-to-one mapping of RTOS tasks to threads. I have, on several occasions, seen designs in which the entire application is implemented with one process containing 40 or more threads. I want to spend some time considering whether this is a good idea or not. Let's begin with some definitions.

A **process** is a memory address space and a thread of execution, as shown in the following diagram. The address space is private to the process and so threads running in different processes cannot access it. This **memory separation** is created by the memory management subsystem in the kernel, which keeps a memory page mapping for each process and re-programs the memory management unit on each context switch. I will describe how this works in detail in Chapter 13, *Managing Memory*. Part of the address space is mapped to a file that contains the code and static data that the program is running, as shown here:

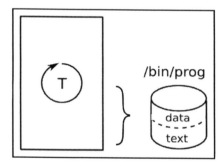

As the program runs, it will allocate resources such as stack space, heap memory, references to files, and so on. When the process terminates, these resources are reclaimed by the system: all the memory is freed up and all the file descriptors are closed.

Processes can communicate with each other using **inter-process communication (IPC)**, such as local sockets. I will talk about IPC later on.

A **thread** is a thread of execution within a process. All processes begin with one thread that runs the `main()` function and is called the main thread. You can create additional threads, for example, using the POSIX function `pthread_create(3)`, which results in multiple threads executing in the same address space, as shown in the following diagram:

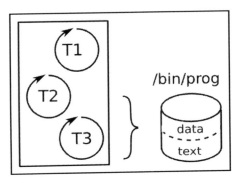

Being in the same process, the threads share resources with each other. They can read and write the same memory and use the same file descriptors. Communication between threads is easy as long as you take care of the synchronization and locking issues.

So, based on these brief details, you can imagine two extreme designs for a hypothetical system with 40 RTOS tasks being ported to Linux.

You could map tasks to processes and have 40 individual programs communicating through IPC, for example, with messages sent through sockets. You would greatly reduce memory corruption problems since the main thread running in each process is protected from the others, and you would reduce resource leakage since each process is cleaned up after it exits. However, the message interface between processes is quite complex and, where there is tight cooperation between a group of processes, the number of messages might be large and become a limiting factor in the performance of the system. Furthermore, any one of the 40 processes may terminate, perhaps because of a bug causing it to crash, leaving the other 39 to carry on. Each process would have to handle the case that its neighbors are no longer running and recover gracefully.

At the other extreme, you could map tasks to threads and implement the system as a single process containing 40 threads. Cooperation becomes much easier because they share the same address space and file descriptors. The overhead of sending messages is reduced or eliminated, and context switches between threads are faster than between processes. The downside is that you have introduced the possibility of one task corrupting the heap or the stack of another. If any one of the threads encounters a fatal bug, the whole process will terminate, taking all the threads with it. Finally, debugging a complex multithreaded process can be a nightmare.

The conclusion you should draw is that neither design is ideal and that there is a better way. But before we get to that point, I will delve a little more deeply into the APIs and the behavior of processes and threads.

Processes

A process holds the environment in which threads can run: it holds the memory mappings, the file descriptors, the user and group IDs, and more. The first process is the init process, which is created by the kernel during boot and has a PID of one. Thereafter, processes are created by duplication in an operation known as **forking**.

Creating a new process

The POSIX function to create a process is fork(2). It is an odd function because for each successful call, there are two returns: one in the process that made the call, known as the **Parent**, and one in the newly created process, known as the **Child** , as shown in the following diagram:

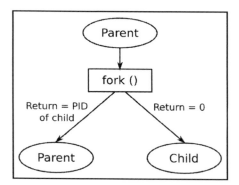

Immediately after the call, the child is an exact copy of the parent: it has the same stack, the same heap, the same file descriptors, and it executes the same line of code, the one following fork. The only way the programmer can tell them apart is by looking at the return value of fork: it is *zero* for the child and *greater than zero* for the parent. Actually, the value returned to the parent is the PID of the newly created child process. There is a third possibility, which is that the return value is negative, which means that the fork call failed and there is still only one process.

Although the two processes are initially identical, they are in separate address spaces. Changes made to a variable by one will not be seen by the other. Under the hood, the kernel does not make a physical copy of the parent's memory, which would be quite a slow operation and consume memory unnecessarily. Instead, the memory is shared but marked with a **copy-on-write (CoW)** flag. If either parent or child modifies this memory, the kernel first makes a copy and then writes to the copy. This has the benefit of an efficient fork function while retaining the logical separation of process address spaces. I will discuss CoW in Chapter 13, *Managing Memory*.

Terminating a process

A process may be stopped voluntarily by calling the *exit(3)* function or, involuntarily, by receiving a signal that is not handled. One signal, in particular, SIGKILL, cannot be handled and so will always kill a process. In all cases, terminating the process will stop all threads, close all file descriptors, and release all memory. The system sends a signal, SIGCHLD, to the parent so that it knows this has happened.

Processes have a return value that is composed of either the argument to exit, if it terminated normally, or the signal number if it was killed. The chief use for this is in shell scripts: it allows you to test the return value from a program. By convention, 0 indicates success and other values indicate a failure of some sort.

The parent can collect the return value with the *wait(2)* or *waitpid(2)* functions. This causes a problem: there will be a delay between a child terminating and its parent collecting the return value. In that period, the return value must be stored somewhere, and the PID number of the now dead process cannot be reused. The process in this state is a **zombie**, which is displayed as state Z in the ps and top commands. As long as the parent calls wait or waitpid whenever it is notified of a child's termination (by means of the SIGCHLD signal; refer to *Linux System Programming, Robert Love, O'Reilly Media* or *The Linux Programming Interface, Michael Kerrisk, No Starch Press* for details on handling signals). Usually zombies exist for too short a time to show up in process listings. But they will become a problem if the parent fails to collect the return value because eventually, there will not be enough resources to create any more processes.

The program in MELP/chapter_12/fork-demo illustrates process creation and termination:

```
#include <stdio.h>
#include <stdlib.h>
#include <unistd.h>
#include <sys/types.h>
#include <sys/wait.h>
```

```
int main(void)
{
  int pid;
  int status;
  pid = fork();
  if (pid == 0) {
    printf("I am the child, PID %d\n", getpid());
    sleep(10);
    exit(42);
  } else if (pid > 0) {
    printf("I am the parent, PID %d\n", getpid());
    wait(&status);
    printf("Child terminated, status %d\n", WEXITSTATUS(status));
  } else
    perror("fork:");
  return 0;
}
```

The `wait` function blocks until a child process exits and stores the exit status. When you run it, you see something like this:

```
I am the parent, PID 13851
I am the child, PID 13852
Child terminated with status 42
```

The child process inherits most of the attributes of the parent, including the user and group IDs, all open file descriptors, signal handling, and scheduling characteristics.

Running a different program

The `fork` function creates a copy of a running program, but it does not run a different program. For that, you need one of the `exec` functions:

```
int execl(const char *path, const char *arg, ...);
int execlp(const char *file, const char *arg, ...);
int execle(const char *path, const char *arg,
           ..., char * const envp[]);
int execv(const char *path, char *const argv[]);
int execvp(const char *file, char *const argv[]);
int execvpe(const char *file, char *const argv[],
           ..., char *const envp[]);
```

Each takes a path to the program file to load and run. If the function succeeds, the kernel discards all the resources of the current process, including memory and file descriptors, and allocates memory to the new program being loaded. When the thread that called exec* returns, it returns not to the line of code after the call but to the main() function of the new program. There is an example of a command launcher in MELP/chapter_12/exec-demo: it prompts for a command, for example, /bin/ls, and forks and executes the string you enter. Here is the code:

```
#include <stdio.h>
#include <stdlib.h>
#include <string.h>
#include <unistd.h>
#include <sys/types.h>
#include <sys/wait.h>
int main(void)
{
  char command_str[128];
  int pid;
  int child_status;
  int wait_for = 1;
  while (1) {
    printf("sh> ");
    scanf("%s", command_str);
    pid = fork();
    if (pid == 0) {
      /* child */
      printf("cmd '%s'\n", command_str);
      execl(command_str, command_str, (char *)NULL);
      /* We should not return from execl, so only get
       to this line if it failed */
      perror("exec");
      exit(1);
    }
    if (wait_for) {
      waitpid(pid, &child_status, 0);
      printf("Done, status %d\n", child_status);
    }
  }
  return 0;
}
```

Here is what you will see when you run it:

```
# ./exec-demo
sh> /bin/ls
cmd '/bin/ls'
bin etc lost+found proc sys var
boot home media run tmp
dev lib mnt sbin usr
Done, status 0
sh>
```

You terminate the program by typing Ctrl-C.

It might seem odd to have one function that duplicates an existing process and another that discards its resources and loads a different program into memory, especially since it is common for a fork to be followed almost immediately by one of the exec functions. Most operating systems combine the two actions into a single call.

There are distinct advantages, however. For example, it makes it very easy to implement redirection and pipes in the shell. Imagine that you want to get a directory listing. This is the sequence of events:

1. You type ls in the shell prompt.
2. The shell forks a copy of itself.
3. The child execs /bin/ls.
4. The ls program prints the directory listing to stdout (file descriptor 1), which is attached to the Terminal. You see the directory listing.
5. The ls program terminates and the shell regains control.

Now imagine that you want the directory listing to be written to a file by redirecting the output using the > character. Now the sequence is as follows:

1. You type ls > listing.txt.
2. The shell forks a copy of itself.
3. The child opens and truncates the listing.txt file and uses dup2(2) to copy the file descriptor of the file over file descriptor 1 (stdout).
4. The child execs /bin/ls.
5. The program prints the listing as before, but this time, it is writing to listing.txt.
6. The ls program terminates and the shell regains control.

There was an opportunity in step three to modify the environment of the child process before executing the program. The `ls` program does not need to know that it is writing to a file rather than a terminal. Instead of a file, `stdout` could be connected to a pipe and so the `ls` program, still unchanged, can send output to another program. This is part of the Unix philosophy of combining many small components that each do a job well, as described in *The Art of Unix Programming*, by Eric Steven Raymond, Addison Wesley (23 Sept, 2003) ISBN 978-0131429017, especially in the *Pipes, Redirection, and Filters* section.

Daemons

We have encountered daemons in several places already. A daemon is a process that runs in the background, owned by the `init` process and not connected to a controlling Terminal. The steps to create a daemon are as follows:

1. Call `fork` to create a new process, after which the parent should exit, thus creating an orphan which will be re-parented to `init`.
2. The child process calls *setsid(2)*, creating a new session and process group of which it is the sole member. The exact details do not matter here; you can simply consider this a way of isolating the process from any controlling terminal.
3. Change the working directory to the `root` directory.
4. Close all file descriptors and redirect `stdin`, `stdout`, and `stderr` (descriptors 0, 1, and 2) to `/dev/null` so that there is no input and all output is hidden.

Thankfully, all of the preceding steps can be achieved with a single function call, *daemon(3)*.

Inter-process communication

Each process is an island of memory. You can pass information from one to another in two ways. Firstly, you can copy it from one address space to the other. Secondly, you can create an area of memory that both can access and share the data.

The first is usually combined with a queue or buffer so that there is a sequence of messages passing between processes. This implies copying the message twice: first to a holding area and then to the destination. Some examples of this are sockets, pipes, and message queues.

The second way requires not only a method of creating memory that is mapped into two (or more) address spaces at once, but it is also a means of synchronizing access to that memory, for example, using semaphores or mutexes.

POSIX has functions for all of these. There is an older set of APIs known as **System V IPC**, which provides message queues, shared memory, and semaphores, but it is not as flexible as the POSIX equivalents so I will not describe them here. The manual page on *svipc(7)* gives an overview of the facilities, and there are more details in *The Linux Programming Interface*, by Michael Kerrisk, and *Unix Network Programming, Volume 2*, by W. Richard Stevens.

Message-based protocols are usually easier to program and debug than shared memory but are slow if the messages are large or many.

Message-based IPC

There are several options, which I will summarize as follows. The attributes that differentiate one from the other are as follows:

- Whether the message flow is uni- or bi-directorial.
- Whether the data flow is a byte stream with no message boundary or discrete messages with boundaries preserved. In the latter case, the maximum size of a message is important.
- Whether messages are tagged with a priority.

The following table summarizes these properties for FIFOs, sockets, and message queues:

Property	FIFO	Unix socket: stream	Unix socket: datagram	POSIX message queue
Message boundary	Byte stream	Byte stream	Discrete	Discrete
Uni/bi-directional	Uni	Bi	Uni	Uni
Max message size	Unlimited	Unlimited	In the range of 100 KiB to 250 KiB	Default: 8 KiB, absolute maximum: 1 MiB
Priority levels	None	None	None	0 to 32767

Unix (or local) sockets

Unix sockets fulfill most requirements and coupled with the familiarity of the sockets API, they are by far the most common mechanism.

Unix sockets are created with the AF_UNIX address family and bound to a pathname. Access to the socket is determined by the access permission of the socket file. As with internet sockets, the socket type can be SOCK_STREAM or SOCK_DGRAM, the former giving a bidirectional byte stream and the latter providing discrete messages with preserved boundaries. Unix socket datagrams are reliable, which means that they will not be dropped or reordered. The maximum size for a datagram is system-dependent and is available via /proc/sys/net/core/wmem_max. It is typically 100 KiB or more.

Unix sockets do not have a mechanism to indicate the priority of a message.

FIFOs and named pipes

FIFO and *named pipe* are just different terms for the same thing. They are an extension of the anonymous pipe that is used to communicate between parent and child processes when implementing pipes in the shell.

A FIFO is a special sort of file, created by the *mkfifo(1)* command. As with Unix sockets, the file access permissions determine who can read and write. They are unidirectional, which means that there is one reader and usually one writer, though there may be several. The data is a pure byte stream but with a guarantee of the atomicity of messages that are smaller than the buffer associated with the pipe. In other words, writes less than this size will not be split into several smaller writes and so you will read the whole message in one go as long as the size of the buffer at your end is large enough. The default size of the FIFO buffer is 64 KiB on modern kernels and can be increased using *fcntl(2)* with F_SETPIPE_SZ up to the value in /proc/sys/fs/pipe-max-size, typically 1 MiB. There is no concept of priority.

POSIX message queues

Message queues are identified by a name, which must begin with a forward slash / and contain only one / character: message queues are actually kept in a pseudo filesystem of the type mqueue. You create a queue and get a reference to an existing queue through *mq_open(3)*, which returns a file descriptor. Each message has a priority, and messages are read from the queue based on priority and then on the age order. Messages can be up to /proc/sys/kernel/msgmax bytes long.

The default value is 8 KiB, but you can set it to be any size in the range 128 bytes to 1 MiB by writing the value to `/proc/sys/kernel/msgmax` bytes. Each message has a priority. They are read from the queue based on the priority then the age order. Since the reference is a file descriptor, you can use *select(2)*, *poll(2)*, and other similar functions to wait for activity in the queue.

Refer to the Linux main page *mq_overview(7)* for more detail.

Summary of message-based IPC

Unix sockets are used most often because they offer all that is needed, except perhaps message priority. They are implemented on most operating systems, and so they confer maximum portability.

FIFOs are less used, mostly because they lack an equivalent to a **datagram.** On the other hand, the API is very simple, being the normal *open(2)*, *close(2)*, *read(2)*, and *write(2)* file calls.

Message queues are the least commonly used of this group. The code paths in the kernel are not optimized in the way that socket (network) and FIFO (filesystem) calls are.

There are also higher-level abstractions, in particular, D-Bus, which are moving from mainstream Linux to embedded devices. D-Bus uses Unix sockets and shared memory under the surface.

Shared memory-based IPC

Sharing memory removes the need for copying data between address spaces, but introduces the problem of synchronizing accesses to it. Synchronization between processes is commonly achieved using semaphores.

POSIX shared memory

To share memory between processes, you first have to create a new area of memory and then map it to the address space of each process that wants access to it, as shown in the following diagram:

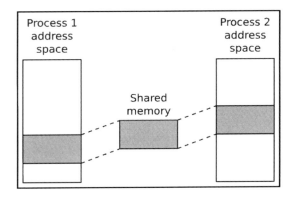

The naming of POSIX shared memory segments follows the pattern we encountered with message queues. The segments are identified by names that begin with a / character and have exactly one such character. The *shm_open(3)* function takes the name and returns a file descriptor for it. If it does not exist already and the O_CREAT flag is set, then a new segment is created. Initially, it has a size of zero. You can use the (misleadingly named) *ftruncate(2)* function to expand it to the desired size.

Once you have a descriptor for the shared memory, you map it to the address space of the process using *mmap(2)*, and so threads in different processes can access the memory.

The program in MELP/chapter_12/shared-mem-demo gives an example of using a shared memory segment to communicate between processes. Here is the code:

```
#include <stdio.h>
#include <stdlib.h>
#include <string.h>
#include <unistd.h>
#include <sys/mman.h>
#include <sys/stat.h>   /* For mode constants */
#include <fcntl.h>
#include <sys/types.h>
#include <errno.h>
#include <semaphore.h>
#define SHM_SEGMENT_SIZE 65536
#define SHM_SEGMENT_NAME "/demo-shm"
#define SEMA_NAME "/demo-sem"

static sem_t *demo_sem;

/*
 * If the shared memory segment does not exist already, create it
 * Returns a pointer to the segment or NULL if there is an error
 */
```

```
static void *get_shared_memory(void)
{
  int shm_fd;
  struct shared_data *shm_p;
  /* Attempt to create the shared memory segment */
  shm_fd = shm_open(SHM_SEGMENT_NAME, O_CREAT | O_EXCL | O_RDWR,
     0666);

  if (shm_fd > 0) {
    /* succeeded: expand it to the desired size (Note: dont't do
     "this every time because ftruncate fills it with zeros) */
    printf ("Creating shared memory and setting size=%d\n",
    SHM_SEGMENT_SIZE);

    if (ftruncate(shm_fd, SHM_SEGMENT_SIZE) < 0) {
      perror("ftruncate");
      exit(1);
    }
    /* Create a semaphore as well */
    demo_sem = sem_open(SEMA_NAME, O_RDWR | O_CREAT, 0666, 1);

    if (demo_sem == SEM_FAILED)
      perror("sem_open failed\n");
  }
  else if (shm_fd == -1 && errno == EEXIST) {
    /* Already exists: open again without O_CREAT */
    shm_fd = shm_open(SHM_SEGMENT_NAME, O_RDWR, 0);
    demo_sem = sem_open(SEMA_NAME, O_RDWR);

    if (demo_sem == SEM_FAILED)
      perror("sem_open failed\n");
  }

  if (shm_fd == -1) {
    perror("shm_open " SHM_SEGMENT_NAME);
    exit(1);
  }
  /* Map the shared memory */
  shm_p = mmap(NULL, SHM_SEGMENT_SIZE, PROT_READ | PROT_WRITE,
    MAP_SHARED, shm_fd, 0);

  if (shm_p == NULL) {
    perror("mmap");
    exit(1);
  }
  return shm_p;
}
```

```
int main(int argc, char *argv[])
{
  char *shm_p;
  printf("%s PID=%d\n", argv[0], getpid());
  shm_p = get_shared_memory();

  while (1) {
    printf("Press enter to see the current contents of shm\n");
    getchar();
    sem_wait(demo_sem);
    printf("%s\n", shm_p);
    /* Write our signature to the shared memory */
    sprintf(shm_p, "Hello from process %d\n", getpid());
    sem_post(demo_sem);
  }
  return 0;
}
```

The program uses a shared memory segment to communicate a message from one process to another. The message is the Hello from process string followed by its PID. The get_shared_memory function is responsible for creating the memory segment, if it does not exist, or getting the file descriptor for it if it does. It returns a pointer to the memory segment. In the main function, there is a semaphore to synchronize access to the memory so that one process does not overwrite the message from another.

To try it out, you need two instances of the program running in separate terminal sessions. In the first terminal, you will see something like this:

```
# ./shared-mem-demo
./shared-mem-demo PID=271
Creating shared memory and setting size=65536
Press enter to see the current contents of shm

Press enter to see the current contents of shm

Hello from process 271
```

Because this is the first time the program is run, it creates the memory segment. Initially, the message area is empty, but after one run through the loop, it contains the PID of this process, 271. Now, you can run a second instance in another terminal:

```
# ./shared-mem-demo
./shared-mem-demo PID=279
Press enter to see the current contents of shm

Hello from process 271

Press enter to see the current contents of shm

Hello from process 279
```

It does not create the shared memory segment because it exists already, and it displays the message that it contains already, which is PID of the other program. Pressing *Enter* causes it to write its own PID, which the first program would be able to see. In this way, the two programs can communicate with each other.

The POSIX IPC functions are part of the POSIX real-time extensions, and so you need to link with librt. Oddly, the POSIX semaphores are implemented in the POSIX threads library, so you need to link with the pthreads library as well. Hence the compilation arguments are as follows:

```
$ arm-cortex_a8-linux-gnueabihf-gcc shared-mem-demo.c -lrt -pthread \
-o arm-cortex_a8-linux-gnueabihf-gcc
```

Threads

Now it is time to look at multithreaded processes. The programming interface for threads is the POSIX threads API, which was first defined in the IEEE POSIX 1003.1c standard (1995) and is commonly known as **pthreads**. It is implemented as an additional part of the C-library, libpthread.so. There have been two implementations of pthreads over the last 15 years or so: **LinuxThreads** and **Native POSIX Thread Library** (**NPTL**). The latter is much more compliant with the specification, particularly with regard to the handling of signals and process IDs. It is pretty dominant now, but you may come across some older versions of uClibc that use LinuxThreads.

Creating a new thread

The function to create a thread is *pthread_create(3)*:

```
int pthread_create(pthread_t *thread, const pthread_attr_t *attr,
    void *(*start_routine) (void *), void *arg);
```

It creates a new thread of execution that begins in the function start_routine and places a descriptor in the pthread_t pointed to by thread. It inherits the scheduling parameters of the calling thread, but these can be overridden by passing a pointer to the thread attributes in attr. The thread will begin to execute immediately.

pthread_t is the main way to refer to the thread within the program, but the thread can also be seen from outside using a command such as ps -eLf:

```
UID    PID  PPID  LWP   C  NLWP  STIME    TTY          TIME CMD
...
chris  6072  5648  6072  0   3   21:18  pts/0 00:00:00 ./thread-demo
chris  6072  5648  6073  0   3   21:18  pts/0 00:00:00 ./thread-demo
```

In the output from ps shown above, the program thread-demo has two threads. The PID and PPID columns show that they all belong to the same process and have the same parent, as you would expect. The column marked LWP is interesting, though. LWP stands for **Light Weight Process**, which, in this context, is another name for a thread. The numbers in that column are also known as **Thread IDs** or **TIDs**. In the main thread, the TID is the same as the PID, but for the others, it is a different (higher) value. You can use a TID in places where the documentation states that you must give a PID, but be aware that this behavior is specific to Linux and is not portable. Here is a simple program that illustrates the life cycle of a thread (the code is in MELP/chapter_12/thread-demo):

```
#include <stdio.h>
#include <unistd.h>
#include <pthread.h>
#include <sys/syscall.h>

static void *thread_fn(void *arg)
{
  printf("New thread started, PID %d TID %d\n",
         getpid(), (pid_t)syscall(SYS_gettid));
  sleep(10);
  printf("New thread terminating\n");
  return NULL;
}

int main(void)
{
```

```
    pthread_t t;
    printf("Main thread, PID %d TID %d\n",
           getpid(), (pid_t)syscall(SYS_gettid));
    pthread_create(&t, NULL, thread_fn, NULL);
    pthread_join(t, NULL);
    return 0;
}
```

Note that in the function `thread_fn` I am retrieving the TID using `syscall(SYS_gettid)`. There is a manual page for *gettid(2)*, which explains that you have to call Linux directly through a `syscall` because there is no C-library wrapper for it.

There is a limit to the total number of threads that a given kernel can schedule. The limit scales according to the size of the system, from around 1,000 on small devices up to tens of thousands on larger embedded devices. The actual number is available in `/proc/sys/kernel/threads-max`. Once you reach this limit, `fork` and `pthread_create` will fail.

Terminating a thread

A thread terminates when:

- It reaches the end of its `start_routine`
- It calls *pthread_exit(3)*
- It is canceled by another thread calling *pthread_cancel(3)*
- The process that contains the thread terminates, for example, because of a thread calling *exit(3)*, or the process receives a signal that is not handled, masked, or ignored

Note that if a multithreaded program calls `fork`, only the thread that made the call will exist in the new child process. Fork does not replicate all threads.

A thread has a return value, which is a void pointer. One thread can wait for another to terminate and collect its return value by calling *pthread_join(2)*. There is an example in the code for `thread-demo`, mentioned in the preceding section. This produces a problem that is very similar to the zombie problem among processes: the resources of the thread, for example, the stack, cannot be freed up until another thread has joined with it. If threads remain *unjoined*, there is a resource leak in the program.

Compiling a program with threads

The support for POSIX threads is part of the C-library in the `libpthread.so` library. However, there is more to building programs with threads than linking the library: there have to be changes to the way the compiler generates code to make sure that certain global variables, such as `errno`, have one instance per thread rather than one for the whole process.

When building a threaded program, you must add the `-pthread` switch in the compile and link stages.

Inter-thread communication

The big advantage of threads is that they share the address space and can share memory variables. This is also a big disadvantage because it requires synchronization to preserve data consistency in a manner similar to memory segments shared between processes but with the proviso that, with threads, all memory is shared. In fact, threads can create private memory using **thread local storage** (**TLS**), but I will not cover that here.

The `pthreads` interface provides the basics necessary to achieve synchronization: mutexes and condition variables. If you want more complex structures, you will have to build them yourself.

It is worth noting that all of the IPC methods described earlier, that is sockets, pipes and message queues, work equally well between threads in the same process.

Mutual exclusion

To write robust programs, you need to protect each shared resource with a mutex lock, and make sure that every code path that reads or writes the resource has locked the mutex first. If you apply this rule consistently, most of the problems should be solved. The ones that remain are associated with the fundamental behavior of mutexes. I will list them briefly here but will not go into detail:

- **Deadlock**: This occurs when mutexes become permanently locked. A classic situation is the **deadly embrace** in which two threads each require two mutexes and have managed to lock one of them but not the other. Each thread blocks, waiting for the lock the other has, and so they remain as they are. One simple rule to avoid the deadly embrace problem is to make sure that mutexes are always locked in the same order. Other solutions involve timeouts and back-off periods.

- **Priority inversion**: The delays caused by waiting for a mutex can cause a real-time thread to miss deadlines. The specific case of priority inversion happens when a high priority thread becomes blocked waiting for a mutex locked by a low priority thread. If the low priority thread is preempted by other threads of intermediate priority, the high priority thread is forced to wait for an unbounded length of time. There are mutex protocols called **priority inheritance** and **priority ceiling** that resolve the problem at the expense of greater processing overhead in the kernel for each lock and unlock call.

- **Poor performance**: Mutexes introduce minimal overhead to the code as long as threads don't have to block on them most of the time. If your design has a resource that is needed by a lot of threads, however, the contention ratio becomes significant. This is usually a design issue that can be resolved using finer grained locking or a different algorithm.

Changing conditions

Cooperating threads need a method of alerting one another that something has changed and needs attention. That thing is called a **condition** and the alert is sent through a **condition variable**, or **condvar**.

A condition is just something that you can test to give a `true` or `false` result. A simple example is a buffer that contains either zero or some items. One thread takes items from the buffer and sleeps when it is empty. Another thread places items into the buffer and signals the other thread that it has done so because the condition that the other thread is waiting on has changed. If it is sleeping, it needs to wake up and do something. The only complexity is that the condition is, by definition, a shared resource and so has to be protected by a mutex.

Here is a simple program with two threads. The first is the producer: it wakes every second and puts an item of data into a global variable and then signals that there has been a change. The second thread is the consumer: it waits on the condition variable and tests the condition (that there is a string in the buffer of nonzero length) each time it wakes up. You can find the code in MELP/chapter_12/condvar-demo:

```c
#include <stdio.h>
#include <stdlib.h>
#include <pthread.h>
#include <unistd.h>
#include <string.h>

char g_data[128];
pthread_cond_t cv = PTHREAD_COND_INITIALIZER;
pthread_mutex_t mutx = PTHREAD_MUTEX_INITIALIZER;

void *consumer(void *arg)
{
    while (1) {
      pthread_mutex_lock(&mutx);
      while (strlen(g_data) == 0)
        pthread_cond_wait(&cv, &mutx);

      /* Got data */
      printf("%s\n", g_data);
      /* Truncate to null string again */
      g_data[0] = 0;
      pthread_mutex_unlock(&mutx);
      }
    return NULL;
}

void *producer(void *arg)
{
    int i = 0;

    while (1) {
      sleep(1);
      pthread_mutex_lock(&mutx);
      sprintf(g_data, "Data item %d", i);
      pthread_mutex_unlock(&mutx);
      pthread_cond_signal(&cv);
      i++;
      }
    return NULL;
}
```

Note that when the consumer thread blocks on the condvar, it does so while holding a locked mutex, which would seem to be a recipe for deadlock the next time the producer thread tries to update the condition. To avoid this, *pthread_condwait(3)* unlocks the mutex after the thread is blocked, and then locks it again before waking it and returning from the wait.

Partitioning the problem

Now that we have covered the basics of processes and threads and the ways in which they communicate, it is time to see what we can do with them.

Here are some of the rules I use when building systems:

- **Rule 1**: Keep tasks that have a lot of interaction together: It is important to minimize overheads by keeping closely inter-operating threads together in one process.
- **Rule 2**: Don't put all your threads in one basket: On the other hand, try and keep components with limited interaction in separate processes, in the interests of resilience and modularity.
- **Rule 3**: Don't mix critical and noncritical threads in the same process: This is an amplification of Rule 2: the critical part of the system, which might be a machine control program, should be kept as simple as possible and written in a more rigorous way than other parts. It must be able to continue even if other processes fail. If you have real-time threads, by definition, they must be critical and should go into a process by themselves.
- **Rule 4**: Threads shouldn't get too intimate: One of the temptations when writing a multithreaded program is to intermingle the code and variables between threads because it is all in one program and easy to do. Keep the threads modular, with well-defined interactions.
- **Rule 5**: Don't think that threads are for free: It is very easy to create additional threads, but there is a cost, not least in the additional synchronization necessary to coordinate their activities.
- **Rule 6**: Threads can work in parallel: Threads can run simultaneously on a multicore processor, giving higher throughput. If you have a large computing job, you can create one thread per core and make maximum use of the hardware. There are libraries to help you do this, such as OpenMP. You should probably not be coding parallel programming algorithms from scratch.

The Android design is a good illustration. Each application is a separate Linux process that helps modularize memory management and ensures that one app crashing does not affect the whole system. The process model is also used for access control: a process can only access the files and resources that its UID and GIDs allow it to. There are a group of threads in each process. There is one to manage and update the user interface, one to handle signals from the operating system, several to manage dynamic memory allocation and the freeing up of Java objects, and a worker pool of at least two threads to receive messages from other parts of the system using the Binder protocol.

To summarize, processes provide resilience because each process has a protected memory space, and when the process terminates, all resources including memory and file descriptors are freed up, reducing resource leaks. On the other hand, threads share resources and can communicate easily through shared variables and can cooperate by sharing access to files and other resources. Threads give parallelism through worker pools and other abstractions, which is useful in multicore processors.

Scheduling

The second big topic I want to cover in this chapter is scheduling. The Linux scheduler has a queue of threads that are ready to run, and its job is to schedule them on CPUs as they become available. Each thread has a scheduling policy that may be time-shared or real-time. The time-shared threads have a **niceness** value that increases or reduces their entitlement to CPU time. The real-time threads have a **priority** such that a higher priority thread will preempt a lower one. The scheduler works with threads, not processes. Each thread is scheduled regardless of which process it is running in.

The scheduler runs when:

- A thread is blocked by calling `sleep()` or another blocking system call
- A time-shared thread exhausts its time slice
- An interruption causes a thread to be unblocked, for example, because of I/O completing

For background information on the Linux scheduler, I recommend that you read the chapter on process scheduling in *Linux Kernel Development, 3rd edition* by *Robert Love*.

Fairness versus determinism

I have grouped the scheduling policies into categories of time-shared and real-time. Time-shared policies are based on the principal of *fairness*. They are designed to make sure that each thread gets a fair amount of processor time and that no thread can hog the system. If a thread runs for too long, it is put to the back of the queue so that others can have a go. At the same time, a fairness policy needs to adjust to threads that are doing a lot of work and give them the resources to get the job done. Time-shared scheduling is good because of the way it automatically adjusts to a wide range of workloads.

On the other hand, if you have a real-time program, fairness is not helpful. Instead, you then want a policy that is **deterministic**, which will give you at least minimal guarantees that your real-time threads will be scheduled at the right time so that they don't miss their deadlines. This means that a real-time thread must preempt time-shared threads. Real-time threads also have a static priority that the scheduler can use to choose between them when there are several of them to run at once. The Linux real-time scheduler implements a fairly standard algorithm that runs the highest priority real-time thread. Most RTOS schedulers are also written in this way.

Both types of thread can coexist. Those requiring deterministic scheduling are scheduled first and the time remaining is divided between the time-shared threads.

Time-shared policies

Time-shared policies are designed for fairness. From Linux 2.6.23 onward, the scheduler used has been **Completely Fair Scheduler (CFS)**. It does not use timeslices in the normal sense of the word. Instead, it calculates a running tally of the length of time a thread would be entitled to run if it had its fair share of CPU time, and it balances that with the actual amount of time it has run for. If it exceeds its entitlement and there are other time-shared threads waiting to run, the scheduler will suspend the thread and run a waiting thread instead.

The time-shared policies are as follows:

- SCHED_NORMAL (also known as SCHED_OTHER): This is the default policy. The vast majority of Linux threads use this policy.
- SCHED_BATCH: This is similar to SCHED_NORMAL except that threads are scheduled with a larger granularity; that is, they run for longer but have to wait longer until they are scheduled again. The intention is to reduce the number of context switches for background processing (batch jobs) and reduce the amount of CPU cache churn.

- SCHED_IDLE: These threads are run only when there are no threads of any other policy ready to run. It is the lowest possible priority.

There are two pairs of functions to get and set the policy and priority of a thread. The first pair takes a PID as a parameter and affects the main thread in a process:

```
struct sched_param {
  ...
  int sched_priority;
  ...
};

int sched_setscheduler(pid_t pid, int policy,
                       const struct sched_param *param);

int sched_getscheduler(pid_t pid);
```

The second pair operates on pthread_t and can change the parameters of the other threads in a process:

```
int pthread_setschedparam(pthread_t thread, int policy,
                          const struct sched_param *param);

int pthread_getschedparam(pthread_t thread, int *policy,
                          struct sched_param *param);
```

Niceness

Some time-shared threads are more important than others. You can indicate this with the nice value, which multiplies a thread's CPU entitlement by a scaling factor. The name comes from the function call, *nice(2)*, which has been part of Unix since the early days. A thread becomes nice by reducing its load on the system, or moves in the opposite direction by increasing it. The range of values is from 19, which is really nice, to −20, which is really not nice. The default value is 0, which is averagely nice, or so-so.

The nice value can be changed for SCHED_NORMAL and SCHED_BATCH threads. To reduce niceness, which increases the CPU load, you need the CAP_SYS_NICE capability, which is available to the root user.

Almost all the documentation for functions and commands that change the `nice` value (*nice(2)* and the `nice` and `renice` commands) talks in terms of processes. However, it really relates to threads. As mentioned in the preceding section, you can use a TID in place of a PID to change the `nice` value of an individual thread. One other discrepancy in the standard descriptions of `nice` is this: the `nice` value is referred to as the priority of a thread (or sometimes, mistakenly, a process). I believe this is misleading and confuses the concept with real-time priority, which is a completely different thing.

Real-time policies

Real-time policies are intended for determinism. The real-time scheduler will always run the highest priority real-time thread that is ready to run. Real-time threads always preempt timeshare threads. In essence, by selecting a real-time policy over a timeshare policy, you are saying that you have inside knowledge of the expected scheduling of this thread and wish to override the scheduler's built-in assumptions.

There are two real-time policies:

- `SCHED_FIFO`: This is a **run to completion** algorithm, which means that once the thread starts to run, it will continue until it is preempted by a higher priority real-time thread, it is blocked in a system call, or until it terminates (completes).
- `SCHED_RR`: This a **round robin** algorithm that will cycle between threads of the same priority if they exceed their time slice, which is 100 ms by default. Since Linux 3.9, it has been possible to control the `timeslice` value through `/proc/sys/kernel/sched_rr_timeslice_ms`. Apart from this, it behaves in the same way as `SCHED_FIFO`.

Each real-time thread has a priority in the range 1 to 99, with 99 being the highest.

To give a thread a real-time policy, you need `CAP_SYS_NICE`, which is given only to the root user by default.

One problem with real-time scheduling, both in Linux and elsewhere, is that of a thread that becomes compute bound, often because a bug has caused it to loop indefinitely, will prevent real-time threads of lower priority from running along with all the timeshare threads. In this case, the system becomes erratic and may lock up completely. There are a couple of ways to guard against this possibility.

First, since Linux 2.6.25, the scheduler has, by default, reserved 5% of CPU time for non-real-time threads so that even a runaway real-time thread cannot completely halt the system. It is configured via two kernel controls:

- `/proc/sys/kernel/sched_rt_period_us`
- `/proc/sys/kernel/sched_rt_runtime_us`

They have default values of 1,000,000 (1 second) and 950,000 (950 ms), respectively, which means that out of every second, 50 ms is reserved for non-real-time processing. If you want real-time threads to be able to take 100%, then set `sched_rt_runtime_us` to −1.

The second option is to use a watchdog, either hardware or software, to monitor the execution of key threads and take action when they begin to miss deadlines. I mentioned watchdogs in `Chapter 10`, *Starting Up – The init Program*.

Choosing a policy

In practice, time-shared policies satisfy the majority of computing workloads. Threads that are I/O-bound spend a lot of time blocked and always have some spare entitlement in hand. When they are unblocked, they will be scheduled almost immediately. Meanwhile, CPU-bound threads will naturally take up any CPU cycles left over. Positive nice values can be applied to the less important threads and negative values to the more important ones.

Of course, this is only average behavior; there are no guarantees that this will always be the case. If more deterministic behavior is needed, then real-time policies will be required. The things that mark out a thread as being real-time are as follows:

- It has a deadline by which it must generate an output
- Missing the deadline would compromise the effectiveness of the system
- It is event-driven
- It is not compute-bound

Examples of real-time tasks include the classic robot arm servo controller, multimedia processing, and communication processing. I will discuss real-time system design later on in `Chapter 16`, *Real-Time Programming*.

Choosing a real-time priority

Choosing real-time priorities that work for all expected workloads is a tricky business and a good reason to avoid real-time policies in the first place.

The most widely used procedure for choosing priorities is known as **Rate Monotonic Analysis (RMA)**, after the 1973 paper by Liu and Layland. It applies to real-time systems with periodic threads, which is a very important class. Each thread has a period and a utilization, which is the proportion of the period it will be executing. The goal is to balance the load so that all threads can complete their execution phase before the next period. RMA states that this can be achieved if:

- The highest priorities are given to the threads with the shortest periods
- The total utilization is less than 69%

The total utilization is the sum of all of the individual utilizations. It also makes the assumption that the interaction between threads or the time spent blocked on mutexes and the like is negligible.

Further reading

The following resources have further information on the topics introduced in this chapter:

- *The Art of Unix Programming,* by Eric Steven Raymond, Addison Wesley; (23 Sept, 2003) ISBN 978-0131429017
- *Linux System Programming, 2nd edition,* by Robert Love, *O'Reilly Media;* (8 Jun, 2013) ISBN-10: 1449339530
- *Linux Kernel Development, 3rd edition by* Robert Love, *Addison-Wesley Professional;* (July 2, 2010) ISBN-10: 0672329468
- *The Linux Programming Interface,* by Michael Kerrisk, *No Starch Press;* (October 2010) ISBN 978-1-59327-220-3
- *UNIX Network Programming: v. 2: Interprocess Communications, 2nd Edition,* by W. Richard Stevens, Prentice Hall; (25 Aug, 1998) ISBN-10: 0132974290
- *Programming with POSIX Threads,* by Butenhof, David R, *Addison-Wesley Professional*
- *Scheduling Algorithm for multiprogramming in a Hard-Real-Time Environment,* by C. L. Liu and James W. Layland, *Journal of ACM,* 1973, vol 20, no 1, pp. 46-61

Summary

The long Unix heritage that is built into Linux and the accompanying C libraries provides almost everything you need in order to write stable and resilient embedded applications. The issue is that for every job, there are at least two ways to achieve the end you desire.

In this chapter, I focused on two aspects of system design: partitioning into separate processes, each with one or more threads to get the job done, and scheduling of those threads. I hope that I shed some light on this and have given you the basis for further study into all of them.

In the next chapter, I will examine another important aspect of system design: memory management.

13
Managing Memory

This chapter covers issues related to memory management, which is an important topic for any Linux system but especially for embedded Linux, where system memory is usually in limited supply. After a brief refresher on virtual memory, I will show you how to measure memory usage, how to detect problems with memory allocation, including memory leaks, and what happens when you run out of memory. You will have to understand the tools that are available, from simple tools such as `free` and `top`, to complex tools such as mtrace and Valgrind.

In this chapter, we will cover the following topics:

- Virtual memory basics.
- Kernel space memory layout.
- User space memory layout.
- The process memory map.
- Swapping.
- Mapping memory with mmap.
- How much memory does my application use?
- Per-process memory usage.
- Identifying memory leaks.
- Running out of memory.

Virtual memory basics

To recap, Linux configures the **memory management unit** (**MMU**) of the CPU to present a virtual address space to a running program that begins at zero and ends at the highest address, 0xffffffff, on a 32-bit processor. This address space is divided into pages of 4 KiB (there are rare examples of systems using other page sizes).

Linux divides this virtual address space into an area for applications, called **user space**, and an area for the kernel, called **kernel space**. The split between the two is set by a kernel configuration parameter named PAGE_OFFSET. In a typical 32-bit embedded system, PAGE_OFFSET is 0xc0000000, giving the lower 3 gigabytes to user space and the top gigabyte to kernel space. The user address space is allocated per process so that each process runs in a sandbox, separated from the others. The kernel address space is the same for all processes: there is only one kernel.

Pages in this virtual address space are mapped to physical addresses by the MMU, which uses page tables to perform the mapping.

Each page of virtual memory may be:

- Unmapped, so that trying to access these addresses will result in a SIGSEGV
- Mapped to a page of physical memory that is private to the process
- Mapped to a page of physical memory that is shared with other processes
- Mapped and shared with a **copy on write (CoW)** flag set: a write is trapped in the kernel, which makes a copy of the page and maps it to the process in place of the original page before allowing the write to take place
- Mapped to a page of physical memory that is used by the kernel

The kernel may additionally map pages to reserved memory regions, for example, to access registers and memory buffers in device drivers.

An obvious question is this: why do we do it this way instead of simply referencing physical memory directly, as a typical RTOS would?

There are numerous advantages to virtual memory, some of which are described here:

- Invalid memory accesses are trapped and applications are alerted by SIGSEGV
- Processes run in their own memory space, isolated from others
- Efficient use of memory through the sharing of common code and data, for example, in libraries
- The possibility of increasing the apparent amount of physical memory by adding swap files, although swapping on embedded targets is rare

These are powerful arguments, but we have to admit that there are some disadvantages as well. It is difficult to determine the actual memory budget of an application, which is one of the main concerns of this chapter. The default allocation strategy is to over-commit, which leads to tricky out-of-memory situations, which I will also discuss later on. Finally, the delays introduced by the memory management code in handling exceptions—page faults—make the system less deterministic, which is important for real-time programs. I will cover this in `Chapter 16`, *Real-Time Programming*.

Memory management is different for kernel space and user space. The upcoming sections describe the essential differences and the things you need to know.

Kernel space memory layout

Kernel memory is managed in a fairly straightforward way. It is not demand-paged, which means that for every allocation using `kmalloc()` or a similar function, there is real physical memory. Kernel memory is never discarded or paged out.

Some architectures show a summary of the memory mapping at boot time in the kernel log messages. This trace is taken from a 32-bit ARM device (a BeagleBone Black):

```
Memory: 511MB = 511MB total
Memory: 505980k/505980k available, 18308k reserved, 0K highmem
Virtual kernel memory layout:
    vector  : 0xffff0000 - 0xffff1000   (    4 kB)
    fixmap  : 0xfff00000 - 0xfffe0000   (  896 kB)
    vmalloc : 0xe0800000 - 0xff000000   (  488 MB)
    lowmem  : 0xc0000000 - 0xe0000000   (  512 MB)
    pkmap   : 0xbfe00000 - 0xc0000000   (    2 MB)
    modules : 0xbf800000 - 0xbfe00000   (    6 MB)
      .text : 0xc0008000 - 0xc0763c90   ( 7536 kB)
      .init : 0xc0764000 - 0xc079f700   (  238 kB)
      .data : 0xc07a0000 - 0xc0827240   (  541 kB)
       .bss : 0xc0827240 - 0xc089e940   (  478 kB)
```

The figure of 505980 KiB available is the amount of free memory the kernel sees when it begins execution but before it begins making dynamic allocations.

Consumers of kernel space memory include the following:

- The kernel itself, in other words, the code and data loaded from the kernel image file at boot time. This is shown in the preceding kernel log in the segments .text, .init, .data, and .bss. The .init segment is freed once the kernel has completed initialization.
- Memory allocated through the slab allocator, which is used for kernel data structures of various kinds. This includes allocations made using kmalloc(). They come from the region marked **lowmem**.
- Memory allocated via vmalloc(), usually for larger chunks of memory than is available through kmalloc(). These are in the **vmalloc** area.
- Mapping for device drivers to access registers and memory belonging to various bits of hardware, which you can see by reading /proc/iomem. These also come from the **vmalloc** area, but since they are mapped to physical memory that is outside of main system memory, they do not take up any real memory.
- Kernel modules, which are loaded into the area marked **modules**.
- Other low-level allocations that are not tracked anywhere else.

How much memory does the kernel use?

Unfortunately, there isn't a complete answer to the question 'how much memory does the kernel use, but what follows is as close as we can get.

Firstly, you can see the memory taken up by the kernel code and data in the kernel log shown previously, or you can use the size command, as follows:

```
$ arm-poky-linux-gnueabi-size vmlinux
text      data      bss       dec        hex       filename
9013448   796868    8428144   18238460   1164bfc   vmlinux
```

Usually, the amount of memory taken by the kernel for the static code and data segments shown here is small when compared to the total amount of memory. If that is not the case, you need to look through the kernel configuration and remove the components that you don't need. There is an ongoing effort to allow small kernels to be built: search for **Linux Kernel Tinification**. There is a project page for it at https://tiny.wiki.kernel.org/.

You can get more information about memory usage by reading /proc/meminfo:

```
# cat /proc/meminfo
MemTotal:          509016  kB
MemFree:           410680  kB
Buffers:             1720  kB
Cached:             25132  kB
SwapCached:             0  kB
Active:             74880  kB
Inactive:            3224  kB
Active(anon):       51344  kB
Inactive(anon):      1372  kB
Active(file):       23536  kB
Inactive(file):      1852  kB
Unevictable:            0  kB
Mlocked:                0  kB
HighTotal:              0  kB
HighFree:               0  kB
LowTotal:          509016  kB
LowFree:           410680  kB
SwapTotal:              0  kB
SwapFree:               0  kB
Dirty:                 16  kB
Writeback:              0  kB
AnonPages:          51248  kB
Mapped:             24376  kB
Shmem:               1452  kB
Slab:               11292  kB
SReclaimable:        5164  kB
SUnreclaim:          6128  kB
KernelStack:         1832  kB
PageTables:          1540  kB
NFS_Unstable:           0  kB
Bounce:                 0  kB
WritebackTmp:           0  kB
CommitLimit:       254508  kB
Committed_AS:      734936  kB
VmallocTotal:      499712  kB
VmallocUsed:        29576  kB
VmallocChunk:      389116  kB
```

There is a description of each of these fields on the manual page `proc(5)`. The kernel memory usage is the sum of the following:

- `Slab`: The total memory allocated by the slab allocator
- `KernelStack`: The stack space used when executing kernel code
- `PageTables`: The memory used to store page tables
- `VmallocUsed`: The memory allocated by `vmalloc()`

In the case of slab allocations, you can get more information by reading `/proc/slabinfo`. Similarly, there is a breakdown of allocations in `/proc/vmallocinfo` for the vmalloc area. In both cases, you need detailed knowledge of the kernel and its subsystems in order to see exactly which subsystem is making the allocations and why, which is beyond the scope of this discussion.

With modules, you can use `lsmod` to find out the memory space taken up by the code and data:

```
# lsmod
Module            Size   Used by
g_multi          47670   2
libcomposite     14299   1 g_multi
mt7601Usta      601404   0
```

This leaves the low-level allocations of which there is no record and that prevent us from generating an accurate account of kernel space memory usage. This will appear as missing memory when we add up all the kernel and user space allocations that we know about.

User space memory layout

Linux employs a lazy allocation strategy for user space, only mapping physical pages of memory when the program accesses it. For example, allocating a buffer of 1 MiB using `malloc(3)` returns a pointer to a block of memory addresses but no actual physical memory. A flag is set in the page table entries such that any read or write access is trapped by the kernel. This is known as a **page fault**. Only at this point does the kernel attempt to find a page of physical memory and add it to the page table mapping for the process. It is worthwhile demonstrating this with a simple program, `MELP/chapter_13/pagefault-demo`:

```
#include <stdio.h>
#include <stdlib.h>
#include <string.h>
#include <sys/resource.h>
```

```
#define BUFFER_SIZE (1024 * 1024)

void print_pgfaults(void)
{
  int ret;
  struct rusage usage;
  ret = getrusage(RUSAGE_SELF, &usage);
  if (ret == -1) {
    perror("getrusage");
  } else {
    printf ("Major page faults %ld\n", usage.ru_majflt);
    printf ("Minor page faults %ld\n", usage.ru_minflt);
  }
}

int main (int argc, char *argv[])
{
  unsigned char *p;
  printf("Initial state\n");
  print_pgfaults();
  p = malloc(BUFFER_SIZE);
  printf("After malloc\n");
  print_pgfaults();
  memset(p, 0x42, BUFFER_SIZE);
  printf("After memset\n");
  print_pgfaults();
  memset(p, 0x42, BUFFER_SIZE);
  printf("After 2nd memset\n");
  print_pgfaults();
  return 0;
}
```

When you run it, you will see something like this:

```
Initial state
Major page faults 0
Minor page faults 172
After malloc
Major page faults 0
Minor page faults 186
After memset
Major page faults 0
Minor page faults 442
After 2nd memset
Major page faults 0
Minor page faults 442
```

There were 172 minor page faults encountered after initializing the program's environment and a further 14 when calling getrusage(2) (these numbers will vary depending on the architecture and the version of the C library you are using). The important part is the increase when filling the memory with data: *442 - 186 = 256*. The buffer is 1 MiB, which is 256 pages. The second call to memset(3) makes no difference because all the pages are now mapped.

As you can see, a page fault is generated when the kernel traps an access to a page that has not been mapped. In fact, there are two kinds of page faults: **minor** and **major**. With a minor fault, the kernel just has to find a page of physical memory and map it to the process address space, as shown in the preceding code. A major page fault occurs when the virtual memory is mapped to a file, for example, using mmap(2), which I will describe shortly. Reading from this memory means that the kernel not only has to find a page of memory and map it in, but it also has to fill it with data from the file. Consequently, major faults are much more expensive in time and system resources.

The process memory map

You can see the memory map for a process through the proc filesystem. As an example, here is the map for the init process, PID 1:

```
# cat /proc/1/maps
00008000-0000e000 r-xp 00000000 00:0b 23281745    /sbin/init
00016000-00017000 rwxp 00006000 00:0b 23281745    /sbin/init
00017000-00038000 rwxp 00000000 00:00 0           [heap]
b6ded000-b6f1d000 r-xp 00000000 00:0b 23281695    /lib/libc-2.19.so
b6f1d000-b6f24000 ---p 00130000 00:0b 23281695    /lib/libc-2.19.so
b6f24000-b6f26000 r-xp 0012f000 00:0b 23281695    /lib/libc-2.19.so
b6f26000-b6f27000 rwxp 00131000 00:0b 23281695    /lib/libc-2.19.so
b6f27000-b6f2a000 rwxp 00000000 00:00 0
b6f2a000-b6f49000 r-xp 00000000 00:0b 23281359    /lib/ld-2.19.so
b6f4c000-b6f4e000 rwxp 00000000 00:00 0
b6f4f000-b6f50000 r-xp 00000000 00:00 0           [sigpage]
b6f50000-b6f51000 r-xp 0001e000 00:0b 23281359    /lib/ld-2.19.so
b6f51000-b6f52000 rwxp 0001f000 00:0b 23281359    /lib/ld-2.19.so
beea1000-beec2000 rw-p 00000000 00:00 0           [stack]
ffff0000-ffff1000 r-xp 00000000 00:00 0           [vectors]
```

The first three columns show the start and end virtual addresses and the permissions for each mapping. The permissions are shown here:

- r: Read
- w: Write

- x: Execute
- s: Shared
- p: Private (copy on write)

If the mapping is associated with a file, the filename appears in the final column, and columns four, five, and six contain the offset from the start of the file, the block device number, and the inode of the file. Most of the mappings are to the program itself and the libraries it is linked with. There are two areas where the program can allocate memory, marked [heap] and [stack]. Memory allocated using malloc comes from the former (except for very large allocations, which we will come to later); allocations on the stack come from the latter. The maximum size of both areas is controlled by the process's ulimit:

- **Heap**: ulimit -d, default unlimited
- **Stack**: ulimit -s, default 8 MiB

Allocations that exceed the limit are rejected by SIGSEGV.

When running out of memory, the kernel may decide to discard pages that are mapped to a file and are read-only. If that page is accessed again, it will cause a major page fault and be read back in from the file.

Swapping

The idea of swapping is to reserve some storage where the kernel can place pages of memory that are not mapped to a file so that it can free up the memory for other uses. It increases the effective size of physical memory by the size of the swap file. It is not a panacea: there is a cost to copying pages to and from a swap file, which becomes apparent on a system that has too little real memory for the workload it is carrying and so swapping becomes the main activity. This is sometimes known as **disk thrashing**.

Swap is seldom used on embedded devices because it does not work well with flash storage, where constant writing would wear it out quickly. However, you may want to consider swapping to compressed RAM (zram).

Swapping to compressed memory (zram)

The **zram** driver creates RAM-based block devices named /dev/zram0, /dev/zram1, and so on. Pages written to these devices are compressed before being stored. With compression ratios in the range of 30% to 50%, you can expect an overall increase in free memory of about 10% at the expense of more processing and a corresponding increase in power usage.

To enable zram, configure the kernel with these options:

```
CONFIG_SWAP
CONFIG_CGROUP_MEM_RES_CTLR
CONFIG_CGROUP_MEM_RES_CTLR_SWAP
CONFIG_ZRAM
```

Then, mount zram at boot time by adding this to /etc/fstab:

```
/dev/zram0 none swap defaults zramsize=<size in bytes>,
swapprio=<swap partition priority>
```

You can turn swap on and off using these commands:

```
# swapon /dev/zram0
# swapoff /dev/zram0
```

Mapping memory with mmap

A process begins life with a certain amount of memory mapped to the text (the code) and data segments of the program file, together with the shared libraries that it is linked with. It can allocate memory on its heap at runtime using malloc(3) and on the stack through locally scoped variables and memory allocated through alloca(3). It may also load libraries dynamically at runtime using dlopen(3). All of these mappings are taken care of by the kernel. However, a process can also manipulate its memory map in an explicit way using mmap(2):

```
void *mmap(void *addr, size_t length, int prot, int flags,
        int fd, off_t offset);
```

This function maps length bytes of memory from the file with the descriptor fd, starting at offset in the file, and returns a pointer to the mapping, assuming it is successful. Since the underlying hardware works in pages, length is rounded up to the nearest whole number of pages. The protection parameter, prot, is a combination of read, write, and execute permissions and the flags parameter contains at least MAP_SHARED or MAP_PRIVATE. There are many other flags, which are described in the main page.

There are many things you can do with mmap. I will show some of them in the upcoming sections.

Using mmap to allocate private memory

You can use mmap to allocate an area of private memory by setting MAP_ANONYMOUS in the flags parameter and setting the file descriptor fd to −1. This is similar to allocating memory from the heap using malloc, except that the memory is page-aligned and in multiples of pages. The memory is allocated in the same area as that used for libraries. In fact, this area is referred to by some as the mmap area for this reason.

Anonymous mappings are better for large allocations because they do not pin down the heap with chunks of memory, which would make fragmentation more likely. Interestingly, you will find that malloc (in glibc at least) stops allocating memory from the heap for requests over 128 KiB and uses mmap in this way, so in most cases, just using malloc is the right thing to do. The system will choose the best way of satisfying the request.

Using mmap to share memory

As we saw in Chapter 12, *Learning About Processes and Threads*, POSIX shared memory requires mmap to access the memory segment. In this case, you set the MAP_SHARED flag and use the file descriptor from shm_open():

```
int shm_fd;
char *shm_p;

shm_fd = shm_open("/myshm", O_CREAT | O_RDWR, 0666);
ftruncate(shm_fd, 65536);
shm_p = mmap(NULL, 65536, PROT_READ | PROT_WRITE,
             MAP_SHARED, shm_fd, 0);
```

Using mmap to access device memory

As I mentioned in Chapter 9, *Interfacing with Device Drivers*, it is possible for a driver to allow its device node to be mmaped and share some of the device memory with an application. The exact implementation is dependent on the driver.

One example is the Linux framebuffer, /dev/fb0. The interface is defined in /usr/include/linux/fb.h, including an ioctl function to get the size of the display and the bits per pixel. You can then use mmap to ask the video driver to share the framebuffer with the application and read and write pixels:

```
int f;
int fb_size;
unsigned char *fb_mem;

f = open("/dev/fb0", O_RDWR);
/* Use ioctl FBIOGET_VSCREENINFO to find the display dimensions
   and calculate fb_size */
fb_mem = mmap(0, fb_size, PROT_READ | PROT_WRITE, MAP_SHARED, fd, 0);
/* read and write pixels through pointer fb_mem */
```

A second example is the streaming video interface, Video 4 Linux, version 2, or V4L2, which is defined in /usr/include/linux/videodev2.h. Each video device has a node named /dev/videoN, starting with /dev/video0. There is an ioctl function to ask the driver to allocate a number of video buffers that you can mmap into user space. Then, it is just a question of cycling the buffers and filling or emptying them with video data, depending on whether you are playing back or capturing a video stream.

How much memory does my application use?

As with kernel space, the different ways of allocating, mapping, and sharing user space memory make it quite difficult to answer this seemingly simple question.

To begin, you can ask the kernel how much memory it thinks is available, which you can do using the free command. Here is a typical example of the output:

```
              total       used       free     shared    buffers     cached
Mem:         509016     504312       4704          0      26456     363860
-/+ buffers/cache:      113996     395020
Swap:             0          0          0
```

At first sight, this looks like a system that is almost out of memory with only 4704 KiB free out of 509,016 KiB: less than 1%. However, note that 26,456 KiB is in buffers and a whopping 363,860 KiB is in caches. Linux believes that free memory is wasted memory and the kernel uses free memory for buffers and caches with the knowledge that they can be shrunk when the need arises. Removing buffers and cache from the measurement provides true free memory, which is 395,020 KiB: 77% of the total. When using `free`, the numbers on the second line marked `-/+ buffers/cache` are the important ones.

You can force the kernel to free up caches by writing a number between 1 and 3 to `/proc/sys/vm/drop_caches`:

```
# echo 3 > /proc/sys/vm/drop_caches
```

The number is actually a bit mask that determines which of the two broad types of caches you want to free: 1 for the page cache and 2 for the dentry and inode caches combined. The exact roles of these caches are not particularly important here, only that there is memory that the kernel is using but that can be reclaimed at short notice.

Per-process memory usage

There are several metrics to measure the amount of memory a process is using. I will begin with the two that are easiest to obtain: the **virtual set size (vss)** and the **resident memory size (rss)**, both of which are available in most implementations of the `ps` and `top` commands:

- **Vss**: Called VSZ in the `ps` command and VIRT in `top`, this is the total amount of memory mapped by a process. It is the sum of all the regions shown in `/proc/<PID>/map`. This number is of limited interest since only part of the virtual memory is committed to physical memory at any time.
- **Rss**: Called RSS in `ps` and RES in `top`, this is the sum of memory that is mapped to physical pages of memory. This gets closer to the actual memory budget of the process, but there is a problem: if you add the Rss of all the processes, you will get an overestimate of the memory in use because some pages will be shared.

Using top and ps

The versions of top and ps from BusyBox provide very limited information. The examples that follow use the full version from the procps package.

The ps command shows **Vss (VSZ)** and **Rss (RSS)** with the options -Aly, or you can use a custom format that includes vsz and rss, as shown here:

```
# ps -eo pid,tid,class,rtprio,stat,vsz,rss,comm
   PID   TID CLS RTPRIO STAT     VSZ    RSS COMMAND
     1     1 TS       - Ss      4496   2652 systemd
  [...]
   205   205 TS       - Ss      4076   1296 systemd-journal
   228   228 TS       - Ss      2524   1396 udevd
   581   581 TS       - Ss      2880   1508 avahi-daemon
   584   584 TS       - Ss      2848   1512 dbus-daemon
   590   590 TS       - Ss      1332    680 acpid
   594   594 TS       - Ss      4600   1564 wpa_supplicant
```

Likewise, top shows a summary of the free memory and memory usage per process:

```
top - 21:17:52 up 10:04,  1 user,  load average: 0.00, 0.01, 0.05
Tasks:  96 total,   1 running,  95 sleeping,   0 stopped,   0 zombie
%Cpu(s):  1.7 us,  2.2 sy,  0.0 ni, 95.9 id,  0.0 wa,  0.0 hi
KiB Mem:  509016 total,  278524 used,  230492 free,   25572 buffers
KiB Swap:      0 total,       0 used,       0 free,  170920 cached
PID USER      PR  NI  VIRT  RES  SHR S  %CPU %MEM    TIME+  COMMAND
595 root      20   0 64920 9.8m 4048 S   0.0  2.0  0:01.09 node
866 root      20   0 28892 9152 3660 S   0.2  1.8  0:36.38 Xorg
[...]
```

These simple commands give you a feel of the memory usage and provide the first indication that you have a memory leak when you see that the Rss of a process keeps on increasing. However, they are not very accurate in the absolute measurements of memory usage.

Using smem

In 2009, Matt Mackall began looking at the problem of accounting for shared pages in process memory measurement and added two new metrics called **unique set size**, or Uss, and **proportional set size**, or **Pss**:

- **Uss**: This is the amount of memory that is committed to physical memory and is unique to a process; it is not shared with any other. It is the amount of memory that would be freed if the process were to terminate.
- **Pss**: This splits the accounting of shared pages that are committed to physical memory between all the processes that have them mapped. For example, if an area of library code is 12-pages long and is shared by six processes, each will accumulate two pages in Pss. Thus, if you add the Pss numbers for all processes, you will get the actual amount of memory being used by those processes. In other words, Pss is the number we have been looking for.

Information about Pss is available in `/proc/<PID>/smaps`, which contains additional information for each of the mappings shown in `/proc/<PID>/maps`. Here is a section from such a file that provides information on the mapping for the `libc` code segment:

```
b6e6d000-b6f45000 r-xp 00000000 b3:02 2444 /lib/libc-2.13.so
Size:                 864 kB
Rss:                  264 kB
Pss:                    6 kB
Shared_Clean:         264 kB
Shared_Dirty:           0 kB
Private_Clean:          0 kB
Private_Dirty:          0 kB
Referenced:           264 kB
Anonymous:              0 kB
AnonHugePages:          0 kB
Swap:                   0 kB
KernelPageSize:         4 kB
MMUPageSize:            4 kB
Locked:                 0 kB
VmFlags: rd ex mr mw me
```

Note that the Rss is 264 KiB, but because it is shared between many other processes, the Pss is only 6 KiB.

There is a tool named **smem** that collates information from the `smaps` files and presents it in various ways, including as pie or bar charts. The project page for smem is `https://www.selenic.com/smem`. It is available as a package in most desktop distributions. However, since it is written in Python, installing it on an embedded target requires a Python environment, which may be too much trouble for just one tool. To help with this, there is a small program named `smemcap` that captures the state from `/proc` on the target and saves it to a TAR file that can be analyzed later on the host computer. It is part of BusyBox, but it can also be compiled from the `smem` source.

Running `smem` natively, as `root`, you will see these results:

```
# smem -t
  PID User    Command                  Swap      USS      PSS      RSS
  610 0       /sbin/agetty -s tty00 11    0      128      149      720
 1236 0       /sbin/agetty -s ttyGS0 1    0      128      149      720
  609 0       /sbin/agetty tty1 38400     0      144      163      724
  578 0       /usr/sbin/acpid             0      140      173      680
  819 0       /usr/sbin/cron              0      188      201      704
  634 103     avahi-daemon: chroot hel    0      112      205      500
  980 0       /usr/sbin/udhcpd -S /etc    0      196      205      568
  ...
  836 0       /usr/bin/X :0 -auth /var    0     7172     7746     9212
  583 0       /usr/bin/node autorun.js    0     8772     9043    10076
 1089 1000    /usr/bin/python -O /usr/    0     9600    11264    16388
-------------------------------------------------------------------
   53 6                                   0    65820    78251   146544
```

You can see from the last line of the output that in this case, the total Pss is about a half of the Rss.

If you don't have or don't want to install Python on your target, you can capture the state using `smemcap`, again as `root`:

```
# smemcap > smem-bbb-cap.tar
```

Then, copy the TAR file to the host and read it using `smem -S`, though this time, there is no need to run as `root`:

```
$ smem -t -S smem-bbb-cap.tar
```

The output is identical to the output we get when running smem natively.

Other tools to consider

Another way to display Pss is via `ps_mem` (`https://github.com/pixelb/ps_mem`), which prints much the same information but in a simpler format. It is also written in Python.

Android also has a tool that displays a summary of Uss and Pss for each process, named `procrank`, which can be cross-compiled for embedded Linux with a few small changes. You can get the code from `https://github.com/csimmonds/procrank_linux`.

Identifying memory leaks

A memory leak occurs when memory is allocated but not freed when it is no longer needed. Memory leakage is by no means unique to embedded systems, but it becomes an issue partly because targets don't have much memory in the first place and partly because they often run for long periods of time without rebooting, allowing the leaks to become a large puddle.

You will realize that there is a leak when you run `free` or `top` and see that free memory is continually going down even if you drop caches, as shown in the preceding section. You will be able to identify the culprit (or culprits) by looking at the Uss and Rss per process.

There are several tools to identify memory leaks in a program. I will look at two: mtrace and Valgrind.

mtrace

mtrace is a component of glibc that traces calls to `malloc`, `free`, and related functions, and identifies areas of memory not freed when the program exits. You need to call the `mtrace()` function from within the program to begin tracing and then at runtime, write a path name to the `MALLOC_TRACE` environment variable in which the trace information is written. If `MALLOC_TRACE` does not exist or if the file cannot be opened, the `mtrace` hooks are not installed. While the trace information is written in ASCII, it is usual to use the `mtrace` command to view it.

Here is an example:

```
#include <mcheck.h>
#include <stdlib.h>
#include <stdio.h>

int main(int argc, char *argv[])
```

```
{
  int j;
  mtrace();
  for (j = 0; j < 2; j++)
    malloc(100);    /* Never freed:a memory leak */
  calloc(16, 16);   /* Never freed:a memory leak */
  exit(EXIT_SUCCESS);
}
```

Here is what you might see when running the program and looking at the trace:

```
$ export MALLOC_TRACE=mtrace.log
$ ./mtrace-example
$ mtrace mtrace-example mtrace.log

Memory not freed:
-----------------
          Address      Size     Caller
0x0000000001479460     0x64   at /home/chris/mtrace-example.c:11
0x00000000014794d0     0x64   at /home/chris/mtrace-example.c:11
0x0000000001479540    0x100   at /home/chris/mtrace-example.c:15
```

Unfortunately, mtrace does not tell you about leaked memory while the program runs. It has to terminate first.

Valgrind

Valgrind is a very powerful tool used to discover memory problems including leaks and other things. One advantage is that you don't have to recompile the programs and libraries that you want to check, although it works better if they have been compiled with the -g option so that they include debug symbol tables. It works by running the program in an emulated environment and trapping execution at various points. This leads to the big downside of Valgrind, which is that the program runs at a fraction of normal speed, which makes it less useful in testing anything with real-time constraints.

 Incidentally, the name is often mispronounced: it says in the Valgrind FAQ that the *grind* part is pronounced with a short *i*, as in grinned (rhymes with tinned) rather than grind (rhymes with find). The FAQ, documentation, and downloads are available at http://valgrind.org.

Valgrind contains several diagnostic tools:

- memcheck: This is the default tool, and it detects memory leaks and general misuse of memory
- cachegrind: This calculates the processor cache hit rate
- callgrind: This calculates the cost of each function call
- helgrind: This highlights the misuse of the Pthread API, including potential deadlocks, and race conditions
- DRD: This is another Pthread analysis tool
- massif: This profiles the usage of the heap and stack

You can select the tool you want with the –tool option. Valgrind runs on the major embedded platforms: ARM (cortex A), PPC, MIPS, and x86 in 32- and 64-bit variants. It is available as a package in both the Yocto Project and Buildroot.

To find our memory leak, we need to use the default memcheck tool, with the --leakcheck=full option to print the lines where the leak was found:

```
$ valgrind --leak-check=full ./mtrace-example
==17235== Memcheck, a memory error detector
==17235== Copyright (C) 2002-2013, and GNU GPL'd, by Julian Seward
    et al.==17235== Using Valgrind-3.10.0.SVN and LibVEX; rerun with -h for
    copyright info
==17235== Command: ./mtrace-example
==17235==
==17235==
==17235== HEAP SUMMARY:
==17235==    in use at exit: 456 bytes in 3 blocks
==17235==    total heap usage: 3 allocs, 0 frees, 456 bytes
    allocated
==17235==
==17235== 200 bytes in 2 blocks are definitely lost in loss record
    1 of 2==17235==    at 0x4C2AB80: malloc (in
    /usr/lib/valgrind/vgpreload_memcheck-linux.so)
==17235==       by 0x4005FA: main (mtrace-example.c:12)
==17235==
==17235== 256 bytes in 1 blocks are definitely lost in loss record
    2 of 2==17235==    at 0x4C2CC70: calloc (in
    /usr/lib/valgrind/vgpreload_memcheck-linux.so)
==17235==       by 0x400613: main (mtrace-example.c:14)
==17235==
==17235== LEAK SUMMARY:
==17235==    definitely lost: 456 bytes in 3 blocks
==17235==    indirectly lost: 0 bytes in 0 blocks
==17235==      possibly lost: 0 bytes in 0 blocks
```

```
==17235==        still reachable: 0 bytes in 0 blocks
==17235==            suppressed: 0 bytes in 0 blocks
==17235==
==17235== For counts of detected and suppressed errors, rerun
   with: -v==17235== ERROR SUMMARY: 2 errors from 2 contexts (suppressed: 0
   from 0)
```

Running out of memory

The standard memory allocation policy is to **over-commit**, which means that the kernel will allow more memory to be allocated by applications than there is physical memory. Most of the time, this works fine because it is common for applications to request more memory than they really need. This also helps in the implementation of `fork(2)`: it is safe to make a copy of a large program because the pages of memory are shared with the copy on write flag set. In the majority of cases, `fork` is followed by an `exec` function call, which unshares the memory and then loads a new program.

However, there is always the possibility that a particular workload will cause a group of processes to try to cash in on the allocations they have been promised simultaneously and so demand more than there really is. This is an **out of memory** situation, or **OOM**. At this point, there is no other alternative but to kill off processes until the problem goes away. This is the job of the **out of memory killer**.

Before we get to that, there is a tuning parameter for kernel allocations in `/proc/sys/vm/overcommit_memory`, which you can set to the following:

- 0: Heuristic over-commit
- 1: Always over-commit; never check
- 2: Always check; never over-commit

Option 0 is the default and is the best choice in the majority of cases.

Option 1 is only really useful if you run programs that work with large sparse arrays and allocate large areas of memory but write to a small proportion of them. Such programs are rare in the context of embedded systems.

Option 2, never over-commit, seems to be a good choice if you are worried about running out of memory, perhaps in a mission or safety-critical application. It will fail allocations that are greater than the commit limit, which is the size of swap space plus the total memory multiplied by the over-commit ratio. The over-commit ratio is controlled by `/proc/sys/vm/overcommit_ratio` and has a default value of 50%.

As an example, suppose you have a device with 512 MB of system RAM and you set a really conservative ratio of 25%:

```
# echo 25 > /proc/sys/vm/overcommit_ratio
# grep -e MemTotal -e CommitLimit /proc/meminfo
MemTotal:            509016 kB
CommitLimit:         127252 kB
```

There is no swap, so the commit limit is 25% of `MemTotal`, as expected.

There is another important variable in `/proc/meminfo`: `Committed_AS`. This is the total amount of memory that is needed to fulfill all the allocations made so far. I found the following on one system:

```
# grep -e MemTotal -e Committed_AS /proc/meminfo
MemTotal:            509016 kB
Committed_AS:        741364 kB
```

In other words, the kernel had already promised more memory than the available memory. Consequently, setting `overcommit_memory` to 2 would mean that all allocations would fail regardless of `overcommit_ratio`. To get to a working system, I would have to either install double the amount of RAM or severely reduce the number of running processes, of which there were about 40.

In all cases, the final defense is `oom-killer`. It uses a heuristic method to calculate a badness score between 0 and 1,000 for each process, and then terminates those with the highest score until there is enough free memory. You should see something like this in the kernel log:

```
[44510.490320] eatmem invoked oom-killer: gfp_mask=0x200da,
 order=0, oom_score_adj=0
...
```

You can force an OOM event using `echo f > /proc/sysrq-trigger`.

You can influence the badness score for a process by writing an adjustment value to `/proc/<PID>/oom_score_adj`. A value of `-1000` means that the badness score can never be greater than zero and so it will never be killed; a value of `+1000` means that it will always be greater than 1000 and so it will always be killed.

Further reading

The following resources have further information on the topics introduced in this chapter:

- *Linux Kernel Development, 3rd Edition,* by Robert Love, Addison Wesley, *O'Reilly Media*; (June, 2010) ISBN-10: 0672329468
- *Linux System Programming, 2nd Edition,* by Robert Love, *O'Reilly Media*; (8 June, 2013) ISBN-10: 1449339530
- *Understanding the Linux VM Manager* by Mel Gorman: `https://www.kernel.org/doc/gorman/pdf/understand.pdf`
- *Valgrind 3.3 - Advanced Debugging and Profiling for Gnu/Linux Applications* by J Seward, N. Nethercote, and J. Weidendorfer, *Network Theory Ltd*; (1 Mar, 2008) ISBN 978-0954612054

Summary

Accounting for every byte of memory used in a virtual memory system is just not possible. However, you can find a fairly accurate figure for the total amount of free memory, excluding that taken by buffers and cache, using the `free` command. By monitoring it over a period of time and with different workloads, you should become confident that it will remain within a given limit.

When you want to tune memory usage or identify sources of unexpected allocations, there are resources that give more detailed information. For kernel space, the most useful information is in `/proc`: `meminfo`, `slabinfo`, and `vmallocinfo`.

When it comes to getting accurate measurements for user space, the best metric is Pss, as shown by `smem` and other tools. For memory debugging, you can get help from simple tracers such as `mtrace`, or you have the heavyweight option of the Valgrind memcheck tool.

If you have concerns about the consequence of an out of memory situation, you can fine-tune the allocation mechanism via `/proc/sys/vm/overcommit_memory` and you can control the likelihood of particular processes being killed though the `oom_score_adj` parameter.

The next chapter is all about debugging user space and kernel code using the GNU debugger and the insights you can gain from watching code as it runs, including the memory management functions I have described here.

14
Debugging with GDB

Bugs happen. Identifying and fixing them is part of the development process. There are many different techniques for finding and characterizing program defects, including static and dynamic analysis, code review, tracing, profiling, and interactive debugging. I will look at tracers and profilers in the next chapter, but here I want to concentrate on the traditional approach of watching code execution through a debugger, which in our case is the **GNU Project Debugger** (**GDB**). GDB is a powerful and flexible tool. You can use it to debug applications, examine the postmortem files (`core` files) that are created after a program crash, and even step through kernel code.

In this chapter, we will cover the following topics:

- The GNU debugger
- Preparing to debug
- Debugging applications
- Just-in-time debugging
- Debugging forks and threads
- Core files
- GDB user interfaces
- Debugging kernel code

The GNU debugger

GDB is a source-level debugger for compiled languages, primarily C and C++, although there is also support for a variety of other languages such as Go and Objective-C. You should read the notes for the version of GDB you are using to find out the current status of support for the various languages.

The project website is `http://www.gnu.org/software/gdb` and it contains a lot of useful information, including the GDB User Manual, *Debugging with GDB*.

Out of the box, GDB has a command-line user interface, which some people find off-putting, although in reality, it is easy to use with a little practice. If command-line interfaces are not to your liking, there are plenty of front-end user interfaces to GDB, and I will describe three of them later.

Preparing to debug

You need to compile the code you want to debug with debug symbols. GCC offers two options for this: `-g` and `-ggdb`. The latter adds debug information that is specific to GDB, whereas the former generates information in an appropriate format for whichever target operating system you are using, making it the more portable option. In our particular case, the target operating system is always Linux, and it makes little difference whether you use `-g` or `-ggdb`. Of more interest is the fact that both options allow you to specify the level of debug information, from 0 to 3:

- 0: This produces no debug information at all and is equivalent to omitting the `-g` or `-ggdb` switch
- 1: This produces minimal information, but which includes function names and external variables, which is enough to generate a backtrace
- 2: This is the default and includes information about local variables and line numbers so that you can perform source-level debugging and single-step through the code
- 3: This includes extra information which, among other things, means that GDB can handle macro expansions correctly

In most cases, `-g` suffices: reserve `-g3` or `-ggdb3` for if you are having problems stepping through code, especially if it contains *macros*.

The next issue to consider is the level of code optimization. Compiler optimization tends to destroy the relationship between lines of source code and machine code, which makes stepping through the source unpredictable. If you experience problems like this, you will most likely need to compile without optimization, leaving out the `-O` compile switch, or using `-Og`, which enables optimizations that do not interfere with debugging.

A related issue is that of stack-frame pointers, which are needed by GDB to generate a backtrace of function calls up to the current one. On some architectures, GCC will not generate stack-frame pointers with the higher levels of optimization (-O2 and above). If you find yourself in the situation that you really have to compile with -O2 but still want backtraces, you can override the default behavior with -fno-omit-frame-pointer. Also look out for code that has been hand-optimized to leave out frame pointers through the addition of -fomit-frame-pointer: you may want to temporarily remove those bits.

Debugging applications

You can use GDB to debug applications in one of two ways: if you are developing code to run on desktops and servers, or indeed any environment where you compile and run the code on the same machine, it is natural to run GDB natively. However, most embedded development is done using a cross toolchain, and hence you want to debug code running on the device but control it from the cross-development environment, where you have the source code and the tools. I will focus on the latter case since it is the most likely scenario for embedded developers, but I will also show you how to set up a system for native debugging. I am not going to describe the basics of using GDB here since there are many good references on that topic already, including the GDB user manual and the suggested *Further reading* at the end of the chapter.

Remote debugging using gdbserver

The key component for remote debugging is the debug agent, gdbserver, which runs on the target and controls execution of the program being debugged. gdbserver connects to a copy of GDB running on the host machine via a network connection or a serial interface.

Debugging through gdbserver is almost, but not quite, the same as debugging natively. The differences are mostly centered around the fact that there are two computers involved and they have to be in the right state for debugging to take place. Here are some things to look out for:

- At the start of a debug session, you need to load the program you want to debug on the target using gdbserver, and then separately load GDB from your cross toolchain on the host.
- GDB and gdbserver need to connect to each other before a debug session can begin.
- GDB, running on the host, needs to be told where to look for debug symbols and source code, especially for shared libraries.

- The GDB `run` command does not work as expected.
- gdbserver will terminate when the debug session ends, and you will need to restart it if you want another debug session.
- You need debug symbols and source code for the binaries you want to debug on the host, but not on the target. Often, there is not enough storage space for them on the target, and they will need to be stripped before deploying to the target.
- The GDB/gdbserver combination does not support all the features of natively running GDB: for example, gdbserver cannot follow the child process after a `fork`, whereas native GDB can.
- Odd things can happen if GDB and gdbserver are of different versions, or are the same version but configured differently. Ideally, they should be built from the same source using your favorite build tool.

Debug symbols increase the size of executables dramatically, sometimes by a factor of 10. As mentioned in `Chapter 5`, *Building a Root Filesystem*, it can be useful to remove debug symbols without recompiling everything. The tool for the job is `strip` from your cross toolchain. You can control the aggressiveness of `strip` with these switches:

- `--strip-all`: This removes all symbols (default)
- `--strip-unneeded`: This removes symbols not needed for relocation processing
- `--strip-debug`: This removes only debug symbols

> For applications and shared libraries, `--strip-all` (the default) is fine, but when it comes to kernel modules, you will find that it will stop the module from loading. Use `--strip-unneeded` instead. I am still working on a use case for `-strip-debug`.

With that in mind, let's look at the specifics involved in debugging with the Yocto Project and Buildroot.

Setting up the Yocto Project for remote debugging

There are two things to be done to debug applications remotely when using the Yocto Project: you need to add gdbserver to the target image, and you need to create an SDK that includes GDB and has debug symbols for the executables that you plan to debug.

First, then, to include gdbserver in the target image, you can add the package explicitly by adding this to `conf/local.conf`:

```
IMAGE_INSTALL_append = " gdbserver"
```

Alternatively, you can add `tools-debug` to `EXTRA_IMAGE_FEATURES`, which will add gdbserver, native `gdb`, and strace to the target image (I will talk about strace in the next chapter):

```
EXTRA_IMAGE_FEATURES = "debug-tweaks tools-debug"
```

For the second part, you just need to build an SDK as I described in Chapter 6, *Selecting a Build System*:

```
$ bitbake -c populate_sdk <image>
```

The SDK contains a copy of GDB. It also contains a `sysroot` for the target with debug symbols for all the programs and libraries that are part of the target image. Finally, the SDK contains the source code for the executables. For example, looking at an SDK built for the BeagleBone Black and generated by version 2.2.1 of the Yocto Project, it is installed by default into `/opt/poky/2.2.1/`. The `sysroot` for the target is `/opt/poky/2.2.1/sysroots/cortexa8hf-neon-poky-linux-gnueabi/`. The programs are in `/bin/`, `/sbin/`, `/usr/bin/` and `/usr/sbin/`, relative to the `sysroot`, and the libraries are in `/lib/` and `/usr/lib/`. In each of these directories, you will find a subdirectory named `.debug/` that contains the symbols for each program and library. GDB knows to look in `.debug/` when searching for symbol information. The source code for the executables is stored in `/usr/src/debug/`, relative to the `sysroot`.

Setting up Buildroot for remote debugging

Buildroot does not make a distinction between the build environment and that used for application development: there is no SDK. Assuming that you are using the Buildroot internal toolchain, you need to enable these options to build the cross GDB for the host and to build gdbserver for the target:

- BR2_PACKAGE_HOST_GDB, in **Toolchain | Build cross gdb for the host**
- BR2_PACKAGE_GDB, in **Target packages | Debugging, profiling and benchmark->gdb**
- BR2_PACKAGE_GDB_SERVER, in **Target packages | Debugging, profiling and benchmark | gdbserver**

You also need to build executables with debug symbols, for which you need to enable BR2_ENABLE_DEBUG, in **Build options | build packages with debugging symbols**.

This will create libraries with debug symbols in output/host/usr/<arch>/sysroot.

Starting to debug

Now that you have gdbserver installed on the target and a cross GDB on the host, you can start a debug session.

Connecting GDB and gdbserver

The connection between GDB and gdbserver can be through a network or serial interface. In the case of a network connection, you launch gdbserver with the TCP port number to listen on and, optionally, an IP address to accept connections from. In most cases, you don't care which IP address is going to connect, so you can just provide the port number. In this example, gdbserver waits for a connection on port 10000 from any host:

```
# gdbserver :10000 ./hello-world
Process hello-world created; pid = 103
Listening on port 10000
```

Next, start the copy of GDB from your toolchain, pointing it at an unstripped copy of the program so that GDB can load the symbol table:

```
$ arm-poky-linux-gnueabi-gdb hello-world
```

In GDB, use the command target remote to make the connection to gdbserver, giving it the IP address or hostname of the target and the port it is waiting on:

```
(gdb) target remote 192.168.1.101:10000
```

When gdbserver sees the connection from the host, it prints the following:

```
Remote debugging from host 192.168.1.1
```

The procedure is similar for a serial connection. On the target, you tell gdbserver which serial port to use:

```
# gdbserver /dev/ttyO0 ./hello-world
```

You may need to configure the port *baud rate* beforehand using `stty(1)` or a similar program. A simple example would be as follows:

```
# stty -F /dev/ttyO0 115200
```

There are many other options to `stty`, so read the manual page for more details. It is worthwhile noting that the port must not be being used for anything else. For example, you can't use a port that is being used as the system console.

On the host, you make the connection to gdbserver using `target remote` plus the serial device at the host end of the cable. In most cases, you will want to set the baud rate of the host serial port first, using the GDB command `set serial baud`:

```
(gdb) set serial baud 115200
(gdb) target remote /dev/ttyUSB0
```

Setting the sysroot

GDB needs to know where to find debug information and source code for the program and shared libraries you are debugging. When debugging natively, the paths are well known and built in to GDB, but when using a cross toolchain, GDB has no way to guess where the root of the target filesystem is. You have to give it this information.

If you built your application using the Yocto Project SDK, the `sysroot` is within the SDK, and so you can set it in GDB like this:

```
(gdb) set sysroot /opt/poky/2.2.1/sysroots/cortexa8hf-neon-poky-linux-gnueabi
```

If you are using Buildroot, you will find that the `sysroot` is in `output/host/usr/<toolchain>/sysroot`, and that there is a symbolic link to it in `output/staging`. So, for Buildroot, you would set the `sysroot` like this:

```
(gdb) set sysroot /home/chris/buildroot/output/staging
```

GDB also needs to find the source code for the files you are debugging. GDB has a search path for source files, which you can see using the command `show directories`:

```
(gdb) show directories
Source directories searched: $cdir:$cwd
```

These are the defaults: $cwd is the current working directory of the GDB instance running on the host; $cdir is the directory where the source was compiled. The latter is encoded into the object files with the tag DW_AT_comp_dir. You can see these tags using objdump --dwarf, like this, for example:

```
$ arm-poky-linux-gnueabi-objdump --dwarf ./helloworld | grep DW_AT_comp_dir
[...]
<160> DW_AT_comp_dir : (indirect string, offset: 0x244):
/home/chris/helloworld
[...]
```

In most cases, the defaults, $cdir:$cwd, are sufficient, but problems arise if the directories have been moved between compilation and debugging. One such case occurs with the Yocto Project. Taking a deeper look at the DW_AT_comp_dir tags for a program compiled using the Yocto Project SDK, you may notice this:

```
$ arm-poky-linux-gnueabi-objdump --dwarf ./helloworld | grep DW_AT_comp_dir
<2f> DW_AT_comp_dir : /usr/src/debug/glibc/2.24-r0/git/csu
<79> DW_AT_comp_dir : (indirect string, offset: 0x139):
/usr/src/debug/glibc/2.24-r0/git/csu
<116> DW_AT_comp_dir : /usr/src/debug/glibc/2.24-r0/git/csu
<160> DW_AT_comp_dir : (indirect string, offset: 0x244):
/home/chris/helloworld
[...]
```

Here, you can see multiple references to the directory /usr/src/debug/glibc/2.24-r0/git, but where is it? The answer is that it is in the sysroot for the SDK, so the full path is /opt/poky/2.2.1/sysroots/cortexa8hf-neon-poky-linux-gnueabi/usr/src/debug/glibc/2.24-r0/git. The SDK contains source code for all of the programs and libraries that are in the target image. GDB has a simple way to cope with an entire directory tree being moved like this: substitute-path. So, when debugging with the Yocto Project SDK, you need to use these commands:

```
(gdb) set sysroot /opt/poky/2.2.1/sysroots/cortexa8hf-neon-poky-linux-gnueabi
(gdb) set substitute-path /usr/src/debug
/opt/poky/2.2.1/sysroots/cortexa8hf-neon-poky-linux-gnueabi/usr/src/debug
```

You may have additional shared libraries that are stored outside the sysroot. In that case, you can use set solib-search-path, which can contain a colon-separated list of directories to search for shared libraries. GDB searches solib-search-path only if it cannot find the binary in the sysroot.

A third way of telling GDB where to look for source code, for both libraries and programs, is using the `directory` command:

```
(gdb) directory /home/chris/MELP/src/lib_mylib
Source directories searched: /home/chris/MELP/src/lib_mylib:$cdir:$cwd
```

Paths added in this way take precedence because they are searched *before* those from `sysroot` or `solib-search-path`.

GDB command files

There are some things that you need to do each time you run GDB, for example, setting the `sysroot`. It is convenient to put such commands into a command file and run them each time GDB is started. GDB reads commands from `$HOME/.gdbinit`, then from `.gdbinit` in the current directory, and then from files specified on the command line with the `-x` parameter. However, recent versions of GDB will refuse to load `.gdbinit` from the current directory for security reasons. You can override that behavior for by adding a line like this to your `$HOME/.gdbinit`:

```
set auto-load safe-path /
```

Alternatively, if you don't want to enable auto-loading globally, you can specify a particular directory like this:

```
add-auto-load-safe-path /home/chris/myprog
```

My personal preference is to use the `-x` parameter to point to the command file, which exposes the location of the file so that I don't forget about it.

To help you set up GDB, Buildroot creates a GDB command file containing the correct `sysroot` command in `output/staging/usr/share/buildroot/gdbinit`. It will contain a line similar to this one:

```
set sysroot /home/chris/buildroot/output/host/usr/arm-buildroot-linux-
gnueabi/sysroot
```

Overview of GDB commands

GDB has a great many commands, which are described in the online manual and in the resources mentioned in the *Further reading* section. To help you get going as quickly as possible, here is a list of the most commonly used commands. In most cases there, is a short form for the command, which is listed in the tables following.

Breakpoints

These are the commands for managing breakpoints:

Command	Short-form command	Use
break <location>	b <location>	Set a breakpoint on a function name, line number, or line. Examples of locations are main, 5, and sortbug.c:42.
info breakpoints	i b	List breakpoints.
delete breakpoint <N>	d b <N>	Delete breakpoint <N>.

Running and stepping

These are commands for controlling the execution of a program:

Command	Short-form command	Use
run	r	Load a fresh copy of the program into memory and start running it. *This does not work for remote debug using gdbserver.*
continue	c	Continue execution from a breakpoint.
Ctrl-C	-	Stop the program being debugged.
step	s	Step one line of code, stepping *into* any function that is called.
next	n	Step one line of code, stepping *over* a function call.
finish	-	Run until the current function returns.

Getting information

These are commands for getting information about the debugger:

Command	Short-form command	Use
`backtrace`	`bt`	List the call stack
`info threads`	`i th`	Display information about the threads executing in the program
`info sharedlibrary`	`i share`	Display information about shared libraries currently loaded by the program
`print <variable>`	`p <variable>`	Print the value of a variable, for example `print foo`
`list`	`l`	List lines of code around the current program counter

Running to a breakpoint

Gdbserver loads the program into memory and sets a breakpoint at the first instruction, then waits for a connection from GDB. When the connection is made, you enter into a debug session. However, you will find that if you try to single-step immediately, you will get this message:

```
Cannot find bounds of current function
```

This is because the program has been halted in code written in assembly which creates the runtime environment for C and C++ programs. The first line of C or C++ code is the `main()` function. Supposing that you want to stop at `main()`, you would set a breakpoint there and then use the `continue` command (abbreviation c) to tell gdbserver to continue from the breakpoint at the start of the program and stop at `main()`:

```
(gdb) break main
Breakpoint 1, main (argc=1, argv=0xbefffe24) at helloworld.c:8
printf("Hello, world!\n");
(gdb) c
```

At this point, you may see the following:

```
Reading /lib/ld-linux.so.3 from remote target...
warning: File transfers from remote targets can be slow. Use "set sysroot"
to access files locally instead.
```

With older versions of GDB, you may instead see this:

```
warning: Could not load shared library symbols for 2 libraries, e.g.
/lib/libc.so.6.
```

In both cases, the problem is that you have forgotten to set the `sysroot`! Take another look at the earlier section on `sysroot`.

This is all very different to starting a program natively, where you just type `run`. In fact, if you try typing `run` in a remote debug session, you will either see a message saying that the remote target does not support the `run` command, or in older versions of GDB, it will just hang without any explanation.

Native debugging

Running a native copy of GDB on the target is not as common as doing it remotely, but it is possible. As well as installing GDB in the target image, you will also need unstripped copies of the executables you want to debug and the corresponding source code installed in the target image. Both the Yocto Project and Buildroot allow you to do this.

While native debugging is not a common activity for embedded developers, running profile and trace tools on the target is very common. These tools usually work best if you have unstripped binaries and source code on the target, which is half of the story I am telling here. I will return to the topic in the next chapter.

The Yocto Project

To begin with, you need to add `gdb` to the target image by adding this to `conf/local.conf`:

```
IMAGE_INSTALL_append = " gdb"
```

Next, you need the debug information for the packages you want to debug. The Yocto Project builds debug variants of packages, which contain unstripped binaries and the source code. You can add these debug packages selectively to your target image by adding `<package name>-dbg` to your `conf/local.conf`. Alternatively, you can simply install *all* debug packages by adding `dbg-pkgs` to `EXTRA_IMAGE_FEATURES`. Be warned that this will increase the size of the target image dramatically, perhaps by several hundreds of megabytes.

```
EXTRA_IMAGE_FEATURES = "dbg-pkgs"
```

The source code is installed into `/usr/src/debug/<package name>` in the target image. This means that GDB will pick it up without needing to run `set substitute-path`. If you don't need the source, you can prevent it from being installed by adding this to your `conf/local.conf` file:

```
PACKAGE_DEBUG_SPLIT_STYLE = "debug-without-src"
```

Buildroot

With Buildroot, you can tell it to install a native copy of GDB in the target image by enabling this option:

- `BR2_PACKAGE_GDB_DEBUGGER` in **Target packages | Debugging, profiling and benchmark | Full debugger**

Then, to build binaries with debug information and to install them in the target image without stripping, enable these two options:

- `BR2_ENABLE_DEBUG` in **Build options | Build packages with debugging symbols**
- `BR2_STRIP_none` in **Build options | Strip command for binaries on target**

Just-in-time debugging

Sometimes a program will start to misbehave after it has been running for a while, and you would like to know what it is doing. The GDB *attach* feature does exactly this. I call it just-in-time debugging. It is available with both native and remote debug sessions.

In the case of remote debugging, you need to find the PID of the process to be debugged and pass it to `gdbserver` with the `--attach` option. For example, if the PID is 109, you would type this:

```
# gdbserver --attach :10000 109
Attached; pid = 109
Listening on port 10000
```

This forces the process to stop as if it were at a breakpoint, allowing you to start your cross GDB in the normal way and connect to gdbserver. When you are done, you can detach, allowing the program to continue running without the debugger:

```
(gdb) detach
Detaching from program: /home/chris/MELP/helloworld/helloworld, process 109
Ending remote debugging.
```

Debugging forks and threads

What happens when the program you are debugging forks? Does the debug session follow the parent process or the child? This behavior is controlled by follow-fork-mode, which may be parent or child, with parent being the default. Unfortunately, current versions of gdbserver do not support this option, so it only works for native debugging. If you really need to debug the child process while using gdbserver, a workaround is to modify the code so that the child loops on a variable immediately after the fork, giving you the opportunity to attach a new gdbserver session to it and then to set the variable so that it drops out of the loop.

When a thread in a multi-threaded process hits a breakpoint, the default behavior is for all threads to halt. In most cases, this is the best thing to do as it allows you to look at static variables without them being changed by the other threads. When you recommence execution of the thread, all the stopped threads start up, even if you are single-stepping, and it is especially this last case that can cause problems. There is a way to modify the way in which GDB handles stopped threads, through a parameter called scheduler-locking. Normally it is off, but if you set it to on, only the thread that was stopped at the breakpoint is resumed and the others remain stopped, giving you a chance to see what the thread alone does without interference. This continues to be the case until you turn scheduler-locking off. Gdbserver supports this feature.

Core files

Core files capture the state of a failing program at the point that it terminates. You don't even have to be in the room with a debugger when the bug manifests itself. So, when you see Segmentation fault (core dumped), don't shrug; investigate the core file and extract the goldmine of information in there.

The first observation is that core files are not created by default, but only when the core file resource limit for the process is non-zero. You can change it for the current shell using `ulimit -c`. To remove all limits on the size of core files, type the following command:

```
$ ulimit -c unlimited
```

By default, the core file is named `core` and is placed in the current working directory of the process, which is the one pointed to by `/proc/<PID>/cwd`. There are a number of problems with this scheme. Firstly, when looking at a device with several files named `core`, it is not obvious which program generated each one. Secondly, the current working directory of the process may well be in a read-only filesystem, there may not be enough space to store the core file, or the process may not have permissions to write to the current working directory.

There are two files that control the naming and placement of core files. The first is `/proc/sys/kernel/core_uses_pid`. Writing a 1 to it causes the PID number of the dying process to be appended to the filename, which is somewhat useful as long as you can associate the PID number with a program name from log files.

Much more useful is `/proc/sys/kernel/core_pattern`, which gives you a lot more control over core files. The default pattern is core, but you can change it to a pattern composed of these meta characters:

- `%p`: The PID
- `%u`: The real UID of the dumped process
- `%g`: The real GID of the dumped process
- `%s`: The number of the signal causing the dump
- `%t`: The time of dump, expressed as seconds since the Epoch, 1970-01-01 00:00:00 +0000 (UTC)
- `%h`: The hostname
- `%e`: The executable filename
- `%E`: The path name of the executable, with slashes (/) replaced by exclamation marks (!)
- `%c`: The core file size soft resource limit of the dumped process

You can also use a pattern that begins with an absolute directory name so that all core files are gathered together in one place. As an example, the following pattern puts all core files into the directory `/corefiles` and names them with the program name and the time of the crash:

```
# echo /corefiles/core.%e.%t > /proc/sys/kernel/core_pattern
```

Following a `core` dump, you would find something like this:

```
# ls /corefiles
core.sort-debug.1431425613
```

For more information, refer to the manual page `core(5)`.

Using GDB to look at core files

Here is a sample GDB session looking at a `core` file:

```
$ arm-poky-linux-gnueabi-gdb sort-debug
/home/chris/rootfs/corefiles/core.sort-debug.1431425613
[...]
Core was generated by `./sort-debug'.
Program terminated with signal SIGSEGV, Segmentation fault.
#0 0x000085c8 in addtree (p=0x0, w=0xbeac4c60 "the") at sort-debug.c:41
41 p->word = strdup (w);
```

That shows that the program stopped at line 41. The `list` command shows the code in the vicinity:

```
(gdb) list
37 static struct tnode *addtree (struct tnode *p, char *w)
38 {
39   int cond;
40
41   p->word = strdup (w);
42   p->count = 1;
43   p->left = NULL;
44   p->right = NULL;
45
```

The backtrace command (shortened to `bt`) shows how we got to this point:

```
(gdb) bt
#0 0x000085c8 in addtree (p=0x0, w=0xbeac4c60 "the") at sort-debug.c:41
#1 0x00008798 in main (argc=1, argv=0xbeac4e24) at sort-debug.c:89
```

An obvious mistake: `addtree()` was called with a null pointer.

GDB user interfaces

GDB is controlled at a low level through the GDB machine interface, GDB/MI, which can be used to wrap GDB in a user interface or as part of a larger program, and it considerably extends the range of options available to you.

In this section, I will describe three that are well suited to debugging embedded targets: the Terminal user interface, TUI; the data display debugger, DDD; and the Eclipse C-development Toolkit (CDT).

Terminal user interface

Terminal user interface (TUI) is an optional part of the standard GDB package. The main feature is a code window that shows the line of code about to be executed, together with any breakpoints. It is a definite improvement on the `list` command in command-line mode GDB.

The attraction of TUI is that it just works without any extra setup, and since it is in text mode it is possible to use over an SSH terminal session, for example, when running `gdb` natively on a target. Most cross toolchains configure GDB with TUI. Simply add `-tui` to the command line and you will see the following:

```
                   Terminal
 File  Edit  View  Search  Terminal  Help
    ┌─sort-debug.c─────────────────────────────────────────
    │36          * the count, otherwise add a new node */
    │37         static struct tnode *addtree (struct tnode *p, char *w)
    │38         {
    │39                  int cond;
    │40
 B+>│41                  p->word = strdup (w);
    │42                  p->count = 1;
    │43                  p->left = NULL;
    │44                  p->right = NULL;
    │45
    │46                  cond = strcmp (w, p->word);
    │47
    │48                  if (cond == 0)
 remote Thread 95 In: addtree                    Line: 41    PC: 0x85b4
 Breakpoint 1, main (argc=1, argv=0xbefffe24) at sort-debug.c:72
 (gdb) break addtree
 Breakpoint 2 at 0x85b4: file sort-debug.c, line 41.
 (gdb) c
 Continuing.

 Breakpoint 2, addtree (p=0x0, w=0xbefffc60 "the") at sort-debug.c:41
 (gdb)
```

Data display debugger

Data display debugger (DDD) is a simple standalone program that gives you a graphical user interface to GDB with minimal fuss and bother, and although the UI controls look dated, it does everything that is necessary.

The `--debugger` option tells DDD to use GDB from your toolchain, and you can use the `-x` argument to give the path to a GDB command file:

```
$ ddd --debugger arm-poky-linux-gnueabi-gdb -x gdbinit sort-debug
```

The following screenshot shows off one of the nicest features: the data window, which contains items in a grid that you can rearrange as you wish. If you double-click on a pointer, it is expanded into a new data item and the link is shown with an arrow:

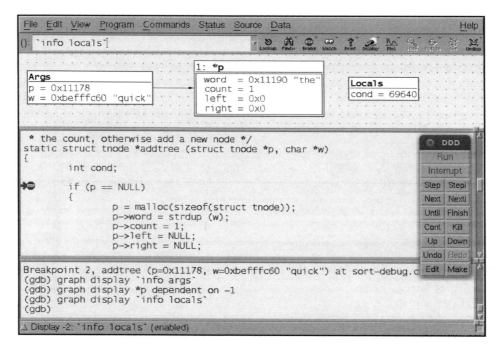

Eclipse

Eclipse, with the **CDT plugin**, supports debugging with GDB, including remote debugging. If you use Eclipse for all your code development, this is the obvious tool to use, but if you are not a regular Eclipse user, it is probably not worth the effort of setting it up just for this task. It would take me a whole chapter to explain adequately how to configure CDT to work with a cross toolchain and connect to a remote device, so I will refer you to the references at the end of the chapter for more information. The screenshot that follows shows the debug perspective of CDT. In the top-right window, you see the stack frames for each of the threads in the process, and at the top right is the watch window, showing variables. In the middle is the code window, showing the line of code where the debugger has stopped the program:

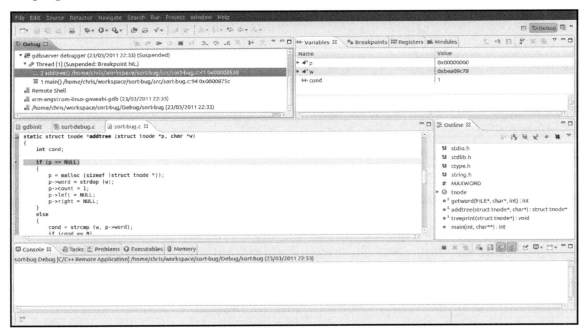

Debugging kernel code

You can use `kgdb` for source-level debugging, in a manner similar to remote debugging with `gdbserver`. There is also a self-hosted kernel debugger, `kdb`, that is handy for lighter-weight tasks such as seeing whether an instruction is executed and getting the backtrace to find out how it got there. Finally, there are kernel *Oops* messages and panics, which tell you a lot about the cause of a kernel exception.

Debugging kernel code with kgdb

When looking at kernel code using a source debugger, you must remember that the kernel is a complex system, with real-time behaviors. Don't expect debugging to be as easy as it is for applications. Stepping through code that changes the memory mapping or switches context is likely to produce odd results.

kgdb is the name given to the kernel GDB stubs that have been part of mainline Linux for many years now. There is a user manual in the kernel DocBook, and you can find an online version at `https://www.kernel.org/doc/htmldocs/kgdb/index.html`.

In most cases, you will connect to kgdb over the serial interface, which is usually shared with the serial console. Hence, this implementation is called **kgdboc**, which is short for **kgdb over console**. To work, it requires a platform `tty` driver that supports I/O polling instead of interrupts, since kgdb has to disable interrupts when communicating with GDB. A few platforms support kgdb over USB, and there have been versions that work over Ethernet but, unfortunately, none of those have found their way into mainline Linux.

The same caveats about optimization and stack frames apply to the kernel, with the limitation that the kernel is written to assume an optimization level of at least −01. You can override the kernel compile flags by setting KCFLAGS before running `make`.

These, then, are the kernel configuration options you will need for kernel debugging:

- CONFIG_DEBUG_INFO is in the menu **Kernel hacking** | **Compile-time checks and compiler options** | **Compile the kernel with debug info**
- CONFIG_FRAME_POINTER may be an option for your architecture, and is in the menu **Kernel hacking** | **Compile-time checks and compiler options** | **Compile the kernel with frame pointers**
- CONFIG_KGDB is in the menu **Kernel hacking** | **KGDB: kernel debugger**
- CONFIG_KGDB_SERIAL_CONSOLE is in the menu **Kernel hacking** | **KGDB: kernel debugger** | **KGDB: use kgdb over the serial console**

In addition to the zImage or uImage compressed kernel image, you will need the kernel image in ELF object format so that GDB can load the symbols into memory. This is the file called vmlinux that is generated in the directory where Linux is built. In Yocto, you can request that a copy be included in the target image and SDK. It is built as a package named kernel-vmlinux, which you can install like any other, for example, by adding it to the IMAGE_INSTALL list.

The file is put into the sysroot boot directory, with a name such as this:

```
/opt/poky/2.2.1/sysroots/cortexa8hf-neon-poky-linux-
gnueabi/boot/vmlinux-4.8.12-yocto-standard
```

In Buildroot, you will find vmlinux in the directory where the kernel was built, which is in output/build/linux-<version string>/vmlinux.

A sample debug session

The best way to show you how it works is with a simple example.

You need to tell kgdb which serial port to use, either through the kernel command line or at runtime via sysfs. For the first option, add kgdboc=<tty>,<baud rate> to the command line, as shown here:

kgdboc=ttyO0,115200

For the second option, boot the device up and write the terminal name to the file /sys/module/kgdboc/parameters/kgdboc, as shown here:

 # echo ttyO0 > /sys/module/kgdboc/parameters/kgdboc

Note that you cannot set the baud rate in this way. If it is the same tty as the console, then it is set already. If not use, stty or a similar program.

Now you can start GDB on the host, selecting the vmlinux file that matches the running kernel:

$ arm-poky-linux-gnueabi-gdb ~/linux/vmlinux

GDB loads the symbol table from vmlinux and waits for further input.

Next, close any terminal emulator that is attached to the console: you are about to use it for GDB, and if both are active at the same time, some of the debug strings might get corrupted.

Now, you can return to GDB and attempt to connect to kgdb. However, you will find that the response you get from target remote at this time is unhelpful:

```
(gdb) set serial baud 115200
(gdb) target remote /dev/ttyUSB0
Remote debugging using /dev/ttyUSB0
Bogus trace status reply from target: qTStatus
```

The problem is that kgdb is not listening for a connection at this point. You need to interrupt the kernel before you can enter into an interactive GDB session with it. Unfortunately, just typing *Ctrl + C* in GDB, as you would with an application, does not work. You have to force a trap into the kernel by launching another shell on the target, via SSH for example, and writing a g to /proc/sysrq-trigger on the target board:

```
# echo g > /proc/sysrq-trigger
```

The target stops dead at this point. Now you can connect to kgdb via the serial device at the host end of the cable:

```
(gdb) set serial baud 115200
(gdb) target remote /dev/ttyUSB0
Remote debugging using /dev/ttyUSB0
0xc009a59c in arch_kgdb_breakpoint ()
```

At last, GDB is in charge. You can set breakpoints, examine variables, look at backtraces, and so on. As an example, set a break on sys_sync, as follows:

```
(gdb) break sys_sync
Breakpoint 1 at 0xc0128a88: file fs/sync.c, line 103.
(gdb) c
Continuing.
```

Now the target comes back to life. Typing sync on the target calls sys_sync and hits the breakpoint:

```
[New Thread 87]
[Switching to Thread 87]
Breakpoint 1, sys_sync () at fs/sync.c:103
```

If you have finished the debug session and want to disable kgdboc, just set the kgdboc terminal to null:

```
# echo "" > /sys/module/kgdboc/parameters/kgdboc
```

Debugging early code

The preceding example works in cases where the code you are interested in is executed when the system is fully booted. If you need to get in early, you can tell the kernel to wait during boot by adding kgdbwait to the command line, after the kgdboc option:

```
kgdboc=ttyO0,115200 kgdbwait
```

Now, when you boot, you will see this on the console:

```
[    1.103415] console [ttyO0] enabled
[    1.108216] kgdb: Registered I/O driver kgdboc.
[    1.113071] kgdb: Waiting for connection from remote gdb...
```

At this point, you can close the console and connect from GDB in the usual way.

Debugging modules

Debugging kernel modules presents an additional challenge because the code is relocated at runtime, and so you need to find out at what address it resides. The information is presented through `sysfs`. The relocation addresses for each section of the module are stored in `/sys/module/<module name>/sections`. Note that since ELF sections begin with a dot (`.`), they appear as hidden files, and you will have to use `ls -a` if you want to list them. The important ones are `.text`, `.data`, and `.bss`.

Take as an example a module named `mbx`:

```
# cat /sys/module/mbx/sections/.text
0xbf000000
# cat /sys/module/mbx/sections/.data
0xbf0003e8
# cat /sys/module/mbx/sections/.bss
0xbf0005c0
```

Now you can use these numbers in GDB to load the symbol table for the module at those addresses:

```
(gdb) add-symbol-file /home/chris/mbx-driver/mbx.ko 0xbf000000 \
-s .data 0xbf0003e8 -s .bss 0xbf0005c0
add symbol table from file "/home/chris/mbx-driver/mbx.ko" at
  .text_addr = 0xbf000000
  .data_addr = 0xbf0003e8
  .bss_addr = 0xbf0005c0
```

Everything should now work as normal: you can set breakpoints and inspect global and local variables in the module just as you can in `vmlinux`:

```
(gdb) break mbx_write
Breakpoint 1 at 0xbf00009c: file /home/chris/mbx-driver/mbx.c, line 93.
(gdb) c
Continuing.
```

Then, force the device driver to call `mbx_write`, and it will hit the breakpoint:

```
Breakpoint 1, mbx_write (file=0xde7a71c0, buffer=0xadf40 "hello\n\n",
    length=6, offset=0xde73df80)
    at /home/chris/mbx-driver/mbx.c:93
```

Debugging kernel code with kdb

Although `kdb` does not have the features of `kgdb` and GDB, it does have its uses, and being self-hosted, there are no external dependencies to worry about. `kdb` has a simple command-line interface that you can use on a serial console. You can use it to inspect memory, registers, process lists, and `dmesg` and even set breakpoints to stop at a certain location.

To configure your kernel so that you can call `kdb` via a serial console, enable `kgdb` as shown previously, and then enable this additional option:

- CONFIG_KGDB_KDB, which is in the menu **KGDB: Kernel hacking | kernel debugger | KGDB_KDB: Include kdb frontend for kgdb**

Now, when you force the kernel into a trap, instead of entering into a GDB session, you will see the `kdb` shell on the console:

```
# echo g > /proc/sysrq-trigger
[   42.971126] SysRq : DEBUG
Entering kdb (current=0xdf36c080, pid 83) due to Keyboard Entry
kdb>
```

There are quite a few things you can do in the `kdb` shell. The `help` command will print all of the options. Here is an overview:

- **Getting information**:
    - ps: This displays active processes
    - ps A: This displays all processes
    - lsmod: This lists modules
    - dmesg: This displays the kernel log buffer
- **Breakpoints**:
    - bp: This sets a breakpoint
    - bl: This lists breakpoints
    - bc: This clears a breakpoint
    - bt: This prints a backtrace
    - go: This continues execution

- **Inspect memory and registers**:
    - md: This displays memory
    - rd: This displays registers

Here is a quick example of setting a breakpoint:

```
kdb> bp sys_sync
Instruction(i) BP #0 at 0xc01304ec (sys_sync)
    is enabled   addr at 00000000c01304ec, hardtype=0 installed=0
kdb> go
```

The kernel returns to life and the console shows the normal shell prompt. If you type sync, it hits the breakpoint and enters kdb again:

```
Entering kdb (current=0xdf388a80, pid 88) due to Breakpoint @0xc01304ec
```

kdb is not a source-level debugger, so you can't see the source code or single-step. However, you can display a backtrace using the bt command, which is useful to get an idea of program flow and call hierarchy.

Looking at an Oops

When the kernel performs an invalid memory access or executes an illegal instruction, a kernel **Oops** message is written to the kernel log. The most useful part of this is the backtrace, and I want to show you how to use the information there to locate the line of code that caused the fault. I will also address the problem of preserving Oops messages if they cause the system to crash.

This Oops message was generated by writing to the mailbox driver in MELP/chapter_14/mbx-driver-oops:

```
Unable to handle kernel NULL pointer dereference at virtual address
00000004
pgd = dd064000
[00000004] *pgd=9e58a831, *pte=00000000, *ppte=00000000
Internal error: Oops: 817 [#1] PREEMPT ARM
Modules linked in: mbx(O)
CPU: 0 PID: 408 Comm: sh Tainted: G O 4.8.12-yocto-standard #1
Hardware name: Generic AM33XX (Flattened Device Tree)
task: dd2a6a00 task.stack: de596000
PC is at mbx_write+0x24/0xbc [mbx]
LR is at __vfs_write+0x28/0x48
pc : [<bf0000f0>] lr : [<c024ff40>] psr: 800e0013
sp : de597f18 ip : de597f38 fp : de597f34
```

```
r10: 00000000 r9 : de596000 r8 : 00000000
r7 : de597f80 r6 : 000fda00 r5 : 00000002 r4 : 00000000
r3 : de597f80 r2 : 00000002 r1 : 000fda00 r0 : de49ee40
Flags: Nzcv IRQs on FIQs on Mode SVC_32 ISA ARM Segment none
Control: 10c5387d Table: 9d064019 DAC: 00000051
Process sh (pid: 408, stack limit = 0xde596210)
```

The line of the Oops that reads PC is at mbx_write+0x24/0xbc [mbx] tells you most of what you want to know: the last instruction was in the mbx_write function of a kernel module named mbx. Furthermore, it was at offset 0x24 bytes from the start of the function, which is 0xbc bytes long.

Next, take a look at the backtrace:

```
Stack: (0xde597f18 to 0xde598000)
7f00: bf0000cc 00000002
7f20: 000fda00 de597f80 de597f4c de597f38 c024ff40 bf0000d8 de49ee40
00000002
7f40: de597f7c de597f50 c0250c40 c024ff24 c026eb04 c026ea70 de49ee40
de49ee40
7f60: 000fda00 00000002 c0107908 de596000 de597fa4 de597f80 c025187c
c0250b80
7f80: 00000000 00000000 00000002 000fda00 b6eecd60 00000004 00000000
de597fa8
7fa0: c0107700 c0251838 00000002 000fda00 00000001 000fda00 00000002
00000000
7fc0: 00000002 000fda00 b6eecd60 00000004 00000002 00000002 000ce80c
00000000
7fe0: 00000000 bef77944 b6e1afbc b6e73d00 600e0010 00000001 d3bbdad3
d54367bf
[<bf0000f0>] (mbx_write [mbx]) from [<c024ff40>] (__vfs_write+0x28/0x48)
[<c024ff40>] (__vfs_write) from [<c0250c40>] (vfs_write+0xcc/0x158)
[<c0250c40>] (vfs_write) from [<c025187c>] (SyS_write+0x50/0x88)
[<c025187c>] (SyS_write) from [<c0107700>] (ret_fast_syscall+0x0/0x3c)
Code: e590407c e3520b01 23a02b01 e1a05002 (e5842004)
---[ end trace edcc51b432f0ce7d ]---
```

In this case, we don't learn much more, merely that mbx_write was called from the virtual filesystem function _vfs_write.

It would be very nice to find the line of code that relates to `mbx_write+0x24`, for which we can use the GDB command `disassemble` with the `/s` modifier so that it shows source and assembler code together. In this example, the code is in the module `mbx.ko`, so we load that into gdb:

```
$ arm-poky-linux-gnueabi-gdb mbx.ko
[...]
(gdb) disassemble /s mbx_write
Dump of assembler code for function mbx_write:
99  {
  0x000000f0 <+0>:   mov    r12, sp
  0x000000f4 <+4>:   push   {r4, r5, r6, r7, r11, r12, lr, pc}
  0x000000f8 <+8>:   sub    r11, r12, #4
  0x000000fc <+12>:  push   {lr}              ; (str lr, [sp, #-4]!)
  0x00000100 <+16>:  bl     0x100 <mbx_write+16>

100   struct mbx_data *m = (struct mbx_data *)file->private_data;
  0x00000104 <+20>:  ldr    r4, [r0, #124] ; 0x7c
  0x00000108 <+24>:  cmp    r2, #1024        ; 0x400
  0x0000010c <+28>:  movcs  r2, #1024        ; 0x400

101   if (length > MBX_LEN)
102       length = MBX_LEN;
103   m->mbx_len = length;
  0x00000110 <+32>:  mov    r5, r2
  0x00000114 <+36>:  str    r2, [r4, #4]
```

The Oops told us that the error occurred at `mbx_write+0x24`. From the disassembly, we can see that `mbx_write` is at address `0xf0`. Adding `0x24` gives `0x114`, which is generated by the code on line `103`.

You may think that I have got the wrong instruction, because the listing reads `0x00000114 <+36>: str r2, [r4, #4]`. Surely we are looking for +24, not +36? Ah, but the authors of GDB are trying to confuse us here. The offsets are displayed in decimal, not *hex: 36 = 0x24*, so I got the right one after all!

You can see from line `100` that `m` has the type `struct mbx_data *`. Here is the place where that structure is defined:

```
#define MBX_LEN 1024
struct mbx_data {
  char mbx[MBX_LEN];
  int mbx_len;
};
```

So it looks like the m variable is a null pointer, and that is what is causing the Oops. Looking at the code where m is initialized, we can see that there is a line missing. With the driver modified to initialize the pointer, as shown highlighted in the following code block, it works fine, without the Oops:

```
static int mbx_open(struct inode *inode, struct file *file)
{
    if (MINOR(inode->i_rdev) >= NUM_MAILBOXES) {
        printk("Invalid mbx minor number\n");
        return -ENODEV;
    }
    file->private_data = &mailboxes[MINOR(inode->i_rdev)];
    return 0;
}
```

Preserving the Oops

Decoding an Oops is only possible if you can capture it in the first place. If the system crashes during boot before the console is enabled, or after a suspend, you won't see it. There are mechanisms to log kernel Oops and messages to an MTD partition or to persistent memory, but here is a simple technique that works in many cases and needs little prior thought.

So long as the contents of memory are not corrupted during a reset (and usually they are not), you can reboot into the bootloader and use it to display memory. You need to know the location of the kernel log buffer, remembering that it is a simple ring buffer of text messages. The symbol is __log_buf. Look this up in System.map for the kernel:

```
$ grep __log_buf System.map
c0f72428 b __log_buf
```

Then, map that kernel logical address into a physical address that U-Boot can understand by subtracting PAGE_OFFSET and adding the physical start of RAM. PAGE_OFFSET is almost always 0xc0000000, and the start address of the RAM is 0x80000000 on a BeagleBone, so the calculation becomes c0f72428 - 0xc0000000 + 0x80000000 = 80f72428.

Now you can use the U-Boot md command to show the log:

```
U-Boot #
md 80f72428
80f72428: 00000000 00000000 00210034 c6000000    ........4.!.....
80f72438: 746f6f42 20676e69 756e694c 6e6f2078    Booting Linux on
80f72448: 79687020 61636973 5043206c 78302055     physical CPU 0x
80f72458: 00000030 00000000 00000000 00730084    0............s.
80f72468: a6000000 756e694c 65762078 6f697372    ....Linux versio
80f72478: 2e34206e 30312e31 68632820 40736972    n 4.1.10 (chris@
80f72488: 6c697562 29726564 63672820 65762063    builder) (gcc ve
80f72498: 6f697372 2e34206e 20312e39 6f726328    rsion 4.9.1 (cro
80f724a8: 6f747373 4e2d6c6f 2e312047 302e3032    sstool-NG 1.20.0
80f724b8: 20292029 53203123 5720504d 4f206465    ) ) #1 SMP Wed O
80f724c8: 32207463 37312038 3a31353a 47203533    ct 28 17:51:53 G
```

 From Linux 3.5 onward, there is a 16-byte binary header for each line in the kernel log buffer that encodes a timestamp, a log level, and other things. There is a discussion about it in the Linux weekly news titled *Toward more reliable logging* at `https://lwn.net/Articles/492125/`.

Further reading

The following resources have further information about the topics introduced in this chapter:

- *The Art of Debugging with GDB, DDD, and Eclipse,* by Norman Matloff and Peter Jay Salzman, *No Starch Press*; 1st edition (28 Sept, 2008), ISBN 978-1593271749
- *GDB Pocket Reference* by Arnold Robbins, *O'Reilly Media*; 1st edition (12 May, 2005), ISBN 978-0596100278
- *Getting to grips with Eclipse: cross compiling,* `http://2net.co.uk/tutorial/eclipse-cross-compile`
- *Getting to grips with Eclipse: remote access and debugging,* `http://2net.co.uk/tutorial/eclipse-rse`

Summary

Knowing how to use GDB for interactive debugging is a useful tool in the embedded developer's tool-chest. It is a stable, well-documented, and well-known entity. It has the ability to debug remotely by placing an agent on the target, be it `gdbserver` for applications or `kgdb` for kernel code, and although the default command-line user interface takes a while to get used to, there are many alternative frontends. The three I mentioned were TUI, DDD, and Eclipse CDT, which should cover most situations, but there are other frontends around that you can try.

A second and equally important way to approach debugging is to collect crash reports and analyze them offline. In this category, we looked at application core dumps and kernel Oops messages.

However, this is only one way of identifying flaws in programs. In the next chapter, I will talk about profiling and tracing as ways of analyzing and optimizing programs.

15
Profiling and Tracing

Interactive debugging using a source-level debugger, as described in the previous chapter, can give you an insight into the way a program works, but it constrains your view to a small body of code. In this chapter, we will look at the larger picture to see whether the system is performing as intended.

Programmers and system designers are notoriously bad at guessing where bottlenecks are. So if your system has performance issues, it is wise to start by looking at the full system and then work down, using more sophisticated tools as you go. In this chapter, I'll begin with the well-known command `top` as a means of getting an overview. Often the problem can be localized to a single program, which you can analyze using the Linux profiler, `perf`. If the problem is not so localized and you want to get a broader picture, `perf` can do that as well. To diagnose problems associated with the kernel, I will describe the trace tools, `Ftrace` and `LTTng`, as a means of gathering detailed information.

I will also cover Valgrind, which, because of its sandboxed execution environment, can monitor a program and report on code as it runs. I will complete the chapter with a description of a simple trace tool, `strace`, which reveals the execution of a program by tracing the system calls it makes.

In this chapter, we will cover the following topics:

- The observer effect
- Beginning to profile
- Profiling with `top`
- Poor man's profiler
- Introducing `perf`
- Other profilers—`OProfile` and `gprof`
- Tracing events

- Introducing `Ftrace`
- Using `LTTng`
- Using Valgrind
- Using `strace`

The observer effect

Before diving into the tools, let's talk about what the tools will show you. As is the case in many fields, measuring a certain property affects the observation itself. Measuring the electric current in a power supply line requires measuring the voltage drop over a small resistor. However, the resistor itself affects the current. The same is true for profiling: every system observation has a cost in CPU cycles, and that resource is no longer spent on the application. Measurement tools also mess up caching behavior, eat memory space, and write to disk, which all make it worse. There is no measurement without overhead.

I've often heard engineers say that the results of a profiling job were totally misleading. That is usually because they were performing the measurements on something not approaching a real situation. Always try to measure on the target, using release builds of the software, with a valid data set, using as few extra services as possible.

Symbol tables and compile flags

We will hit a problem right away. While it is important to observe the system in its natural state, the tools often need additional information to make sense of the events.

Some tools require special kernel options. For the tools we are examining in this chapter, this applies to `perf`, `Ftrace`, and `LTTng`. Therefore, you will probably have to build and deploy a new kernel for these tests.

Debug symbols are very helpful in translating raw program addresses into function names and lines of code. Deploying executables with debug symbols does not change the execution of the code, but it does require that you have copies of the binaries and the kernel compiled with debug information, at least for the components you want to profile. Some tools work best if you have these installed on the target system: `perf`, for example. The techniques are the same as for general debugging, as I discussed in `Chapter 14`, *Debugging with GDB*.

If you want a tool to generate call graphs, you may have to compile with stack frames enabled. If you want the tool to attribute addresses with lines of code accurately, you may need to compile with lower levels of optimization.

Finally, some tools require instrumentation to be inserted into the program to capture samples, so you will have to recompile those components. This applies to gprof for applications and Ftrace and LTTng for the kernel.

Be aware that the more you change the system you are observing, the harder it is to relate the measurements you make to the production system.

It is best to adopt a wait-and-see approach, making changes only when the need is clear, and being mindful that each time you do so, you will change what you are measuring.

Beginning to profile

When looking at the entire system, a good place to start is with a simple tool such as top, which gives you an overview very quickly. It shows you how much memory is being used, which processes are eating CPU cycles, and how this is spread across different cores and time.

If top shows that a single application is using up all the CPU cycles in user space, then you can profile that application using perf.

If two or more processes have a high CPU usage, there is probably something that is coupling them together, perhaps data communication. If a lot of cycles are spent in system calls or handling interrupts, then there may be an issue with the kernel configuration or with a device driver. In either case, you need to start by taking a profile of the whole system, again using perf.

If you want to find out more about the kernel and the sequencing of events there, you would use Ftrace or LTTng.

There could be other problems that top will not help you with. If you have multi-threaded code and there are problems with lockups, or if you have random data corruption, then **Valgrind** plus the **Helgrind** plugin might be helpful. Memory leaks also fit into this category: I covered memory-related diagnosis in Chapter 13, *Managing Memory*.

Profiling with top

The `top` program is a simple tool that doesn't require any special kernel options or symbol tables. There is a basic version in BusyBox and a more functional version in the `procps` package, which is available in the Yocto Project and Buildroot. You may also want to consider using `htop`, which is functionally similar to `top` but has a nicer user interface (some people think).

To begin with, focus on the summary line of `top`, which is the second line if you are using BusyBox and the third line if using `top` from `procps`. Here is an example, using BusyBox `top`:

```
Mem: 57044K used, 446172K free, 40K shrd, 3352K buff, 34452K cached
CPU:  58% usr   4% sys   0% nic   0% idle  37% io   0% irq   0% sirq
Load average: 0.24 0.06 0.02 2/51 105
  PID  PPID USER     STAT   VSZ %VSZ %CPU COMMAND
  105   104 root      R    27912   6%  61% ffmpeg -i track2.wav
[...]
```

The summary line shows the percentage of time spent running in various states, as shown in this table:

procps	BusyBox	Description
us	usr	User space programs with default nice value
sy	sys	Kernel code
ni	nic	User space programs with non-default nice value
id	idle	Idle
wa	io	I/O wait
hi	irq	Hardware interrupts
si	sirq	Software interrupts
st	-	Steal time: only relevant in virtual environments

In the preceding example, almost all of the time (58%) is spent in user mode, with a small amount (4%) in system mode, so this is a system that is CPU-bound in user space. The first line after the summary shows that just one application is responsible: `ffmpeg`. Any efforts toward reducing CPU usage should be directed there.

Here is another example:

```
Mem: 13128K used, 490088K free, 40K shrd, 0K buff, 2788K cached
CPU:    0% usr  99% sys   0% nic   0% idle   0% io   0% irq   0% sirq
Load average: 0.41 0.11 0.04 2/46 97
  PID  PPID USER     STAT    VSZ %VSZ %CPU COMMAND
   92    82 root     R      2152   0% 100% cat /dev/urandom
[...]
```

This system is spending almost all of the time in kernel space (99% sys), as a result of cat reading from /dev/urandom. In this artificial case, profiling cat by itself would not help, but profiling the kernel functions that cat calls might be.

The default view of top shows only processes, so the CPU usage is the total of all the threads in the process. Press *H* to see information for each thread. Likewise, it aggregates the time across all CPUs. If you are using the procps version of top you can see a summary per CPU by pressing the *1* key.

Poor man's profiler

You can profile an application just by using GDB to stop it at arbitrary intervals to see what it is doing. This is the **poor man's profiler**. It is easy to set up and is one way of gathering profile data.

The procedure is simple:

1. Attach to the process using gdbserver (for a remote debug) or GDB (for a native debug). The process stops.
2. Observe the function it stopped in. You can use the backtrace GDB command to see the call stack.
3. Type continue so that the program resumes.
4. After a while, type *Ctrl + C* to stop it again, and go back to step 2.

If you repeat steps 2 to 4 several times, you will quickly get an idea of whether it is looping or making progress, and if you repeat them often enough, you will get an idea of where the hot spots in the code are.

There is a whole web page dedicated to the idea at http://poormansprofiler.org, together with scripts that make it a little easier. I have used this technique many times over the years with various operating systems and debuggers.

This is an example of **statistical profiling,** in which you sample the program state at intervals. After a number of samples, you begin to learn the statistical likelihood of the functions being executed. It is surprising how few you really need. Other statistical profilers are perf record, OProfile, and gprof.

Sampling using a debugger is intrusive because the program is stopped for a significant period while you collect the sample. Other tools can do this with much lower overhead.

Introducing perf

perf is an abbreviation of the Linux **performance event counter subsystem,** perf_events, and also the name of the command-line tool for interacting with perf_events. Both have been part of the kernel since Linux 2.6.31. There is plenty of useful information in the Linux source tree in tools/perf/Documentation as well as at https://perf.wiki.kernel.org.

The initial impetus for developing perf was to provide a unified way to access the registers of the **performance measurement unit (PMU),** which is part of most modern processor cores. Once the API was defined and integrated into Linux, it became logical to extend it to cover other types of performance counters.

At its heart, perf is a collection of event counters with rules about when they actively collect data. By setting the rules, you can capture data from the whole system, or just the kernel, or just one process and its children, and do it across all CPUs or just one CPU. It is very flexible. With this one tool, you can start by looking at the whole system, then zero in on a device driver that seems to be causing problems, or an application that is running slowly, or a library function that seems to be taking longer to execute than you thought.

The code for the perf command-line tool is part of the kernel, in the tools/perf directory. The tool and the kernel subsystem are developed hand in hand, meaning that they must be from the same version of the kernel. perf can do a lot. In this chapter, I will examine it only as a profiler. For a description of its other capabilities, read the perf man pages and refer to the documentation mentioned at the start of this section.

Configuring the kernel for perf

You need a kernel that is configured for perf_events, and you need the perf command cross compiled to run on the target. The relevant kernel configuration is CONFIG_PERF_EVENTS, present in the menu **General setup** | **Kernel Performance Events And Counters**.

If you want to profile using tracepoints—more on this subject later—also enable the options described in the section about `Ftrace`. While you are there, it is worthwhile enabling `CONFIG_DEBUG_INFO` as well.

The `perf` command has many dependencies, which makes cross compiling it quite messy. However, both the Yocto Project and Buildroot have target packages for it.

You will also need debug symbols on the target for the binaries that you are interested in profiling; otherwise, `perf` will not be able to resolve addresses to meaningful symbols. Ideally, you want debug symbols for the whole system, including the kernel. For the latter, remember that the debug symbols for the kernel are in the `vmlinux` file.

Building perf with the Yocto Project

If you are using the standard `linux-yocto` kernel, `perf_events` is enabled already, so there is nothing more to do.

To build the `perf` tool, you can add it explicitly to the target image dependencies, or you can add the tools-profile feature, which also brings in `gprof`. As I mentioned previously, you will probably want debug symbols on the target image and also the kernel `vmlinux` image. In total, this is what you will need in `conf/local.conf`:

```
EXTRA_IMAGE_FEATURES = "debug-tweaks dbg-pkgs tools-profile"
IMAGE_INSTALL_append = "kernel-vmlinux"
```

Building perf with Buildroot

Many Buildroot kernel configurations do not include `perf_events`, so you should begin by checking that your kernel includes the options mentioned in the preceding section.

To cross compile `perf`, run the Buildroot `menuconfig` and select the following:

- `BR2_LINUX_KERNEL_TOOL_PERF` in **Kernel | Linux Kernel Tools**.

To build packages with debug symbols and install them unstripped on the target, select these two settings:

- `BR2_ENABLE_DEBUG` in the menu **Build options | build packages with debugging symbols**.
- `BR2_STRIP = none` in the menu **Build options | strip command for binaries on target**.

Then, run `make clean`, followed by `make`.

When you have built everything, you will have to copy `vmlinux` into the target image manually.

Profiling with perf

You can use `perf` to sample the state of a program using one of the event counters and accumulate samples over a period of time to create a profile. This is another example of statistical profiling. The default event counter is called **cycles**, which is a generic hardware counter that is mapped to a PMU register representing a count of cycles at the core clock frequency.

Creating a profile using `perf` is a two-stage process: the `perf record` command captures samples and writes them to a file named `perf.data` (by default), and then `perf report` analyzes the results. Both commands are run on the target. The samples being collected are filtered for the process and children of a command you specify. Here is an example profiling a shell script that searches for the string `linux`:

```
# perf record sh -c "find /usr/share | xargs grep linux > /dev/null"
[ perf record: Woken up 2 times to write data ]
[ perf record: Captured and wrote 0.368 MB perf.data (~16057 samples) ]
# ls -l perf.data
-rw-------    1 root      root      387360 Aug 25  2015 perf.data
```

Now you can show the results from `perf.data` using the command `perf report`. There are three user interfaces you can select on the command line:

- `--stdio`: This is a pure text interface with no user interaction. You will have to launch `perf report` and annotate for each view of the trace.
- `--tui`: This is a simple text-based menu interface with traversal between screens.
- `--gtk`: This is a graphical interface that otherwise acts in the same way as `--tui`.

The default is TUI, as shown in this example:

```
Samples: 9K of event 'cycles', Event count (approx.): 2006177260
 11.29%   grep   libc-2.20.so        [.] re_search_internal
  8.80%   grep   busybox.nosuid      [.] bb_get_chunk_from_file
  5.55%   grep   libc-2.20.so        [.] _int_malloc
  5.40%   grep   libc-2.20.so        [.] _int_free
  3.74%   grep   libc-2.20.so        [.] realloc
  2.59%   grep   libc-2.20.so        [.] malloc
  2.51%   grep   libc-2.20.so        [.] regexec@@GLIBC_2.4
  1.64%   grep   busybox.nosuid      [.] grep_file
  1.57%   grep   libc-2.20.so        [.] malloc_consolidate
  1.33%   grep   libc-2.20.so        [.] strlen
  1.33%   grep   libc-2.20.so        [.] memset
  1.26%   grep   [kernel.kallsyms]   [k] __copy_to_user_std
  1.20%   grep   libc-2.20.so        [.] free
  1.10%   grep   libc-2.20.so        [.] _int_realloc
  0.95%   grep   libc-2.20.so        [.] re_string_reconstruct
  0.79%   grep   busybox.nosuid      [.] xrealloc
  0.75%   grep   [kernel.kallsyms]   [k] __do_softirq
  0.72%   grep   [kernel.kallsyms]   [k] preempt_count_sub
  0.68%   find   [kernel.kallsyms]   [k] __do_softirq
  0.53%   grep   [kernel.kallsyms]   [k] __dev_queue_xmit
  0.52%   grep   [kernel.kallsyms]   [k] preempt_count_add
  0.47%   grep   [kernel.kallsyms]   [k] finish_task_switch.isra.85
Press '?' for help on key bindings
```

perf is able to record the kernel functions executed on behalf of the processes because it collects samples in kernel space.

The list is ordered with the most active functions first. In this example, all but one are captured while grep is running. Some are in a library, libc-2.20, some in a program, busybox.nosuid, and some are in the kernel. We have symbol names for program and library functions because all the binaries have been installed on the target with debug information, and kernel symbols are being read from /boot/vmlinux. If you have vmlinux in a different location, add -k <path> to the perf report command. Rather than storing samples in perf.data, you can save them to a different file using perf record -o <file name> and analyze them using perf report -i <file name>.

By default, perf record samples at a frequency of 1000 Hz using the cycles counter.

A sampling frequency of 1000 Hz may be higher than you really need, and may be the cause of an observer effect. Try with lower rates: 100 Hz is enough for most cases, in my experience. You can set the sample frequency using the -F option.

Call graphs

This is still not really making life easy; the functions at the top of the list are mostly low-level memory operations, and you can be fairly sure that they have already been optimized. It would be nice to step back and see where these functions are being called from. You can do that by capturing the backtrace from each sample, which you can do with the -g option to `perf record`.

Now, `perf report` shows a plus sign (+) where the function is part of a call chain. You can expand the trace to see the functions lower down in the chain:

```
Samples: 10K of event 'cycles', Event count (approx.): 2256721655
-   9.95%   grep  libc-2.20.so        [.] re_search_internal
  - re_search_internal
        95.96% 0
        3.50% 0x208
+   8.19%   grep  busybox.nosuid      [.] bb_get_chunk_from_file
+   5.07%   grep  libc-2.20.so        [.] _int_free
+   4.76%   grep  libc-2.20.so        [.] _int_malloc
+   3.75%   grep  libc-2.20.so        [.] realloc
+   2.63%   grep  libc-2.20.so        [.] malloc
+   2.04%   grep  libc-2.20.so        [.] regexec@@GLIBC_2.4
+   1.43%   grep  busybox.nosuid      [.] grep_file
+   1.37%   grep  libc-2.20.so        [.] memset
+   1.29%   grep  libc-2.20.so        [.] malloc_consolidate
+   1.22%   grep  libc-2.20.so        [.] _int_realloc
+   1.15%   grep  libc-2.20.so        [.] free
+   1.01%   grep  [kernel.kallsyms]   [k] __copy_to_user_std
+   0.98%   grep  libc-2.20.so        [.] strlen
+   0.89%   grep  libc-2.20.so        [.] re_string_reconstruct
+   0.73%   grep  [kernel.kallsyms]   [k] preempt_count_sub
+   0.68%   grep  [kernel.kallsyms]   [k] finish_task_switch.isra.85
+   0.62%   grep  busybox.nosuid      [.] xrealloc
+   0.57%   grep  [kernel.kallsyms]   [k] __do_softirq
Press '?' for help on key bindings
```

 Generating call graphs relies on the ability to extract call frames from the stack, just as is necessary for backtraces in GDB. The information needed to unwind stacks is encoded in the debug information of the executables, but not all combinations of architecture and toolchains are capable of doing so.

perf annotate

Now that you know which functions to look at, it would be nice to step inside and see the code and to have hit counts for each instruction. That is what `perf annotate` does, by calling down to a copy of `objdump` installed on the target. You just need to use `perf annotate` in place of `perf report`.

`perf annotate` requires symbol tables for the executables and `vmlinux`. Here is an example of an annotated function:

```
re search internal  /lib/libc-2.20.so
                    cmp     r1,
                    beq     c362c <gai_strerror+0xcaf8>
                    str     r3, [fp, #-40]        ; 0x28
                    b       c3684 <gai_strerror+0xcb50>
      0.65          ldr     ip, [fp, #-256]      ; 0x100
      0.16          ldr     r0, [fp, #-268]      ; 0x10c
      2.44          add     r3,
      4.15          cmp     r0,
      3.91          strle   r3, [fp, #-40]       ; 0x28
                    ble     c3684 <gai_strerror+0xcb50>
      4.72          ldrb    r1, [r2, #1]!
     10.26          ldrb    r1, [ip, r1]
      6.68          cmp     r1,
                    beq     c3660 <gai_strerror+0xcb2c>
      0.90          str     r3, [fp, #-40]       ; 0x28
      2.12          ldr     r3, [fp, #-40]       ; 0x28
      0.08          ldr     r2, [fp, #-268]      ; 0x10c
      0.33          cmp     r2,
                    bne     c3804 <gai_strerror+0xccd0>
      0.08          mov     r3,
                    ldr     r2, [fp, #-280]      ; 0x118
      0.08          cmp     r3,
Press 'h' for help on key bindings
```

If you want to see the source code interleaved with the assembler, you can copy the relevant source files to the target device. If you are using the Yocto Project and build with the extra image feature `dbg-pkgs`, or have installed the individual `–dbg` package, then the source will have been installed for you in `/usr/src/debug`. Otherwise, you can examine the debug information to see the location of the source code:

```
$ arm-buildroot-linux-gnueabi-objdump --dwarf lib/libc-2.19.so |
  grep DW_AT_comp_dir
  <3f>    DW_AT_comp_dir : /home/chris/buildroot/output/build/host-
  gcc-initial-4.8.3/build/arm-buildroot-linux-gnueabi/libgcc
```

The path on the target should be *exactly the same* as the path you can see in `DW_AT_comp_dir`.

Here is an example of annotation with source and assembler code:

```
re_search_internal  /lib/libc-2.20.so
                              ++match_first;
                              goto forward_match_found_start_or_reached_end;

                          case 6:
                              /* Fastmap without translation, match forward.  */
                              while (BE (match_first < right_lim, 1)
  4.15               cmp    r0,
  3.91               strle  r3, [fp, #-40]         ; 0x28
                     ble    c3684 <gai_strerror+0xcb50>
                                  && !fastmap[(unsigned char) string[match_first]])
  4.72               ldrb   r1, [r2, #1]!
 10.26               ldrb   r1, [ip, r1]
  6.68               cmp    r1,
                     beq    c3660 <gai_strerror+0xcb2c>
  0.90               str    r3, [fp, #-40]         ; 0x28
                              ++match_first;

                          forward_match_found_start_or_reached_end:
                              if (BE (match_first == right_lim, 0))
  2.12               ldr    r3, [fp, #-40]         ; 0x28
  0.08               ldr    r2, [fp, #-268]        ; 0x10c
  0.33               cmp    r2,
Press 'h' for help on key bindings
```

Other profilers – OProfile and gprof

OProfile and gprof are two statistical profilers that predate `perf`. They are both offer subsets of the functionality of `perf`, but they are still quite popular. I will mention them only briefly.

OProfile is a kernel profiler that started out in 2002. Originally, it had its own kernel sampling code, but recent versions use the `perf_events` infrastructure for that purpose. There is more information about it at `http://oprofile.sourceforge.net`. OProfile consists of a kernel-space component and a user space daemon and analysis commands.

OProfile needs these two kernel options to be enabled:

- `CONFIG_PROFILING` in **General setup** | **Profiling support**
- `CONFIG_OPROFILE` in **General setup** | **OProfile system profiling**

If you are using the Yocto Project, the user space components are installed as part of the `tools-profile` image feature. If you are using Buildroot, the package is enabled by `BR2_PACKAGE_OPROFILE`.

You can collect samples using this command:

```
# operf <program>
```

Wait for your application to finish, or press *Ctrl + C*, to stop profiling. The profile data is stored in `<cur-dir>/oprofile_data/samples/current`.

Use `opreport` to generate a profile summary. There are various options, which are documented in the OProfile manual.

`gprof` is part of the GNU toolchain and was one of the earliest open source code-profiling tools. It combines compile-time instrumentation and sampling techniques, using a 100 Hz sample rate. It has the advantage that it does not require kernel support.

To prepare a program for profiling with `gprof`, you add `-pg` to the compile and link flags, which injects code that collects information about the call tree into the function preamble. When you run the program, samples are collected and stored in a buffer, which is written to a file named `gmon.out` when the program terminates.

You use the `gprof` command to read the samples from `gmon.out`, together with the debug information from a copy of the program.

As an example, if you wanted to profile the BusyBox `grep` applet, you would rebuild BusyBox with the `-pg` option, run the command, and view the results:

```
# busybox grep "linux" *
# ls -l gmon.out
-rw-r--r-- 1 root root    473 Nov 24 14:07 gmon.out
```

Then, you would analyze the captured samples on either the target or the host, using the following:

```
# gprof busybox
Flat profile:

Each sample counts as 0.01 seconds.
 no time accumulated

  %   cumulative   self              self     total
 time   seconds   seconds    calls  Ts/call  Ts/call  name
 0.00      0.00     0.00      688     0.00     0.00  xrealloc
 0.00      0.00     0.00      345     0.00     0.00  bb_get_chunk_from_file
 0.00      0.00     0.00      345     0.00     0.00  xmalloc_fgetline
 0.00      0.00     0.00        6     0.00     0.00  fclose_if_not_stdin
 0.00      0.00     0.00        6     0.00     0.00  fopen_for_read
 0.00      0.00     0.00        6     0.00     0.00  grep_file
```

```
[...]
    Call graph

granularity: each sample hit covers 2 byte(s) no time propagated

index  % time    self   children    called       name
                 0.00     0.00      688/688   bb_get_chunk_from_file [2]
[1]      0.0     0.00     0.00      688           xrealloc [1]
-----------------------------------------------------------------
                 0.00     0.00      345/345   xmalloc_fgetline [3]
[2]      0.0     0.00     0.00      345           bb_get_chunk_from_file [2]
                 0.00     0.00      688/688       xrealloc [1]
-----------------------------------------------------------------
                 0.00     0.00      345/345   grep_file [6]
[3]      0.0     0.00     0.00      345           xmalloc_fgetline [3]
                 0.00     0.00      345/345       bb_get_chunk_from_file [2]
-----------------------------------------------------------------
                 0.00     0.00        6/6     grep_main [12]
[4]      0.0     0.00     0.00        6           fclose_if_not_stdin [4]
[...]
```

The execution times are all shown as zero because most of the time was spent in system calls, which are not traced by gprof.

 gprof does not capture samples from threads other than the main thread of a multi-threaded process, and it does not sample kernel space, both of which limit its usefulness.

Tracing events

The tools we have seen so far all use statistical sampling. You often want to know more about the ordering of events so that you can see them and relate them to each other. Function tracing involves instrumenting the code with trace points that capture information about the event, and may include some or all of the following:

- Timestamp
- Context, such as the current PID
- Function parameters and return value
- Callstack

It is more intrusive than statistical profiling, and it can generate a large amount of data. The latter can be mitigated by applying filters when the sample is captured, and later on when viewing the trace.

I will cover two trace tools here: the kernel function tracers, **Ftrace** and **LTTng**.

Introducing Ftrace

The kernel function tracer, Ftrace, evolved from work done by Steven Rostedt, and many others, as they were tracking down the causes of high scheduling latency in real-time applications. Ftrace appeared in Linux 2.6.27 and has been actively developed since then. There are a number of documents describing kernel tracing in the kernel source in `Documentation/trace`.

Ftrace consists of a number of tracers that can log various types of activity in the kernel. Here, I am going to talk about the `function` and `function_graph` tracers and about the event tracepoints. In `Chapter 16`, *Real-Time Programming*, I will revisit Ftrace and use it to show real-time latencies.

The `function` tracer instruments each kernel function so that calls can be recorded and timestamped. As a matter of interest, it compiles the kernel with the `-pg` switch to inject the instrumentation, but the resemblance to `gprof` ends there. The `function_graph` tracer goes further and records both the entry and exit of functions so that it can create a call graph. The event tracepoints feature also records parameters associated with the call.

Ftrace has a very embedded-friendly user interface that is entirely implemented through virtual files in the `debugfs` filesystem, meaning that you do not have to install any tools on the target to make it work. Nevertheless, there are other user interfaces if you prefer: `trace-cmd` is a command-line tool that records and views traces, and is available in Buildroot (`BR2_PACKAGE_TRACE_CMD`) and the Yocto Project (`trace-cmd`). There is a graphical trace viewer named **KernelShark**, which is available as a package for the Yocto Project.

Preparing to use Ftrace

Ftrace and its various options are configured in the kernel configuration menu. You will need the following as a minimum:

- `CONFIG_FUNCTION_TRACER` in the menu **Kernel hacking** | **Tracers** | **Kernel Function Tracer**

For reasons that will become clear later, you would be well advised to turn on these options as well:

- CONFIG_FUNCTION_GRAPH_TRACER in the menu **Kernel hacking | Tracers | Kernel Function Graph Tracer**
- CONFIG_DYNAMIC_FTRACE in the menu **Kernel hacking | Tracers | enable/disable function tracing dynamically**

Since the whole thing is hosted in the kernel, there is no user space configuration to be done.

Using Ftrace

Before you can use Ftrace, you have to mount the debugfs filesystem, which by convention goes in the /sys/kernel/debug directory:

```
# mount -t debugfs none /sys/kernel/debug
```

All the controls for Ftrace are in the /sys/kernel/debug/tracing directory; there is even a mini HOWTO in the README file there.

This is the list of tracers available in the kernel:

```
# cat /sys/kernel/debug/tracing/available_tracers
blk function_graph function nop
```

The active tracer is shown by current_tracer, which initially will be the null tracer, nop.

To capture a trace, select the tracer by writing the name of one of the available_tracers to current_tracer, and then enable tracing for a short while, as shown here:

```
# echo function > /sys/kernel/debug/tracing/current_tracer
# echo 1 > /sys/kernel/debug/tracing/tracing_on
# sleep 1
# echo 0 > /sys/kernel/debug/tracing/tracing_on
```

In that one second, the trace buffer will have been filled with the details of every function called by the kernel. The format of the trace buffer is plain text, as described in Documentation/trace/ftrace.txt. You can read the trace buffer from the trace file:

```
# cat /sys/kernel/debug/tracing/trace
# tracer: function
#
# entries-in-buffer/entries-written: 40051/40051    #P:1
```

```
#
#                              _-----=> irqs-off
#                             / _----=> need-resched
#                            | / _---=> hardirq/softirq
#                            || / _--=> preempt-depth
#                            ||| /     delay
#   TASK-PID    CPU#    ||||     TIMESTAMP  FUNCTION
#    | |         |      ||||        |          |
      sh-361    [000] ...1   992.990646: mutex_unlock <-rb_simple_write
      sh-361    [000] ...1   992.990658: __fsnotify_parent <-vfs_write
      sh-361    [000] ...1   992.990661: fsnotify <-vfs_write
      sh-361    [000] ...1   992.990663: __srcu_read_lock <-fsnotify
      sh-361    [000] ...1   992.990666: preempt_count_add <-
__srcu_read_lock
      sh-361    [000] ...2   992.990668: preempt_count_sub <-
__srcu_read_lock
      sh-361    [000] ...1   992.990670: __srcu_read_unlock <-fsnotify
      sh-361    [000] ...1   992.990672: __sb_end_write <-vfs_write
      sh-361    [000] ...1   992.990674: preempt_count_add <-__sb_end_write
[...]
```

You can capture a large number of data points in just one second: in this case, over 40,000.

As with profilers, it is difficult to make sense of a flat function list like this. If you select the function_graph tracer, Ftrace captures call graphs like this:

```
# tracer: function_graph
#
# CPU  DURATION               FUNCTION CALLS
# |     |   |                 |   |   |   |
 0) + 63.167 us   |                 } /* cpdma_ctlr_int_ctrl */
 0) + 73.417 us   |               } /* cpsw_intr_disable */
 0)               |               disable_irq_nosync() {
 0)               |                 __disable_irq_nosync() {
 0)               |                   __irq_get_desc_lock() {
 0)    0.541 us   |                     irq_to_desc();
 0)    0.500 us   |                     preempt_count_add();
 0) + 16.000 us   |                   }
 0)               |                   __disable_irq() {
 0)    0.500 us   |                     irq_disable();
 0)    8.208 us   |                   }
 0)               |                   __irq_put_desc_unlock() {
 0)    0.459 us   |                     preempt_count_sub();
 0)    8.000 us   |                   }
 0) + 55.625 us   |                 }
 0) + 63.375 us   |               }
```

Now you can see the nesting of the function calls, delimited by braces, { and }. At the terminating brace, there is a measurement of the time taken in the function, annotated with a plus sign (+) if it takes more than 10 μs and an exclamation mark (!) if it takes more than 100 μs.

You are often only interested in the kernel activity caused by a single process or thread, in which case you can restrict the trace to the one thread by writing the thread ID to set_ftrace_pid.

Dynamic Ftrace and trace filters

Enabling CONFIG_DYNAMIC_FTRACE allows Ftrace to modify the function trace sites at runtime, which has a couple of benefits. Firstly, it triggers additional build-time processing of the trace function probes, which allows the Ftrace subsystem to locate them at boot time and overwrite them with NOP instructions, thus reducing the overhead of the function trace code to almost nothing. You can then enable Ftrace in production or near-production kernels with no impact on performance.

The second advantage is that you can selectively enable function trace sites rather than tracing everything. The list of functions is put into available_filter_functions; there are several tens of thousands of them. You can selectively enable function traces as you need them by copying the name from available_filter_functions to set_ftrace_filter, and then stop tracing that function by writing the name to set_ftrace_notrace. You can also use wildcards and append names to the list. For example, suppose you are interested in tcp handling:

```
# cd /sys/kernel/debug/tracing
# echo "tcp*" > set_ftrace_filter
# echo function > current_tracer
# echo 1 > tracing_on
```

Run some tests and then look at the trace:

```
# cat trace
# tracer: function
#
# entries-in-buffer/entries-written: 590/590    #P:1
#
#                              _-----=> irqs-off
#                             / _----=> need-resched
#                            | / _---=> hardirq/softirq
#                            || / _--=> preempt-depth
#                            ||| /     delay
```

```
#         TASK-PID    CPU#   ||||    TIMESTAMP   FUNCTION
#           | |        |     ||||        |           |
     dropbear-375    [000]  ...1 48545.022235: tcp_poll <-sock_poll
     dropbear-375    [000]  ...1 48545.022372: tcp_poll <-sock_poll
     dropbear-375    [000]  ...1 48545.022393: tcp_sendmsg <-inet_sendmsg
     dropbear-375    [000]  ...1 48545.022398: tcp_send_mss <-tcp_sendmsg
     dropbear-375    [000]  ...1 48545.022400: tcp_current_mss <-tcp_send_mss
[...]
```

The `set_ftrace_filter` function can also contain commands, for example to start and stop tracing when certain functions are executed. There isn't space to go into these details here, but if you want to find out more, read the `Filter commands` section in `Documentation/trace/ftrace.txt`.

Trace events

The `function` and `function_graph` tracers described in the preceding section record only the time at which the function was executed. The trace events feature also records parameters associated with the call, making the trace more readable and informative. For example, instead of just recording that the function `kmalloc` has been called, a trace event will record the number of bytes requested and the returned pointer. Trace events are used in `perf` and `LTTng` as well as `Ftrace`, but the development of the trace events subsystem was prompted by the `LTTng` project.

It takes effort from kernel developers to create trace events, since each one is different. They are defined in the source code using the `TRACE_EVENT` macro: there are over a thousand of them now. You can see the list of events available at runtime in `/sys/kernel/debug/tracing/available_events`. They are named `subsystem:function`, for example, `kmem:kmalloc`. Each event is also represented by a subdirectory in `tracing/events/[subsystem]/[function]`, as demonstrated here:

```
# ls events/kmem/kmalloc
enable    filter    format    id    trigger
```

The files are as follows:

- `enable`: You write a 1 to this file to enable the event.
- `filter`: This is an expression that must evaluate to true for the event to be traced.
- `format`: This is the format of the event and parameters.

- `id`: This is a numeric identifier.
- `trigger`: This is a command that is executed when the event occurs using the syntax defined in the `Filter` commands section of `Documentation/trace/ftrace.txt`.

I will show you a simple example involving `kmalloc` and `kfree`. Event tracing does not depend on the function tracers, so begin by selecting the `nop` tracer:

```
# echo nop > current_tracer
```

Next, select the events to trace by enabling each one individually:

```
# echo 1 > events/kmem/kmalloc/enable
# echo 1 > events/kmem/kfree/enable
```

You can also write the event names to `set_event`, as shown here:

```
# echo "kmem:kmalloc kmem:kfree" > set_event
```

Now, when you read the trace, you can see the functions and their parameters:

```
# tracer: nop
#
# entries-in-buffer/entries-written: 359/359    #P:1
#
#                              _-----=> irqs-off
#                             / _----=> need-resched
#                            | / _---=> hardirq/softirq
#                            || / _--=> preempt-depth
#                            ||| /     delay
#    TASK-PID    CPU#  ||||    TIMESTAMP  FUNCTION
#      | |        |    ||||       |          |
    cat-382    [000] ...1  2935.586706: kmalloc:call_site=c0554644
ptr=de515a00
                                        bytes_req=384 bytes_alloc=512
gfp_flags=GFP_ATOMIC|GFP_NOWARN|GFP_NOMEMALLOC
    cat-382    [000] ...1  2935.586718: kfree: call_site=c059c2d8
ptr=(null)
```

Exactly the same trace events are visible in `perf` as `tracepoint` events.

Using LTTng

The **Linux Trace Toolkit (LTT)** project was started by Karim Yaghmour as a means of tracing kernel activity and was one of the first trace tools generally available for the Linux kernel. Later, Mathieu Desnoyers took up the idea and re-implemented it as the next-generation trace tool, LTTng. It was then expanded to cover user space traces as well as the kernel. The project website is at `http://lttng.org/` and contains a comprehensive user manual.

LTTng consists of three components:

- A core session manager
- A kernel tracer implemented as a group of kernel modules
- A user space tracer implemented as a library

In addition to those, you will need a trace viewer such as **Babeltrace** (`http://www.efficios.com/babeltrace`) or the **Eclipse Trace Compass** plugin to display and filter the raw trace data on the host or target.

LTTng requires a kernel configured with `CONFIG_TRACEPOINTS`, which is enabled when you select **Kernel hacking | Tracers | Kernel Function Tracer**.

The description that follows refers to LTTng version 2.5; other versions may be different.

LTTng and the Yocto Project

You need to add these packages to the target dependencies in `conf/local.conf`:

```
IMAGE_INSTALL_append = " lttng-tools lttng-modules lttng-ust"
```

If you want to run Babeltrace on the target, also append the package `babeltrace`.

LTTng and Buildroot

You need to enable the following:

- `BR2_PACKAGE_LTTNG_MODULES` in the menu **Target packages | Debugging, profiling and benchmark | lttng-modules**
- `BR2_PACKAGE_LTTNG_TOOLS` in the menu **Target packages | Debugging, profiling and benchmark | lttng-tools**

For user space trace tracing, enable this:

- `BR2_PACKAGE_LTTNG_LIBUST` in the menu **Target packages | Libraries | Other,** enable **lttng-libust**

There is a package called `lttng-babeltrace` for the target. Buildroot builds the host `babeltrace` automatically and places it in `output/host/usr/bin/babeltrace`.

Using LTTng for kernel tracing

LTTng can use the set of `ftrace` events described previously as potential trace points. Initially, they are disabled.

The control interface for LTTng is the `lttng` command. You can list the kernel probes using the following:

```
# lttng list --kernel
Kernel events:
-------------
      writeback_nothread (loglevel: TRACE_EMERG (0)) (type: tracepoint)
      writeback_queue (loglevel: TRACE_EMERG (0)) (type: tracepoint)
      writeback_exec (loglevel: TRACE_EMERG (0)) (type: tracepoint)
[...]
```

Traces are captured in the context of a session, which in this example is called `test`:

```
# lttng create test
Session test created.
Traces will be written in /home/root/lttng-traces/test-20150824-140942
# lttng list
Available tracing sessions:
  1) test (/home/root/lttng-traces/test-20150824-140942) [inactive]
```

Now enable a few events in the current session. You can enable all kernel tracepoints using the `--all` option, but remember the warning about generating too much trace data. Let's start with a couple of scheduler-related trace events:

```
# lttng enable-event --kernel sched_switch,sched_process_fork
```

Check that everything is set up:

```
# lttng list test
Tracing session test: [inactive]
    Trace path: /home/root/lttng-traces/test-20150824-140942
    Live timer interval (usec): 0
```

```
=== Domain: Kernel ===

Channels:
-------------
- channel0: [enabled]

    Attributes:
       overwrite mode: 0
       subbufers size: 26214
       number of subbufers: 4
       switch timer interval: 0
       read timer interval: 200000
       trace file count: 0
       trace file size (bytes): 0
       output: splice()

    Events:
       sched_process_fork (loglevel: TRACE_EMERG (0)) (type: tracepoint)
[enabled]
       sched_switch (loglevel: TRACE_EMERG (0)) (type: tracepoint) [enabled]
```

Now start tracing:

```
# lttng start
```

Run the test load and then stop tracing:

```
# lttng stop
```

Traces for the session are written to the session directory, `lttng-traces/<session>/kernel`.

You can use the Babeltrace viewer to dump the raw trace data in text format. In this case, I ran it on the host computer:

```
$ babeltrace    lttng-traces/test-20150824-140942/kernel
```

The output is too verbose to fit on this page, so I will leave it as an exercise for you to capture and display a trace in this way. The text output from Babeltrace does have the advantage that it is easy to search for strings using `grep` and similar commands.

A good choice for a graphical trace viewer is the Trace Compass plugin for Eclipse, which is now part of the Eclipse IDE for C/C++ developer bundle. Importing the trace data into Eclipse is characteristically fiddly. Briefly, you need to follow these steps:

1. Open the tracing perspective.
2. Create a new project by selecting **File** | **New** | **Tracing project**.

3. Enter a project name and click on **Finish**.

4. Right-click on the **New Project** option in the **Project Explorer** menu and select **Import**.

5. Expand **Tracing** and then select **Trace Import**.

6. Browse to the directory containing the traces (for example, `test-20150824-140942`), tick the box to indicate which subdirectories you want (it might be the kernel), and click on **Finish**.

7. Now, expand the project and, within that, expand **Traces[1]** and, within that, double-click on **kernel**. You should see the trace data shown in the following screenshot:

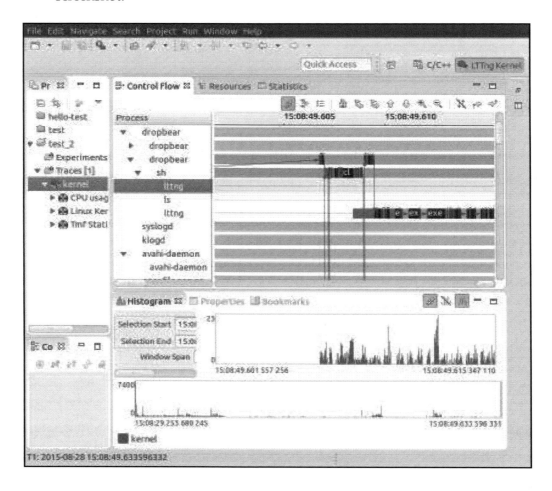

In the preceding screenshot, I have zoomed in on the **Control Flow** view to show state transitions between `dropbear` and a shell, and also some activity of the `lttng` daemon.

Using Valgrind

I introduced Valgrind in Chapter 13, *Managing Memory*, as a tool for identifying memory problems using the `memcheck` tool. Valgrind has other useful tools for application profiling. The two I am going to look at here are **Callgrind** and **Helgrind**. Since Valgrind works by running the code in a sandbox, it is able to check the code as it runs and report certain behaviors, which native tracers and profilers cannot do.

Callgrind

Callgrind is a call-graph-generating profiler that also collects information about processor cache hit rate and branch prediction. Callgrind is only useful if your bottleneck is CPU bound. It's not useful if heavy I/O or multiple processes are involved.

Valgrind does not require kernel configuration, but it does need debug symbols. It is available as a target package in both the Yocto Project and Buildroot (`BR2_PACKAGE_VALGRIND`).

You run Callgrind in Valgrind on the target, like so:

```
# valgrind --tool=callgrind <program>
```

This produces a file called `callgrind.out.<PID>`, which you can copy to the host and analyze with `callgrind_annotate`.

The default is to capture data for all the threads together in a single file. If you add option `--separate-threads=yes` when capturing, there will be profiles for each of the threads in files named `callgrind.out.<PID>-<thread id>`, for example, `callgrind.out.122-01` and `callgrind.out.122-02`.

Callgrind can simulate the processor L1/L2 cache and report on cache misses. Capture the trace with the `--simulate-cache=yes` option. L2 misses are much more expensive than L1 misses, so pay attention to code with high D2mr or D2mw counts.

Helgrind

This is a thread-error detector for detecting synchronization errors in C, C++, and Fortran programs that include POSIX threads.

Helgrind can detect three classes of error. Firstly, it can detect the incorrect use of the API, for example, unlocking a mutex that is already unlocked, unlocking a mutex that was locked by a different thread, or not checking the return value of certain pthread functions. Secondly, it monitors the order in which threads acquire locks and thus detects potential deadlocks that could arise from the formation of cycles of locks, which is also known as the deadly embrace. Finally, it detects data races, which can happen when two threads access a shared memory location without using suitable locks or other synchronization to ensure single-threaded access.

Using Helgrind is simple; you just need this command:

```
# valgrind --tool=helgrind <program>
```

It prints problems and potential problems as it finds them. You can direct these messages to a file by adding `--log-file=<filename>`.

Using strace

I started the chapter with the simple and ubiquitous tool, `top`, and I will finish with another: `strace`. It is a very simple tracer that captures system calls made by a program and, optionally, its children. You can use it to do the following:

- Learn which system calls a program makes
- Find those system calls that fail, together with the error code: I find this useful if a program fails to start but doesn't print an error message or if the message is too general
- Find which files a program opens
- Find out which `syscalls` a running program is making, for example, to see whether it is stuck in a loop

There are many more examples online; just search for `strace tips and tricks`. Everybody has their own favorite story, for example, `http://chadfowler.com /2014/01/26/the-magic-of-strace.html`.

`strace` uses the `ptrace(2)` function to hook calls as they are made from user space to the kernel. If you want to know more about how `ptrace` works, the manual page is detailed and surprisingly readable.

The simplest way to get a trace is to run the command as a parameter to `strace` as shown here (the listing has been edited to make it clearer):

```
# strace ./helloworld
execve("./helloworld", ["./helloworld"], [/* 14 vars */]) = 0
brk(0)                                      = 0x11000
uname({sys="Linux", node="beaglebone", ...}) = 0
mmap2(NULL, 4096, PROT_READ|PROT_WRITE, MAP_PRIVATE|MAP_ANONYMOUS, -
 1, 0) = 0xb6f40000
access("/etc/ld.so.preload", R_OK)          = -1 ENOENT (No such file or
 directory)
open("/etc/ld.so.cache", O_RDONLY|O_CLOEXEC) = 3
fstat64(3, {st_mode=S_IFREG|0644, st_size=8100, ...}) = 0
mmap2(NULL, 8100, PROT_READ, MAP_PRIVATE, 3, 0) = 0xb6f3e000
close(3)                                    = 0
open("/lib/tls/v7l/neon/vfp/libc.so.6", O_RDONLY|O_CLOEXEC) = -1
 ENOENT (No such file or directory)
[...]

open("/lib/libc.so.6", O_RDONLY|O_CLOEXEC) = 3
read(3,
 "\177ELF\1\1\1\0\0\0\0\0\0\0\0\0\3\0(\0\1\0\0\0$`\1\0004\0\0\0"...,
 512) = 512
fstat64(3, {st_mode=S_IFREG|0755, st_size=1291884, ...}) = 0
mmap2(NULL, 1328520, PROT_READ|PROT_EXEC, MAP_PRIVATE|MAP_DENYWRITE,
 3, 0) = 0xb6df9000
mprotect(0xb6f30000, 32768, PROT_NONE)   = 0
mmap2(0xb6f38000, 12288, PROT_READ|PROT_WRITE,
 MAP_PRIVATE|MAP_FIXED|MAP_DENYWRITE, 3, 0x137000) = 0xb6f38000
mmap2(0xb6f3b000, 9608, PROT_READ|PROT_WRITE,
 MAP_PRIVATE|MAP_FIXED|MAP_ANONYMOUS, -1, 0) = 0xb6f3b000
close(3)
[...]

write(1, "Hello, world!\n", 14Hello, world!
 )               = 14
exit_group(0)                                = ?
+++ exited with 0 +++
```

Most of the trace shows how the runtime environment is created. In particular, you can see how the library loader hunts for `libc.so.6`, eventually finding it in `/lib`. Finally, it gets to running the `main()` function of the program, which prints its message and exits.

If you want `strace` to follow any child processes or threads created by the original process, add the `-f` option.

> If you are using `strace` to trace a program that creates threads, you almost certainly want the `-f` option. Better still, use `-ff` and `-o <file name>` so that the output for each child process or thread is written to a separate file named `<filename>.<PID | TID>`.

A common use of `strace` is to discover which files a program tries to open at startup. You can restrict the system calls that are traced through the `-e` option, and you can write the trace to a file instead of `stdout` using the `-o` option:

```
# strace -e open -o ssh-strace.txt ssh localhost
```

This shows the libraries and configuration files `ssh` opens when it is setting up a connection.

You can even use `strace` as a basic profile tool: if you use the `-c` option, it accumulates the time spent in system calls and prints out a summary like this:

```
# strace -c grep linux /usr/lib/* > /dev/null
```

% time	seconds	usecs/call	calls	errors	syscall
78.68	0.012825	1	11098	18	read
11.03	0.001798	1	3551		write
10.02	0.001634	8	216	15	open
0.26	0.000043	0	202		fstat64
0.00	0.000000	0	201		close
0.00	0.000000	0	1		execve
0.00	0.000000	0	1	1	access
0.00	0.000000	0	3		brk
0.00	0.000000	0	199		munmap
0.00	0.000000	0	1		uname
0.00	0.000000	0	5		mprotect
0.00	0.000000	0	207		mmap2
0.00	0.000000	0	15	15	stat64
0.00	0.000000	0	1		getuid32
0.00	0.000000	0	1		set_tls
100.00	0.016300		15702	49	total

Summary

Nobody can complain that Linux lacks options for profiling and tracing. This chapter has given you an overview of some of the most common ones.

When faced with a system that is not performing as well as you would like, start with `top` and try to identify the problem. If it proves to be a single application, then you can use perf record/report to profile it, bearing in mind that you will have to configure the kernel to enable perf and you will need debug symbols for the binaries and kernel. `OProfile` is an alternative to perf record and can tell you similar things. `gprof` is, frankly, outdated, but it does have the advantage of not requiring kernel support. If the problem is not so well localized, use perf (or OProfile) to get a system-wide view.

`Ftrace` comes into its own when you have specific questions about the behavior of the kernel. The `function` and `function_graph` tracers provide a detailed view of the relationship and sequence of function calls. The event tracers allow you to extract more information about functions, including the parameters and return values. `LTTng` performs a similar role, making use of the event trace mechanism, and adds high-speed ring buffers to extract large quantities of data from the kernel. Valgrind has the particular advantage that it runs code in a sandbox and can report on errors that are hard to track down in other ways. Using the Callgrind tool, it can generate call graphs and report on processor cache usage, and with Helgrind, it can report on thread-related problems.

Finally, don't forget `strace`. It is a good standby for finding out which system calls a program is making, from tracking file open calls to finding file path names and checking for system wake-ups and incoming signals.

All the while, be aware of, and try to avoid, the observer effect: make sure that the measurements you are making are valid for a production system. In the next chapter, I will continue the theme as I delve into the latency tracers that help us quantify the real-time performance of a target system.

16
Real-Time Programming

Much of the interaction between a computer system and the real world happens in real time, and so this is an important topic for developers of embedded systems. I have touched on real-time programming in several places so far: in Chapter 12, *Learning About Processes and Threads*, I looked at scheduling policies and priority inversion, and in Chapter 13, *Managing Memory*, I described the problems with page faults and the need for memory locking. Now, it is time to bring these topics together and look at real-time programming in some depth.

In this chapter, I will begin with a discussion about the characteristics of real-time systems and then consider the implications for system design, both at the application and kernel levels. I will describe the real-time kernel patch, PREEMPT_RT, and show how to get it and apply it to a mainline kernel. The final sections will describe how to characterize system latencies using two tools: **cyclictest** and **Ftrace**.

There are other ways to achieve real-time behavior on an embedded Linux device, for instance, using a dedicated microcontroller or a separate real-time kernel alongside the Linux kernel in the way that Xenomai and RTAI do. I am not going to discuss these here because the focus of this book is on using Linux as the core for embedded systems.

In this chapter, we will cover the following topics:

- What is real time?
- Identifying sources of non-determinism.
- Understanding scheduling latency.
- Kernel preemption.
- The real-time Linux kernel (PREEMPT_RT).
- High-resolution timers.

- Avoiding page faults.
- Interrupt shielding.
- Measuring scheduling latencies.

What is real time?

The nature of real-time programming is one of the subjects that software engineers love to discuss at length, often giving a range of contradictory definitions. I will begin by setting out what I think is important about real time.

A task is a real-time task if it has to complete before a certain point in time, known as the **deadline**. The distinction between real-time and nonreal-time tasks is shown by considering what happens when you play an audio stream on your computer while compiling the Linux kernel. The first is a real-time task because there is a constant stream of data arriving at the audio driver, and blocks of audio samples have to be written to the audio interface at the playback rate. Meanwhile, the compilation is not real time because there is no deadline. You simply want it to complete as soon as possible; whether it takes 10 seconds or 10 minutes does not affect the quality of the kernel binaries.

The other important thing to consider is the consequence of missing the deadline, which can range from mild annoyance through to system failure or, in the most extreme cases, injury or death. Here are some examples:

- **Playing an audio stream**: There is a deadline in the order of tens of milliseconds. If the audio buffer underruns, you will hear a click, which is annoying, but you will get over it.
- **Moving and clicking a mouse**: The deadline is also in the order of tens of milliseconds. If it is missed, the mouse moves erratically and button clicks will be lost. If the problem persists, the system will become unusable.
- **Printing a piece of paper**: The deadlines for the paper feed are in the millisecond range, which if missed may cause the printer to jam, and somebody will have to go and fix it. Occasional jams are acceptable, but nobody is going to buy a printer that keeps on jamming.
- **Printing sell-by dates on bottles on a production line**: If one bottle is not printed, the whole production line has to be halted, the bottle removed, and the line restarted, which is expensive.
- **Baking a cake**: There is a deadline of 30 minutes or so. If you miss it by a few minutes, the cake might be ruined. If you miss it by a lot, the house may burn down.

- **A power-surge detection system**: If the system detects a surge, a circuit breaker has to be triggered within 2 milliseconds. Failing to do so causes damage to the equipment and may injure or kill personnel.

In other words, there are many consequences to missed deadlines. We often talk about these different categories:

- **Soft real-time**: The deadline is desirable but is sometimes missed without the system being considered a failure. The first two examples in the previous list are like this.
- **Hard real-time**: Here, missing a deadline has a serious effect. We can further subdivide hard real-time into mission-critical systems, in which there is a cost to missing the deadline, such as the fourth example; and safety-critical systems, in which there is a danger to life and limb, such as the last two examples. I put in the baking example to show that not all hard real-time systems have deadlines measured in milliseconds or microseconds.

Software written for safety-critical systems has to conform to various standards that seek to ensure that it is capable of performing reliably. It is very difficult for a complex operating system such as Linux to meet those requirements.

When it comes to mission-critical systems, it is possible, and common, for Linux to be used for a wide range of control systems. The requirements of the software depend on the combination of the deadline and the confidence level, which can usually be determined through extensive testing.

Therefore, to say that a system is real-time, you have to measure its response times under the maximum anticipated load, and show that it meets the deadline for an agreed proportion of the time. As a rule of thumb, a well-configured Linux system using a mainline kernel is good for soft real-time tasks with deadlines down to tens of milliseconds, and a kernel with the PREEMPT_RT patch is good for soft and hard real-time mission-critical systems with deadlines down to several hundreds of microseconds.

The key to creating a real-time system is to reduce the variability in response times so that you have greater confidence that the deadlines will not be missed; in other words, you need to make the system more deterministic. Often, this is done at the expense of performance. For example, caches make systems run faster by making the average time to access an item of data shorter, but the maximum time is longer in the case of a cache miss. Caches make a system faster but less deterministic, which is the opposite of what we want.

It is a myth of real-time computing that it is fast. This is not so, the more deterministic a system is, the lower the maximum throughput.

The remainder of this chapter is concerned with identifying the causes of latency and the things you can do to reduce it.

Identifying sources of non-determinism

Fundamentally, real-time programming is about making sure that the threads controlling the output in real time are scheduled when needed and so can complete the job before the deadline. Anything that prevents this is a problem. Here are some problem areas:

- **Scheduling**: Real-time threads must be scheduled before others, and so they must have a real-time policy, SCHED_FIFO or SCHED_RR. Additionally, they should have priorities assigned in descending order starting with the one with the shortest deadline, according to the theory of Rate Monotonic Analysis that I described in Chapter 12, *Learning About Processes and Threads*.

- **Scheduling latency**: The kernel must be able to reschedule as soon as an event such as an interrupt or timer occurs, and not be subject to unbounded delays. Reducing scheduling latency is a key topic later on in this chapter.

- **Priority inversion**: This is a consequence of priority-based scheduling, which leads to unbounded delays when a high-priority thread is blocked on a mutex held by a low-priority thread, as I described in Chapter 12, *Learning About Processes and Threads*. User space has priority inheritance and priority ceiling mutexes; in kernel space, we have rt-mutexes, which implement priority inheritance and which I will talk about in the section on the real-time kernel.

- **Accurate timers**: If you want to manage deadlines in the region of low milliseconds or microseconds, you need timers that match. High-resolution timers are crucial and are a configuration option on almost all kernels.

- **Page faults**: A page fault while executing a critical section of code will upset all timing estimates. You can avoid them by locking memory, as I shall describe later on.

- **Interrupts**: They occur at unpredictable times and can result in an unexpected processing overhead if there is a sudden flood of them. There are two ways to avoid this. One is to run interrupts as kernel threads, and the other, on multi-core devices, is to shield one or more CPUs from interrupt handling. I will discuss both possibilities later.

- **Processor caches**: These provide a buffer between the CPU and the main memory and, like all caches, are a source of non-determinism, especially on multi-core devices. Unfortunately, this is beyond the scope of this book, but you may want refer to the references at the end of the chapter for more details.
- **Memory bus contention**: When peripherals access memory directly through a DMA channel, they use up a slice of memory bus bandwidth, which slows down access from the CPU core (or cores) and so contributes to non-deterministic execution of the program. However, this is a hardware issue and is also beyond the scope of this book.

I will expand on the important problems and see what can be done about them in the next sections.

Understanding scheduling latency

Real-time threads need to be scheduled as soon as they have something to do. However, even if there are no other threads of the same or higher priority, there is always a delay from the point at which the wake-up event occurs—an interrupt or system timer—to the time that the thread starts to run. This is called the **scheduling latency**. It can be broken down into several components, as shown in the following diagram:

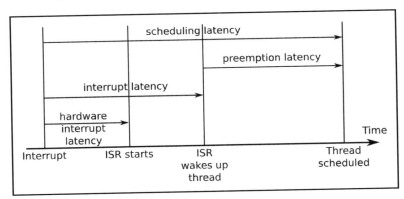

Firstly, there is the hardware interrupt latency from the point at which an interrupt is asserted until the **interrupt service routine (ISR)** begins to run. A small part of this is the delay in the interrupt hardware itself, but the biggest problem is due to interrupts being disabled in software. Minimizing this *IRQ off time* is important.

The next is interrupt latency, which is the length of time until the ISR has serviced the interrupt and woken up any threads waiting on this event. It is mostly dependent on the way the ISR was written. Normally, it should take only a short time, measured in microseconds.

The final delay is the preemption latency, which is the time from the point that the kernel is notified that a thread is ready to run to that at which the scheduler actually runs the thread. It is determined by whether the kernel can be preempted or not. If it is running code in a critical section, then the rescheduling will have to wait. The length of the delay is dependent on the configuration of kernel preemption.

Kernel preemption

Preemption latency occurs because it is not always safe or desirable to preempt the current thread of execution and call the scheduler. Mainline Linux has three settings for preemption, selected via the **Kernel Features** | **Preemption Model** menu:

- CONFIG_PREEMPT_NONE: No preemption
- CONFIG_PREEMPT_VOLUNTARY: This enables additional checks for requests for preemption
- CONFIG_PREEMPT: This allows the kernel to be preempted

With preemption set to none, kernel code will continue without rescheduling until it either returns via a syscall back to user space, where preemption is always allowed, or it encounters a sleeping wait that stops the current thread. Since it reduces the number of transitions between the kernel and user space and may reduce the total number of context switches, this option results in the highest throughput at the expense of large preemption latencies. It is the default for servers and some desktop kernels, where throughput is more important than responsiveness.

The second option enables explicit preemption points, where the scheduler is called if the need_resched flag is set, which reduces the worst-case preemption latencies at the expense of slightly lower throughput. Some distributions set this option on desktops.

The third option makes the kernel preemptible, meaning that an interrupt can result in an immediate reschedule so long as the kernel is not executing in an atomic context, which I will describe in the following section. This reduces worst-case preemption latencies and, therefore, overall scheduling latencies to something in the order of a few milliseconds on typical embedded hardware.

This is often described as a soft real-time option, and most embedded kernels are configured in this way. Of course, there is a small reduction in overall throughput, but that is usually less important than having more deterministic scheduling for embedded devices.

The real-time Linux kernel (PREEMPT_RT)

There is a long-standing effort to reduce latencies still further that goes by the name of the kernel configuration option for these features, PREEMPT_RT. The project was started by Ingo Molnar, Thomas Gleixner, and Steven Rostedt and has had contributions from many more developers over the years. The kernel patches are at https://www.kernel.org/pub/linux/kernel/projects/rt, and there is a wiki, including an FAQ (slightly out of date), at https://rt.wiki.kernel.org.

Many parts of the project have been incorporated into mainline Linux over the years, including high-resolution timers, kernel mutexes, and threaded interrupt handlers. However, the core patches remain outside of the mainline because they are rather intrusive and (some claim) only benefit a small percentage of the total Linux user base. Maybe, one day, the whole patch set will be merged upstream.

The central plan is to reduce the amount of time the kernel spends running in an **atomic context**, which is where it is not safe to call the scheduler and switch to a different thread. Typical atomic contexts are when the kernel is in the following states:

- Running an interrupt or trap handler.
- Holding a spinlock or in an RCU critical section. Spin lock and RCU are kernel-locking primitives, the details of which are not relevant here.
- Between calls to preempt_disable() and preempt_enable().
- Hardware interrupts are disabled (**IRQs off**)

The changes that are part of PREEMPT_RT fall into two main areas: one is to reduce the impact of interrupt handlers by turning them into kernel threads, and the other is to make locks preemptible so that a thread can sleep while holding one. It is obvious that there is a large overhead in these changes, which makes average-case interrupt handling slower but much more deterministic, which is what we are striving for.

Threaded interrupt handlers

Not all interrupts are triggers for real-time tasks, but all interrupts steal cycles from real-time tasks. Threaded interrupt handlers allow a priority to be associated with the interrupt and for it to be scheduled at an appropriate time, as shown in the following diagram:

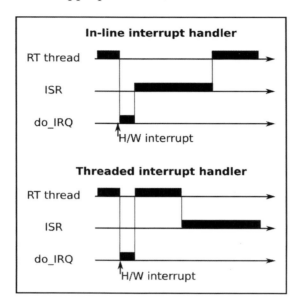

If the interrupt-handler code is run as a kernel thread, there is no reason why it cannot be preempted by a user space thread of higher priority, and so the interrupt handler does not contribute toward scheduling latency of the user space thread. Threaded interrupt handlers have been a feature of mainline Linux since 2.6.30. You can request that an individual interrupt handler be threaded by registering it with `request_threaded_irq()` in place of the normal `request_irq()`. You can make threaded IRQs the default by configuring the kernel with `CONFIG_IRQ_FORCED_THREADING=y`, which makes all handlers into threads unless they have explicitly prevented this by setting the `IRQF_NO_THREAD` flag. When you apply the `PREEMPT_RT` patches, interrupts are, by default, configured as threads in this way. Here is an example of what you might see:

```
# ps -Leo pid,tid,class,rtprio,stat,comm,wchan | grep FF
PID     TID     CLS     RTPRIO  STAT    COMMAND         WCHAN
3       3       FF      1       S       ksoftirqd/0     smpboot_th
7       7       FF      99      S       posixcputmr/0   posix_cpu_
19      19      FF      50      S       irq/28-edma     irq_thread
20      20      FF      50      S       irq/30-edma_err irq_thread
42      42      FF      50      S       irq/91-rtc0     irq_thread
```

43	43	FF	50	S	irq/92-rtc0	irq_thread
44	44	FF	50	S	irq/80-mmc0	irq_thread
45	45	FF	50	S	irq/150-mmc0	irq_thread
47	47	FF	50	S	irq/44-mmc1	irq_thread
52	52	FF	50	S	irq/86-44e0b000	irq_thread
59	59	FF	50	S	irq/52-tilcdc	irq_thread
65	65	FF	50	S	irq/56-4a100000	irq_thread
66	66	FF	50	S	irq/57-4a100000	irq_thread
67	67	FF	50	S	irq/58-4a100000	irq_thread
68	68	FF	50	S	irq/59-4a100000	irq_thread
76	76	FF	50	S	irq/88-OMAP UAR	irq_thread

In this case, a BeagleBone running `linux-yocto-rt`, only the `gp_timer` interrupt was not threaded. It is normal that the timer interrupt handler be run inline.

 The interrupt threads have all been given the default policy `SCHED_FIFO` and a priority of `50`. It doesn't make sense to leave them with the defaults; however, now is your chance to assign priorities according to the importance of the interrupts compared to real-time user space threads.

Here is a suggested order of descending thread priorities:

- The POSIX timers thread, `posixcputmr`, should always have the highest priority.
- Hardware interrupts associated with the highest priority real-time thread.
- The highest priority real-time thread.
- Hardware interrupts for the progressively lower-priority real-time threads, followed by the thread itself.
- The next highest-priority real-time thread.
- Hardware interrupts for nonreal-time interfaces.
- The soft IRQ daemon, `ksoftirqd`, which on RT kernels is responsible for running delayed interrupt routines and, prior to Linux 3.6, was responsible for running the network stack, the block I/O layer, and other things. You may need to experiment with different priority levels to achieve a balance.

You can change the priorities using the `chrt` command as part of the boot script, using a command like this:

```
# chrt -f -p 90 `pgrep irq/28-edma`
```

The `pgrep` command is part of the `procps` package.

Preemptible kernel locks

Making the majority of kernel locks preemptible is the most intrusive change that PREEMPT_RT makes, and this code remains outside of the mainline kernel.

The problem occurs with spin locks, which are used for much of the kernel locking. A spin lock is a busy-wait mutex that does not require a context switch in the contended case, and so it is very efficient as long as the lock is held for a short time. Ideally, they should be locked for less than the time it would take to reschedule twice. The following diagram shows threads running on two different CPUs contending the same spin lock. **CPU 0** gets it first, forcing **CPU 1** to spin, waiting until it is unlocked:

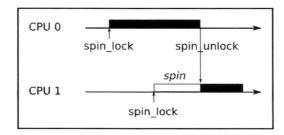

The thread that holds the spin lock cannot be preempted since doing so may make the new thread enter the same code and deadlock when it tries to lock the same spin lock. Consequently, in mainline Linux, locking a spin lock disables kernel preemption, creating an atomic context. This means that a low priority thread that holds a spin lock can prevent a high-priority thread from being scheduled.

 The solution adopted by PREEMPT_RT is to replace almost all spin locks with RT-mutexes. A mutex is slower than a spin lock, but it is fully preemptible. Not only that, but RT-mutexes implement priority inheritance and so are not susceptible to priority inversion.

Getting the PREEMPT_RT patches

The RT developers do not create patch sets for every kernel version because of the amount of effort involved. On average, they create patches for every other kernel. The most recent kernels that are supported at the time of writing are as follows:

- 4.9-rt
- 4.8-rt
- 4.6-rt

- 4.4-rt
- 4.1-rt
- 4.0-rt
- 3.18-rt
- 3.14-rt
- 3.12-rt
- 3.10-rt
- 3.4-rt
- 3.2-rt

The patches are available at
`https://www.kernel.org/pub/linux/kernel/projects/rt`.

If you are using the Yocto Project, there is an `rt` version of the kernel already. Otherwise, it is possible that the place you got your kernel from already has the `PREEMPT_RT` patch applied. If not, you will have to apply the patch yourself. Firstly, make sure that the `PREEMPT_RT` patch version and your kernel version match exactly; otherwise, you will not be able to apply the patches cleanly. Then, you apply it in the normal way, as shown in the following command lines. You will then be able to configure the kernel with `CONFIG_PREEMPT_RT_FULL`.

```
$ cd linux-4.1.10
$ zcat patch-4.1.10-rt11.patch.gz | patch -p1
```

There is a problem in the previous paragraph. The RT patch will only apply if you are using a compatible mainline kernel. You are probably not, because that is the nature of embedded Linux kernels. So you will have to spend some time looking at failed patches and fixing them, and then analyzing the board support for your target and adding any real-time support that is missing. These details are, once again, outside the scope of this book. If you are not sure what to do, you should inquire of the developers of the kernel you are using and on kernel-developer forums.

The Yocto Project and PREEMPT_RT

The Yocto Project supplies two standard kernel recipes: `linux-yocto` and `linux-yocto-rt`, the latter having the real-time patches already applied. Assuming that your target is supported by the Yocto kernels, you just need to select `linux-yocto-rt` as your preferred kernel and declare that your machine is compatible, for example, by adding lines similar to these to your `conf/local.conf`:

```
PREFERRED_PROVIDER_virtual/kernel = "linux-yocto-rt"
COMPATIBLE_MACHINE_beaglebone = "beaglebone"
```

High-resolution timers

Timer resolution is important if you have precise timing requirements, which is typical for real-time applications. The default timer in Linux is a clock that runs at a configurable rate, typically 100 Hz for embedded systems and 250 Hz for servers and desktops. The interval between two timer ticks is known as a **jiffy** and, in the examples given previously, is 10 milliseconds on an embedded SoC and four milliseconds on a server.

Linux gained more accurate timers from the real-time kernel project in version 2.6.18, and now they are available on all platforms, provided that there is a high-resolution timer source and device driver for it—which is almost always the case. You need to configure the kernel with `CONFIG_HIGH_RES_TIMERS=y`.

With this enabled, all the kernel and user space clocks will be accurate down to the granularity of the underlying hardware. Finding the actual clock granularity is difficult. The obvious answer is the value provided by `clock_getres(2)`, but that always claims a resolution of one nanosecond. The `cyclictest` tool that I will describe later has an option to analyze the times reported by the clock to guess the resolution:

```
# cyclictest -R
# /dev/cpu_dma_latency set to 0us
WARN: reported clock resolution: 1 nsec
WARN: measured clock resolution approximately: 708 nsec
```

You can also look at the kernel log messages for strings like this:

```
# dmesg | grep clock
OMAP clockevent source: timer2 at 24000000 Hz
sched_clock: 32 bits at 24MHz, resolution 41ns, wraps every
 178956969942ns
OMAP clocksource: timer1 at 24000000 Hz
Switched to clocksource timer1
```

The two methods provide rather different numbers, for which I have no good explanation, but since both are below one microsecond, I am happy.

Avoiding page faults

A page fault occurs when an application reads or writes to memory that is not committed to physical memory. It is impossible (or very hard) to predict when a page fault will happen, so they are another source of non-determinism in computers.

Fortunately, there is a function that allows you to commit all the memory used by the process and lock it down so that it cannot cause a page fault. It is mlockall(2). These are its two flags:

- MCL_CURRENT: This locks all pages currently mapped
- MCL_FUTURE: This locks pages that are mapped in later

You usually call mlockall during the startup of the application with both flags set to lock all current and future memory mappings.

 MCL_FUTURE is not magic, in that there will still be non-deterministic delay when allocating or freeing heap memory using malloc()/free() or mmap(). Such operations are best done at startup and not in the main control loops.

Memory allocated on the stack is trickier because it is done automatically, and if you call a function that makes the stack deeper than before, you will encounter more memory-management delays. A simple fix is to grow the stack to a size larger than you think you will ever need at startup. The code would look like this:

```
#define MAX_STACK (512*1024)
static void stack_grow (void)
{
  char dummy[MAX_STACK];
  memset(dummy, 0, MAX_STACK);
  return;
}

int main(int argc, char* argv[])
{
  [...]
  stack_grow ();
  mlockall(MCL_CURRENT | MCL_FUTURE);
  [...]
```

The `stack_grow()` function allocates a large variable on the stack and then zeroes it to force those pages of memory to be committed to this process.

Interrupt shielding

Using threaded interrupt handlers helps mitigate interrupt overhead by running some threads at a higher priority than interrupt handlers that do not impact real-time tasks. If you are using a multi-core processor, you can take a different approach and shield one or more cores from processing interrupts completely, allowing them to be dedicated to real-time tasks instead. This works either with a normal Linux kernel or a `PREEMPT_RT` kernel.

Achieving this is a question of pinning the real-time threads to one CPU and the interrupt handlers to a different one. You can set the CPU affinity off a thread or process using the command-line tool `taskset`, or you can use the `sched_setaffinity(2)` and `pthread_setaffinity_np(3)` functions.

To set the affinity of an interrupt, first note that there is a subdirectory for each interrupt number in `/proc/irq/<IRQ number>`. The control files for the interrupt are in there, including a CPU mask in `smp_affinity`. Write a bitmask to that file with a bit set for each CPU that is allowed to handle that IRQ.

Measuring scheduling latencies

All the configuration and tuning you may do will be pointless if you cannot show that your device meets the deadlines. You will need your own benchmarks for the final testing, but I will describe here two important measurement tools: cyclictest and Ftrace.

cyclictest

`cyclictest` was originally written by Thomas Gleixner and is now available on most platforms in a package named `rt-tests`. If you are using the Yocto Project, you can create a target image that includes `rt-tests` by building the real-time image recipe like this:

```
$ bitbake core-image-rt
```

If you are using Buildroot, you need to add the package `BR2_PACKAGE_RT_TESTS` in the menu **Target packages | Debugging, profiling and benchmark | rt-tests**.

`cyclictest` measures scheduling latencies by comparing the actual time taken for a sleep to the requested time. If there was no latency, they would be the same, and the reported latency would be zero. `cyclictest` assumes a timer resolution of less than one microsecond.

It has a large number of command-line options. To start with, you might try running this command as `root` on the target:

```
# cyclictest -l 100000 -m -n -p 99
# /dev/cpu_dma_latency set to 0us
policy: fifo: loadavg: 1.14 1.06 1.00 1/49 320
T: 0 (  320) P:99 I:1000 C: 100000 Min:  9 Act:  13 Avg:  15 Max:   134
```

The options selected are as follows:

- `-l N`: This loops N times (the default is unlimited)
- `-m`: This locks memory with `mlockall`
- `-n`: This uses `clock_nanosleep(2)` instead of `nanosleep(2)`
- `-p N`: This uses the real-time priority N

The result line shows the following, reading from left to right:

- `T:  0`: This was thread 0, the only thread in this run. You can set the number of threads with parameter `-t`.
- `(320)`: This was PID 320.
- `P:99`: The priority was 99.
- `I:1000`: The interval between loops was 1,000 microseconds. You can set the interval with parameter `-i N`.
- `C:100000`: The final loop count for this thread was 100,000.
- `Min:  9`: The minimum latency was 9 microseconds.
- `Act:13`: The actual latency was 13 microseconds. The *actual latency* is the most recent latency measurement, which only makes sense if you are watching `cyclictest` as it runs.
- `Avg:15`: The average latency was 15 microseconds.
- `Max:134`: The maximum latency was 134 microseconds.

This was obtained on an idle system running an unmodified `linux-yocto` kernel as a quick demonstration of the tool. To be of real use, you would run tests over a 24-hour period or longer while running a load representative of the maximum you expect.

Of the numbers produced by `cyclictest`, the maximum latency is the most interesting, but it would be nice to get an idea of the spread of the values. You can get that by adding –h <N> to obtain a histogram of samples that are up to N microseconds late. Using this technique, I obtained three traces for the same target board running kernels with no preemption, with standard preemption, and with RT preemption while being loaded with Ethernet traffic from a **flood ping**. The command line was as shown here:

```
# cyclictest -p 99 -m -n -l 100000 -q -h 500 > cyclictest.data
```

Then, I used `gnuplot` to create the three graphs that follow. If you are curious, the data files and the `gnuplot` command script are in the code archive, in MELP/chapter_16/plot.

The following is the output generated with no preemption:

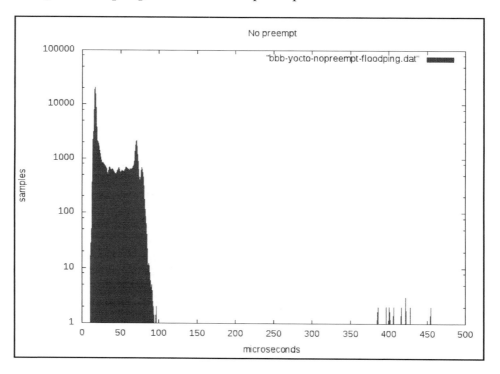

Without preemption, most samples are within 100 microseconds of the deadline, but there are some outliers of up to *500 microseconds*, which is pretty much what you would expect.

This is the output generated with standard preemption:

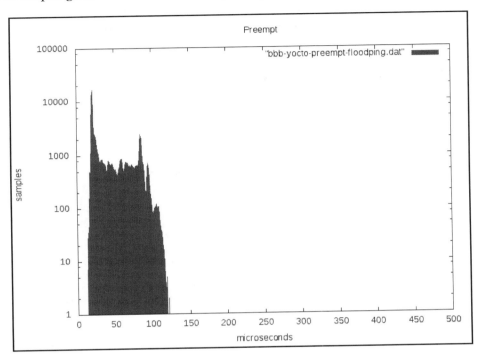

With preemption, the samples are spread out at the lower end, but there is nothing beyond 120 microseconds.

Here is the output generated with RT preemption:

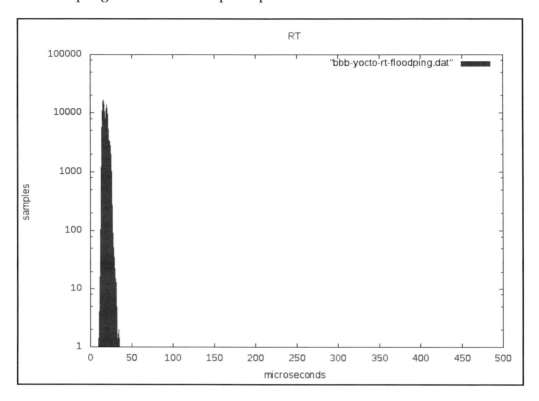

The RT kernel is a clear winner because everything is tightly bunched around the 20-microsecond mark, and there is nothing later than 35 microseconds.

`cyclictest`, then, is a standard metric for scheduling latencies. However, it cannot help you identify and resolve specific problems with kernel latency. To do that, you need `Ftrace`.

Using Ftrace

The kernel function tracer has tracers to help track down kernel latencies—that is what it was originally written for, after all. These tracers capture the trace for the worst-case latency detected during a run, showing the functions that caused the delay.

The tracers of interest, together with the kernel configuration parameters, are as follows:

- `irqsoff`: `CONFIG_IRQSOFF_TRACER` traces code that disables interrupts, recording the worst case
- `preemptoff`: `CONFIG_PREEMPT_TRACER` is similar to `irqsoff`, but traces the longest time that kernel preemption is disabled (only available on preemptible kernels)
- `preemptirqsoff`: combines the previous two traces to record the largest time either `irqs` and/or preemption is disabled for
- `wakeup`: traces and records the maximum latency that it takes for the highest-priority task to get scheduled after it has been woken up
- `wakeup_rt`: this is the same as wake up but only for real-time threads with the `SCHED_FIFO`, `SCHED_RR`, or `SCHED_DEADLINE` policies
- `wakeup_dl`: this is the same but only for deadline-scheduled threads with the `SCHED_DEADLINE` policy

Be aware that running Ftrace adds a lot of latency, in the order of tens of milliseconds, every time it captures a new maximum, which Ftrace itself can ignore. However, it skews the results of user space tracers such as `cyclictest`. In other words, ignore the results of `cyclictest` if you run it while capturing traces.

Selecting the tracer is the same as for the function tracer we looked at in Chapter 15, *Profiling and Tracing*. Here is an example of capturing a trace for the maximum period with preemption disabled for a period of 60 seconds:

```
# echo preemptoff > /sys/kernel/debug/tracing/current_tracer
# echo 0 > /sys/kernel/debug/tracing/tracing_max_latency
# echo 1  > /sys/kernel/debug/tracing/tracing_on
# sleep 60
# echo 0  > /sys/kernel/debug/tracing/tracing_on
```

The resulting trace, heavily edited, looks like this:

```
# cat /sys/kernel/debug/tracing/trace
# tracer: preemptoff
#
# preemptoff latency trace v1.1.5 on 3.14.19-yocto-standard
# --------------------------------------------------------------------
# latency: 1160 us, #384/384, CPU#0 | (M:preempt VP:0, KP:0, SP:0 HP:0)
#    -----------------
#    | task: init-1 (uid:0 nice:0 policy:0 rt_prio:0)
#    -----------------
#  => started at: ip_finish_output
```

```
#   => ended at:    __local_bh_enable_ip
#
#
#                        _------=> CPU#
#                       / _-----=> irqs-off
#                      | / _----=> need-resched
#                      || / _---=> hardirq/softirq
#                      ||| / _--=> preempt-depth
#                      |||| /      delay
#   cmd      pid       ||||| time  |   caller
#      \    /          |||||  \    |   /
    init-1             0..s.    1us+: ip_finish_output
    init-1             0d.s2   27us+: preempt_count_add <-cpdma_chan_submit
    init-1             0d.s3   30us+: preempt_count_add <-cpdma_chan_submit
    init-1             0d.s4   37us+: preempt_count_sub <-cpdma_chan_submit

[...]

    init-1             0d.s2 1152us+: preempt_count_sub <-__local_bh_enable
    init-1             0d..2 1155us+: preempt_count_sub <-__local_bh_enable_ip
    init-1             0d..1 1158us+: __local_bh_enable_ip
    init-1             0d..1 1162us!: trace_preempt_on <-__local_bh_enable_ip
    init-1             0d..1 1340us : <stack trace>
```

Here, you can see that the longest period with kernel preemption disabled while running the trace was 1160 microseconds. This simple fact is available by reading /sys/kernel/debug/tracing/tracing_max_latency, but the previous trace goes further and gives you the sequence of kernel function calls that lead up to that measurement. The column marked delay shows the point on the trail where each function was called, ending with the call to trace_preempt_on() at 1162us, at which point kernel preemption is once again enabled. With this information, you can look back through the call chain and (hopefully) work out whether this is a problem or not.

The other tracers mentioned work in the same way.

Combining cyclictest and Ftrace

If cyclictest reports unexpectedly long latencies, you can use the breaktrace option to abort the program and trigger Ftrace to obtain more information.

You invoke `breaktrace` using `-b<N>` or `--breaktrace=<N>`, where `N` is the number of microseconds of latency that will trigger the trace. You select the `Ftrace` tracer using `-T[tracer name]` or one of the following:

- `-C`: Context switch
- `-E`: Event
- `-f`: Function
- `-w`: Wakeup
- `-W`: Wakeup-RT

For example, this will trigger the `Ftrace` function tracer when a latency greater than `100` microseconds is measured:

```
# cyclictest -a -t -n -p99 -f -b100
```

Further reading

The following resources have further information about the topics introduced in this chapter:

- *Hard Real-Time Computing Systems: Predictable Scheduling Algorithms and Applications* by Buttazzo, Giorgio, Springer, 2011
- *Multicore Application Programming* by Darryl Gove, *Addison Wesley*, 2011

Summary

The term *real-time* is meaningless unless you qualify it with a deadline and an acceptable miss rate. When you have these two pieces of information, you can determine whether or not Linux is a suitable candidate for the operating system and, if so, begin to tune your system to meet the requirements. Tuning Linux and your application to handle real-time events means making it more deterministic so that the real-time threads can meet their deadlines reliably. Determinism usually comes at the price of total throughput, so a real-time system is not going to be able to process as much data as a nonreal-time system.

It is not possible to provide mathematical proof that a complex operating system such as Linux will always meet a given deadline, so the only approach is through extensive testing using tools such as cyclictest and Ftrace and, more importantly, using your own benchmarks for your own application.

To improve determinism, you need to consider both the application and the kernel. When writing real-time applications, you should follow the guidelines given in this chapter about scheduling, locking, and memory.

The kernel has a large impact on the determinism of your system. Thankfully, there has been a lot of work on this over the years. Enabling kernel preemption is a good first step. If you still find that it is missing deadlines more often than you would like, then you might want to consider the PREEMPT_RT kernel patches. They can certainly produce low latencies, but the fact that they are not in the mainline yet means that you may have problems integrating them with the vendor kernel for your particular board. You may instead, or in addition, need to embark on the exercise of finding the cause of the latencies using Ftrace and similar tools.

That brings me to the end of this dissection of embedded Linux. Being an engineer of embedded systems requires a very wide range of skills, which include a low-level knowledge of hardware and how the kernel interacts with it. You need to be an excellent system engineer who is able to configure user applications and tune them to work in an efficient manner. All of this has to be done with hardware that is, often, only just capable of the task. There is a quotation that sums this up: *An engineer can do for a dollar what anyone else can do for two.* I hope that you will be able to achieve this with the information I have presented during the course of this book.

Index

Made in the USA
Middletown, DE
05 July 2018